Angela Schmitz

LATEIN AMERICA IN THE VISOR

VOLUME 1 – SOUTH AMERICA

nzvp BOOKS

Angela Schmitz

LATIN AMERICA IN THE VISOR

VOLUME 1 – SOUTH AMERICA

nzvp BOOKS

This book is dedicated to Axel Hess. Without him, many of the stories and images from this journey would not exist. Apart from the people we met and who greatly enriched our trips, there are good friends who deserve my gratitude for many things. On behalf of all the good souls I should like to mention Peter Stumm, Ralf Mainka, Andrea Behrens, Petra and Michael Böhmer.

Angela Schmitz

THE WORLD IS A BOOK, AND THOSE WHO DO NOT TRAVEL READ ONLY A PAGE

SAINT AUGUSTINE OF TAGASTE (354 UNTIL 430)

THE AUTOR

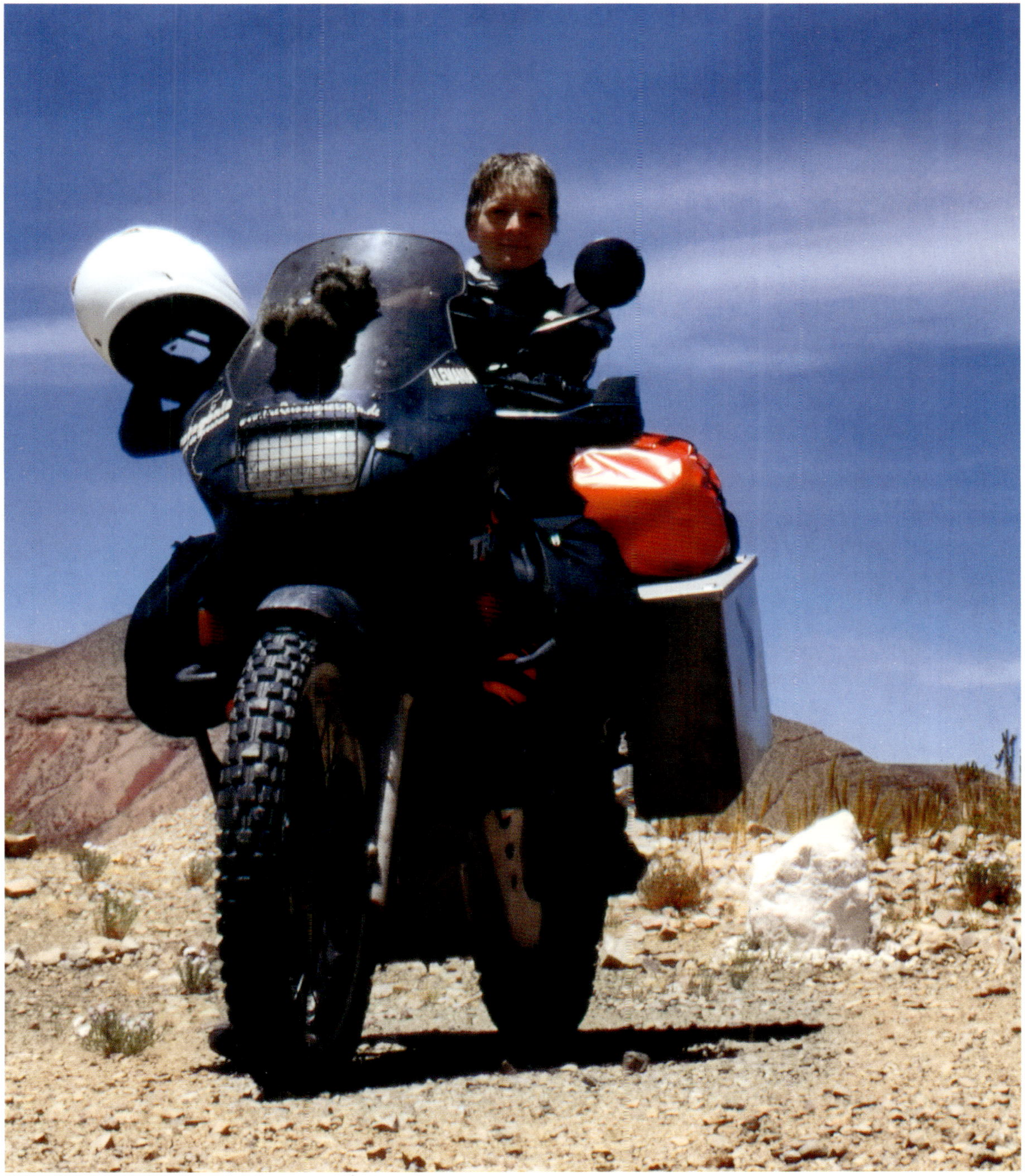

Angela Schmitz

The Duisburg native economist, born in 1966, travelled to Chile several times in the mid-1990s in the course of her research work on development policies. Captivated by this long, narrow country, its people, its wide variety of landscapes, climates and vegetation, the motorbike enthusiast decided to discover the entire continent of América from its southern tip in Tierra del Fuego to its northern border in Mexico on her two wheels. She and her husband Axel Heß quit their jobs and went on several journeys of discovery in Latin America, each lasting a few months. Free from all obligations and independent, they followed only their intuition. The author's passion for Latin America will not let her go. First and foremost, she is fascinated by what is unknown and unforeseeable in foreign countries, which creates openness for other cultures and people. Unusual images, colours and forms of nature inspire her paintings and photography while opening her eyes for different perspectives. In her book "Latin America in the visor –South America", the first of two volumes, Angela Schmitz takes you to South America. The second part, "Latin America in the visor – Central America", tells the story of her journey from Panama to Mexico.

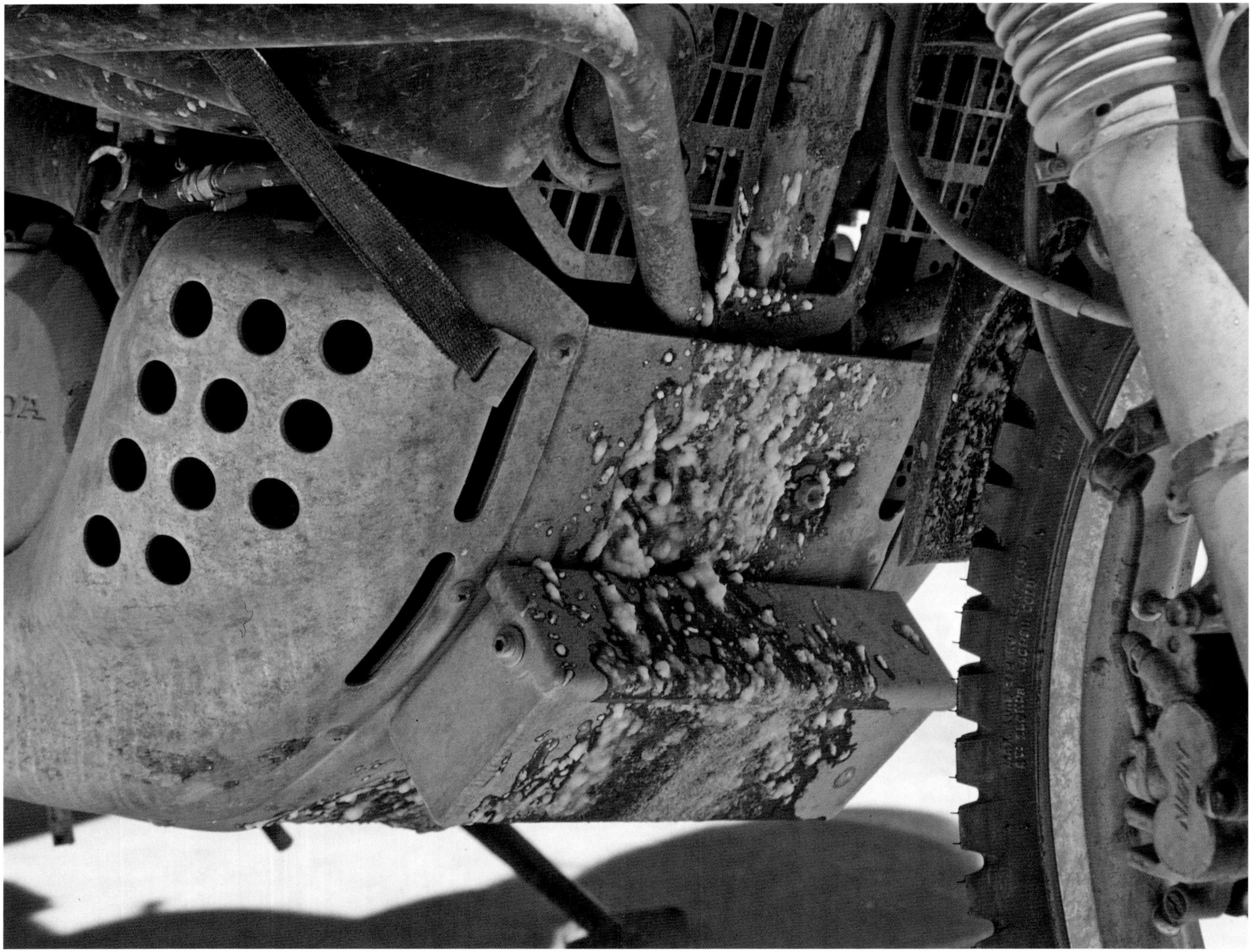

PREPARATION

When you undertake a journey, it's important to prepare everything well. This applies not only to the people but also to the motorbikes, which should be equipped for all possible occurrences. When on the road, they are the most important things you have. In this sense they are on par with travelling companions – and naturally also want to "see the world"! With a few alterations, the 1996 Honda Transalp and the Honda Africa Twin from 2003 have been equipped to be suitable for long distance journeys. The changes meet the objectives even though there are surely varying opinions about whether they are necessary or superfluous.

Grips for the clutch, brake levers, a stable luggage rack and crash bars have been added for protection when falls are unavoidable. An aluminium engine guard and a headlamp guard have also been mounted. A starter and charger plug make it possible to jump start the motorbikes more easily in the case a battery becomes empty while on the road, and also to be able to recharge batteries or for use as a source of energy when camping. An aluminium toolbox screwed to the engine guard provides a place for tools. The Transalp sits quite deep over the steering head. In order to be prepared to do without petrol stations on longer isolated routes, the Africa Twin has been equipped with a 43 litre tank made of polyamide; petrol can be tapped easily using a quick release fastener. The rubber has been removed from the footpegs because the serrated footpegs concealed under the rubber provide a more secure foothold on rough terrain.

Various replacement parts travel with us in the luggage. Camping equipment, cooking utensils and forehead lamps as well as items of clothing carefully selected to be suitable for the most varied of climate zones and weather conditions, have to fit in the limited storage space, along with medications and first-aid kit. Photographic equipment, maps, compass and GPS also cannot be left behind. A variety of documents like passport and vaccination card, an international driving licence, an international registration, bank and credit cards and cash have to be provided. Also vaccinations have to be obtained in time. Finally, reading materials to accompany you on the journey are also essential.

Page 10: Nothing can get to the protective aluminium panels

Bottom: The bits and pieces for the road

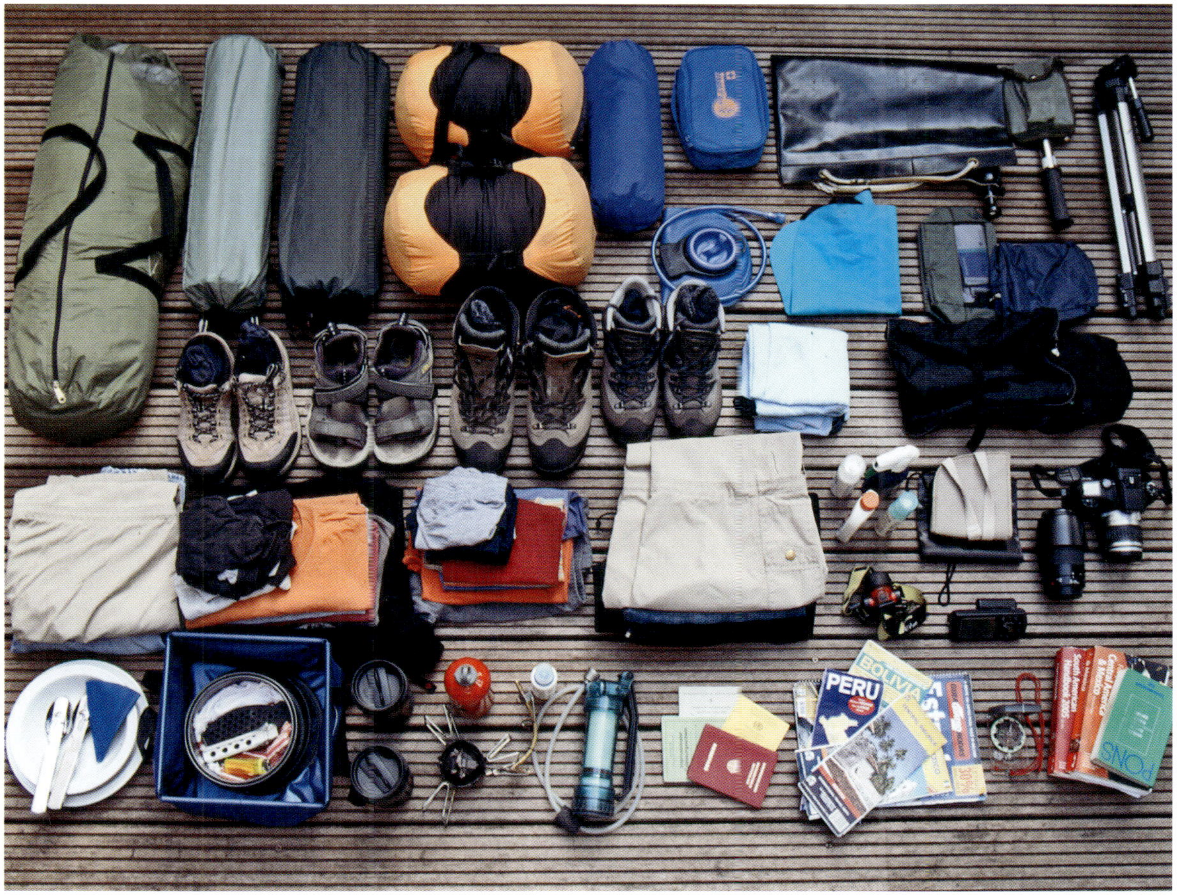

THE ROUTE

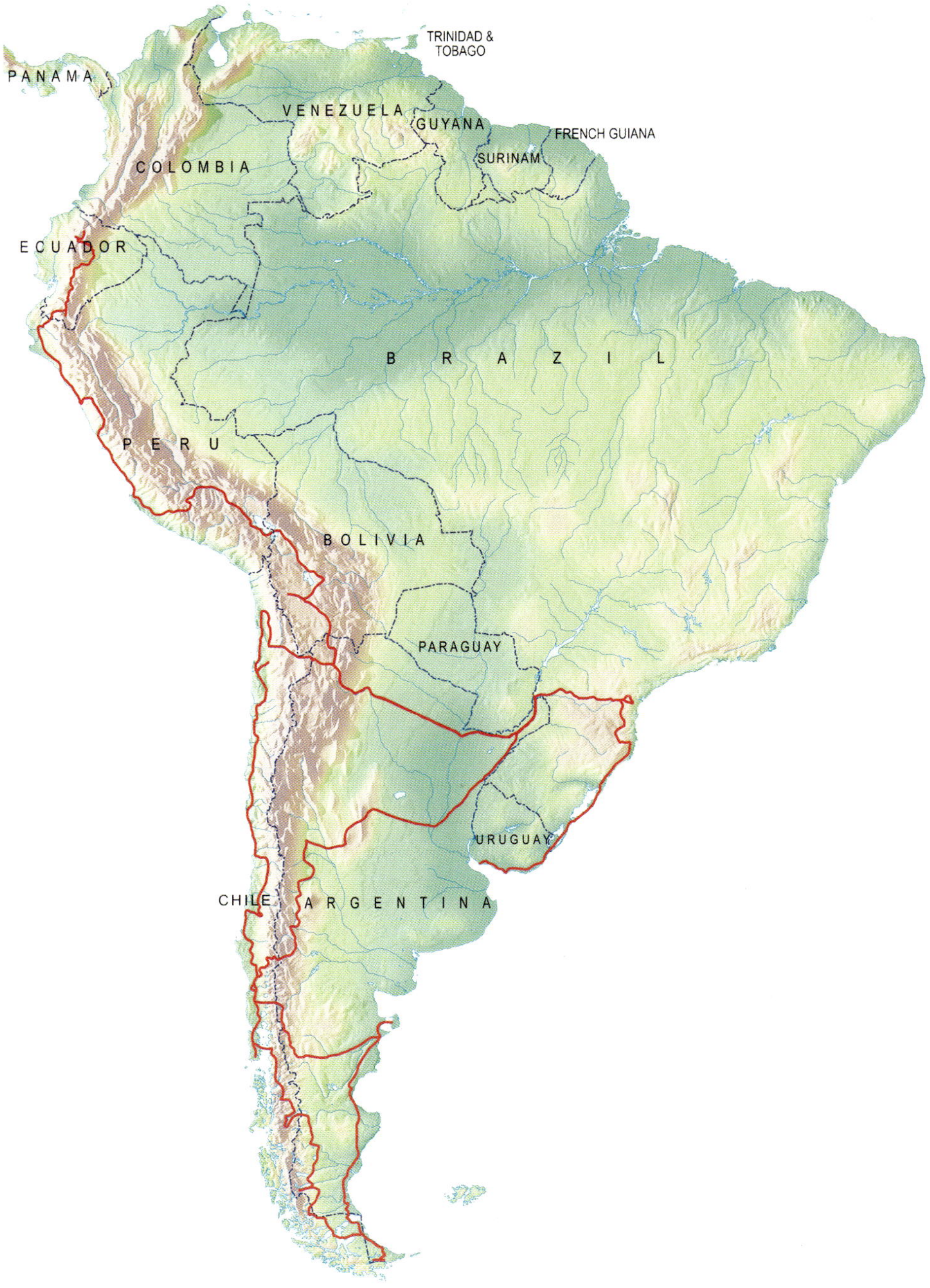
TRINIDAD & TOBAGO
PANAMA
VENEZUELA
GUYANA
FRENCH GUIANA
SURINAM
COLOMBIA
ECUADOR
BRAZIL
PERU
BOLIVIA
PARAGUAY
URUGUAY
CHILE
ARGENTINA

SOUTH AMERICA

About 250 million years ago, the world consisted of the huge continent of Pangaea, which was surrounded by the ocean Panthalassa and jutted out into the Tethys Sea like a huge tongue of land. 115 million years later, the landmass broke apart and the Tethys Sea separated a southern continent: Gondwana. The northern continent divided into North America and Eurasia. In the course of the following millions of years, Gondwana broke up further into pieces that formed South America, Africa, Australia and Antarctica. About 60 million years ago, the Andes folded upward as the backbone of South America. During the ice age, they developed into an Alpine mountain range, the longest in the world, stretching over 7,500 km from Venezuela to Antarctica.

The countries of South America possess a multitude of animals and plants whose habitat often comprises only a small, limited area. Brazil is the home of a third of all species of tropical trees, a fifth of all plant species and a sixth of all species of birds. About 20,000 different plants and 1,500 species of birds live in Ecuador. However, it must also be said that many of these species are endangered because human interferences in nature are depriving them of their habitats. The destruction of forests, commercial overfishing and the flourishing trade in endangered species are the flip side of a fascinating exotic world. Air and water pollution, sewage problems and unauthorised rubbish dumps also in these countries contribute to the destruction of the balance of nature and our conditions for life as well. Regions change all the time. Towns grow, roads are built. A dirt road that is fairly impassable today may be a built-up asphalt road tomorrow. Landscapes, animals and vegetation must yield to it. The land loses some of its primitiveness, which is the greatest attraction on such a trip. From Tierra del Fuego at the end of the world up to Ecuador, the author travels 33,500 km on her motorbike between the 56th parallel south and the equator, through pampas, deserts and dense rainforests, to volcanoes, waterfalls, glaciers and old civilizations. She conquers enormous heights of almost 5,000 m and crosses the most diverse climatic zones. Angela Schmitz avoids the huge metropolises on her bike whenever possible, looking instead for less travelled paths and unspoilt natural landscapes.

The glacier Perito Moreno on Lago Argentino, a climb up the active volcano Villarica, the world's biggest waterfalls at Iguaçu on the border of Argentina, Brazil and Paraguay, or the Desierto de Atacama, the world's driest desert, and the Valle de la Luna transport the author into the enchanted worlds in Chile and Argentina. Quiet Uruguay has an irresistible provincial charm. Brazil impresses with its size, variety and contrasts – not just in nature, but in the ethnic roots of its people. The Puna in Argentina's north-west is colourful and dizzying, while Bolivia's Altiplano fascinates with its mysterious silver mountain at Potosí. In Peru, the author is overwhelmed by the mystic atmosphere of Machu Picchu, the ancient Inca site, and by the wondrous desert lines in Nazca. Dirt roads winding their way through rugged mountain ranges become a challenge for the drivers. After meeting a shaman in the jungle of Ecuador, Angela Schmitz finally stands in the northern hemisphere with one foot and in the southern with the other – as close as anyone can get to the equator.

The landscapes she discovers are much more than pretty scenery for a motorbike trip, they are a framework for discovering and coming to understand other cultures and lifestyles. Countless new impressions and experiences broaden personal horizons, open the mind to new things, and change the way people interact. Simple considerations like the search for a place to sleep, food, fuel for the bike or a passable road become essential. Every day presents a new challenge and sometimes an adventure. The special appeal of this kind of journey lies in the unknown, the unforeseeable. If you embark on it, you need to be prepared for everything, even for the most wonderful experiences.

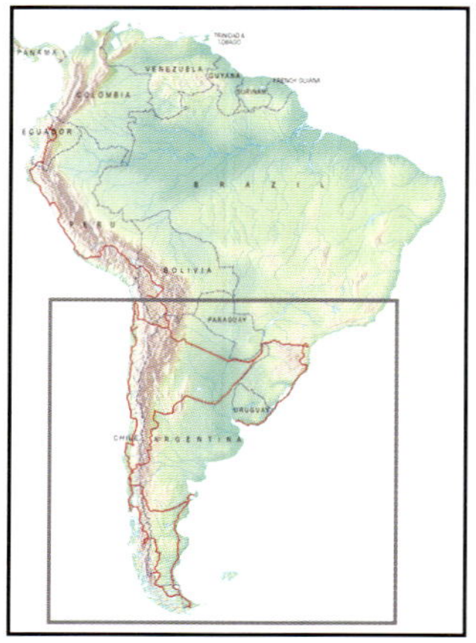

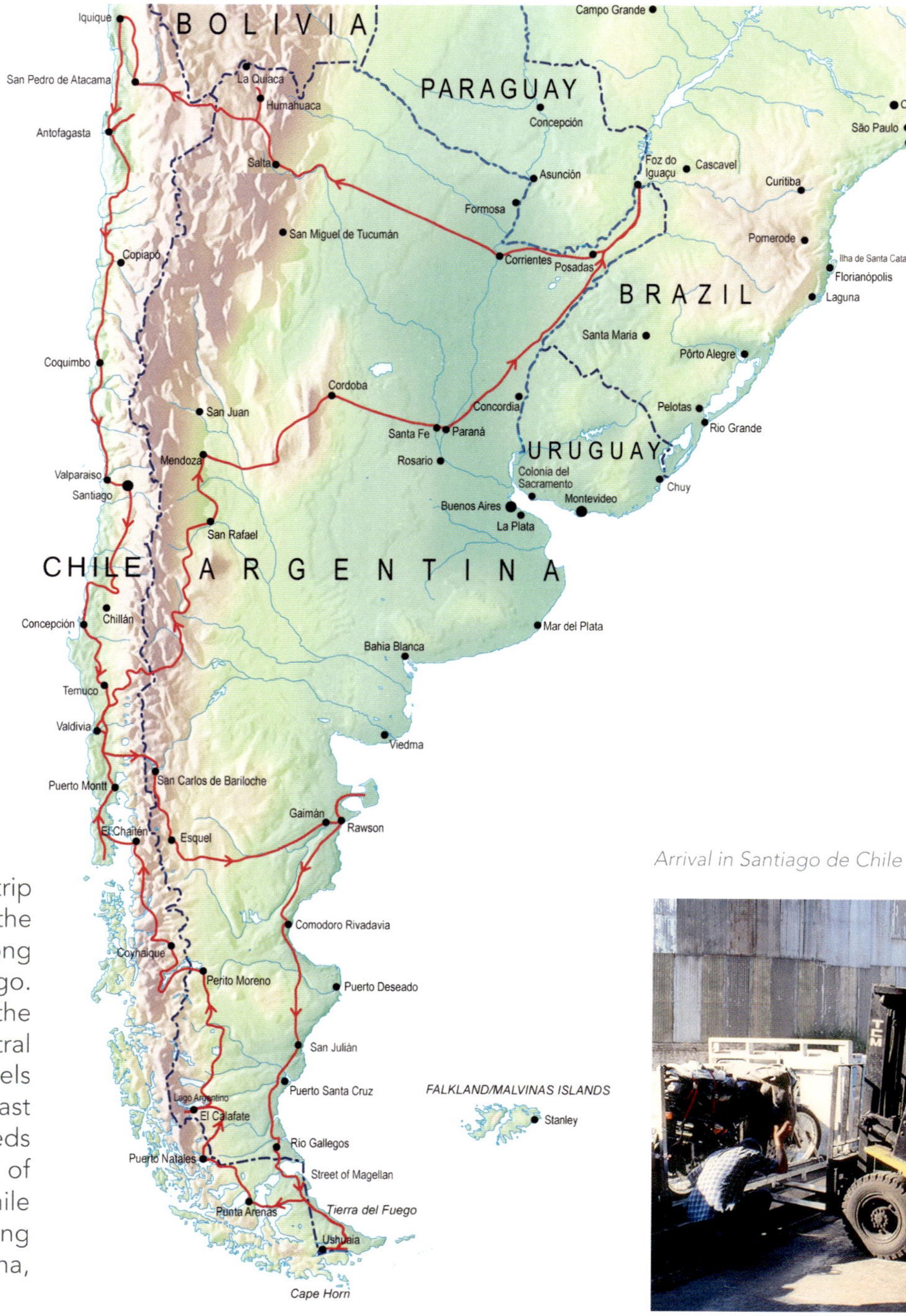

Starting from Santiago de Chile, the trip leads south through the Lake Region over the Andes to Argentina, across Patagonia and along the Atlantic coast down to Tierra del Fuego. From there, constantly crossing borders, the route leads northward over the Carretera Austral to the "Small South" of Chile. The author travels across Argentina from the farthest north-east to the Iguaçu Waterfalls. The route proceeds westward into the Puna in the north-west of Argentina, then over the Andes back to Chile through the Atacama Desert. It returns along the Pacific coast, in part over the Panamericana, to the Chilean capital.

Arrival in Santiago de Chile

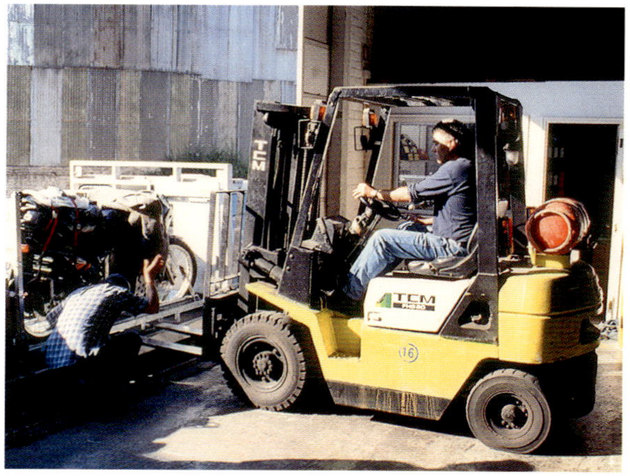

CHILE – ARGENTINA
ENDLESS VASTNESS

IN MAPUCHE COUNTRY

A turbulent day is coming to an end. We are sitting in Carolina and Gregori's living room, sampling the Chilean national drink – Pisco Sour. The clear liquor made from grapes mixed with lemon juice, egg white and powdered sugar tastes great. With 80 proof, it also goes to your head fairly quickly. Utterly exhausted we scramble into our tent pitched next to the empty basin of the local public pool, which our two hosts are currently renovating for the next season. The events of the first day on the roads of Chile flash before my eyes again.

In the morning rush hour of Santiago de Chile, a metropolis with six million inhabitants, we are looking for a way out of the city. Both bikes are loaded up with two aluminium boxes, one on each side of the carrier, and a huge bag strapped across the seat. Over the edge of the rucksack on the tank I can only just make out the speedometer on the cockpit. After a few kilometres, I wonder how I am supposed to manage my unwieldy monstrosity of a motorbike on dirt roads for the next few months. It is difficult to stay orientated in this metropolitan maze. And immediately – while turning onto a street – I wonder why there are cars coming at me on all three lanes, before steering my bike safely to the sidewalk, utterly terrified. Axel follows. I completely overlooked the tiny white arrow on the dark background of the street sign. After this surge of adrenalin, we are able to relax on Ruta 5 that runs due south. Lined by vineyards, the famous Panamericana, a motorway with tollbooths, traverses the narrow country lengthwise. It takes some time to get used to the fact that there are bus stops along the road every few kilometres. People keep crossing the road or ride their bicycles in the lanes so that I have to brake rather sharply a few times. On the straight, monotonous route my mind wanders, while I follow a truck in the right lane that creeps along a construction site. Suddenly there is a loud bang, I'm enveloped in a cloud of dust, and can't see anything for a few seconds while pieces of rubber hurtle through the air. The truck driver slams on the brakes because his right rear tyre has exploded. I just barely manage to swerve to the fast lane and get past the truck unharmed. The second surge of adrenalin, I'm wide awake now. It's enough for today, about 300 km south of Santiago, we turn onto a little country lane to look for a place to stay in a village. People stop in the streets to stare at us in disbelief. We probably look like aliens to them, with our big bikes and heavy cross boots. A few girls in school uniforms start flirting with Axel while one of the locals tells me to ask at the public pool. That is how we met Carolina and Gregori, and now we are snuggling in our sleeping bags. I can't keep my eyes open much longer.

Something tugs on the rope of our tent. A sheep tethered close by in the meadow is chewing happily on it, greeting us just after sunrise. Breakfast is already ready. Carolina's parents have arrived and welcome us into the family right away. Our host persuades me to do a live interview with a reporter from a local radio station. A little while later, the reporter proffers his mobile phone and I describe our first impressions from the trip. It is odd to hear my own voice coming from the radio that stands by the side of the pool 10 m away, while Gregory paints the walls and acts silly. At the end, Axel adds holiday greetings in German and everybody is happy. It is hard to say goodbye, and we drag it out until noon. Our hosts vehemently refuse to take money for the food and lodgings. We are family now, after all, so we don't pay a single peso. After exchanging addresses, Gregori and Carolina accompany us on a 250er to the on-ramp of the motorway.

We reach the Pacific Ocean with a few detours, the sea is very tempting. The camping sites are closed so we spend the night in a little boarding house. After nightfall it proves to be a paradise for insects. I drop the cap of my water bottle and it rolls under the bed. Axel bends down, saying, "I don't think you want that back." Ants have gathered around dead flies, bugs, fat caterpillars, huge beetles with chirping wings, and other creatures are crawling on the walls of the room and

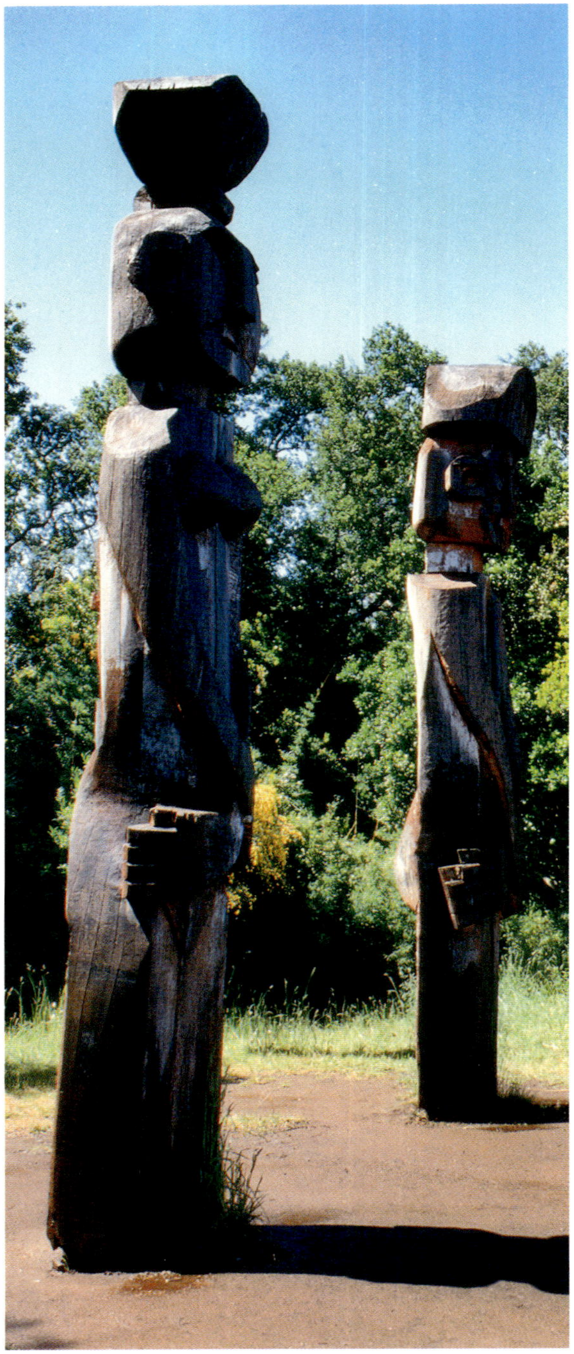

bath. It is too late to look for another place. We don't have any other choice but to share our room with them. I wake up a few times, switch on the light and go to the bathroom. It's a good opportunity to kill a few of the insects, but more critters come crawling all the time. It doesn't get any better in the morning. The landlady brings our breakfast to our room on a sticky tray, because she doesn't want to unlock the dining room just for us. There is instant coffee powder, one teabag, and eggs fried in rancid lard. In the relative safety of our bed, we take two sips of tea before packing our bags in a hurry to get out of here. However, we have to go down to the Pacific Ocean for a little while. The black sand glistens in the sun, an intriguing contrast to our white feet. Tiny puddles form in our footprints. The blue sea throws huge waves at the shore that break on the cliffs with foaming crowns. The air smells of distant lands and adventure.

Past Concepción the road runs along the river Bío-Bío. Until the early 19th century, it was the natural border between the lands of the Mapuche to the south and the Spanish conquerors to the north. German, English, French and Spanish immigrants settled further south with the hope of a better future. In Temuco, the Cerro Ñielol is the location of a "ngullaton", a Mapuche prayer field, with wooden statues that rise up to a height of 3 m as a mark of recognition of the Mapuche culture. In 1881, this "mountain of many ditches", as the name of the hill literally translates, was also the location of one of many so-called "parlamentos", in which the Spanish conquerors negotiated their seizure of land with the Mapuche. A patagua tree was planted to seal the peace between the two parties. Still, 90 % of the Mapuche land was expropriated, and they were driven onto reservations. In the early 1970s, the land was returned to them, but they were dispossessed again in the years of the military dictatorship after 1973. To this day, most of the 500,000 Mapuche live on the outer fringes of society, economically and culturally marginalized, fighting for their rights and their way of life.

Rain beats down on us for days. The further we make our way south, the more persistent it becomes. Our clothes are cold and damp, and the moisture seems to seep into our bones. We had planned to take a boat to the island of Chiloé, but that is impossible under these conditions. We hope that the weather and climate will be better on the other side of the Andes, and take an eastward turn at Osorno, over the Paso Cardenal Antonio Samore towards Argentina. The road leads through impermeable forests. Low clouds and fog make it difficult to see, and wrap the landscape in a fairytale veil. Snow lies on the side of the road. The dirt road is crisscrossed with waterlogged ditches. Not the best route to check the reach of my tank. But exactly this is the case: I run out of petrol. Luckily, I have my mobile filling station with me at all times. In the driving rain, with cold, stiff fingers we fill the canister from Axel's big tank and give the Transalp a few litres of petrol. That should last me a while. We slide through the mud downhill to the Argentinean border station. It takes time to fill in all the forms. The Argentine customs officers do demonstrate a sense of humour when they ask us with straight faces whether our motorbikes are equipped with air conditioning or a radio.

Here the weather changes. The snow ceases, the roads are better, and then suddenly we have a magnificent view of Lago Nahuel Huapi surrounded by a sea of wild plants and flowers. Patagonia's garden greets us with a blue sky, and the sunlight gleams on the snow-topped mountains and the blue surface of the lake. On the eastern shore of the lake lies San Carlos de Bariloche, the sports centre. Mountain-biking, rafting, climbing, skiing, you can do everything here if you have the money. People also display the latest fashion trends. The overall atmosphere reminds me of Switzerland. Many houses have boxes of lush geraniums hanging from their wooden balconies, the "Hotel Edelweiß" stands right next to the "Hostal Seeblick" (Lake View). San Carlos de Bariloche has another specialty. With its 13 chocolate factories, the town is a paradise for chocolate lovers. The scent wafts out of the many small cafés and shops, promising sweet pleasures to aficionados.

At a camping site outside of town, we concentrate on our bikes. My right rear indicator light doesn't work anymore, but the bulb doesn't seem to be burnt out. I switch the left and right bulbs – and it works for some reason. The hose of Axel's chain lubricator is clogged with a slimy substance. He drains off the oil, and the goo flows out with it. This phenomenon will cause occasional trouble on the entire trip, because the substance accumulates, clogs the hose, and the chain stays dry. And then there is the blocked water drain of the filler neck on the Twin. In heavy rain, the water collects there and does not drain off. When Axel removes the lid, the water flows into the tank, watering down the petrol. In order to clean it, the entire 43-litre behemoth has to be taken off. Axel removes the blockage with a long wire, and the water drains properly again.

Page 16: "Ngullaton", prayer field of the Mapuche in Temuco, Chile

Bottom: Fight with the big tank

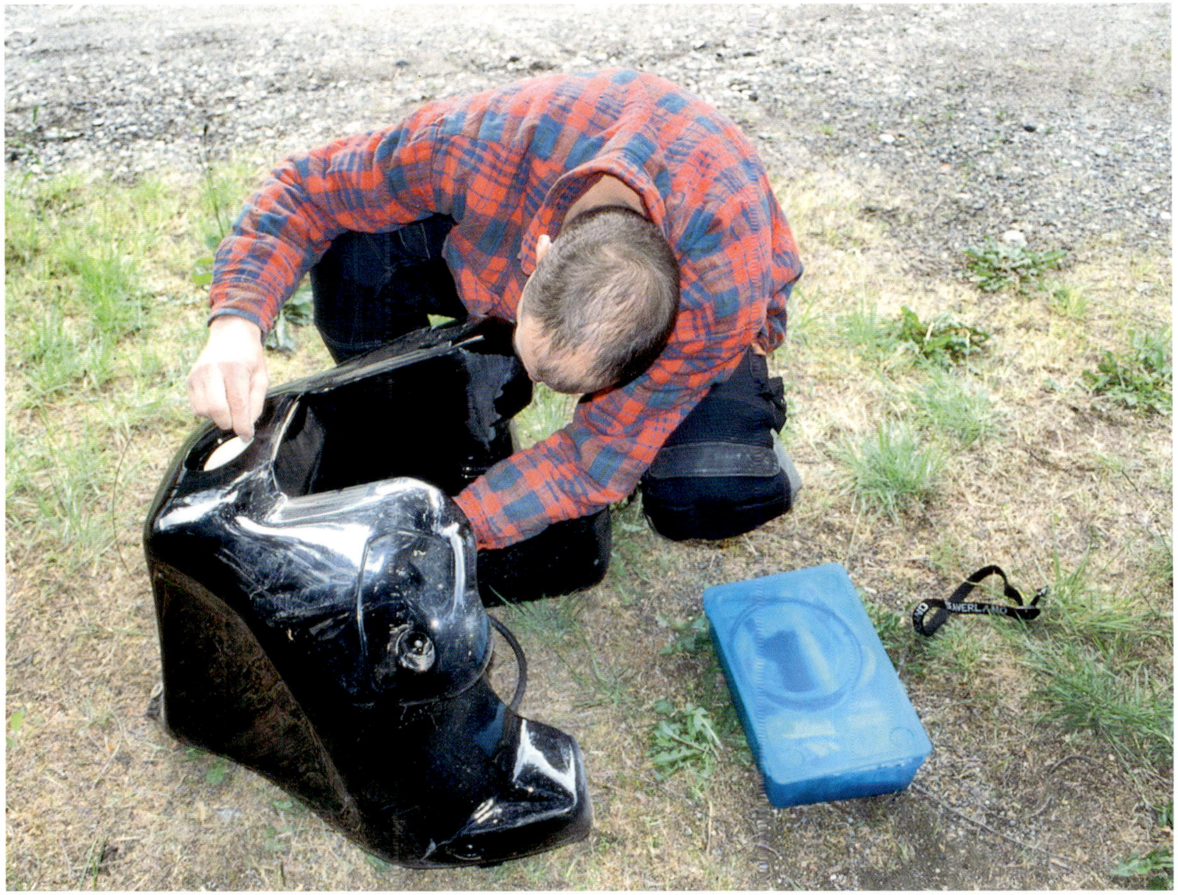

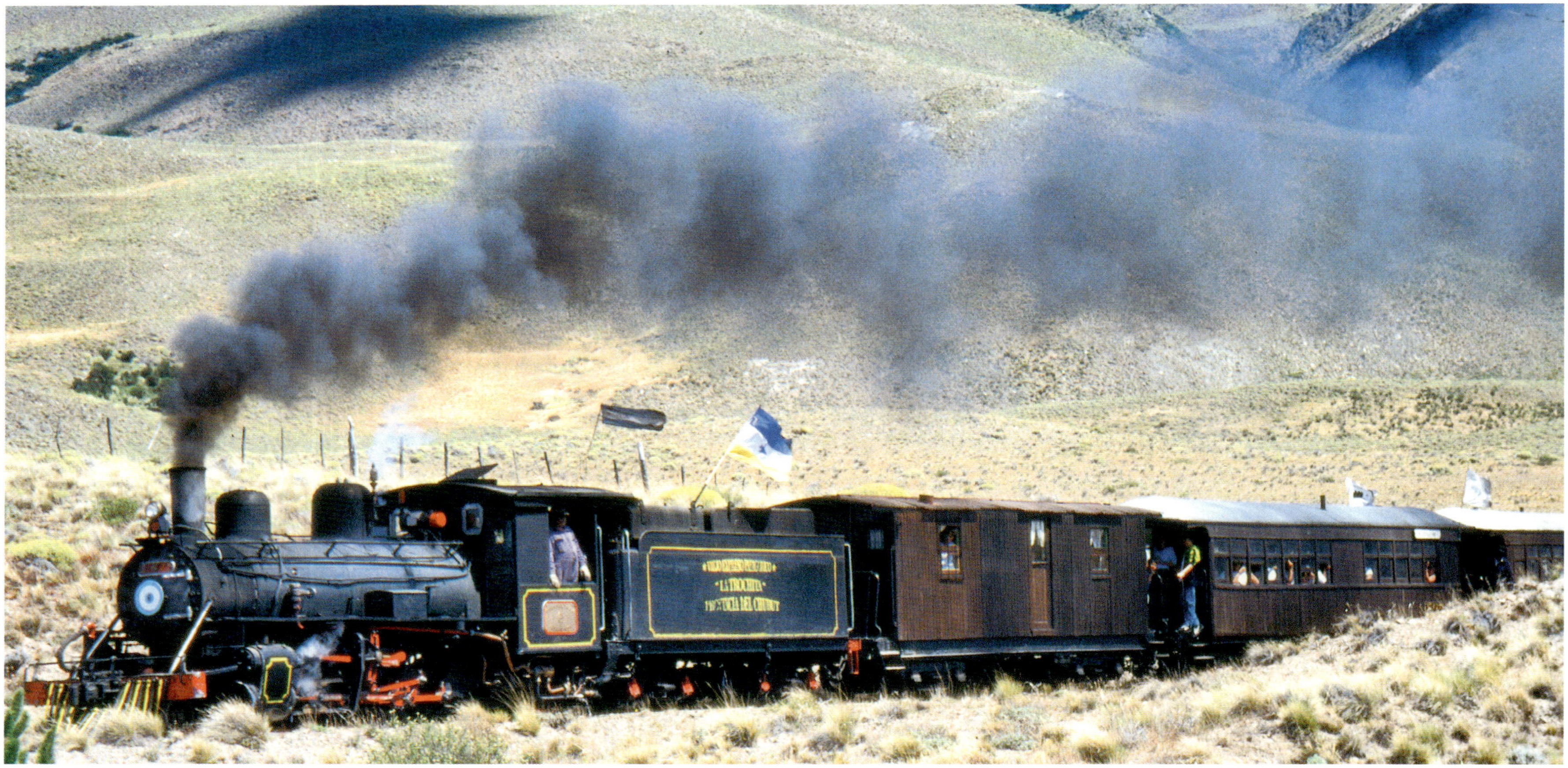

On our way to San Martin de los Andes the next day we come to a police check-point. A strong wind tugs at our clothes. As I reach for my passport, a small piece of paper flutters away. Thinking that it is my immigration form, I call out, "Mi papel!" A policeman chases after it, but the wind drives the paper over a ditch and up the hill towards a fenced-in pasture. The policeman keeps up his hot pursuit. Finally, he manages to grab the paper and proudly returns it to me. I take it back ... it is a supermarket receipt.

We follow the trail of the old Patagonia express La Trochita, a narrow-gauge railway that has been huffing and puffing through the Meseta, the Argentine lowlands, since 1922. The steam engine uses 100 litres of water per track kilometre. In the old days, the train transported wool, cattle, agricultural products and passengers back and forth between the towns of Esquel and Ingeniero Jacobacci. On a route of 400 km, the tracks connected a few estancias along the way. Today, La Trochita is a tourist attraction. Several times a week during the summer season, the train takes passengers to the Mapuche settlement of Nahuel Pan, whose name translates literally as "puma snout". We, too, take the train. Engine No. 6 is coupled up to warm applause from the waiting passengers. The carriages are equipped with wooden benches. Each carriage has a wood stove in the centre that used to provide the necessary warmth in winter. At the end of the corridor, there is even a loo with a hole in the ground. We chug along through the Meseta

Page 18: La Trochita, the old Patagonia Express

Bottom: The train station in Esquel, last stop for the old Patagonia express, Argentina

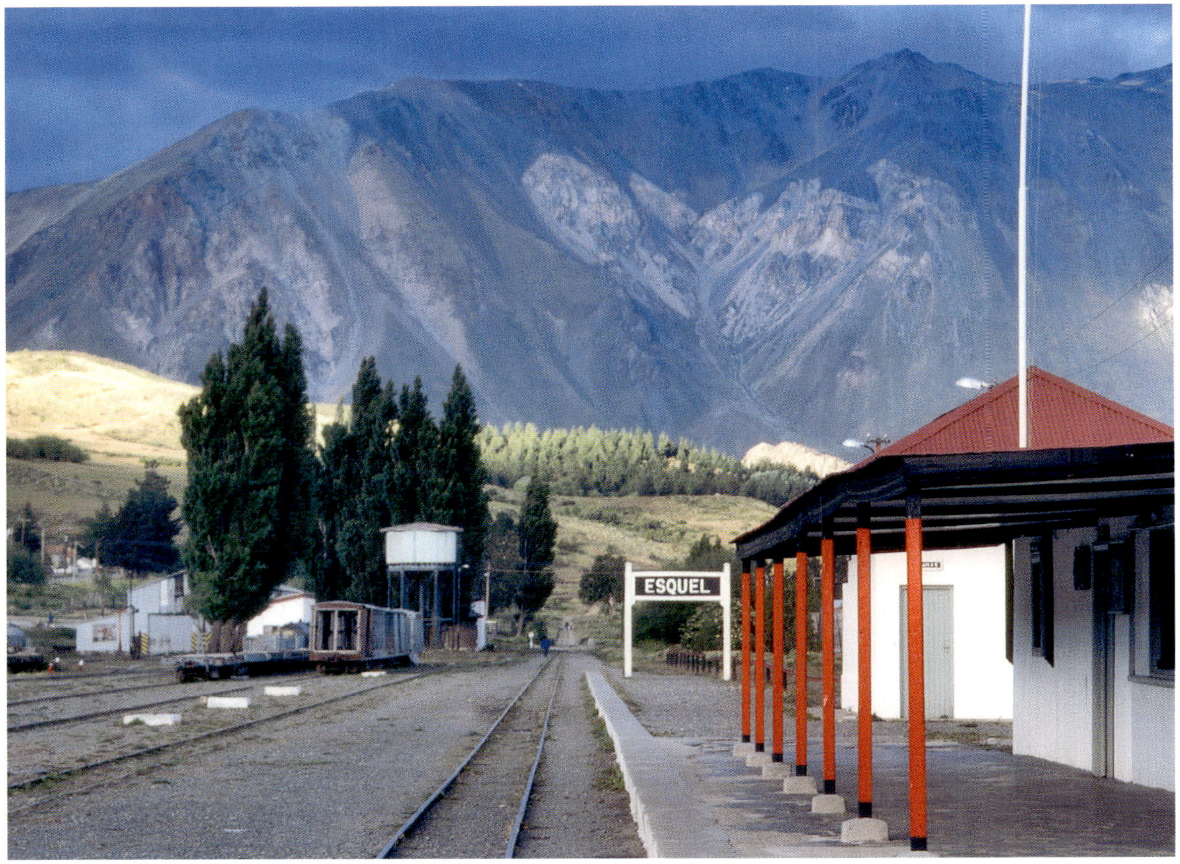

for about two hours at an average speed of 15 km/h. At one point the train stops. The engine doesn't have enough power to conquer a small hill. The entire train rolls back a few hundred metres in order to gather new momentum. It is a close call, but the engine makes it and we reach Nahuel Pan. Nobody lives in the village permanently, even the Mapuche commute by car or on horseback when the train stops here. Still, the village is bustling. Women and men demonstrate their craftsmanship in the houses, explaining how their products are made. They work for a development aid project and their crafts receive a special certificate so that customers can be certain that they are not buying mass-produced goods. Outside, small children can ride a horse and young girls offer homemade cake and cold lemonade.

For 628 km, we cross the Patagonian pampas on our bikes down to the Atlantic coast. Nine hours in the burning heat and not a bit of shade anywhere. The fascination of this region lies in the little things. You have to look closely and take in the landscape. Far away hills shimmer in hues of red and brown, they are several million years old. Not a single tree in sight, just grass and shrubs. I have a feeling of being transported to another time, another place. I spot a hill on the horizon thinking that it is a two days' ride away. Now all we need are vultures circling in the sky above us waiting for our water to run out or the horses to wear out. Axel gives his bike the name La Trochita, because this drive reminds him so much of the old Patagonia express. There are settlements marked on the road map, but most of them are just filling stations that appear out of the blue about a hundred kilometres apart. We meet hardly a soul on our way. Only the men at the stations would provide an opportunity for a chat, if they deigned to talk to me. They are curious, of course, and try to find out about us. But they will only talk to Axel. Spanish is not his thing. Even when he indicates that he doesn't understand a word and points in my direction, you can practically see the wheels turning in their heads. I smile to myself sometimes, wondering which will be stronger: their curiosity or their machismo. I don't understand why they refuse to talk to a woman, but I will have to get used to it. Someone like me, a woman driving a motorbike, going on a journey like this, is a rare sight in these parts and probably a little too emancipated for some men here.

The heat on the east coast is overwhelming. Even in the shade, the thermometer rises above 30° C. Still I want to see the paleontological park near the small village of Gaimán that was founded by Welsh immigrants in the 19th century. The park reflects Patagonia's geological history of the past 40 million years. Sandstone cliffs with a height of 150 m tell the story. From the bottom to the top layer, there are leaps of millions of years from the terrestrial to the maritime and back to the terrestrial era. The top stratum is about 10,000 years old and contains thousands of petrified shells. The way up to the crest of the hill is exhausting, there is no shade anywhere. Equipped with protective hats and big water bottles, we climb up the 1.5 km path in the blazing sun. Many excavated skeletons, fossils of penguins, whales, dolphins, armadillos and their ancestors serve as a clear illustration of a bygone age. At the top, the wind does its best to blow you away, but the fantastic view of the Chubut Valley makes the strenuous climb worthwhile.

Right: Penguin meets motorcycle in Punta Tombo, Argentina

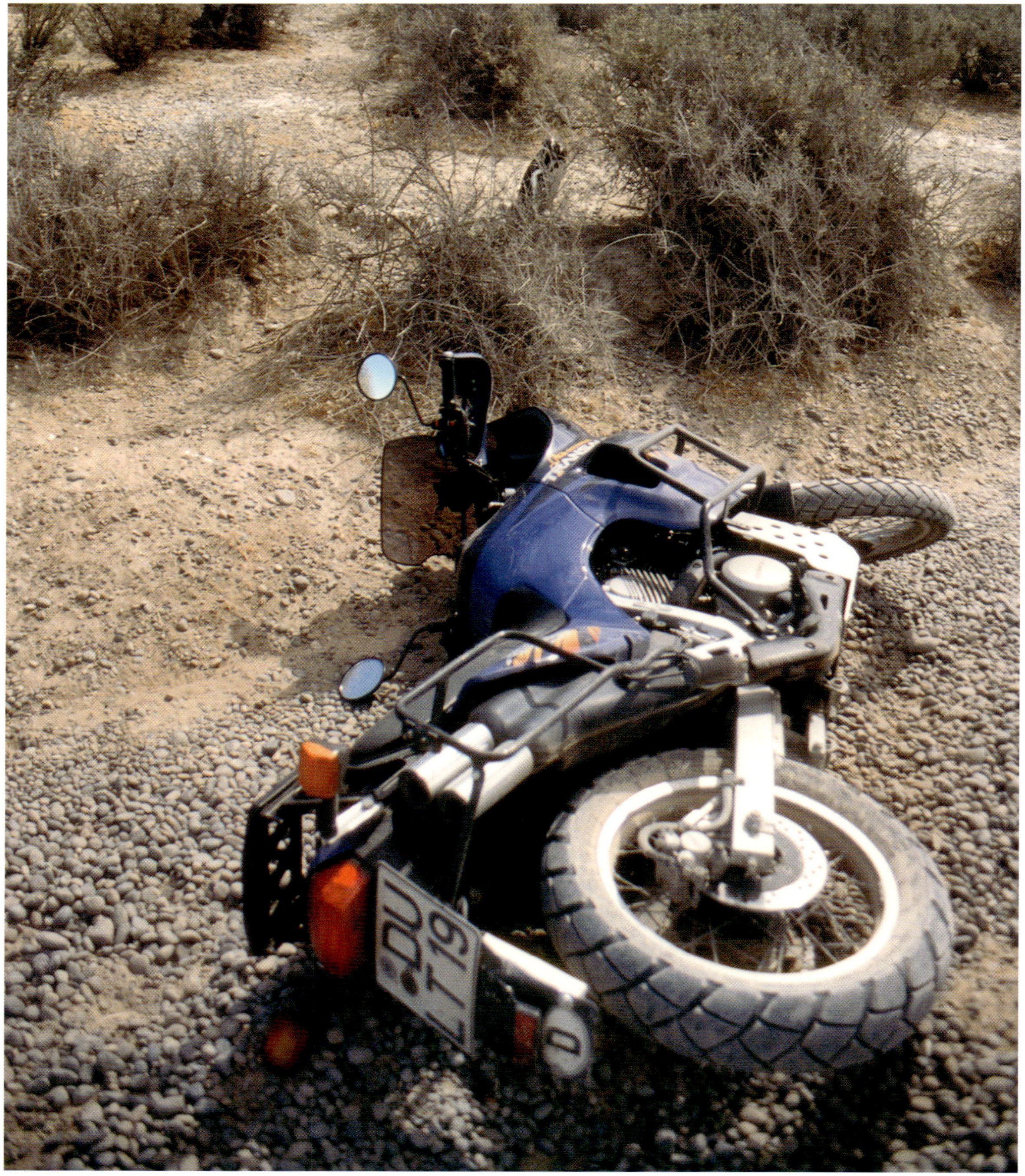

Page 21: In the penguin school Punta Tombo

On a gravel road of 120 km, we reach the penguin colony of Punta Tombo. With 500,000 animals inhabiting a nature reserve of 210 ha, this is the world's biggest accessible colony of Magellan penguins. The last stretch of road to the parking lot is a little rough, the gravel is piled high. My tyres sink in and I start to tilt to the side in slow motion. As I lift my head, I look into two huge penguin eyes watching me in astonishment – what I would give to be able to read the minds of animals right now! Axel has followed me so closely that he has to slam on the brakes and falls over, too. Cars stop, we are blocking the road. Nobody gets out to help. We heave up both motorbikes; I turn the key in the ignition ... no sound, no lights. A ranger appears and barks at me that I can't leave the bike standing here. That isn't the plan, anyway. Axel drives back to the parking lot. then, dripping with sweat, we push my bike back there as well. Since all indicator lights are off, it must be the battery or the fuses. I remove the side panel and spot the problem right away. The screws of the battery terminal have been rattled loose on the past 120 km of dirt road – a small cause with a huge effect. I find the road to the reserve not exactly easy to manage, but the ranger explains the eminent reason for it: an asphalt road would mean the end of the colony, she says. On a well-developed road, the big tour buses would arrive here with countless people, there would be fast food restaurants along the road, the area would turn into an amusement park, and the habitat of the penguins and other animals would be destroyed. This scenario is not only true for Punta Tombo. We decide not to try a second time and take the ranger up on her offer to take us to the colony by car. It is a wonderful experience to be so close to the penguins. They cross the road everywhere and don't care about blocked areas when digging their burrows. Penguins have no natural fear of humans. They let us go first or hurry to waddle from left to right in front of us. They don't tolerate it, however, when we get too close to their offspring. The young are defenced with much hissing and spreading of wings. From a bridge we look down on an "autopista" for the tuxedoed birds that brings them to the sea undisturbed. A penguin stands next to the sign that states clearly who gets the "right of way" here. Our landlord has a photo with the same motif. I wonder if the penguin is real ... When we return from our tour, the spot next to the sign is empty. I laugh about it and tell the story to the ranger later. "No, no," she says with a twinkling eye. Sometimes they place an inflatable penguin there as a photo motif to confuse the tourists.

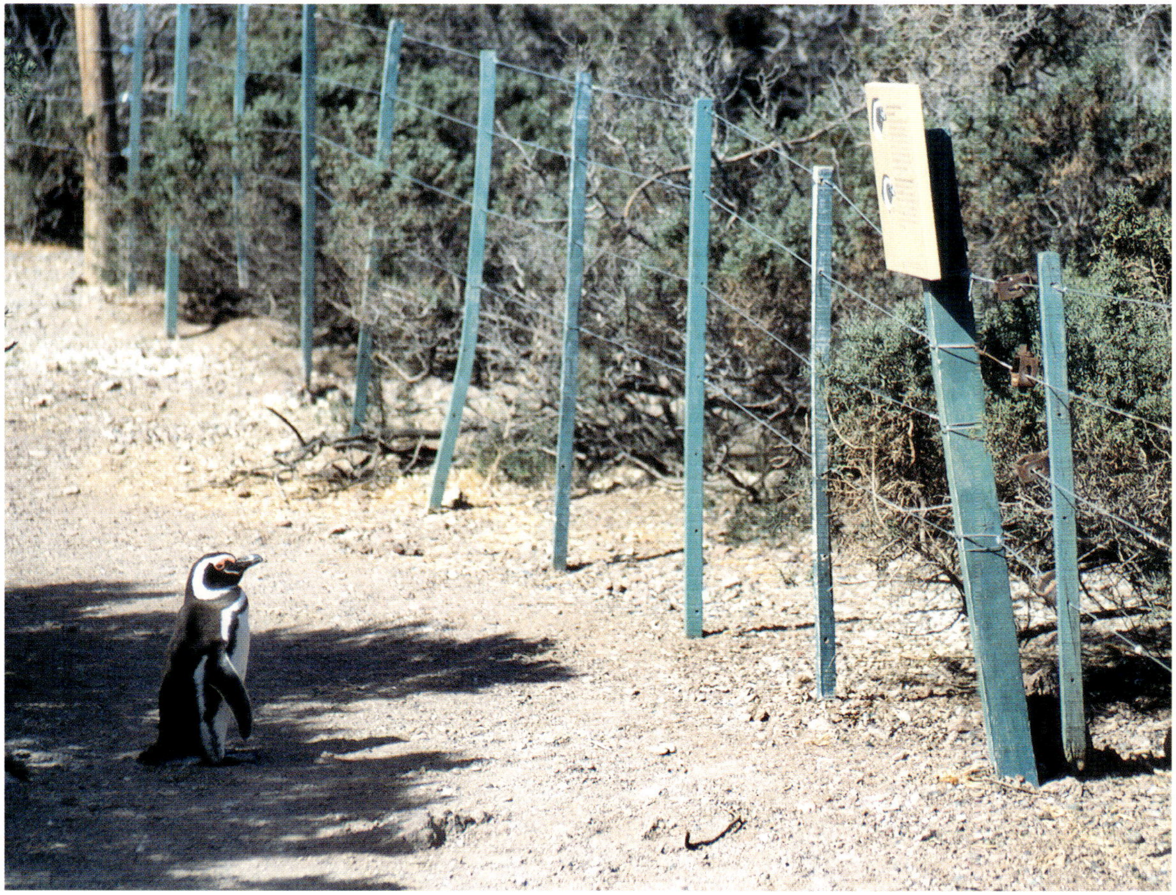

FINIS TERRAE AT THE END OF THE WORLD

On Ruta 3, we cruise along the Atlantic coast with an average speed of 40 km/h in a storm the likes of which we have never seen in Germany. In order to be able to drive "upright", we have to tilt the bikes so far over to the side that we can just barely hang on to the edge of the seat. Every once in a while a gust of wind tries to blow us into the ditch on the other side of the road. On the way we meet six other German bikers who are also driving south. Originally, they wanted to take in the petrified forests, but they don't have enough petrol for that. Since our bikes, too, will need a refill soon, we begin to look for a petrol station together. That turns out to be more difficult than expected. The first station is out of business, the next one, about 180 km further along, is open but the attendant wants to sell us only 10 litres per person. His supplies are getting low, too. He has been waiting for a new delivery for days and

Page 23: Warning sign in Tierra del Fuego, Chile

Bottom: The "high-flier" in San Julián, Argentina

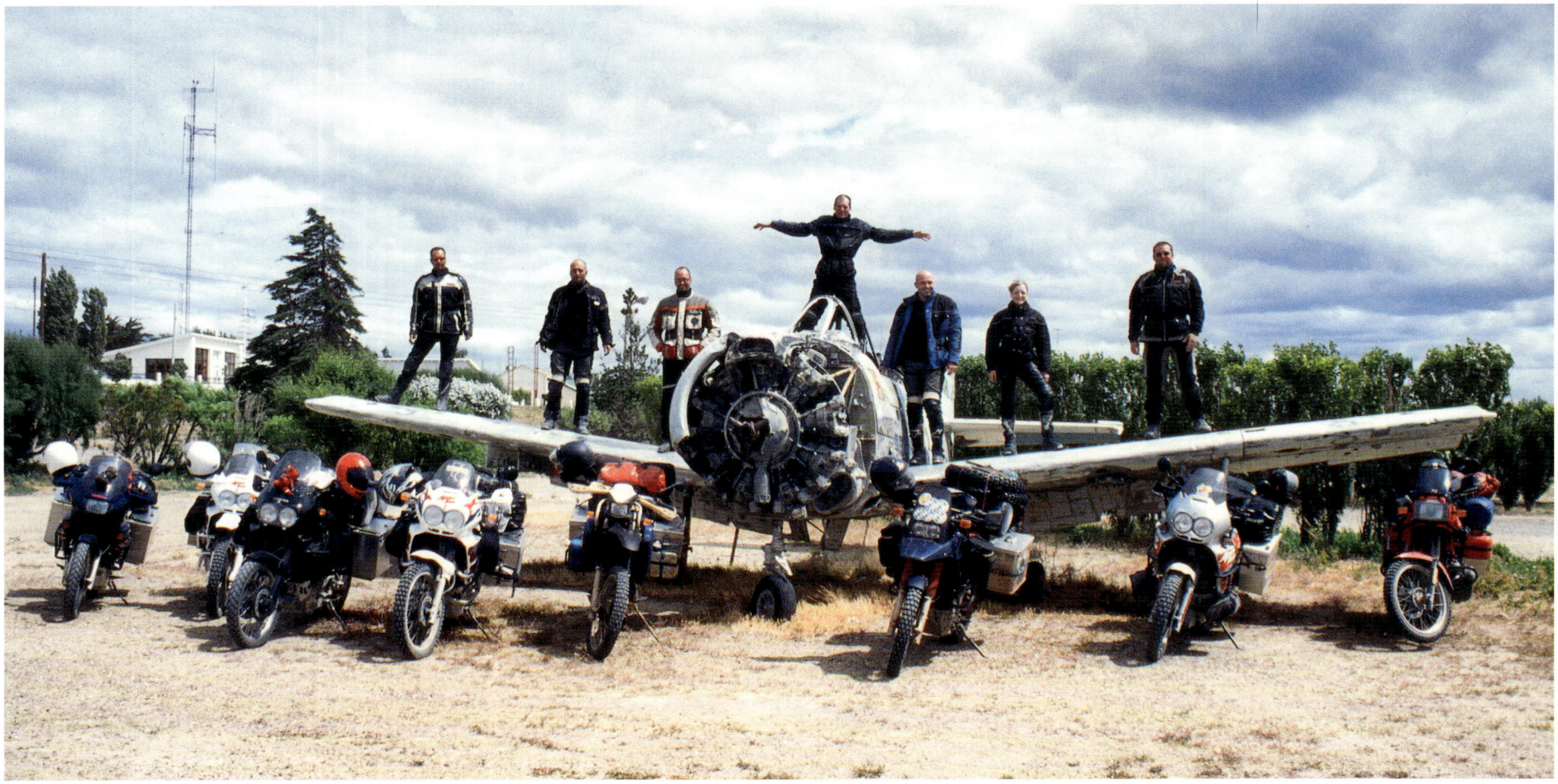

promises, "mañana, mañana." That could mean next week. We take a break at a coffee shop to figure out how much petrol we have together and how far that will take us. If we all get our fuel rations and refrain from any detours, we should be able to make it to San Julián. It works. A camping site on the beach will be our shared home for the next few days. I use the time to take care of my Transalp. It has me a little worried. The engine keeps sputtering. It can't be a lack of petrol. I empty the carburettor and check the spark plugs. After that, the bike runs better.

In 1520, Fernão de Magalhães and his crew discovered not only the waterway that made it possible to pass from the Atlantic to the Pacific Ocean, but also an island named Tierra del Fuego due to its widely visible columns of smoke rising up from the cliffs. They came from the small fireplaces in the huts of the Yamaná, who lived as water nomads on the coast. Late at night, we reach Tierra del Fuego. Although it doesn't get really dark, we refrain from a midnight tour. But where should we sleep? There is nothing here except for a grubby cafeteria in a wooden shed. The owner tells us we can pitch our tents on one of the meadows nearby. At first we don't care that the grounds belong to the Chilean army. After our tents are up, however, I happen to spot a sign in several languages on the meadow next to ours: "Minefield peligro" – dangerous. I brace myself for a night of suspense. Who knows what hides in the grass under our tents, left over from the conflict with Argentina in the late 1970s. Everything remains quiet though, until 6 a.m. The first cars arrive, keeping their engines running while they wait for the ferry. We scramble from our sleeping bags and allow ourselves a cup of tea to wake up properly before getting back on our bikes. The route to Ushuaia is a feast for the eyes because we can finally see forests and trees again after days on the Patagonian pampas. I take a deep breath. I wouldn't have thought that I could miss the lush green of the trees so much. White peaks rise over the tree tops because the foothills of the Andes are snow-covered even in the summer. Chinese lanterns and lichen hang from the branches in a delicate web. We reach Ushuaia, the continent's southernmost city, just before New Year's Eve. In the language of the Yamaná, the name means "the bay penetrating the land to the west". It is a former penal colony that today has more than 50,000 inhabitants. At the end of Ruta 3, which ends in Tierra del Fuego National Park, we reach the southernmost point of our journey, just barely 1,000 km away from Antarctica. I have the feeling of having come a little closer to the end of the world.

This year, 24 bikers from all over the world are meeting at a camping site on the edge of the national park. On a whim we together organize the first Fin del Mundo Rally. Two of the bikers figure out a demanding trial and race course. A local TV station pays a visit, then it starts. I mentally take my helmet off to each of the contestants and we cheer on these brave people at the top of our lungs. The course is marked with twigs and plastic bags, leading through trees, down a steep hill and up again through a narrow bend. The skill and minor mistakes of the drivers are rated according to a simple point system. The course runs through the

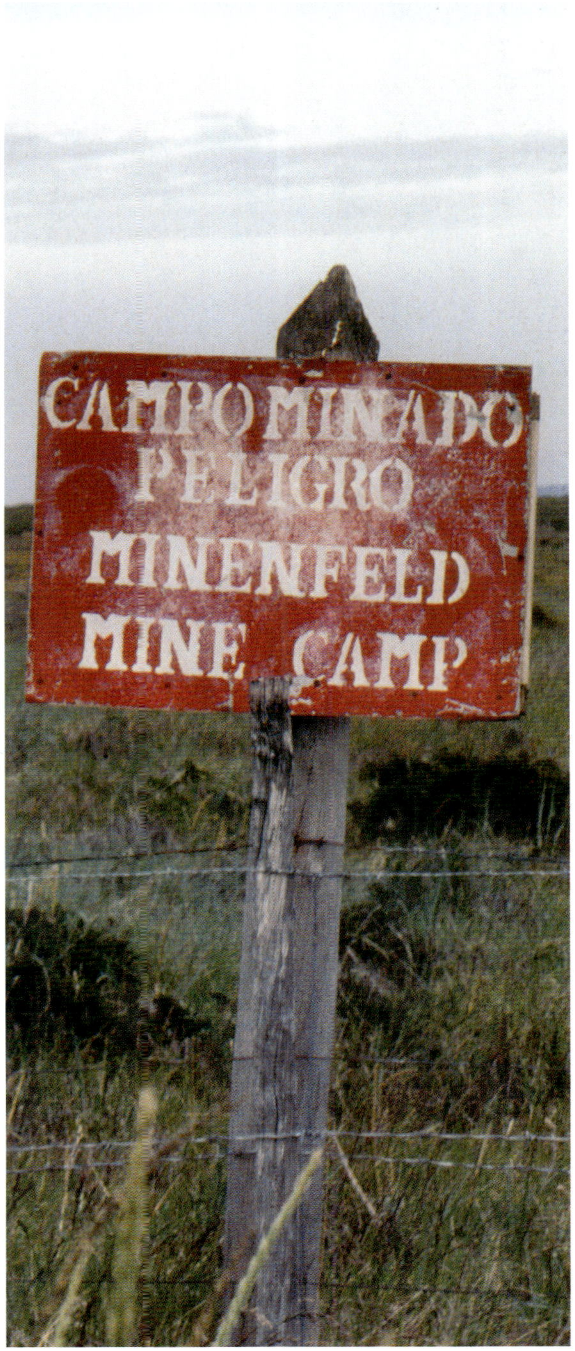

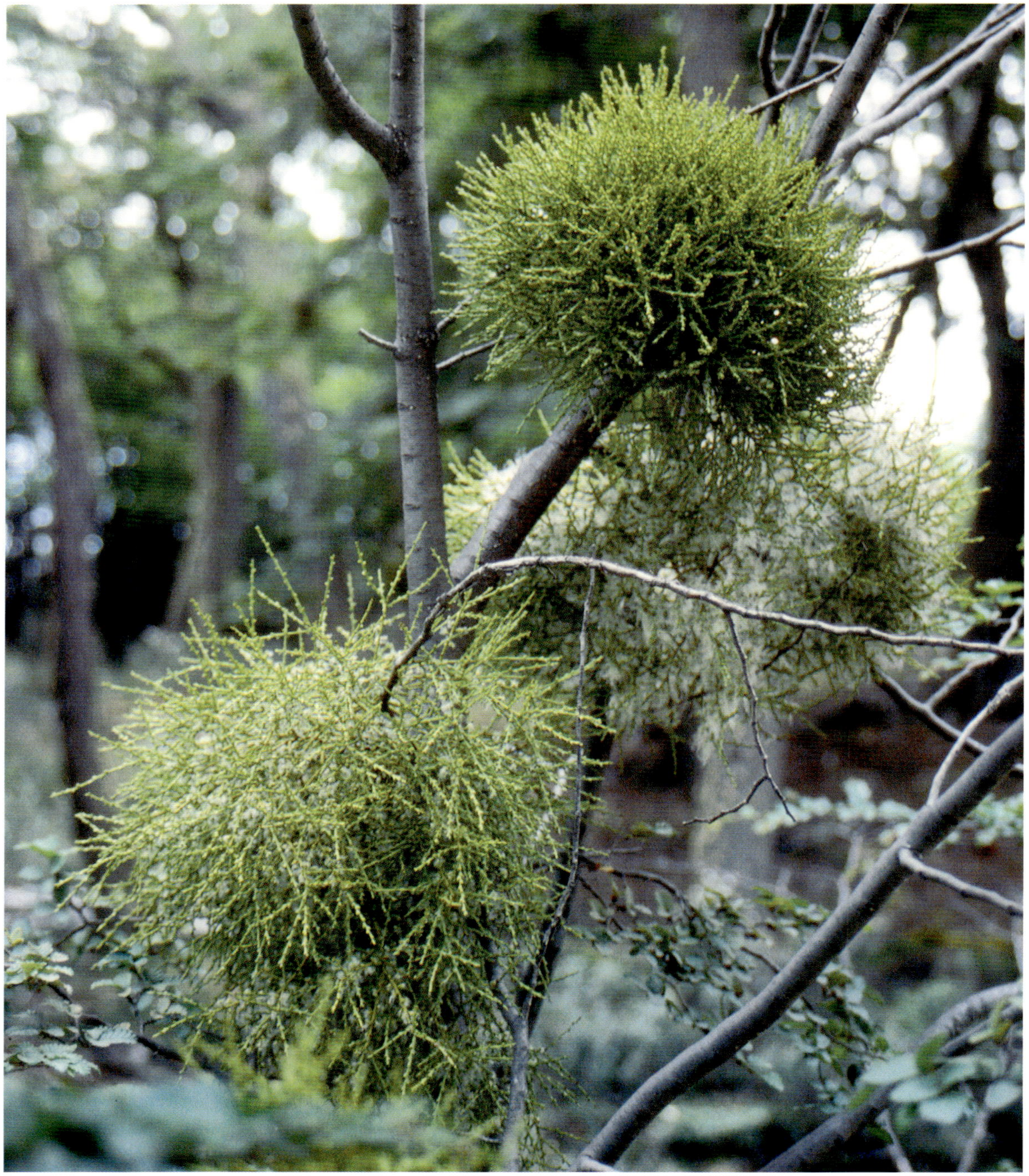

Left: "Chinese Lanterns" in the magic forest of Tierra del Fuego, Argentina

Page 25 top: Ushuaia, the world's southernmost city, Argentina

Page 25 bottom: First Fin del Mundo Rally New Year's Eve 2003 in Ushuaia

river. Three groups start one after the other and enter into a hot competition. Everybody is ambitious and none of the participants is willing to give up. In a muddy bend they begin to race for the finish line. Carsten is chosen as the overall winner and receives a bottle of German schnapps that someone has unearthed from his food bag. After finishing an Asado, a typical Argentinean barbecue, we light a bonfire on the shore. The atmosphere on this New Year's Eve is something special because we celebrate with strangers from all corners of the globe as if they are our best friends, knowing very well that we won't see most of them ever again. We talk about the past and about what the future might bring. Many of them left their jobs as we did and don't know what will happen when they go home. But in the end, all that matters is being together right now, the next leg of the journey, the next day, and rising to the challenges it will bring.

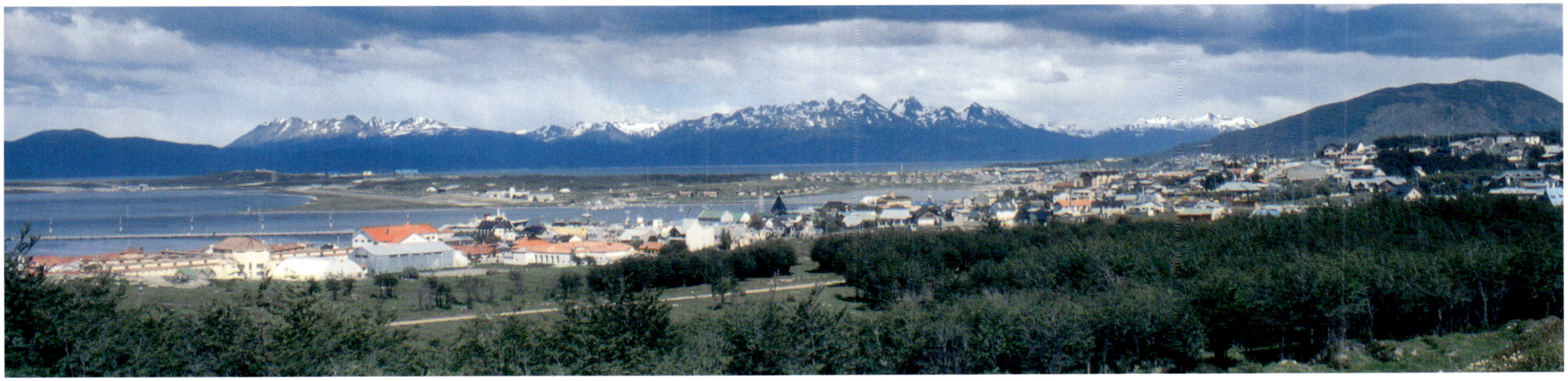

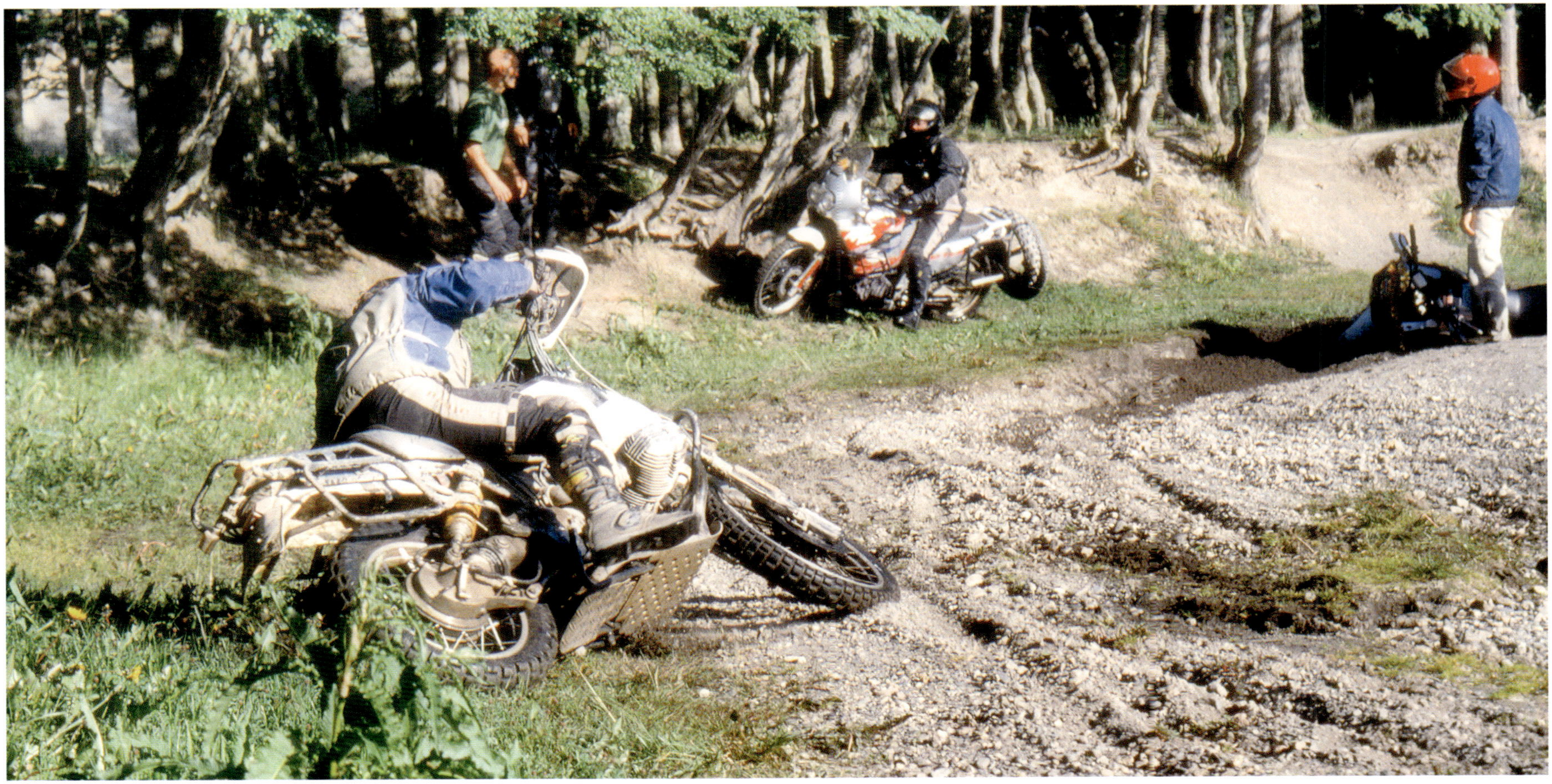

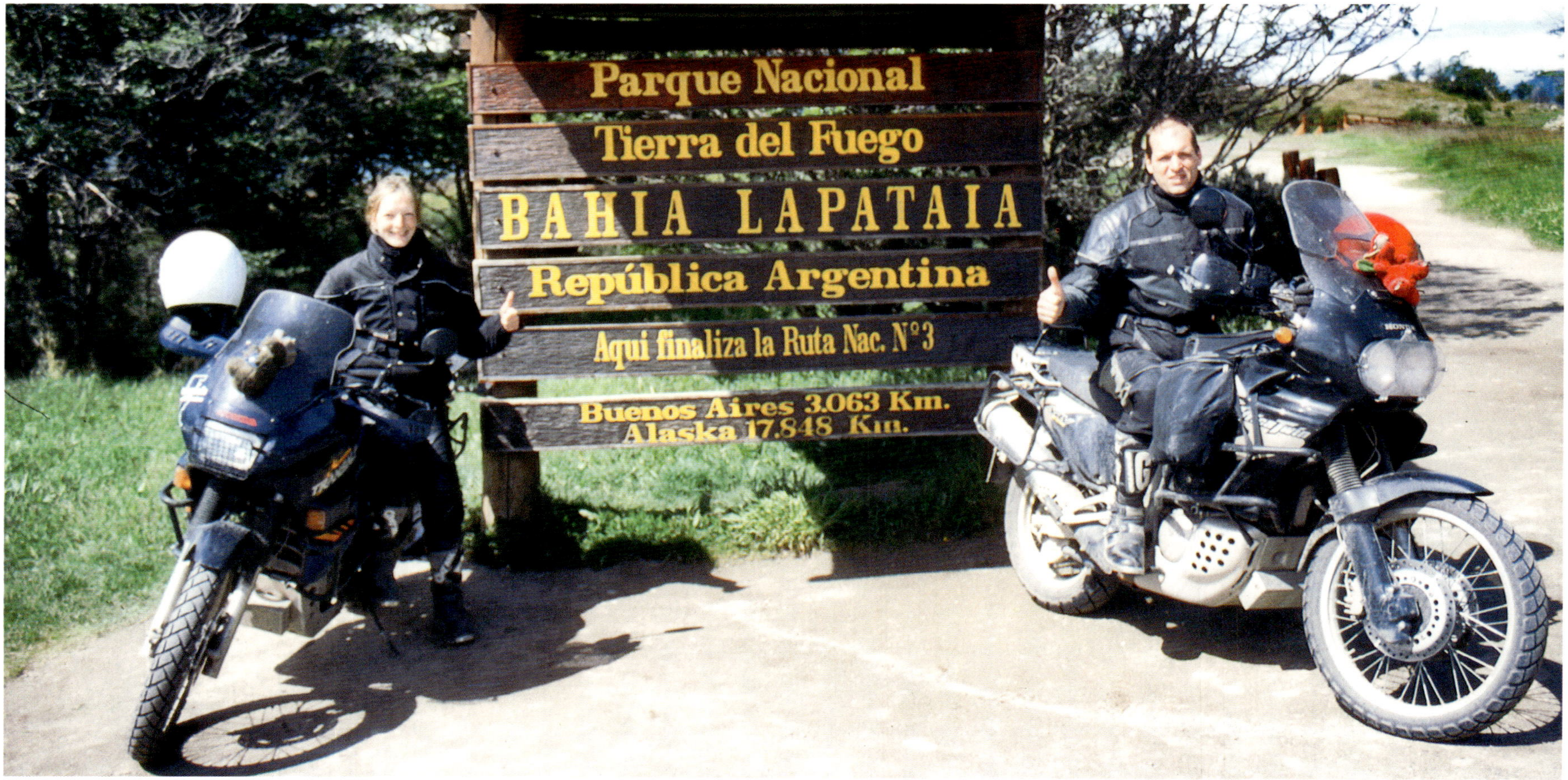

Top: We reach the southernmost place of our journey

ROADS TO SOLITUDE

A few days later we are on our way to the north-western shore of Tierra del Fuego to go back to the mainland. This time, we don't have much luck with the ferry. According to several trustworthy sources it is supposed to cast off at 2 p.m. However, the boat is nowhere to be seen on the quay. At the harbour master's office they tell us that, of course, the ferry always leaves at 8 a.m. Of course. Now we are stuck in the dreary little village of Porvenir for the night. We ask a woman about a place to stay, but she doesn't know whether or not there is one here. Then we ask for directions to the city centre, and she answers, rather astonished, that this is it. I look around and nod. No bank, no shops, a tiny post office on the promenade. In a little side street we come across a boarding house with vacancies. Later, we take a walk and find a minimercado where we can buy a few biscuits and beverages. Translated into English, "Porvenir" means "future", it is, after all, the region's administrative centre. Still, the name

Page 27: Dirt road along the "useless bay" (bahia inútil) in Chile

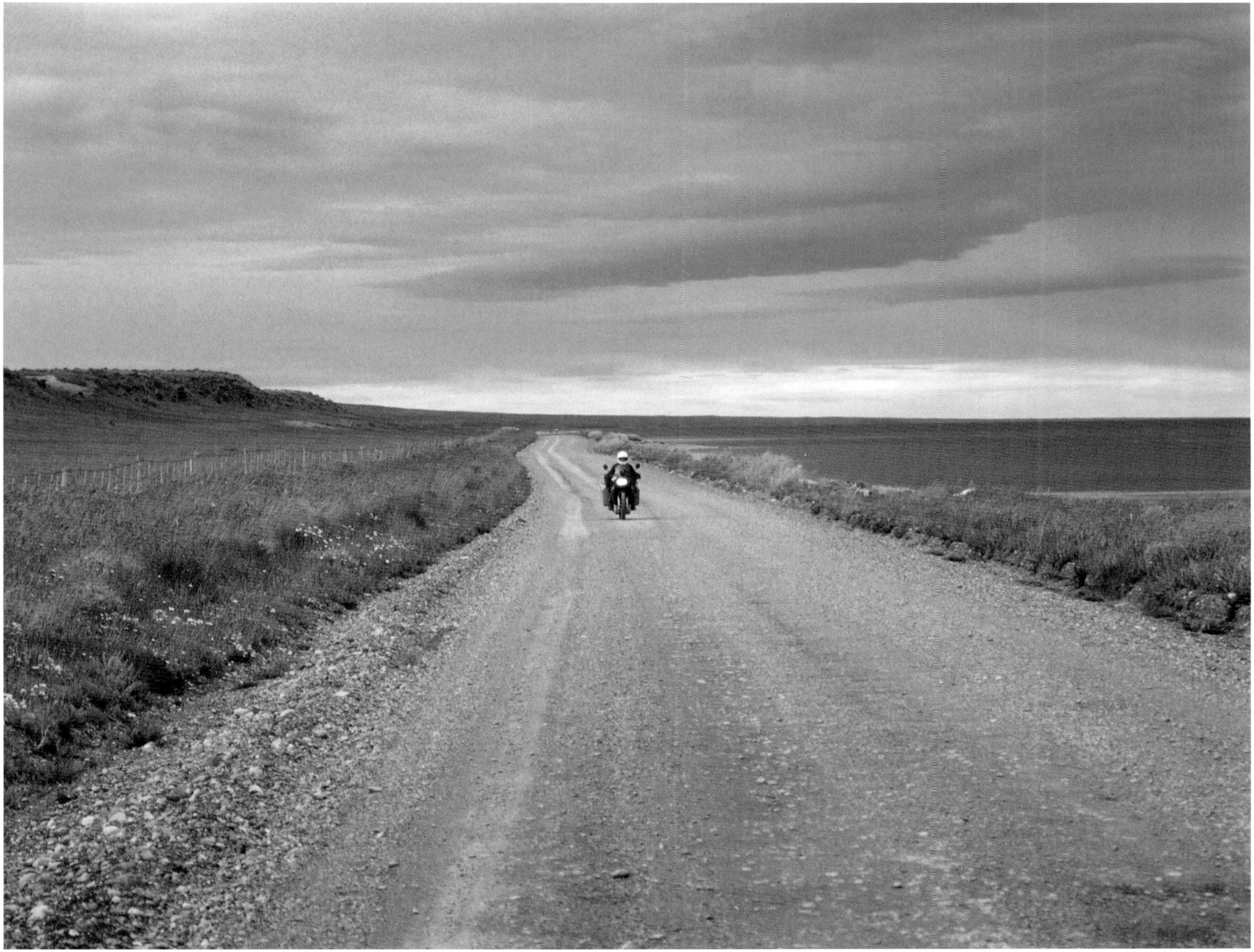

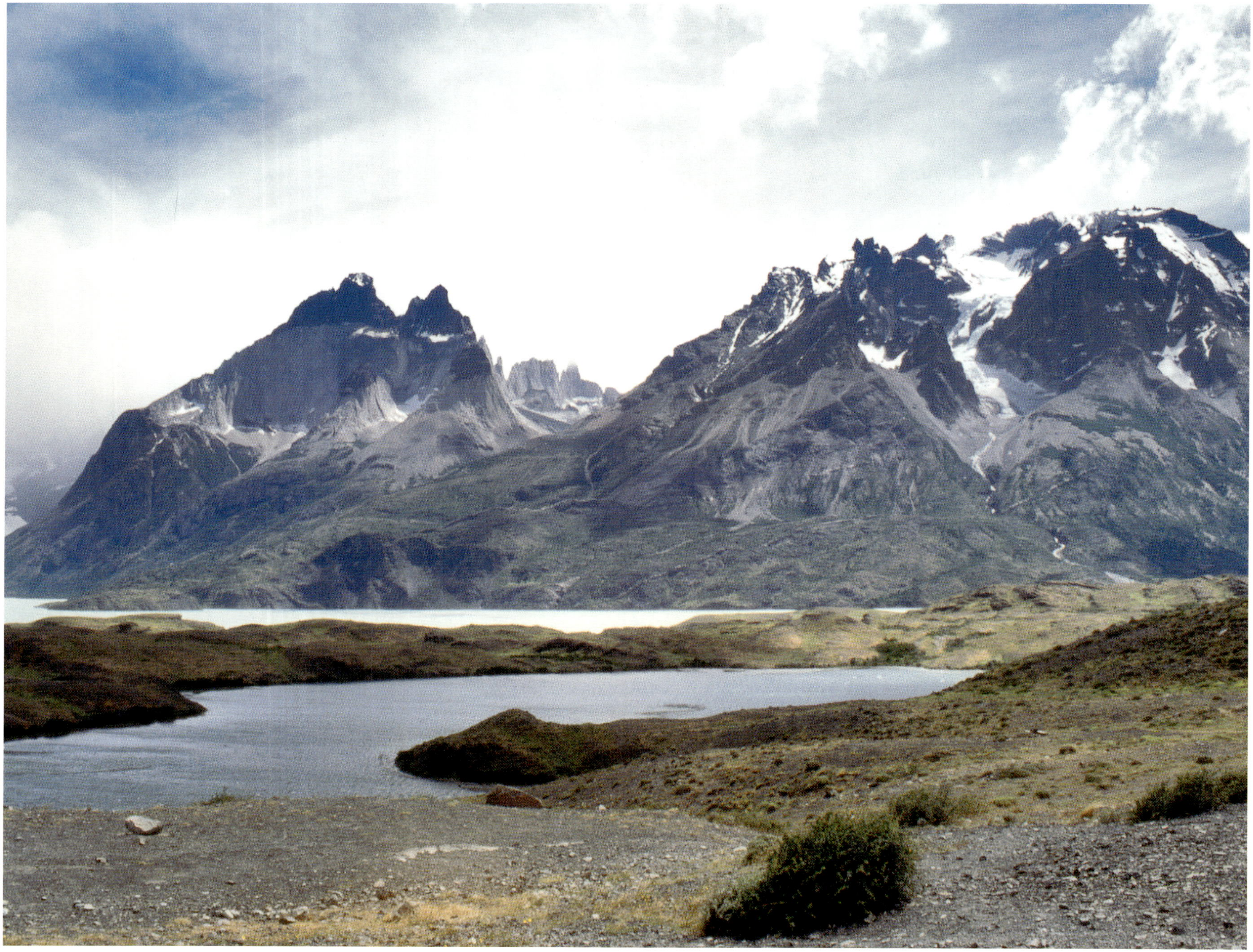

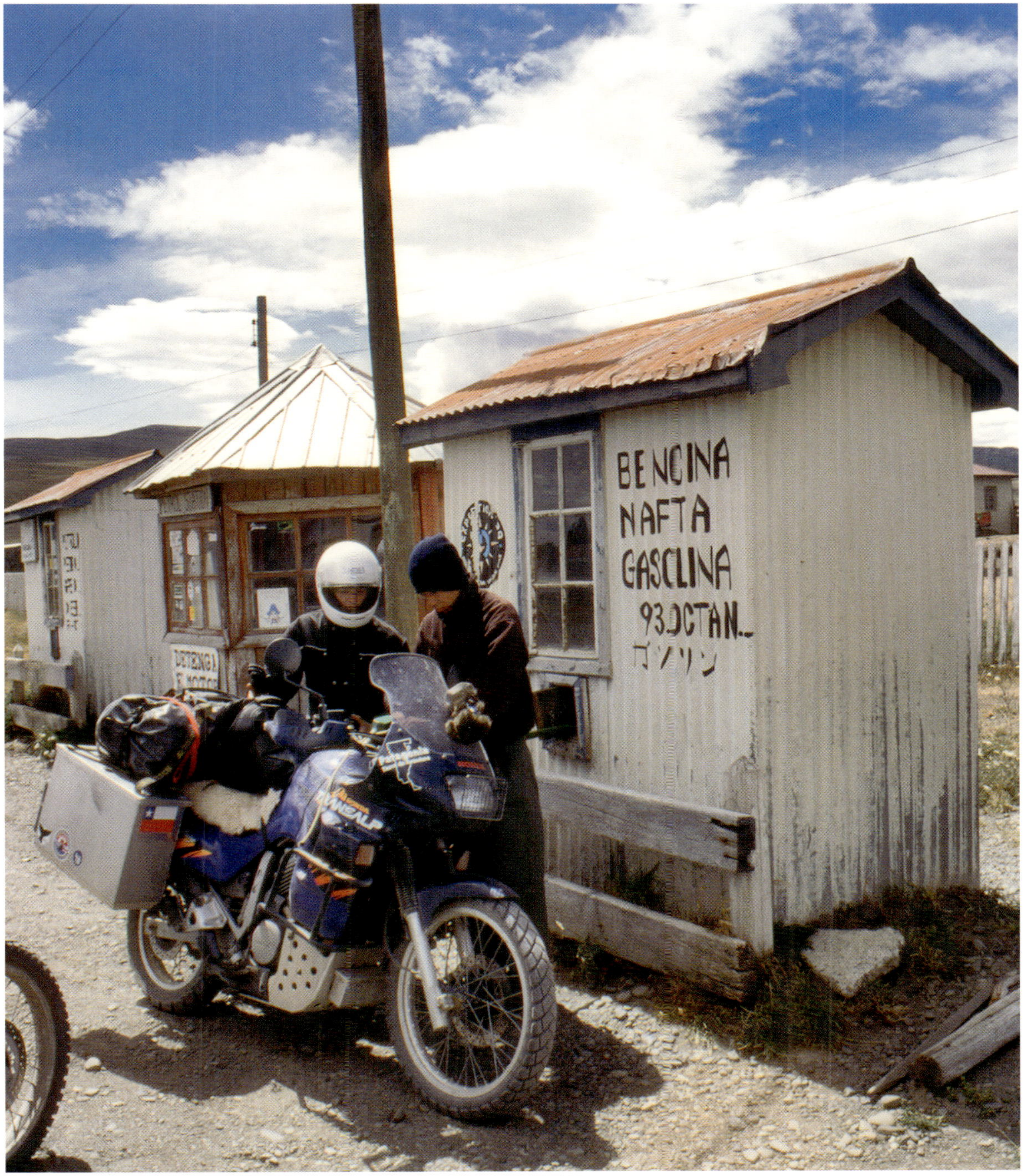

Page 28: "Towers" in the Chilean National Park Torres del Paine

Right: Not all pumps are easily recognizable, Cerro Castillo in Chile

doesn't quite seem to express the spirit of the village, it rather seems to refer to the days when prospectors came through here looking for gold.

The alarm goes off at the crack of dawn, we arrive at the port on time, the boat lies at the quay, but its single loading ramp is frighteningly small. The parking lot is crammed with cars. When the captain sees our big bikes, he shakes his head. This could be a close call. A big truck is manoeuvred back and forth for half an hour before having to drive off again, so there is room to squeeze us into two little corners at the bow. The Transalp is tied to a pick-up with thick ropes. It is a two-hour trip and the sea is quite heavy, so I am glad that the bikes are secured. Following an inspiration, I untie the bikes before we reach the quay, because the driver of the pick-up shoots off without checking the ropes on his bodywork.

Passing Punta Arenas and Puerto Natales, and after an excursion to the Torres del Paine National Park, we switch countries, again on gravelly dirt roads and arrive in Argentina. We struggle with a rocky path where even a bullock cart would have a difficult time and drive on gravel roads to Los Glaciares National Park. Perito Moreno on Lago Argentino is one of 14 glaciers fed by

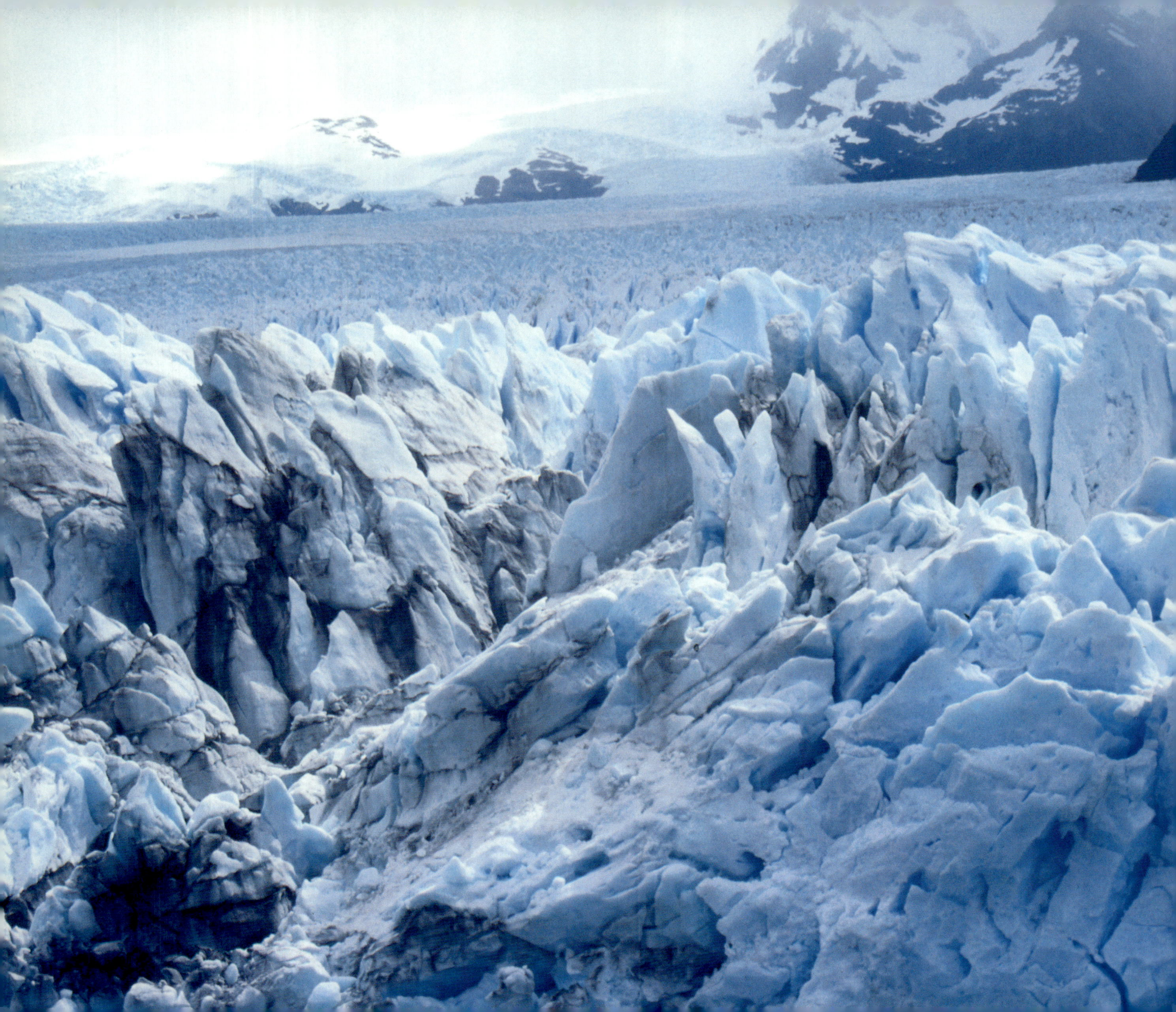

Page 30: The glacier Perito Moreno in Argentina

Bottom right: Seclusion in Patagonia, Ruta 40 in Argentina

the Patagonian ice sheet. The dirt road of 78 km leads through forests to the glacier. As we turn around a bend, it shows itself for the first time. Like a very long tongue, the ice winds its way down the slopes. It is 4 km wide and 70 m high, pushing forward at least 40 cm per day into the lake towards the opposite shore. In 1900, the glacier was still 750 m away from the lake, now the ice separates it into two parts. It is an overwhelming view. The colours of the ice range from deep blue to emerald green to turquoise and even brilliant white. The movement opens holes and fissure in the ice that catch the light to form fantastic shapes. Hundreds of visitors crowd the planks and lookouts. Every time the glacier "calves", meaning that a big chunk of ice breaks off the main mass, there is a thunderous crash and the visitors murmur in awe. A chunk sinks down and bobs back to the surface a few seconds later, spreading circular waves. Then it drifts off, slightly wobbly, as a new little iceberg. It is difficult to catch just the right moment on camera because when you hear the crash the ice has almost vanished into the water. Suddenly it seems as if the wide front of projecting ice is beginning to move. It bobs up and down and for a moment it looks as if a horizontal crack might run along the glacier's lower edge. Then there is complete silence again. We stay for hours, because I can't stop watching the fascinating scene. Every few years, the ice pushing into the lake dams up so much water that its pressure makes a huge block of ice collapse. This time it will take 16 years.Two months later, travelling through Argentina's north-east about 2,000 km away, we watch a live TV broadcast as a 70 m tall wall of ice that had been pushed onto the tongue of land is first hollowed out and then collapses. It is a rather moving spectacle of nature that draws international attention.

620 km of gravel road are ahead of us on the plains. The Andes are far to the west. On the notorious Ruta 40, many travellers have had to cut their journeys short because of the heavy winds. Some days the air hardly moves at all, so travellers don't believe the

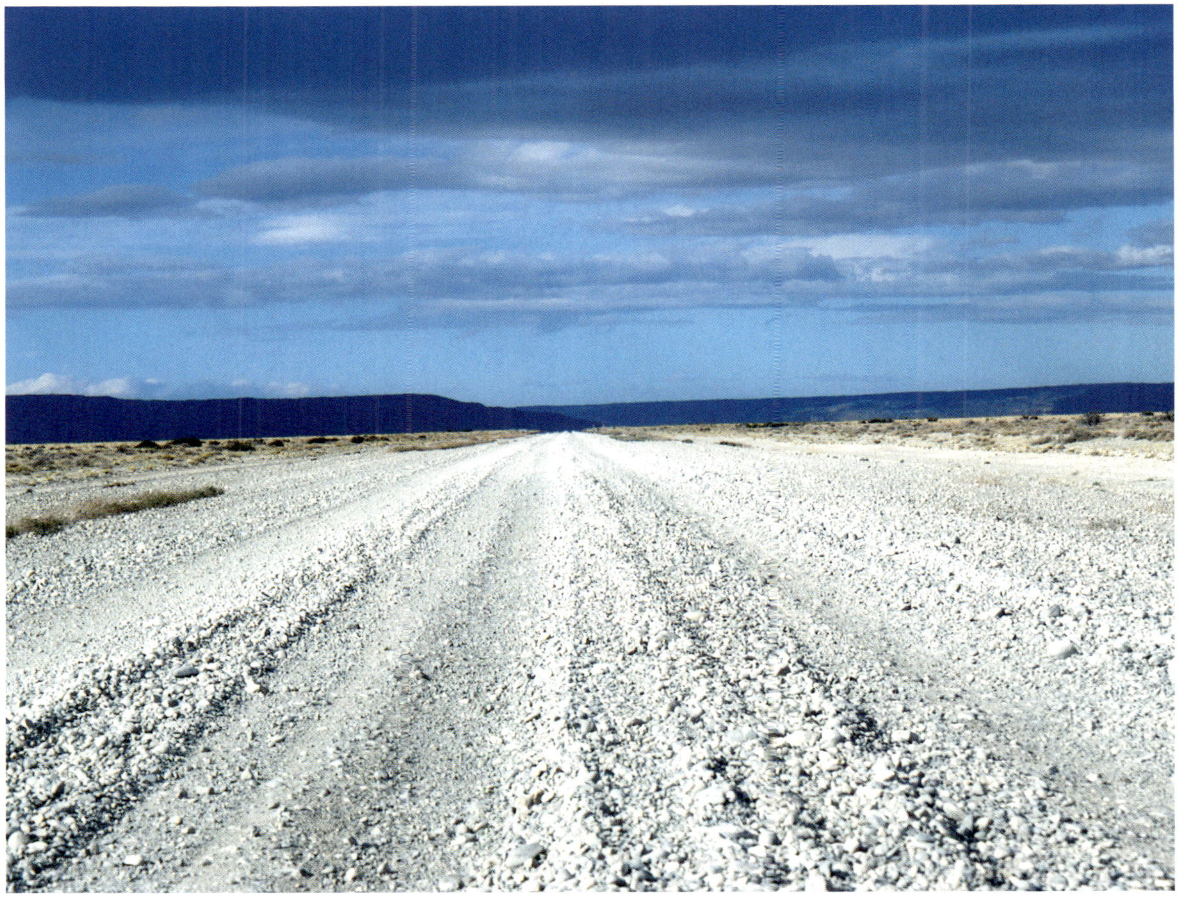

stories about the things that others have experienced on the road. I wonder what will happen to us. With Klaus and Mark, two of the Germans we met, we go on our way. At first we harbour the illusion of being able to make it to Lago Buenos Aires in a day. But the road is terrible. Next to the ruts, just about the width of a car tyre, the gravel is piled high. It is very windy. The gales keep driving me off the road, up a small hill, down the slope, back onto the road. It doesn't take long for me to fall. The guys help me right my heavy, loaded bike. With new determination I get back on my bike and drive. I take two more falls, and the last makes my bike spin on the aluminium suitcase, which is torn off. We park the bikes by the side on the road so that they can't fall over and hunker down in a ditch to repair the fixtures of the case as best we can. The box can be secured again, only the lid doesn't fit well anymore. Meanwhile there is a layer of dust on everything, so the lopsided lid doesn't matter. I'm fed up and exhausted. Mark sums it up perfectly, "Angi is on the ground more than on her bike." At least we haven't lost our sense of humour. We weigh giving up for today and returning to Tres Lagos against going on. The three guys take the easy way out and let me decide. Who knows what the conditions will be tomorrow, we have to move on somehow. So I grit my teeth – let's just do this. During a photo break, Klaus' bike is blown over, and Mark's, too, not a minute later. At least I'm not the only one who needs to repair some things. After 11 hours and 370 km we start looking for a place to stay near Tamel Aike. There is very little choice. On a far away field we can see a deserted ruin without a roof, windows or doors. One house by the side of the road looks inhabited. We knock and ask for permission to pitch our tents next to the house to be sheltered from the wind. Father and son offer us a room in their house. They think that the wind would blow our tents away. There are two Swiss women with bicycles and two bikers from Buenos Aires already staying for the night.

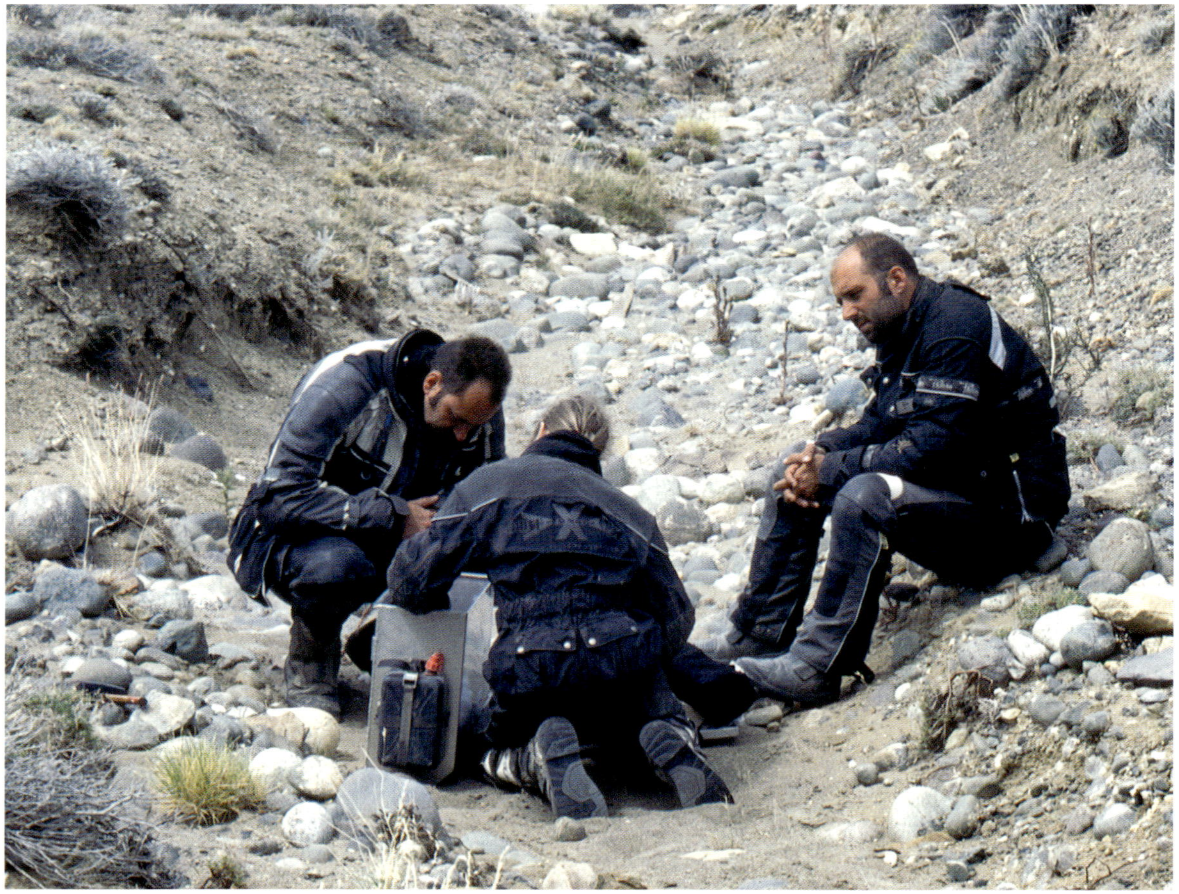

First we adjust the lid of my box and then straighten Mark's out with a jack. Afterwards we all gather in the kitchen and are allowed to cook something on the stove. For father and son, it seems to be completely normal to offer shelter to travellers, almost as if they are having friends over. Our hosts live in very simple conditions and share a room behind the kitchen. The Swiss ladies sleep in a room next to the door. Another room is used for storage, as a feed silo and chicken coop. An animal hide hangs over the back of a chair, dry corn spilling from a ripped feed sack is scattered all over the floor. Mark and Klaus try to sweep away the

Page 32: Forced break on the Ruta 40, Argentina

Bottom: Quarters inTamel Aike, Argentina

worst of the dried-up chicken droppings, feathers and other debris and spread their sleeping bags out on the wooden floor. In the adjoining room taken by the Argentineans, there are three wooden bedsteads piled high with mattresses, and a little hallway leads to a bathroom with two wash basins, a shower and a toilet. These seem to be lodgings for migrant workers. After a glance at the mattresses, Axel and I prefer to roll out our thermomats and sleeping bags on the floor, even though this disturbs the insects on their usual routes. Electricity is supplied by a generator in the barn. The lights go out at 8 p.m. and candles are distributed in the rooms. Soon, everything goes quiet. The two women depart on their bicycles at dawn. We are back on our way around 8:30 a.m. The wind is still blowing strong, let's see what this day has in store for us. After 20 minutes and 14 km, we meet the two women again. It took them three hours to get this far. Compared to them we are making really good time!

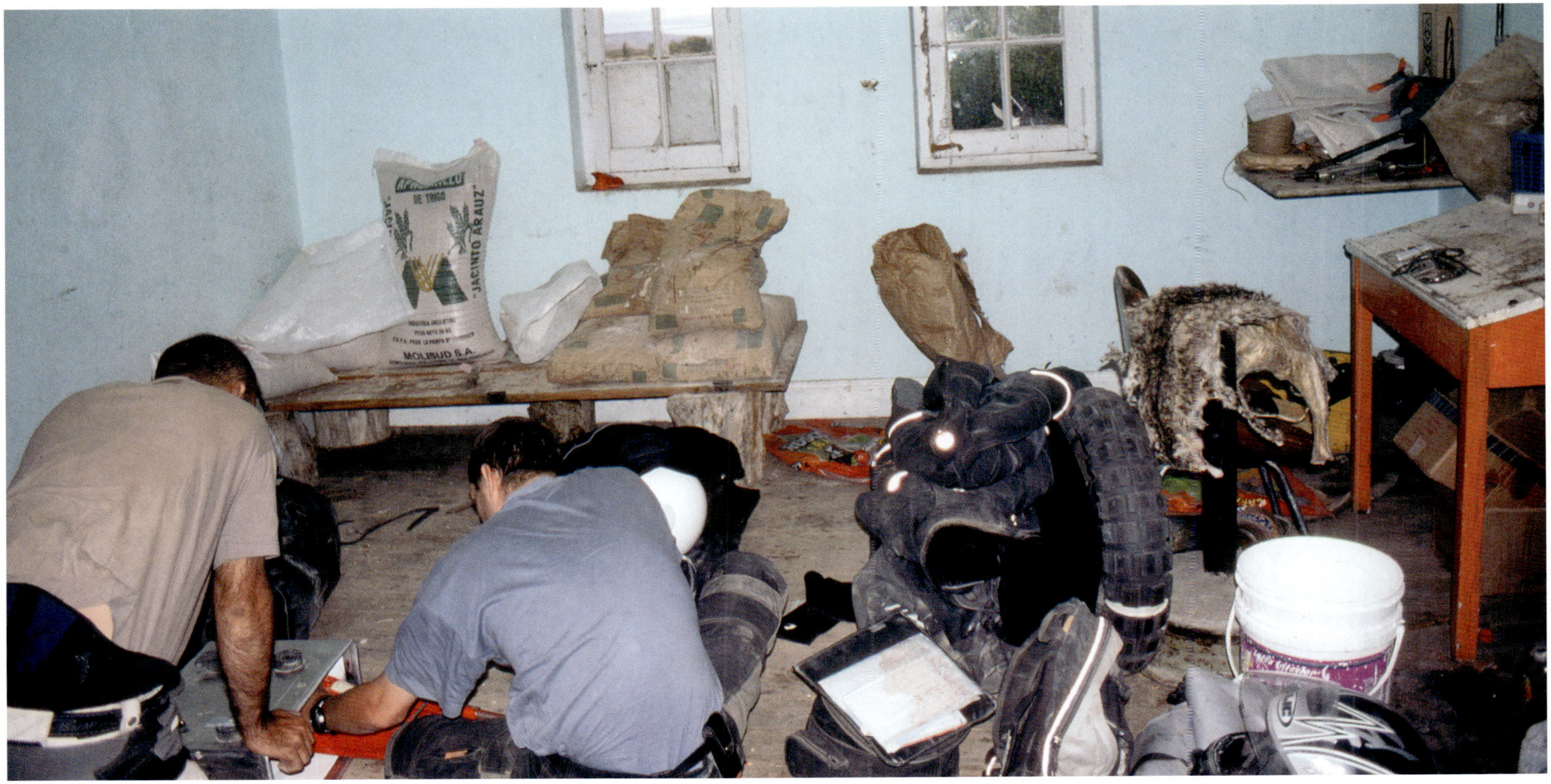

The road turns to the north and after about 120 km we reach Bajo Caracoles, a cluster of houses with a filling station and hotel in the middle of nowhere. Here we get food for ourselves and our bikes. So far the landscape has been rather monotonous, but now that the Andes are within view, it is becoming more interesting – snow-topped mountains are lined up like a string of pearls. The wind drops and we manage to reach an average speed of 50 km/h. We reach Perito Moreno a day later than planned. We turn right around and leave the community camping grounds when the manager and his friends start to paw through our luggage, drunk and completely high on dope. Instead we find Raúl's Minicamping, a clean place with hot running water, something that we certainly don't take for granted. Raúl is quite a character and has a good heart. He is constantly mumbling unintelligible things in a melodic singsong voice, but that doesn't matter. Happily, he wields his cleaning rags all over the place and is always looking out for our welfare.

We need to do a little check-up. The brothers' suitcases need to be straightened out again and our rubber mallet is quickly becoming the most important tool. The speedometer of the Transalp doesn't work and can't be repaired. I take my little bicycle speedometer as a work-around, even though I have just used it as a watch until now. One of the fixtures of the engine casing has shaken loose and is replaced with cable ties. Unfortunately, the chain is rattling like mad and has been for a while. Axel wants to check it out and tries to hoist it up on one of the aluminium boxes. In order to do this, he pulls it over the side stand, which gives way under the weight. I can't believe it. The thread bar that was built in as extra support for the lowered bike has just caved in. Now the bike has no support whatsoever. Right away, Raúl takes us to the village to find a welder. We spend the entire afternoon at the local hardware shop where the mechanic sets about the task with a great amount of dedication. He takes a No. 10 drill and tries to hollow out the bar. When that doesn't work, he takes the No. 12. The outer wall is getting thinner. Then his boss joins us and stops him. He looks for a No. 5 drill which he places carefully in the centre. This works much better, but the hole is too big now to do much good. They are trying to weld on a thread rod. The problem which occurs is that the thread of the nut in the upper part of the stand has metric measurements, while the rod is in imperial system, which is more common in Argentina. The mechanic and his boss are confident that they will find a solution if given a little time. I'm preparing for a long wait and am utterly surprised when they deliver a perfectly functional stand to the camping site that evening. They found a metric screw, sawed the head off and welded it to the stand. It turned out to be a little on the long side, but at least I can support my bike again. At first, the men refuse payment for the work because this is not their regular business but a personal favour. After a while, I am able to persuade them to take 20 pesos, about 7 €. That evening I begin to wonder. My frequent falls are bothering me. Is it my lack of strength or the right method, or are my tyres at fault here? Is it so difficult to hold the bike because of the condition of

Page 35: At Lago General Carrera in the Aisén province, Chile

Bottom: Chilean variation of the Golden Gate Bridge on the Carretera Austral

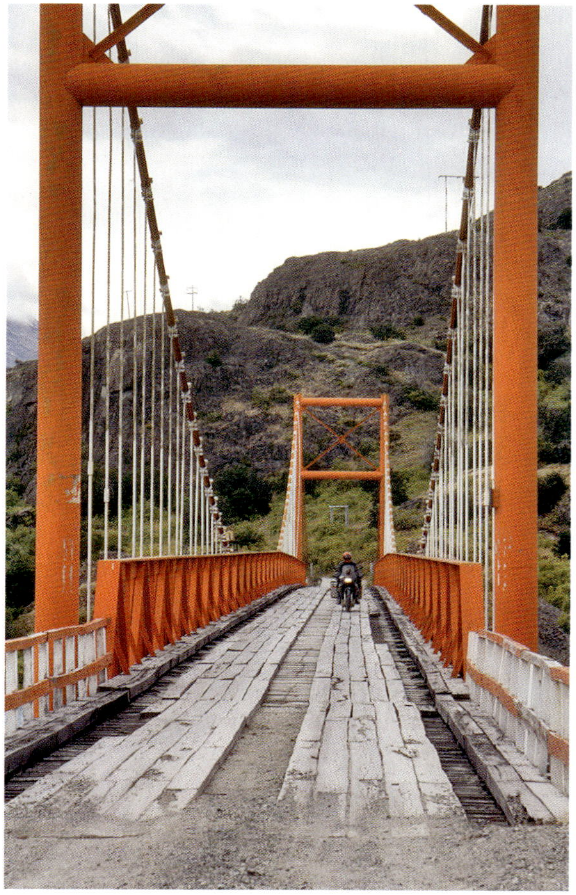

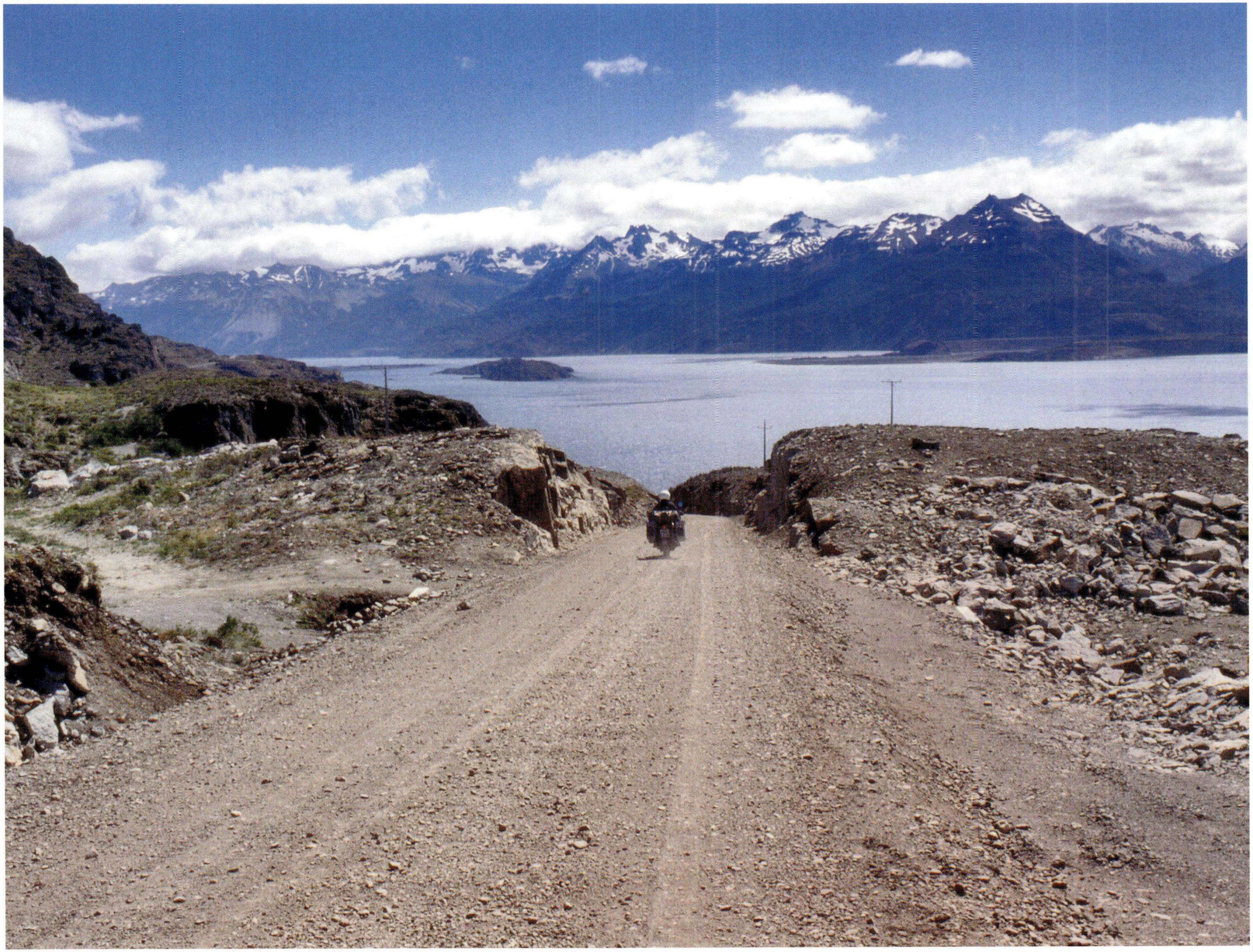

the roads and the heavy winds? Maybe it is a little of everything and the journey is getting to me a little. So many experiences crowd my mind every day, so many impressions are taken in with all my senses, that they can't all be processed by writing in my journal alone. Still, despite the occasional doubts it is an incredible feeling to be so free, to travel on two wheels and feel my bike beneath me.

South America's second-largest lake is called General Carrera in Chile and Buenos Aires in Argentina, because the border between the countries runs straight through it. Along its shore, the lake offers a 120 km roller coaster ride – pure joy. The road winds its way through the mountains, we make it over the crest and plunge down into the valley before conquering the next height, with one bend chasing after the other. Out of Puerto Guadal, we find the Carretera Austral. Ruta 7, as it is called officially and somewhat prosaically, begins to the south-east of Puerto Montt, leading south through lush rainforests and difficult terrain for about 1,100 km to Puerto Yungay, and from there with a ferry across Mitchell Fjord to Villa O'Higgins. Here begins the biggest continuous field of ice outside of Antarctica, the Campo de Hielo Norte. In the 1930s, the first few settlers came to Chile's "great south" and built a few settlements. In the 1970s, Chile's former ruler Augusto Pinochet initiated the big project "Carretera Austral". It was mainly for strategic reasons that he wanted to create a north-south axis along the Argentine border. It was hewn right through the rainforest. Rivers, fjords and mountains were subjected to the construction efforts, but nature rebelled many times against this kind of interference. Even now, the road has many narrow, overgrown places. The Carretera Austral has become an important transit road for trucks even though the conditions hardly allow it.

Due to the rain, we take a room at a boarding house in Rio Tranquilo. Despite the bad weather, we want to cross the lake and go to the marble caves. In the morning, the rain lets up and we set out in a group of ten people. The lake is rather choppy, and we bob on the waves in a little cockle shell of a boat. The marble caves are worth the stormy

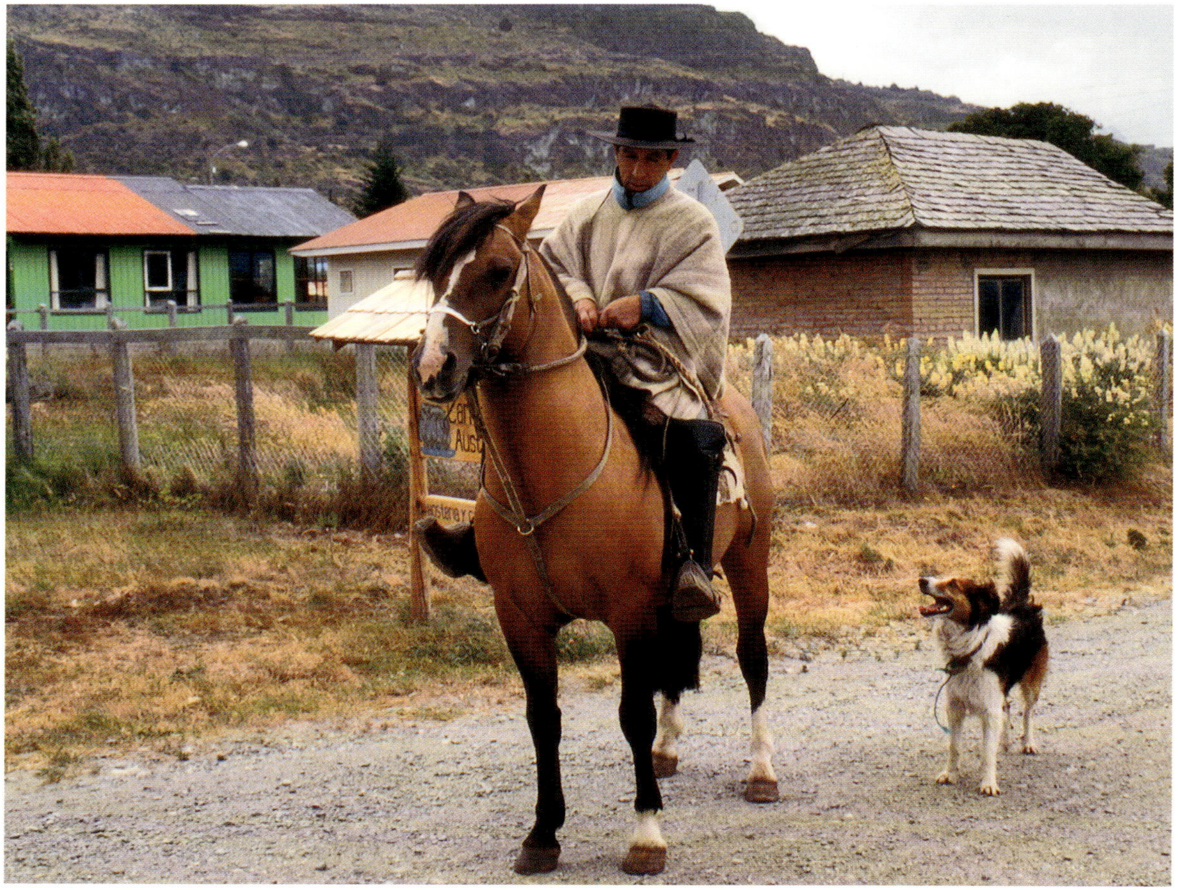

Top: Proud Huaso, as the Chilean drovers are called, with his herd dog Puerto Río Tranquilo

Page 37: Capilla de Mármol, chapel-like marble cave Lago General Carrera, Chile

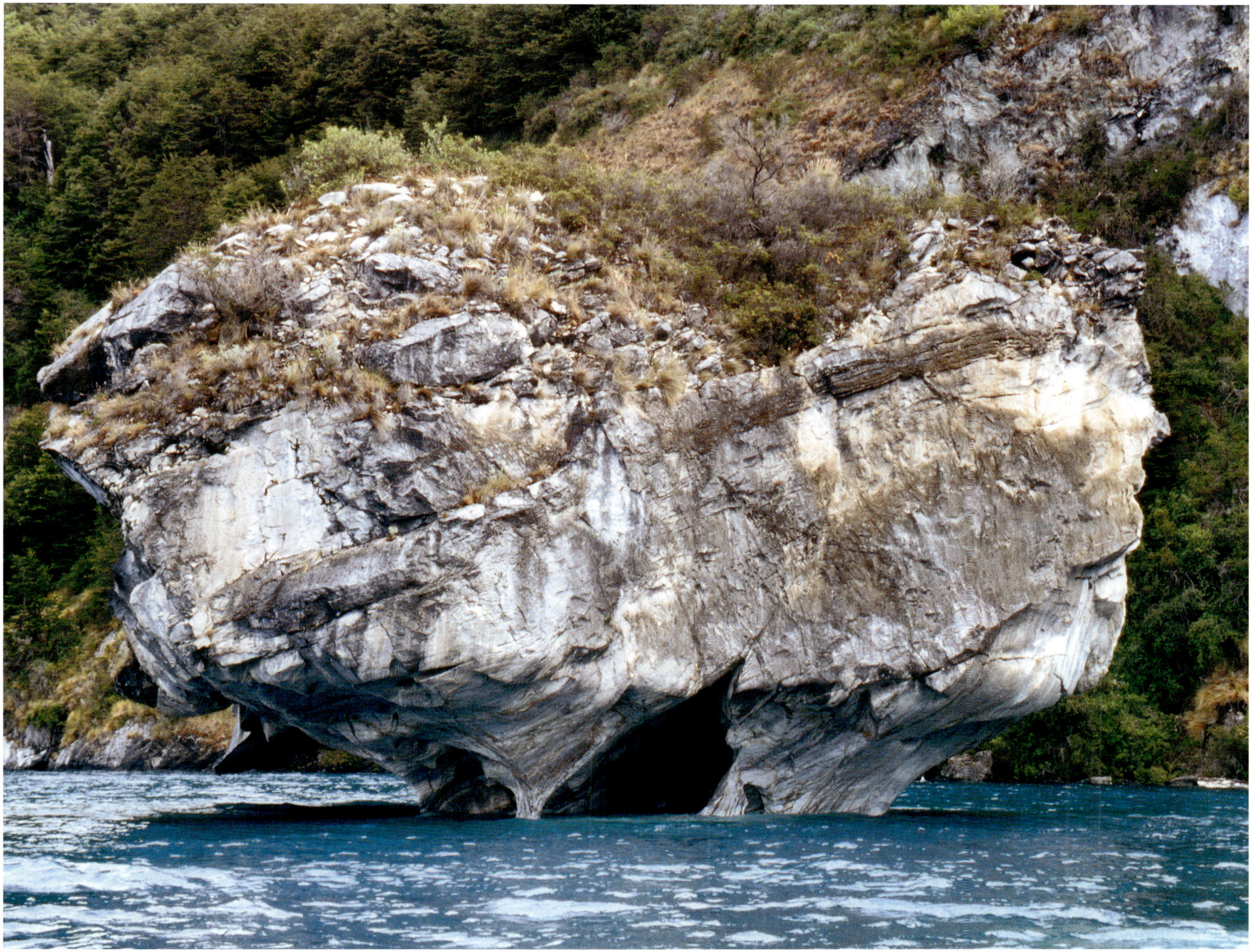

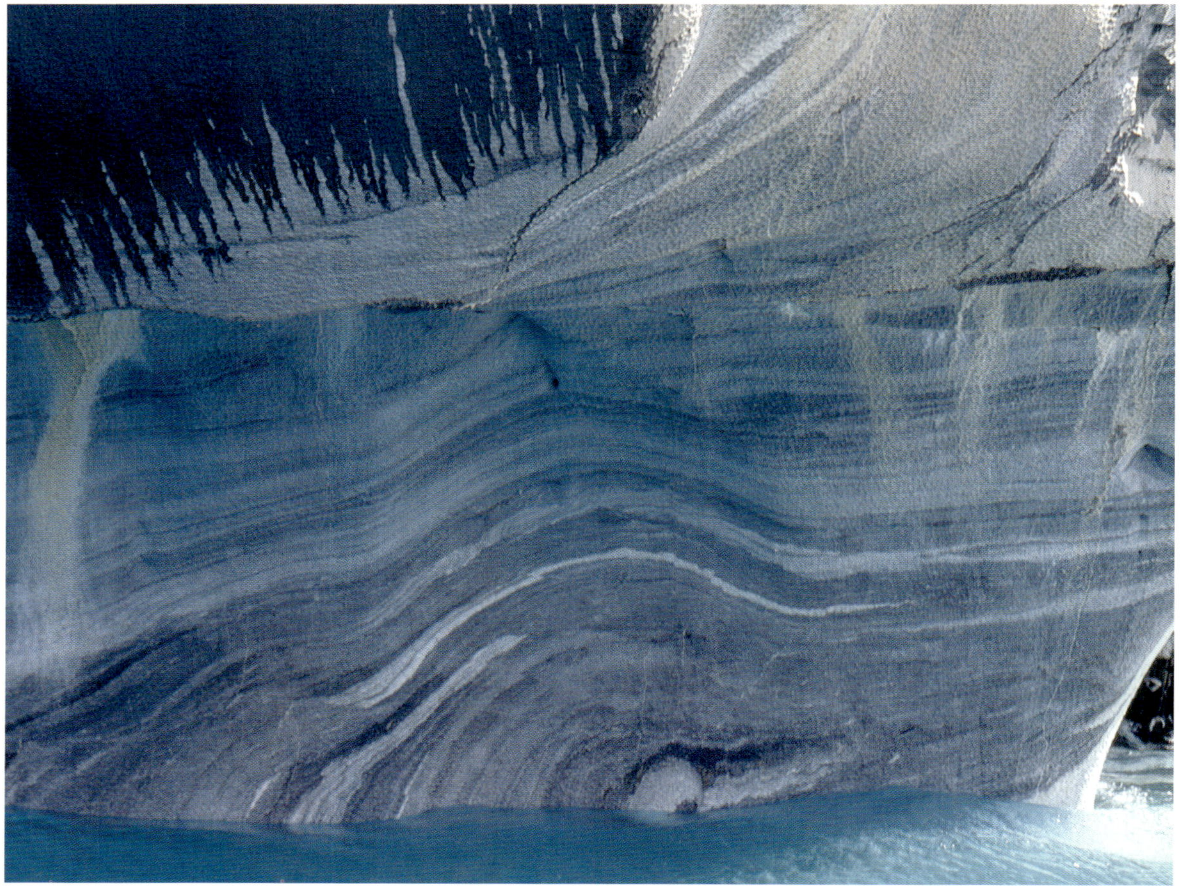

Left: Rough marble polished by water

Page 39: Puerto Puyuhuapi on the Carretera Austral, Chile

Bottom: One of the last of his kind: aluminium propeller welder in Coyhaique, Chile

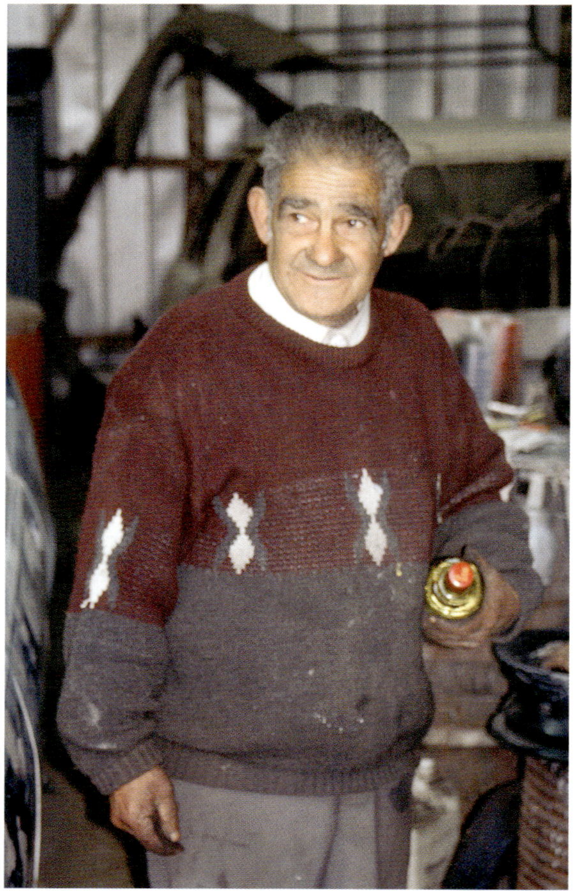

crossing. The sun is peeking out behind the clouds and makes the marble shimmer in many colours. It shimmers blue and green, white and beige, all reflected on the surface of the lake. The water has washed out the rock over the course of many centuries creating bizarre shapes. One of them looks like a skull whose empty black sockets stare at us mysteriously, another one is is Capilla de Mármol, a marble chapel perched on thin pillars at the bottom of the lake. In a certain light, it shines and shimmers like a submerged crystal. On the return trip, the wind picks up again. We have to distribute our weight strategically in the little boat so that it won't capsize in the rough waves. In this little boat on the lake in a storm, I feel completely helpless and subjected to the forces of nature. Now I can understand Axel's fear of flying that comes over him because he can't control the events. The waves throw us off our seats and down again. Foam sprays our faces. But the man at the helm knows what he is doing and gets us safely across the lake in half an hour.

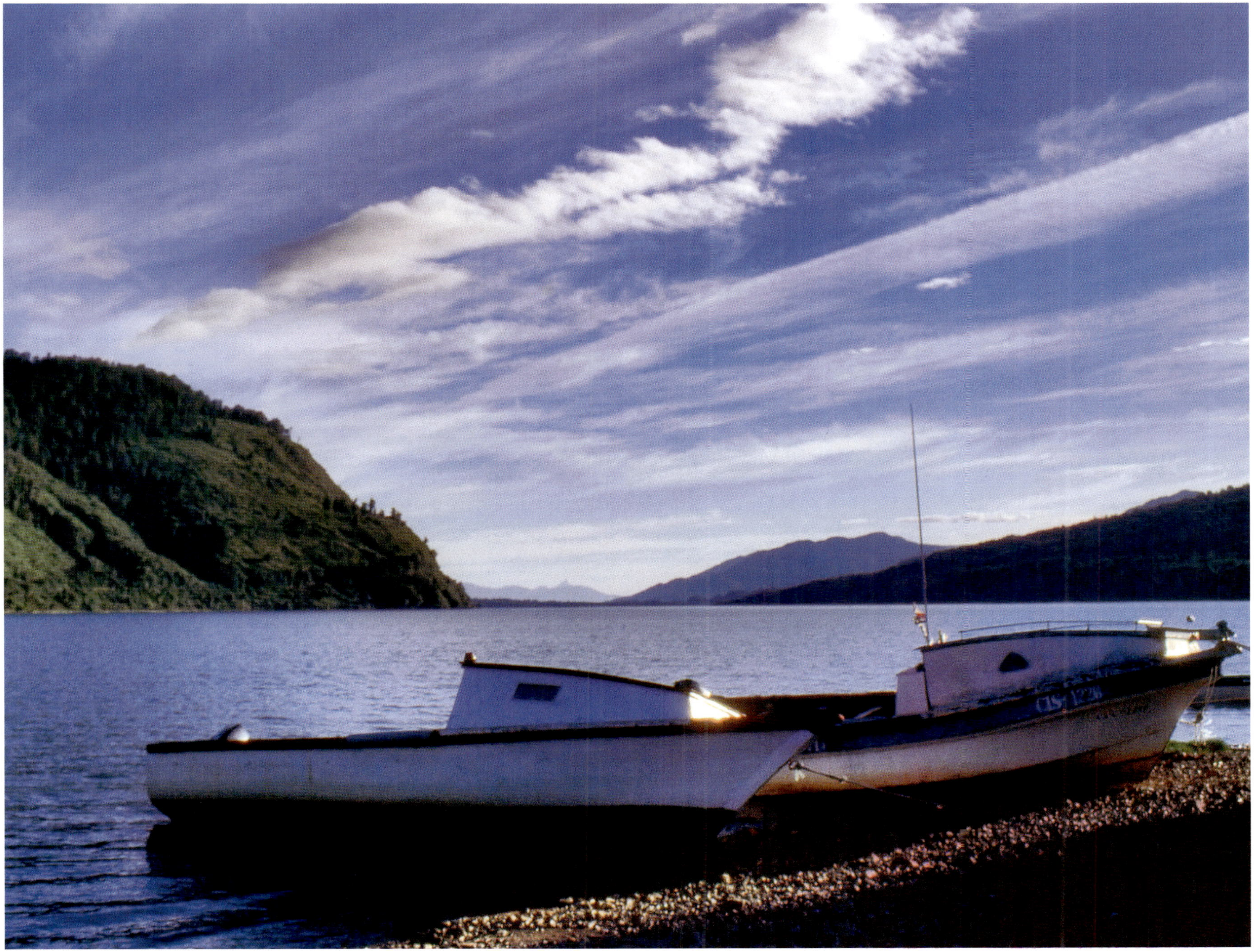

Through a dense forest we stay on the Carretera Austral travelling north. On small paths, passing waterfalls and little rivers, we make our way through the mist, dodging oncoming trucks as best we can. The terrain is difficult and everything is muddy from the rain. In Coyhaique, we look for a welder. We want to stabilize the stand. Completely by accident, we find a true master welder, who is said to be Patagonia's only welder of aluminium ship's propellers. In record time, he gives the stand a sturdy casing and even a new coat of paint – indestructible. From here, Axel and I travel alone to Puyuhuapi where we find ourselves transported to Germany at the beginning of the previous century. The village was established on the north shore of the Seno Ventisquero fjord by four Germans in 1935, and it is still run by the immigrants. Hostal Ludwig, Café Rossbach and numerous German tourists are the defining characteristics of the village, and many residents speak our language. The village is famous for its carpet factory where traditional carpets are still hand-knotted, mainly by women from the island of Chiloé, who are famous for their nimble fingers. The houses with their outer walls covered in wooden slats are built with a mixture of traditions from Germany and Chiloé tradition, which is still kept alive.

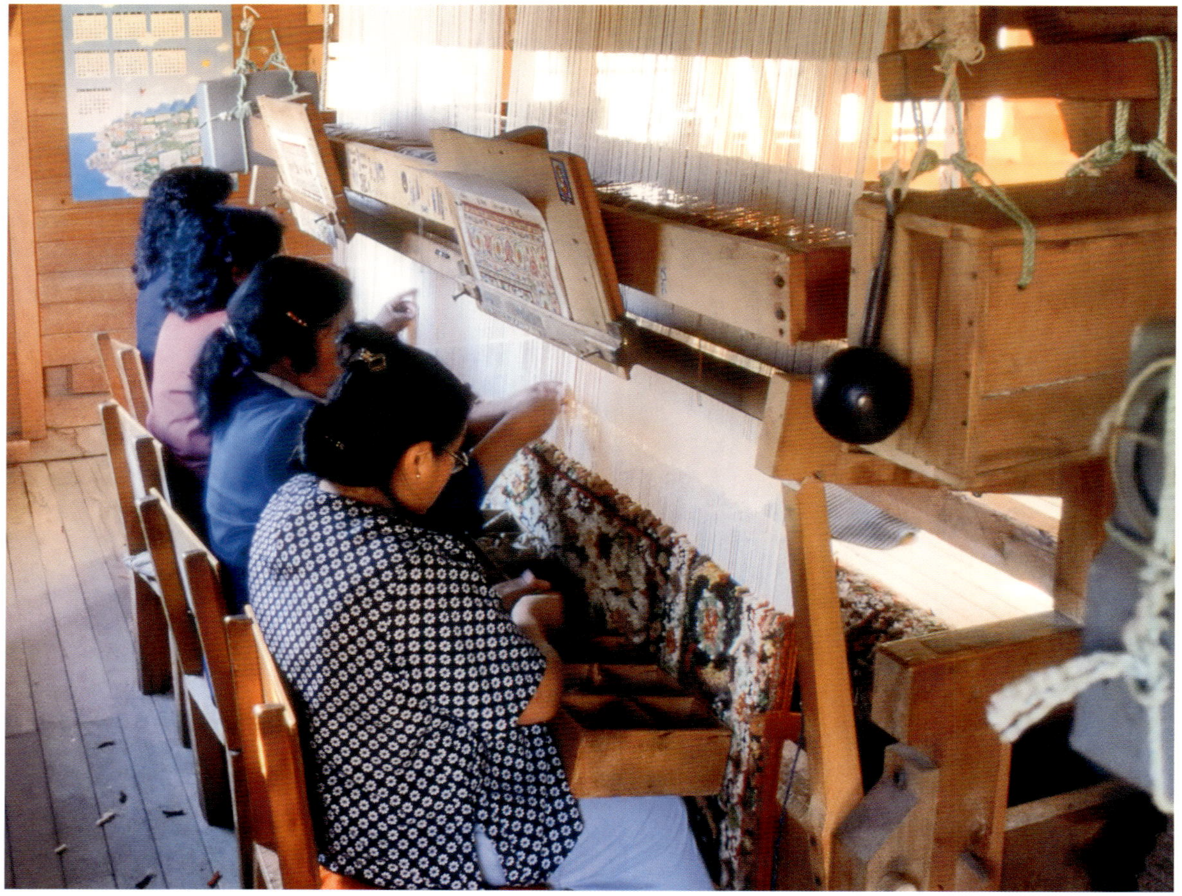

Near Chaitén, the North American Douglas Tompkins, co-founder of a well-known fashion label, has bought more than 320,000 ha of rain forest since the early 1990s to turn it into a nature reserve. At the time of the project "Pumalin Park" was conceived, Chilean opinion about it was divided. Its supporters were people who wanted to preserve the natural forests, the opponents, many of them entrepreneurs and landowners, wanted to prevent a foreigner from buying so much land to turn it into a reserve instead of exploiting it for economic purposes. In other regions of Chile, vast forests were cut down and replaced by plantations with fast-growing eucalyptus and pines, or used as cattle pastures. The export of wood chips is a very profitable business. After a few years and a lot of stubborn negotiations, Douglas Tompkins reached an agreement with the government about the legal framework for the project. A polished concept for gentle eco-tourism opens parts of the reserve to the public. In addition, the local inhabitants practice sustained farming and receive support to market their organic produce. This is a perfect example of preserving the biodiversity of the temperate, evergreen rainforest, one of the last in this form that exist in Chile's south. The Carretera Austral leads us straight into the forest that is veiled in clouds. Every once in a while waterfalls plunge down the mountain, and we pass lakes and see snow-

Page 40: In the carpet manufacture of Puyuhuapi

Bottom left: In the Argentinean national park Los Alerces

Bottom right: Thousands of years old: alerces in the Pumalin Park in Chile

topped mountains. A light drizzle is our steady companion. The air is steamy. Like in a fairy tale forest, lichen grows on the trees wrapping them in a gossamer white and green robe. The volcano Michinmahuida lies before us, the white snow blazes against the blue sky. We walk through the wild, almost impassable forest on a small, marked path, with roots and rocks serving as metres high stairs, pointing us in the right direction. A spider web, still wet from the rain, glistens between the branches, raindrops glide slowly down the leaves like tears and are caught at the tips. Mighty alerce trees stretch proudly towards the sky, cypresses which were 1,000 years old when Europeans first sighted the coast of Chiloé in February of 1540. Some trees are more than 3,000 years old. Who could find better words for our thoughts than the Chilean poet Pablo Neruda: "Quien no conoce el bosque chileno, no conoce este planeta – Anyone who doesn´t know the Chilean forest doesn't know this planet."

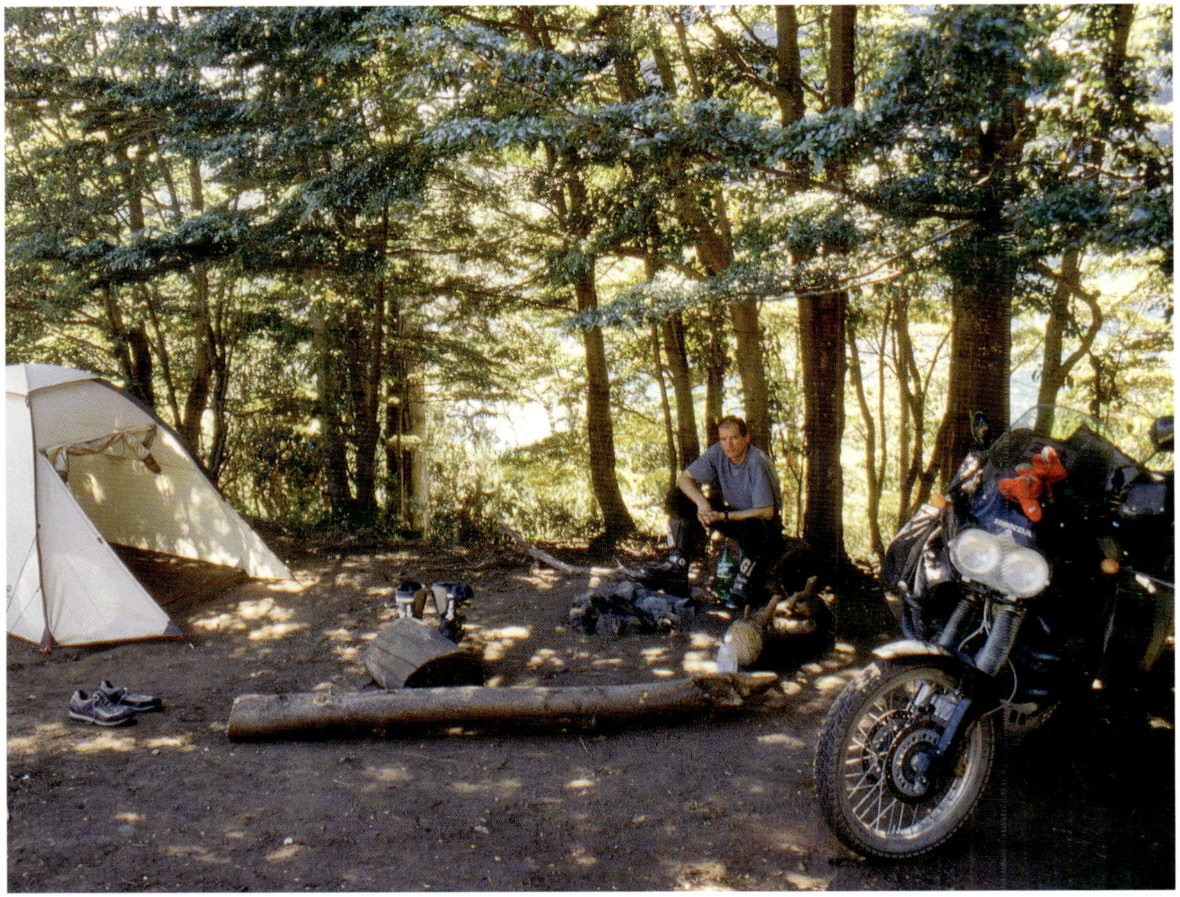

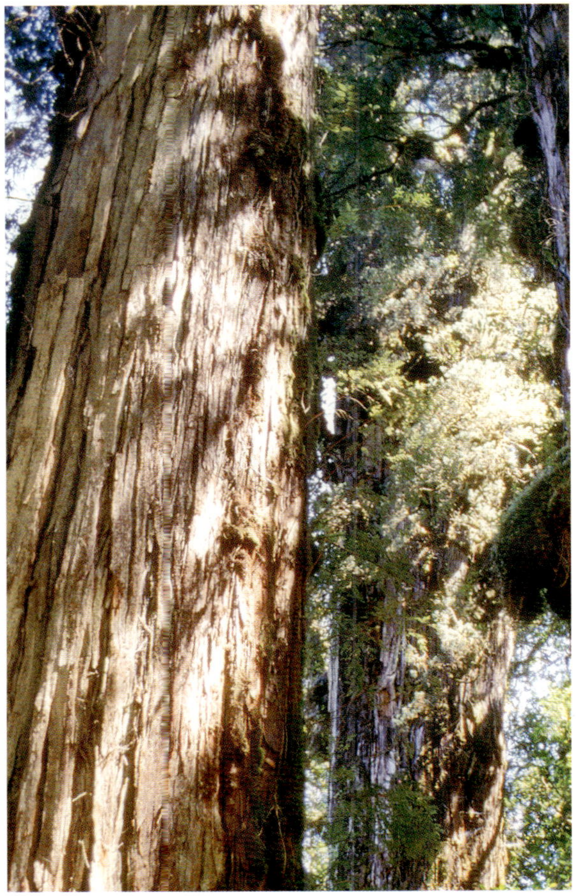

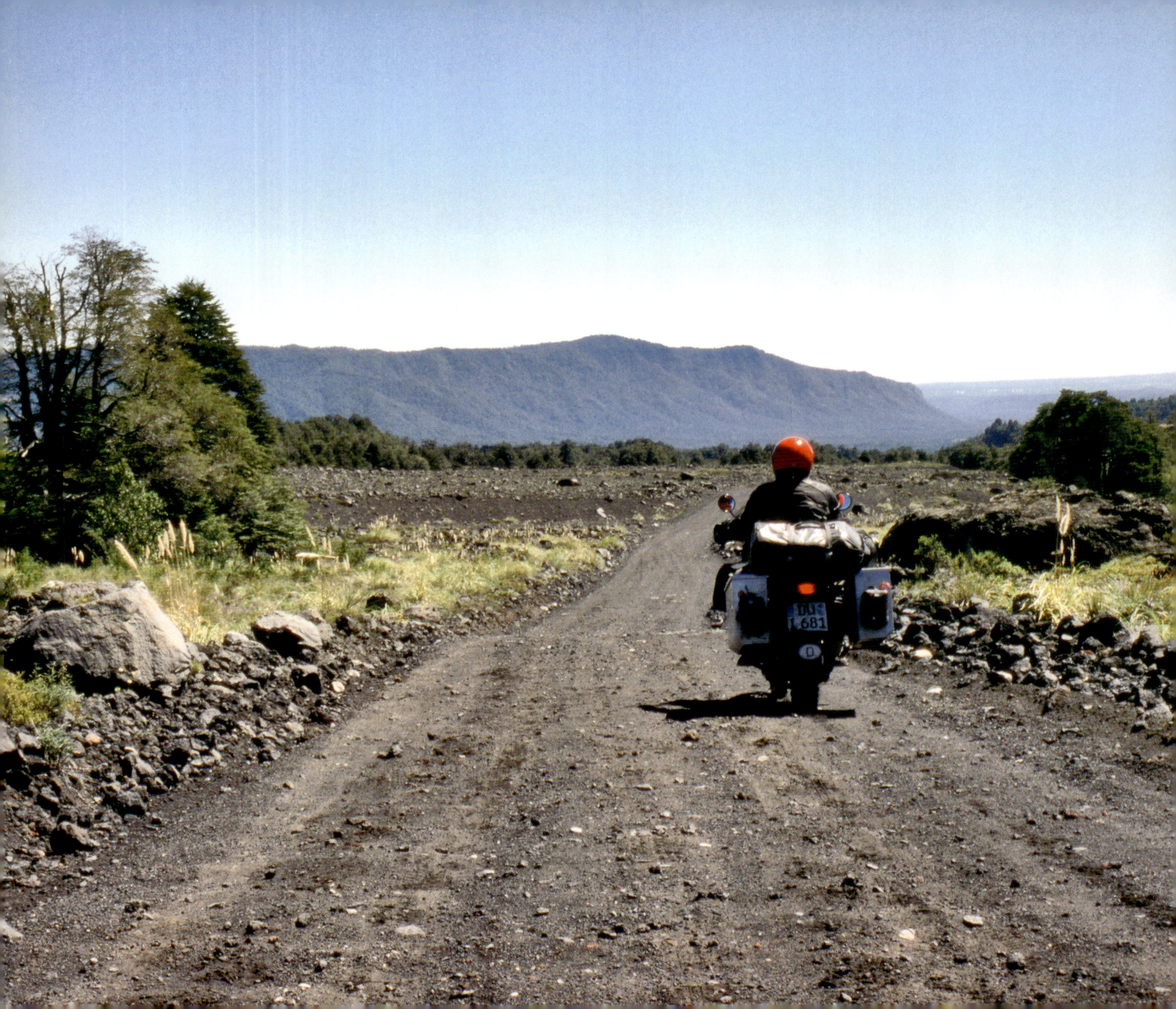

Page 42: Across cold lava ash, the road leads through the national park Conguillio in Chile

Bottom: The volcano Llaima rises 3,125 m, with 48 eruptions between 1640 and 1994 the most active in Chile's "Small South"

LAVA AND ICE

In Chile's "Small South', volcanoes define the landscape. The nights are clear. Millions of stars twinkle and form a white veil in the black sky that looks like the Milky Way. Compared to those dimensions, everything on earth becomes relative, small and insignificant. In contrast, the climb up the still active volcano Villarica is very concrete, high and tremendous. At 7 a.m., the group gathers around Oscar, who will lead the day's hike. Equipped with waterproof pants, jackets, gloves, spats, ice picks and backpacks, after a 30-minute approach to 1,900 m, it is then into the ice. We have slathered our faces with sun cream and shield our eyes from the strong UV rays with sunglasses. We walk single-file and close together, always in the zigzagging footsteps of the person in front of us. I slip and am just able to slam my pick into the ice to save myself from sliding off. I don't want to think about where I would have ended up. The peak is within reach, the

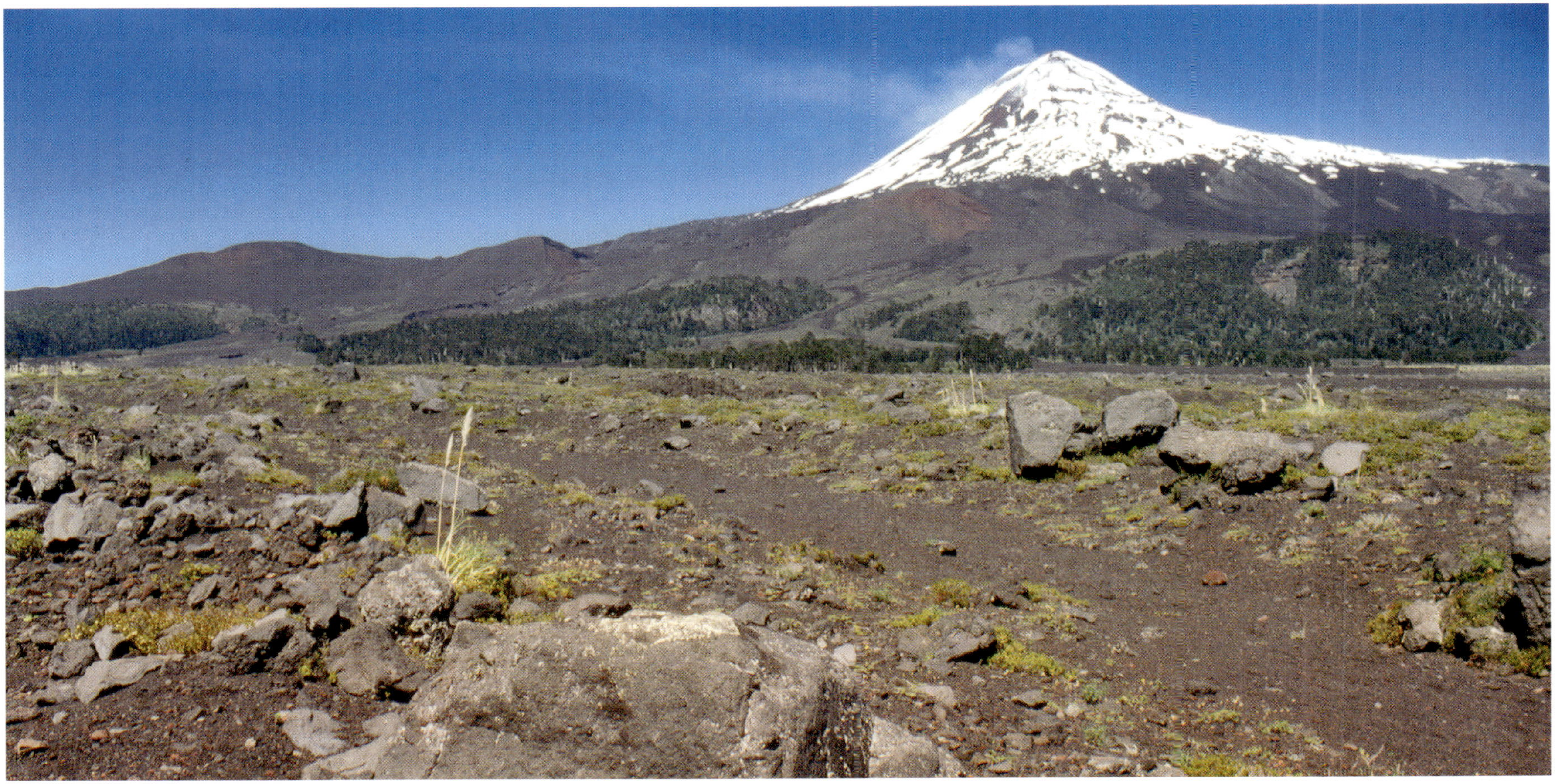

air is getting noticeably thinner, and each step is more exhausting. Only 50 metres in altitude to go. The ice has vanished, and we are making our way with effort through cold lava rubble. I don't think that I can take another step. Exhausted, I sit on a chunk of lava, gasping for breath. My body tells me that it's better to give up, but a little voice inside whispers to me about the wonderful view at the top. I am far too curious about the view of the crater, so I pull myself up and conquer the last few metres. Then, after a climb of three and a half hours, we reach the volcano's conical peak at a height of 2,847 m. Everything seems to be muffled in cotton. Mountain peaks jut out from the clouds. Every once in a while the clouds open and reveal a view of the valley and a few tiny rivers winding their way through the landscape. Far below in the depths of the crater, you can hear the lava bubble. Puffs of yellow sulphur smoke that envelops us and burns in our eyes comes again and again. The rocks on the edge of the crater gleam in shades of green, yellow, red and brown, and a thick layer of ice surrounds the cone. It is not only the sulphur but also the view of these forces of nature, the power and beauty of the volcano that takes our breath away.

The way down is sheer pleasure. We slide over the ice on our backsides. At top speed I race down the slope, hurtle through the air and land with my left foot caught on the track, while the rest of my body slides on. A sharp pain stabs through my knee and I lie still without moving. Axel packs ice around the knee to cool it, it's on hand in great quantities. After a brief rest, Oscar bandages my knee. I can't rely on outside help here in the ice. Somehow, I have to make my way down the mountain. Oscar drags me with the ice pick through the ice runs. The last stretch on the gravel road back to the village I limp supported by two walking sticks step by step to the waiting bus. Even after two days, the pain doesn't go away, so I go to the local hospital. There is no orthopaedist at the hospital and the next is 120 km away. Not thrilled with the prospect of having to take the next bus there, I limp down the steps of the hospital. Something cracks in my knee and the pain is gone. I don't need to go to Temuco after all.

Page 45: The crater of the volcano Villarica, which last erupted in 1985

Bottom: The volcano Villarica near the lake of the same name in Chile's "Small South" is a popular ski resort despite the volcanic activity

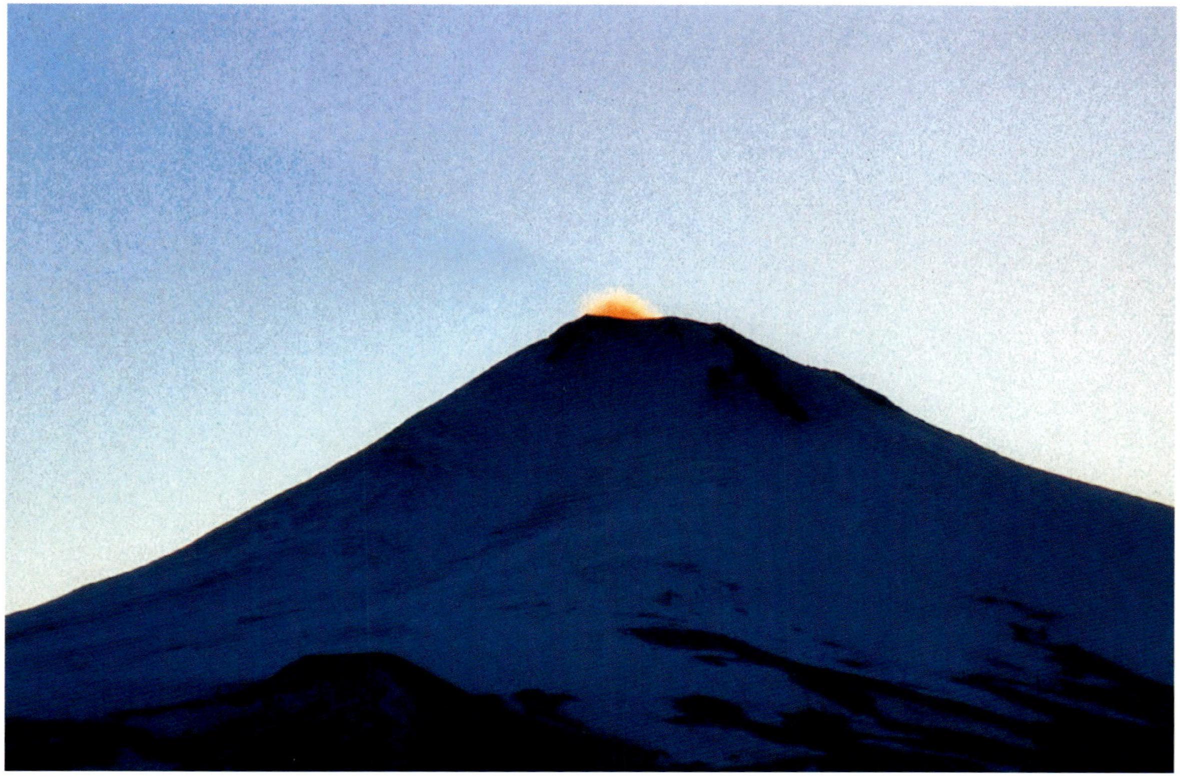

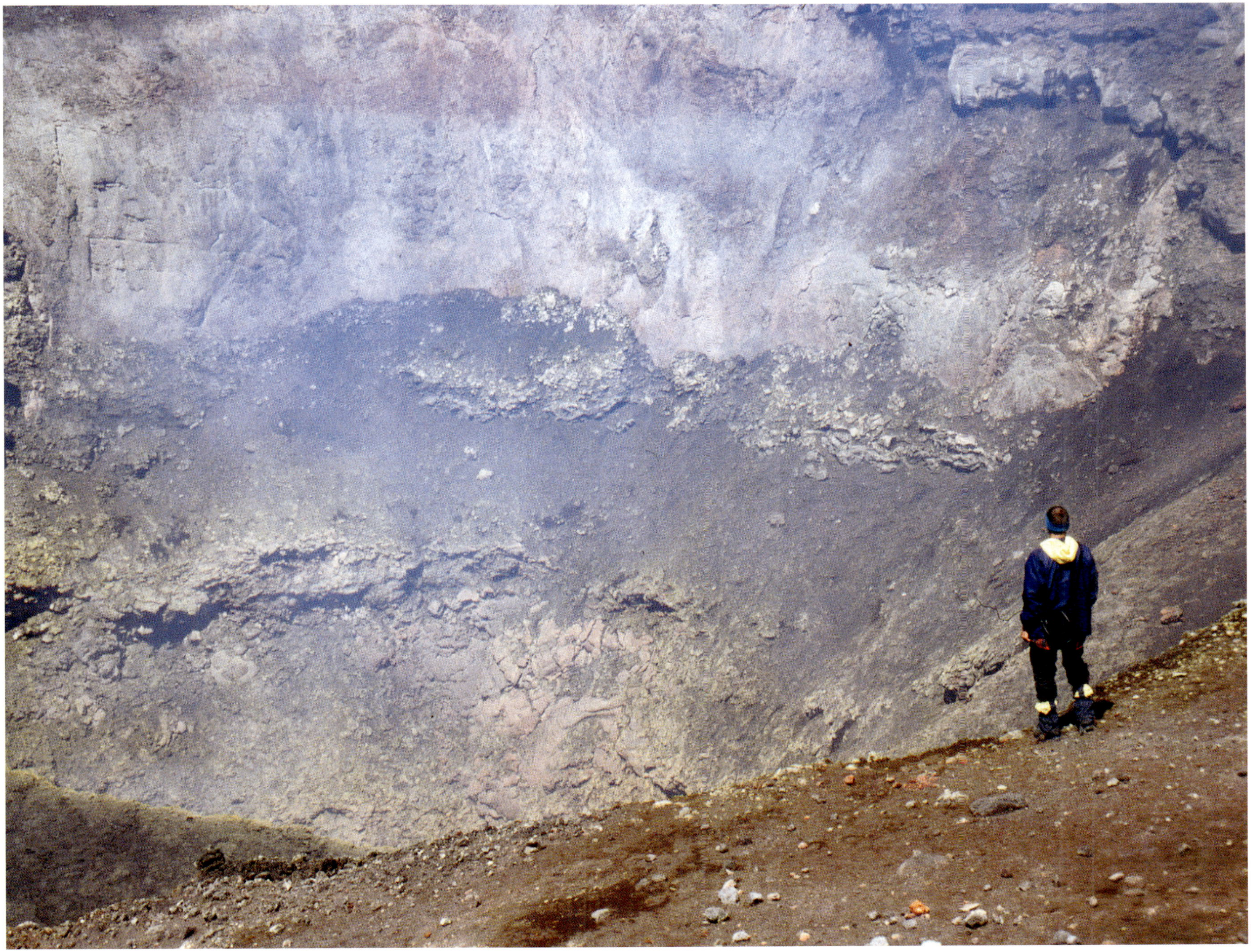

"BIG WATER"

The next days, we have a long drive ahead of us, from the region of Neuquen behind the border through Argentina to the very north-east of the country, to the triangle of Argentina, Brazil and Paraguay. Just before Lonquimay, we take a shortcut through a tunnel in order to have a relaxed break from the many kilometres on dirt roads – we don't yet know what lies ahead. At the entrance we are ordered to drive through the tunnel single-file with the cars at a walking pace. I'm getting wary. After a few metres I understand the reason for these precautions. The 4.5 km tunnel is pitch-black, the damp walls swallow up most of the light from our headlights, and it rains from the ceiling. There is a single dirt lane with ditches left and right, and the track is soaking wet and slippery.

Just great! It's too late to turn back, there are more vehicles entering the black hole behind us. After 3 km, we catch up to a truck making its way slowly up a hill. We have to keep braking and balancing the bikes. The van behind me seems to be having fun coming really close, braking, falling back, coming at me again. A crawler in front, a road hog behind us – I am very relieved to see the shimmer of daylight at the end of the tunnel. We find the Ruta Cuarenta, one of the country's main roads, again. This time the "fun part" is about 200 km long. It starts with hard-packed clay, followed by potholes and jagged rocks in the surface of the road. Some parts of the road are so narrow as to be virtually impassable for trucks, just barely wide enough for a car. The road used to be paved, or at least that is what the remnants of asphalt tell us. But with time, sand drifts covered parts of the road, a few little brooks flood the lanes, a few sections are broken away completely. Nature has reclaimed a part of its property.

There is not a single free bed in Mendoza. The wine festival happens once a year, and we have landed in the middle of it. After three hours of a desperate and unsuccessful search for a place to stay, we drive to a little suburb before it gets dark. We stand at an intersection, helplessly casting our eyes around, when an elder woman with her

Page 47: The region Misiones in Argentina's north-east deserves its name: land of the red earth

Bottom: Sometimes you need a professional to repair cropper damage, shop in Paso de los Libres, Argentina

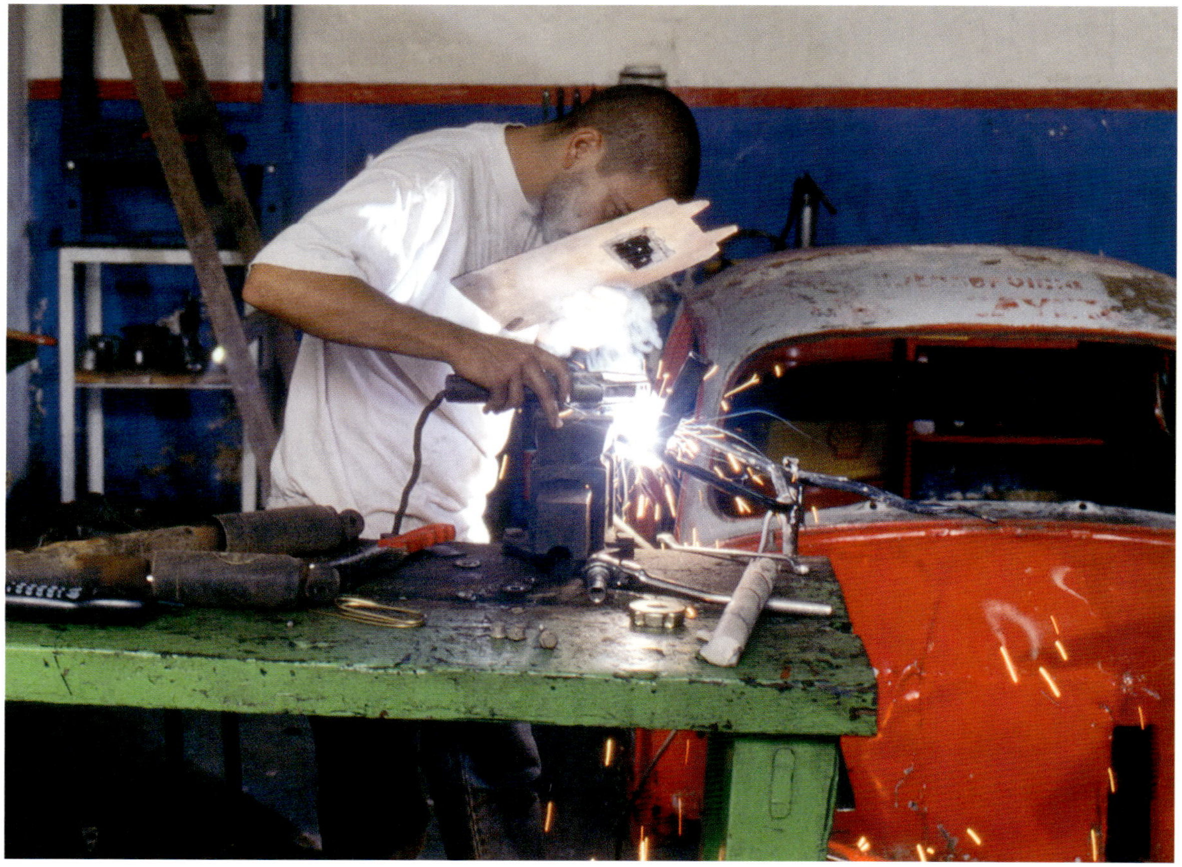

grandson approaches on a moped, stops and asks if we need her help! And how! We are looking for a place to stay, camping site, floor, anything. "Well, the mayor will help you, after all, that is why we elected him," she says. We follow her, through half of the town to the town hall and park our bikes on the sidewalk of the main plaza. The woman introduces herself as Marí. Determined, she marches into the building with me and talks to the mayor's assistant. She makes many calls, but without success. Outside, Axel is plied with tap water by the caretaker while curious onlookers gather around him asking him questions which he can only answer with his hands and feet, but they understand each other. Meanwhile, it is dark outside, 9:30 p.m. I am about to ask if we may sleep on the floor here at the town hall, promising that we will be gone at dawn. At that moment, three cleaning ladies enter the office. One of them, Rosario, offers us a place to stay at her house. It is big enough, she says, and we can park our bikes in her dining room. Curious about her supposedly magnificent villa, we make our way to her house. She is separated from her husband and lives with her three children in a neighbourhood on the outskirts of town. The door is so small that the bikes don't have a chance of getting through. A neighbour permits us to park them in her courtyard. Inside, the house has a room with kitchenette, three small bedrooms and a bathroom. She insists that we take the bed while she sleeps on the floor in the bedroom of her children and won't take no for an answer. We can hardly believe our luck. At the same time, we feel very guilty because we cannot repay her kindness. She

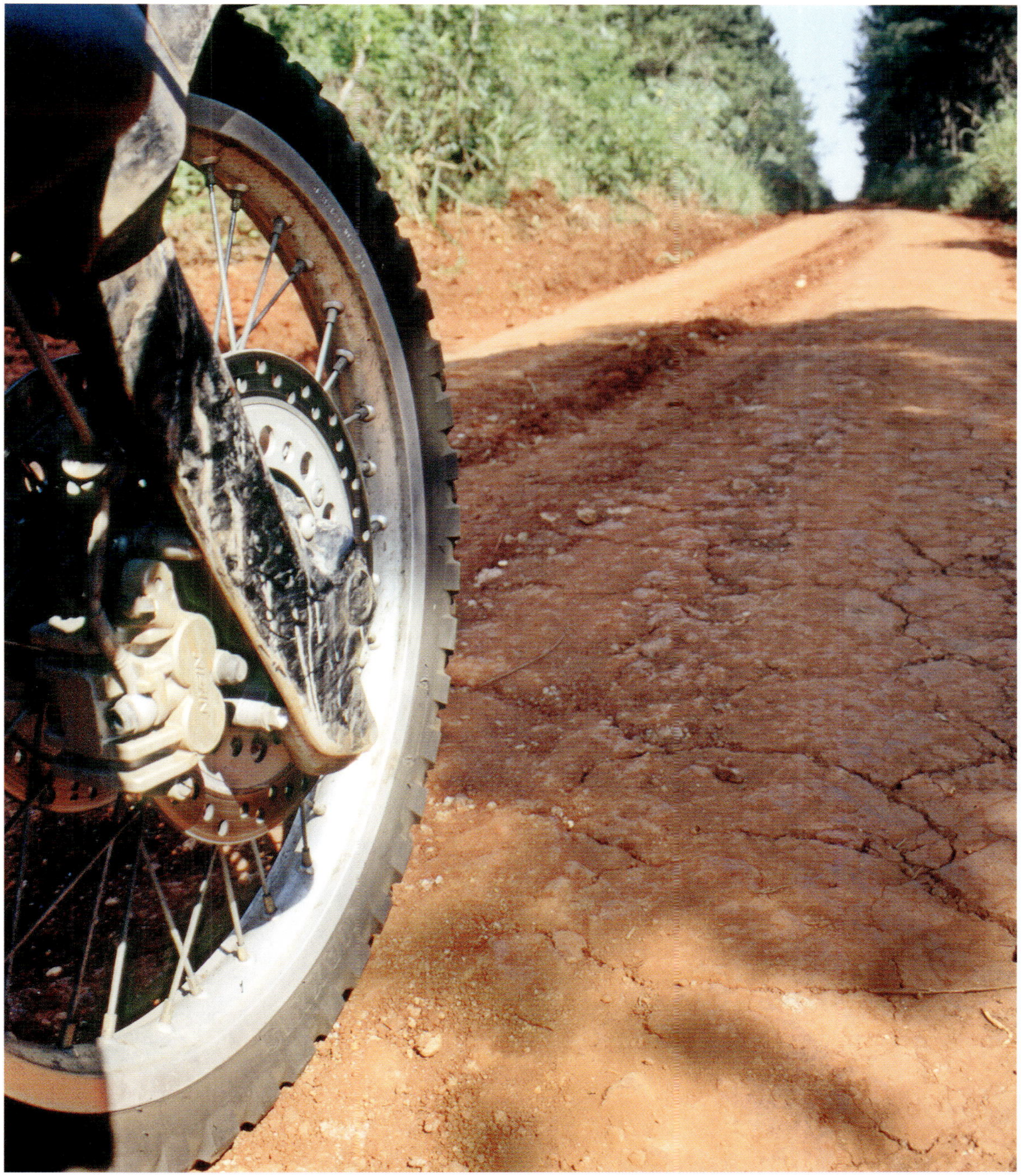

won't take money from us, that would hurt her pride. So we ask if there is anything she needs. She refuses. She says that it will be enough to know that we, too, will help a person in need some day.

Several days later we reach the subtropical region of Misiones. The sky darkens suspiciously, then suddenly a deluge of hailstones beats down on us like pebbles but Axel says that stopping for a few minutes to get out the raingear isn't worth it. After fifteen minutes it is all over – what a wonderful feeling to have our clothes dry slowly in the warm wind! In this region, as the name indicates, Jesuits established missions in this region on behalf of the Spanish Crown in the early 17th century, to control government raids against the natives and convert them to Christianity. Of 11 former Jesuit missions there are three ruins that have more or less remained today. One of them is San Ignacio Mini. We stand in the middle of a lush meadow, surrounded by the remains of red-brick buildings. Roots and tree trunks have been growing in the

Page 49: The Iguaçu waterfalls on the border of Argentina, Brazil and Paraguay, which was created from divine jealousy, as legend has it

Bottom: San Ignacio Mini, former Jesuit mission in the Argentineal jungle

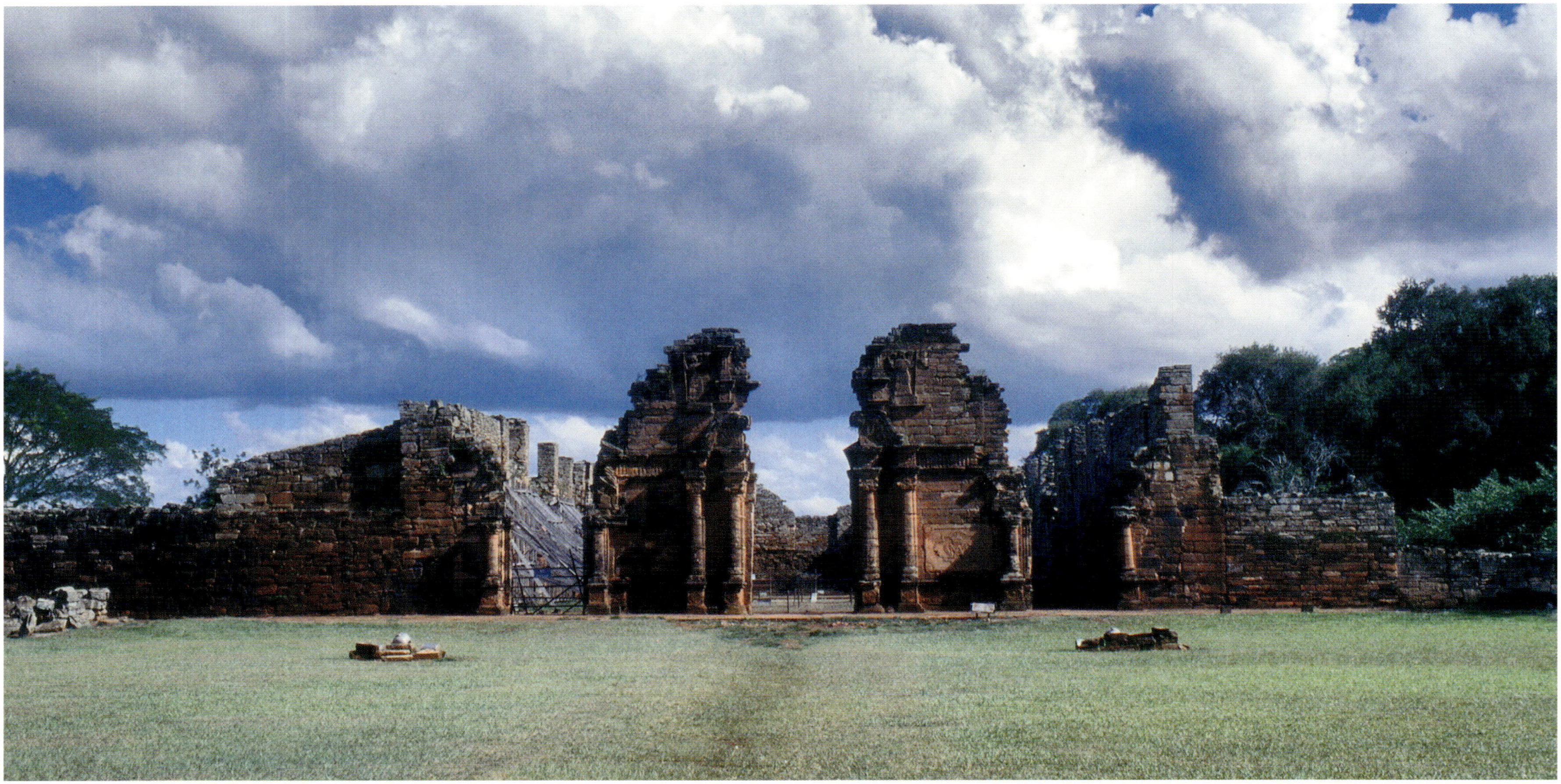

ruin for centuries, merging with it into natural sculptures. Of the many buildings only a few bits of the walls still exist, but they are richly decorated. Corn, manioc, mate, sugarcane, tobacco, potatoes and vegetables were planted. The more the Jesuits taught the natives valuable skills, of working with stone, wood, metal and leather, with which they were very successful economically, the more they also alienated the Guaraní from their traditional way of life. Unhappy with these autonomous settlements in the jungle, Argentina's government forced Spain to expel the Jesuit brothers from the country in 1767 and recommenced the persecution and slaughter of the indigenous population. Long before the days of Spanish conquerors, the Guaraní grew a herb called Yerba. It is used to brew a mate tea, a beverage most common even in nowadays Argentina. The region Misiones offers perfect conditions for growing the herb for Argentina's national beverage on huge farms. After all, the per capita consumption is about 5 kg per year. Argentineans spend their days with a calabash and "bombilla" (mug with a metal drinking straw) in their hands and a thermos with hot water under their arms. All across the country, you can find hot water machines for free refills.

The waterfalls of Iguaçu can hardly be described with words because nature created an utterly unbelievable spectacle here. The Guaraní gave the falls the fitting name of "big water". More than 275 cascades carry an average of 1,700 m^3 per second over the edge at top speed. The border between Argentina and Brazil runs through the middle of the Iguaçu River. It bubbles and gurgles

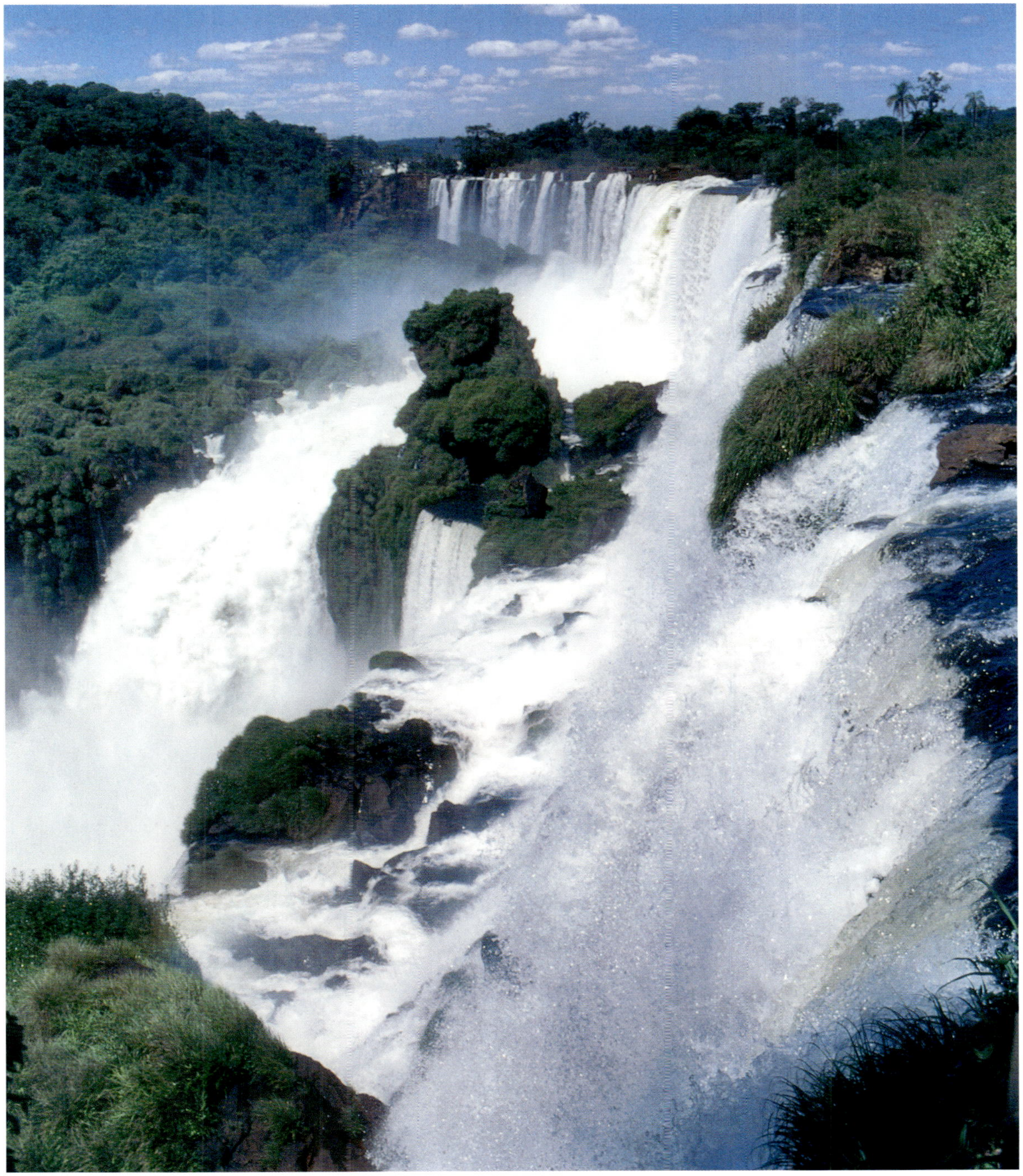

everywhere. If you close your eyes, you feel as if the deafening cascades of water carry you over the edge as well. The spraying water joins the sunbeams to create enchanting rainbows that arch over the abyss. At the "devil's maw", the calm river suddenly plunges down 70 m through a basin with three walls, sweeping everything along with it. We hurtle across the water in a speedboat, the first surging waves soak the entire party, and then we reach a bay and steer below a waterfall. The others were clever enough to wear nothing but swimsuits. The tour guide tells us to put our cameras into plastic bags just before we are all soon showered. It takes our breath away at first, but then we enjoy the tingling, wet, full-body massage. While the women squeal, some of the men shout, "Más, más" – "more!" Our guide grants their wish. Back on the shore we try to dry ourselves in the sun along with our camera, which has sustained a bit of water damage. Whatever, it was great fun!

Page 51: An average of 1,700 m3 water plunge into the depth every second

Bottom: The Iguaçu waterfalls on the Argentinean side

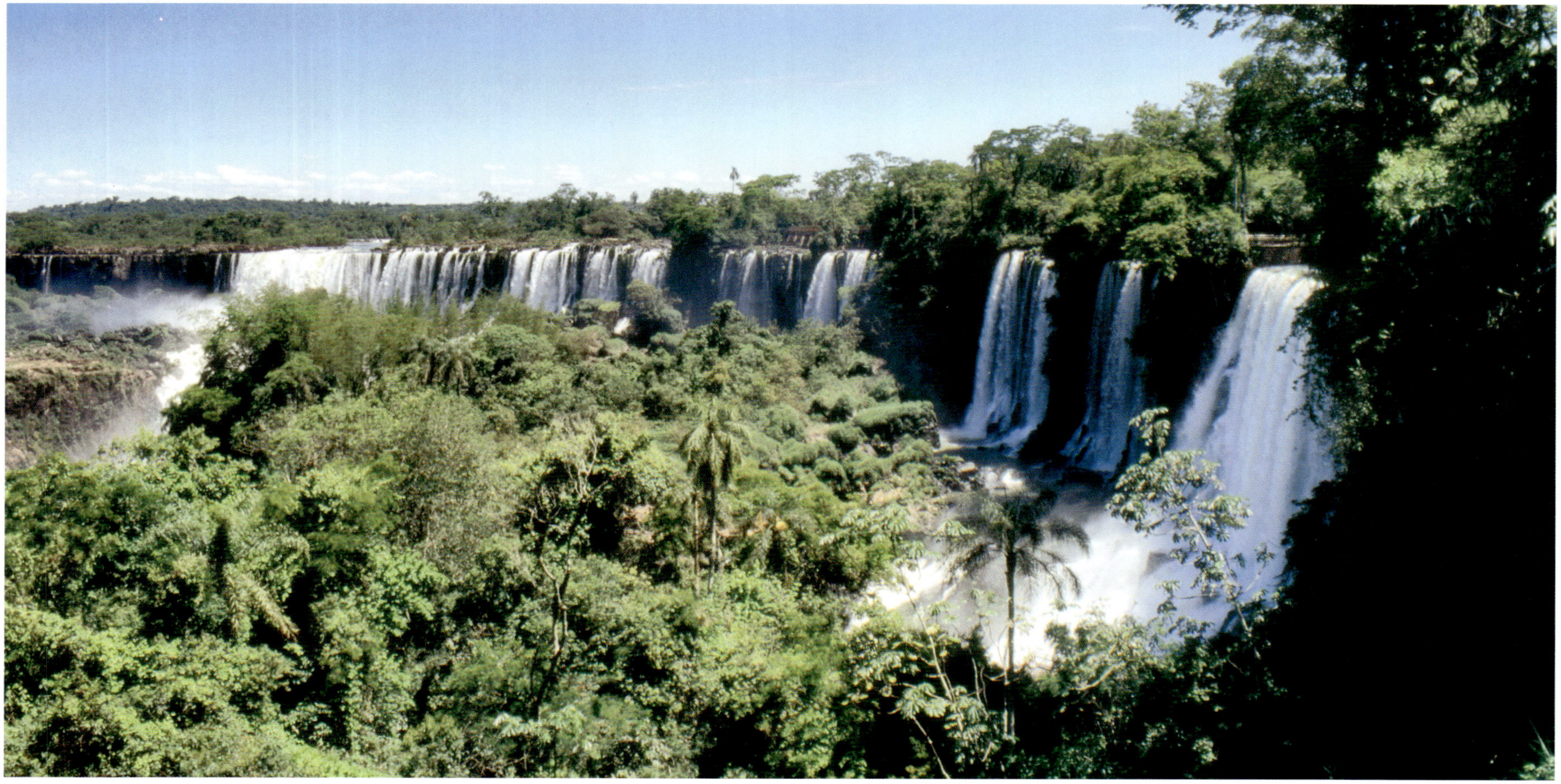

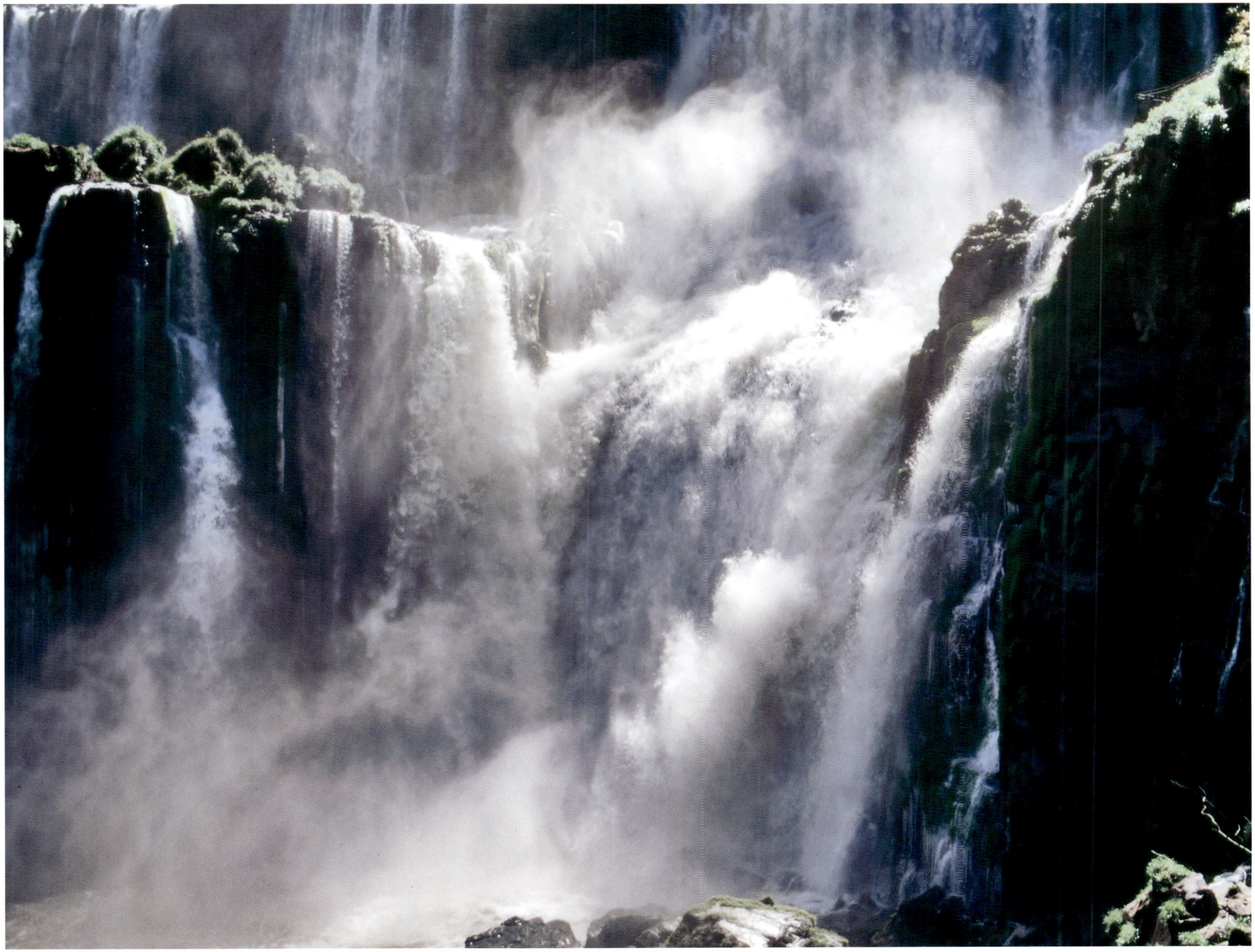

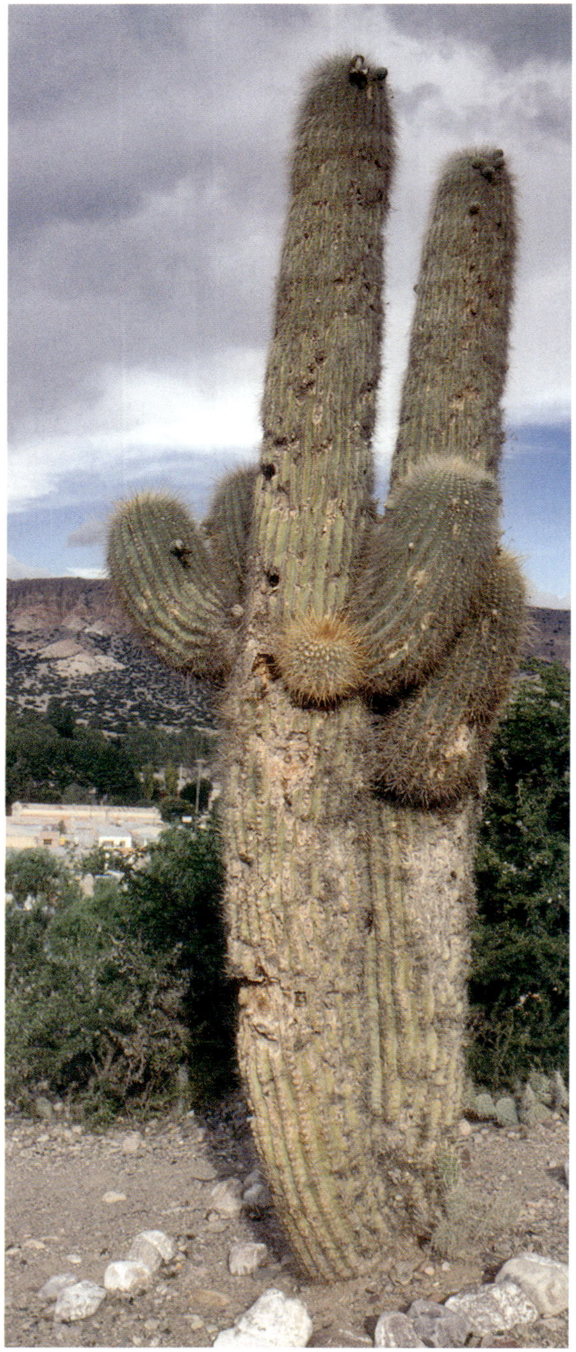

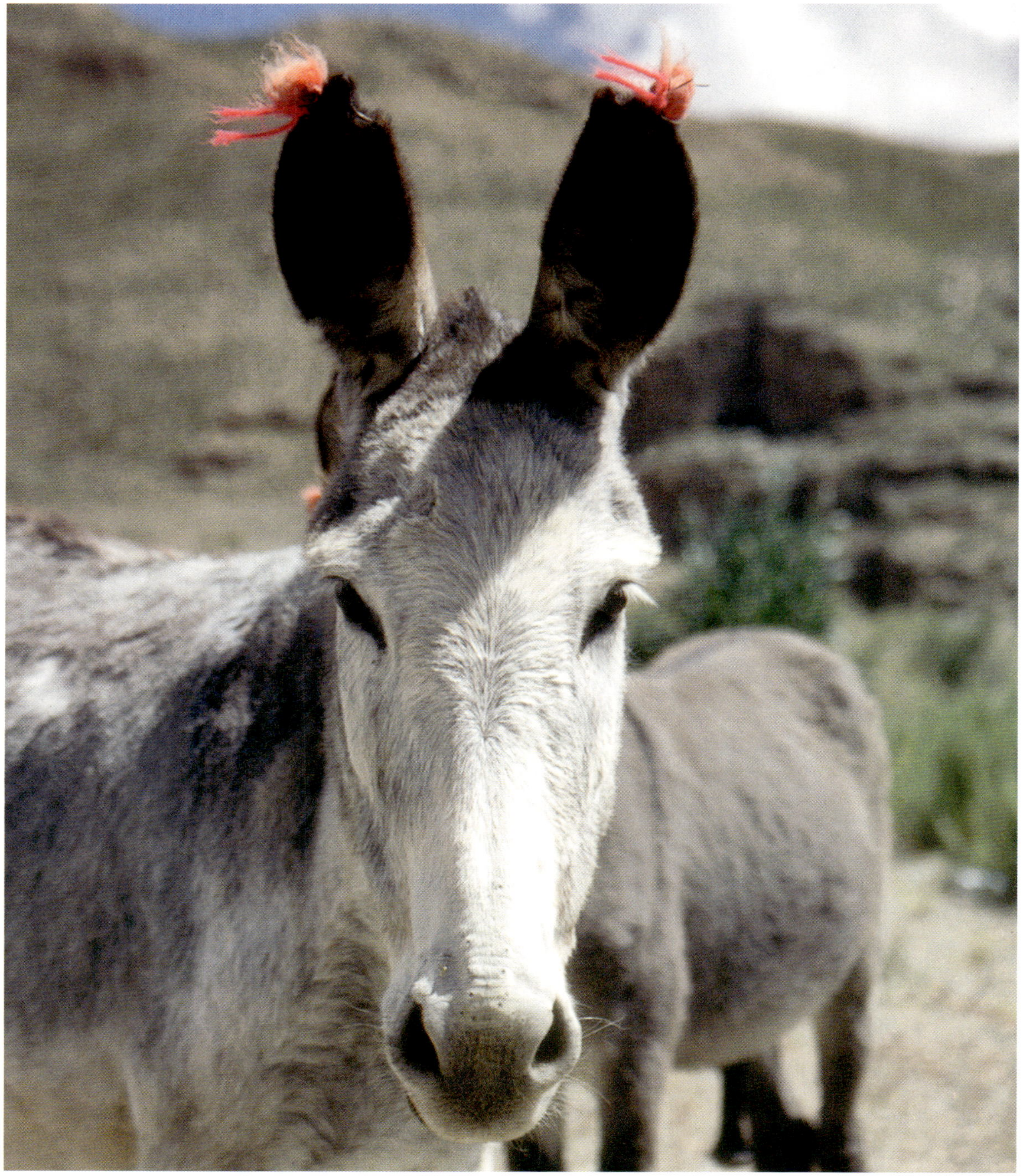

EUPHORIA AND DESERT HEAT

We have been on the road for 100 days and are slowly moving back westward. A dazzling mountain region begins near Volcán. The Quebrada de Humahuaca is characterized by its multicoloured rocks. Wedged between the top and bottom layers of rock lie compressed sediments of sand, clay, marl, and chalk, around 230 to 130 million years old. Various minerals make the rock shine – chocolate brown, yellow, ochre, red turquoise or lilac – and the sun lends its support as well. To the west rise the mighty Andes to a height of 4,000 m, to the east the Zenta Mountains. Huge cactus trees, cardones grow here like weeds. In order to get used to the thin air and avoid the ugly side effects of altitude sickness, we stay in Humahuaca for two days. The naming of this village is connected to a legend, as one of the locals tells us. The Indio girl Dove Heart had a lover in the area. Her father did not accept the relationship and had the boy beheaded. The head was then impaled on a cactus tree. After two days, tears began to run down the cheeks, so that the people in the village cried out, "humahuacac" – "the head is crying!"

At a height of almost 3,000 m, the bikes are still running fine. We don't feel any signs of nausea or headaches either. However, even the slightest exertions make us gasp for breath. A test drive on a gravel-surfaced side road takes us to the mountain village of Iruya. There is nothing but rocks, not a single trace of civilization anywhere. Many kilometres further along, we discover the first secluded homesteads on the plains and begin to wonder how people manage to live here. Some have solar cells on their roofs to produce some electricity at least. It is the obvious solution, because the Puna is one of the places in the world with the most intense solar radiation. At first the road is dreadful, but after crossing 13 brooks conditions improve. Serpentines lead up to Paso de Cóndor at a height of 4,000 m. At an "apacheta", a mystic stone pyramid, I follow the thousands of year old custom of add-

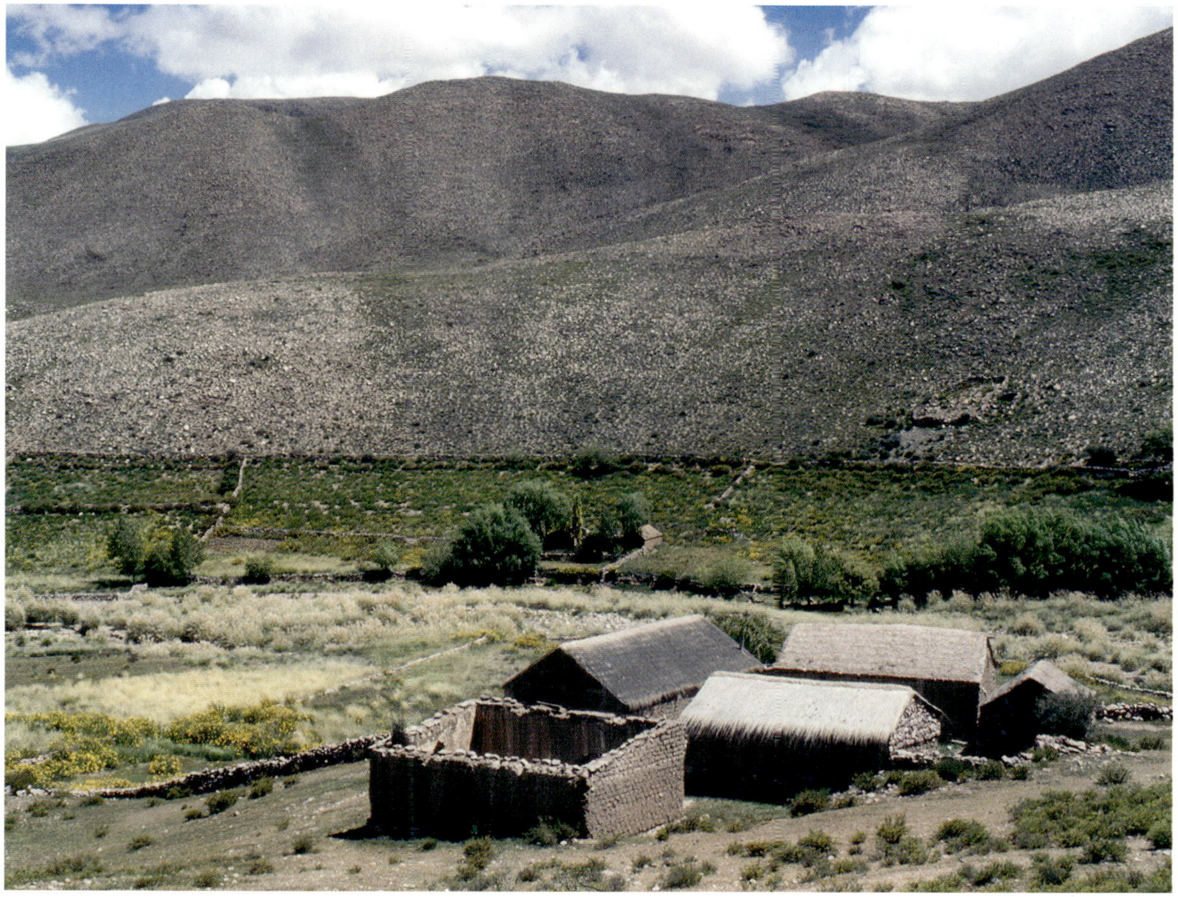

Page 52 left: Cardones, huge cactus trees, define the vegetation in the Puna of Argentina

Page 52 right: Farmers in the Argentinean Puna mark their donkeys with coloured fabric strips

Right: Secluded farms on the way to the Iruya valley

ing a coloured piece of rock to appease the gods, because it can't hurt. After crossing the dried-up bed of the Iruya River we reach the village. Many steep, narrow alleys, paved with river rocks, lead through the village of 300 people. We take a little break to refresh and then we hurry to leave before the bus that is just taking in a few passengers on the market square in order to return to civilization. We would not be able to pass the bus on the way. We and our bikes have mastered the test of heights with flying colours.

Then we tackle the Paso de Jama. The road is tricky. 120 km of corrugated iron sheeting interspersed with sand ditches. Axel almost loses his balance in the first sand ditch. He shoots from right to left and back on the road, just barely catching himself. It's my turn in the second section of deep sand, where I lose control over the bike. A truck with a trailer comes towards me and brakes just a few metres behind me. The case gets it badly again, the lid doesn't close properly anymore and the carrier is tangled in the sid-

Page 55: Bike fun in the Puna

Bottom: On the way to Paso de Jama from Argentina to Chile you cross the Salinas Grandes

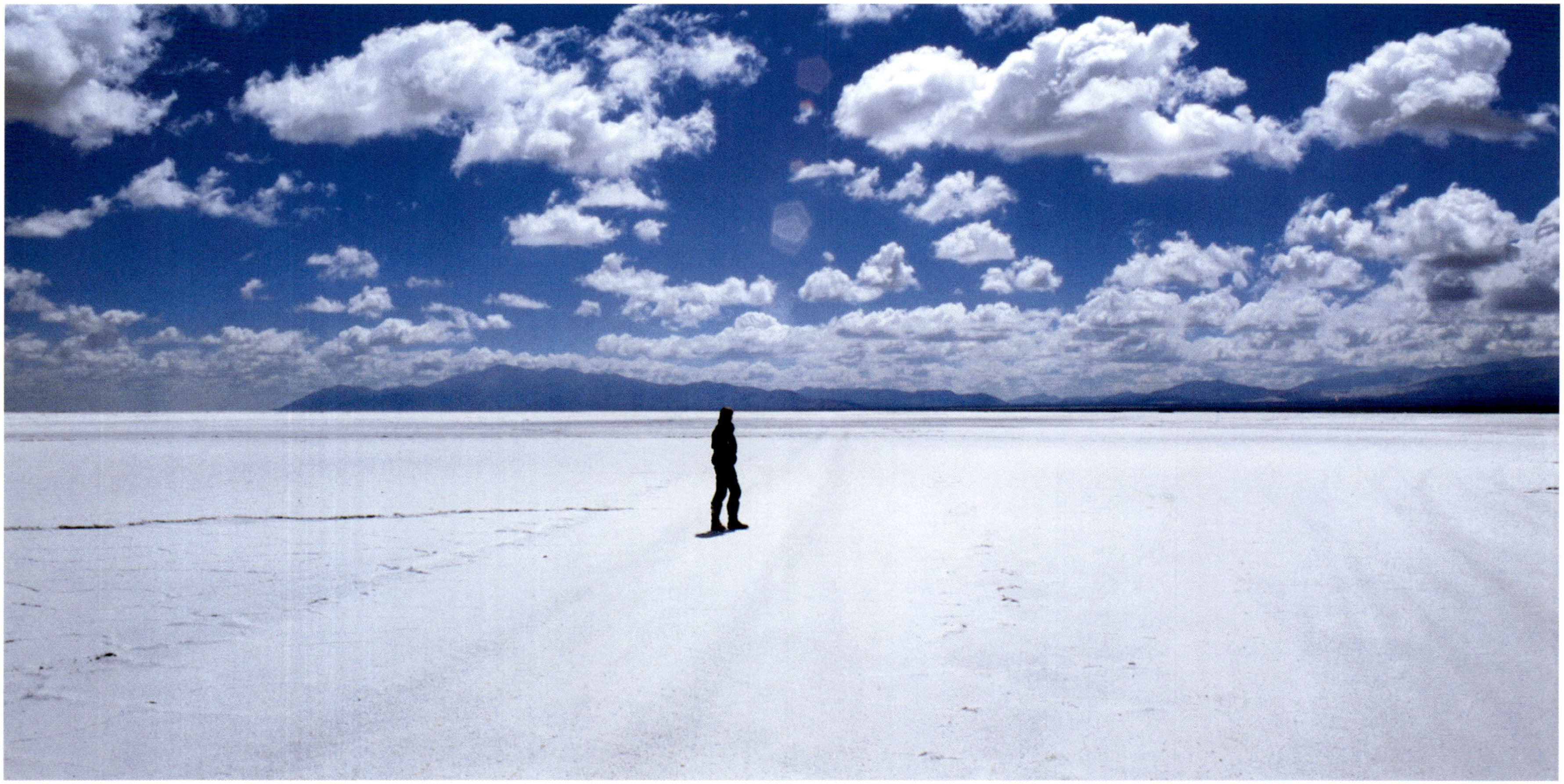

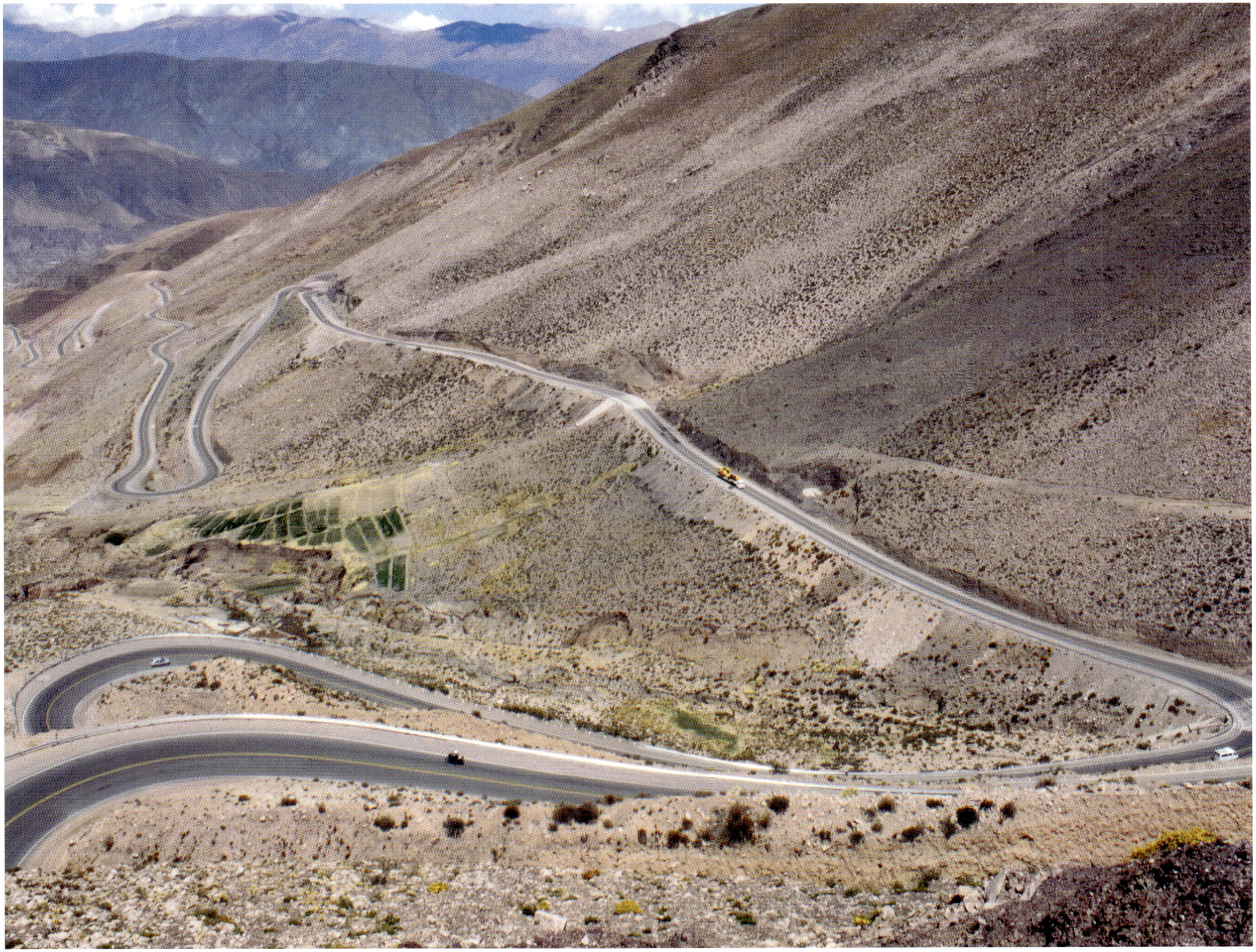

ing. We have a long, time-consuming way before us, so we do without extensive repairs. The road widens on a high plateau. The trucks use the opportunity to step on it and pass us at high speed with not much room to spare. We can't see very far through the billowing clouds of dust. Some trucks break down and the remains of exploded tyres litter the side of the road. The drive is eating away at my strength, so that I start counting down the kilometres to the border. Half left, a third, 30 km ... what was that again about pushing past your own limits? Finally, we can see the Argentinean checkpoint – and an asphalt road. On the Chilean side, the GPS shows 4,848 m as the highest point of the pass. On the last 45 km to San Pedro de Atacama, the road plummets 2,000 m. The ears ache as they do during a plane's landing approach. Far away we see the volcano Licancábur with a height of 5,930 m. In its crater lies the world's highest lake. According to the romantic legend, Licancábur is deeply in love with the volcano Quimal. Her father, the volcano

Page 57: Towards San Pedro de Atacama in Chile

Bottom: Argentina's high plain is the home of the vicuñas

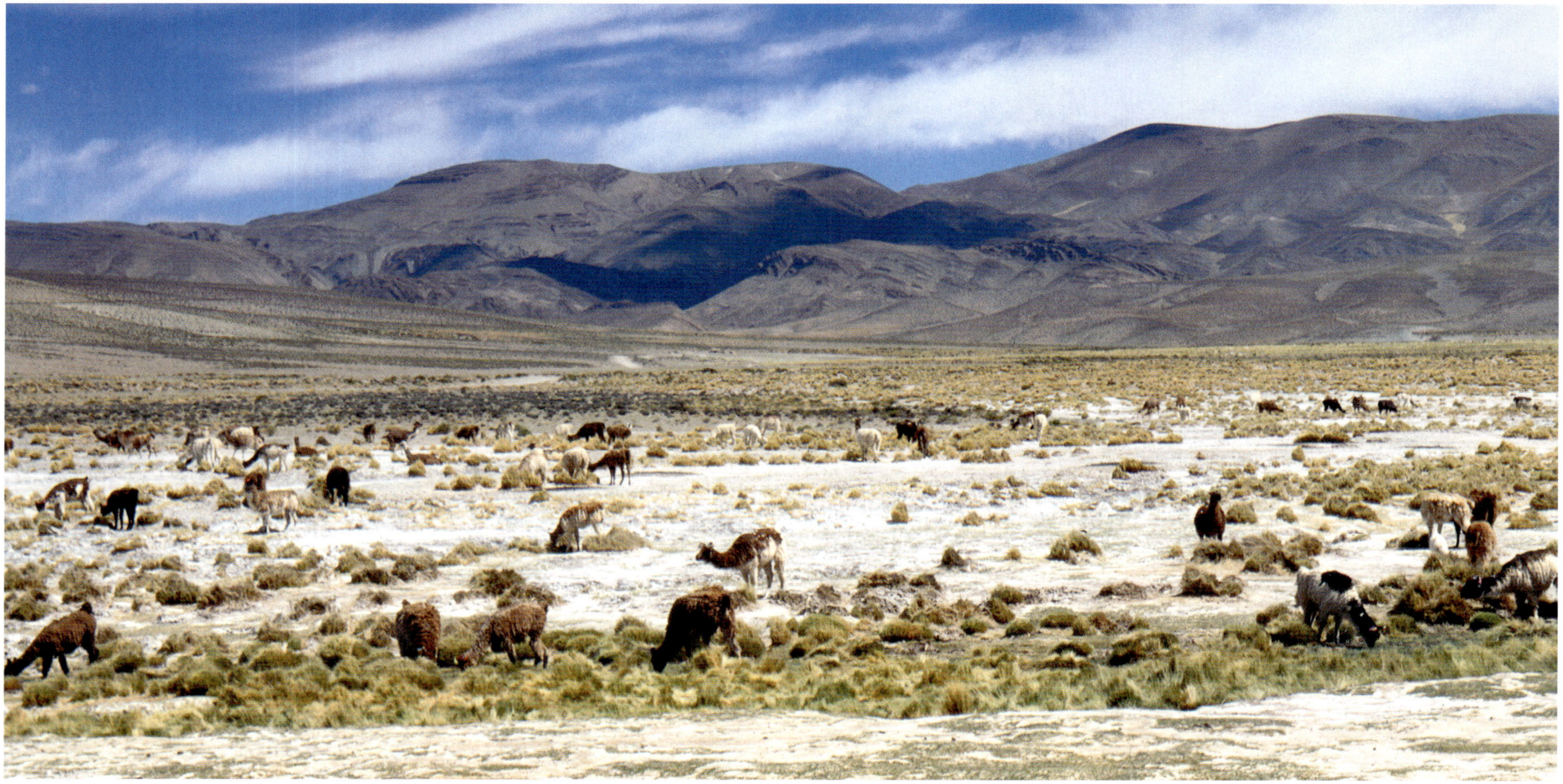

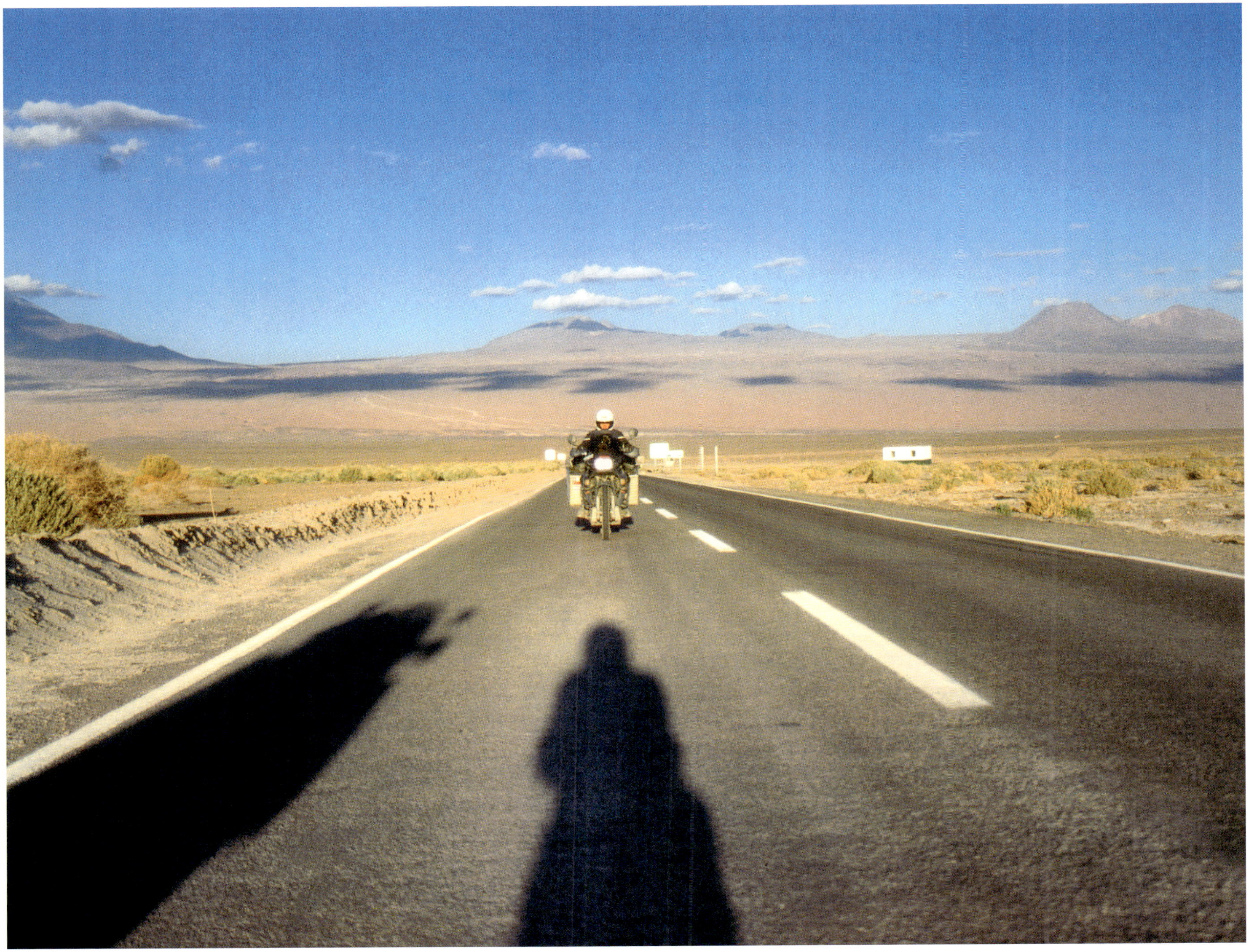

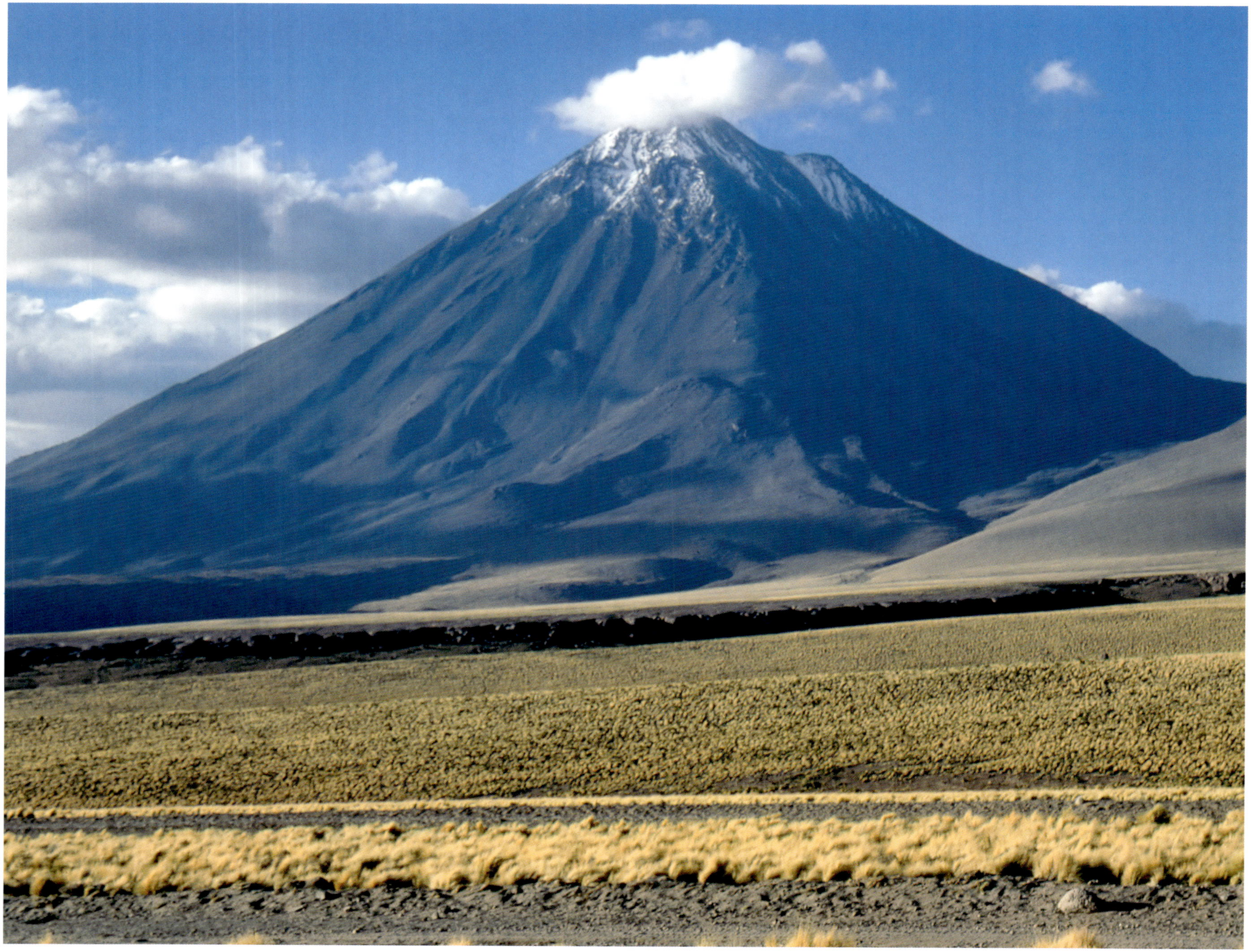

Page 58: The volcano Licancábur in Chile is surrounded by legend

Bottom: The small church in Chilean San Pedro de Atacama was built in 1744

Lascar, fought against their love with a sea of flames that swallowed up the whole valley and separated the two forever. Once a year, on a September morning, the position of the sun allows Licancábur to throw his shadow on his beloved Quimal.

In the late 1980s, the first backpackers discovered the adobe village of San Pedro de Atacama. At first glance, the alleys and houses look rather desolate and uninviting. The adobe architecture is typical for the region, however, and for very practical reasons, too: the adobe bricks store the heat of the day and protect the interior from the cold nights. They keep the temperature at a pleasant balance all day. There are only a few doors and small windows to let the sun into the buildings. But the dreary facades hide cosy restaurants and nice shops to browse to your heart's content. Several buses arrive at the station every day to bring tourists to the village that exudes a hint of a dropout mentality and a hippie lifestyle. And all that in the driest desert on earth. Clouds will often

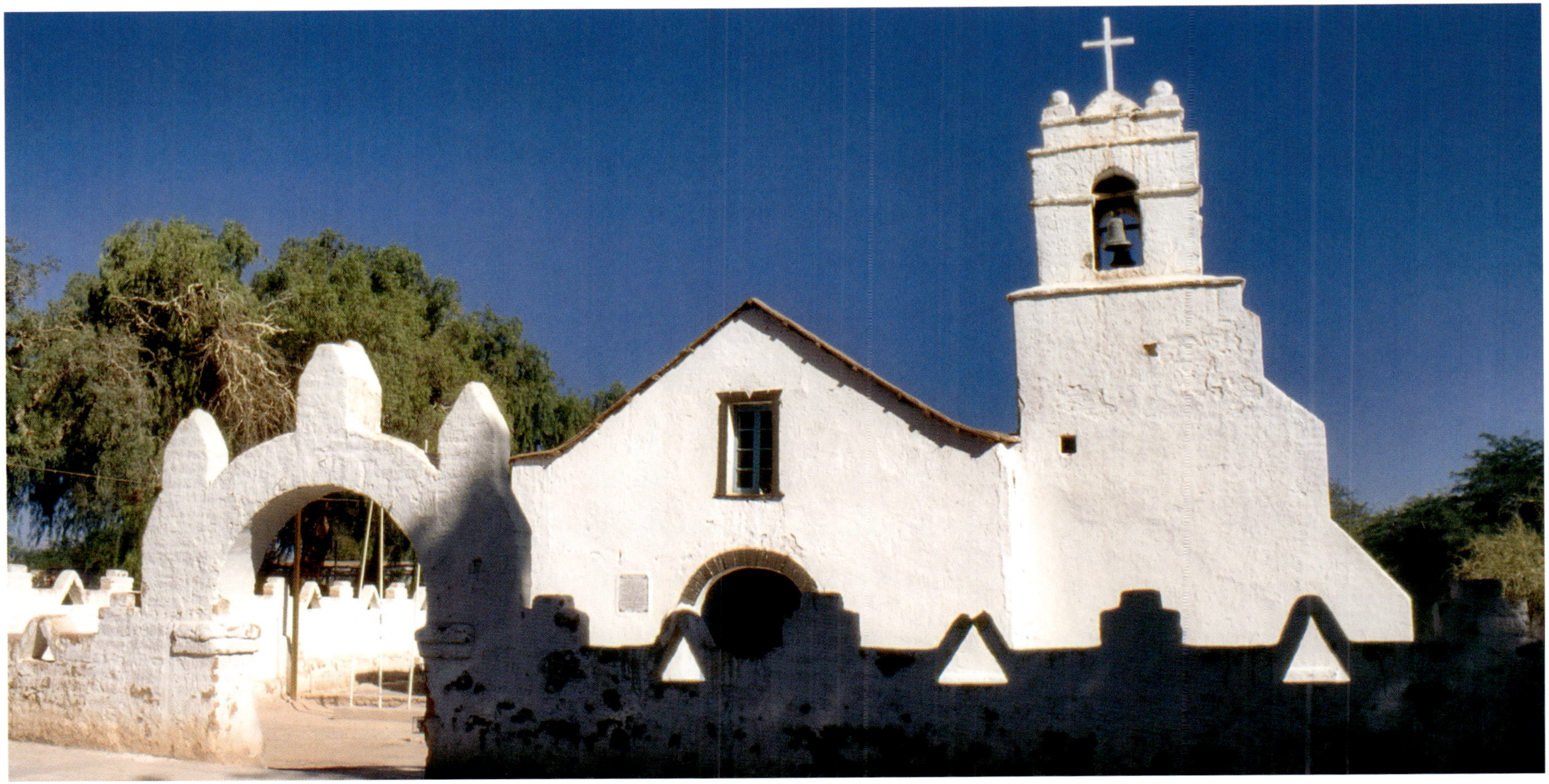

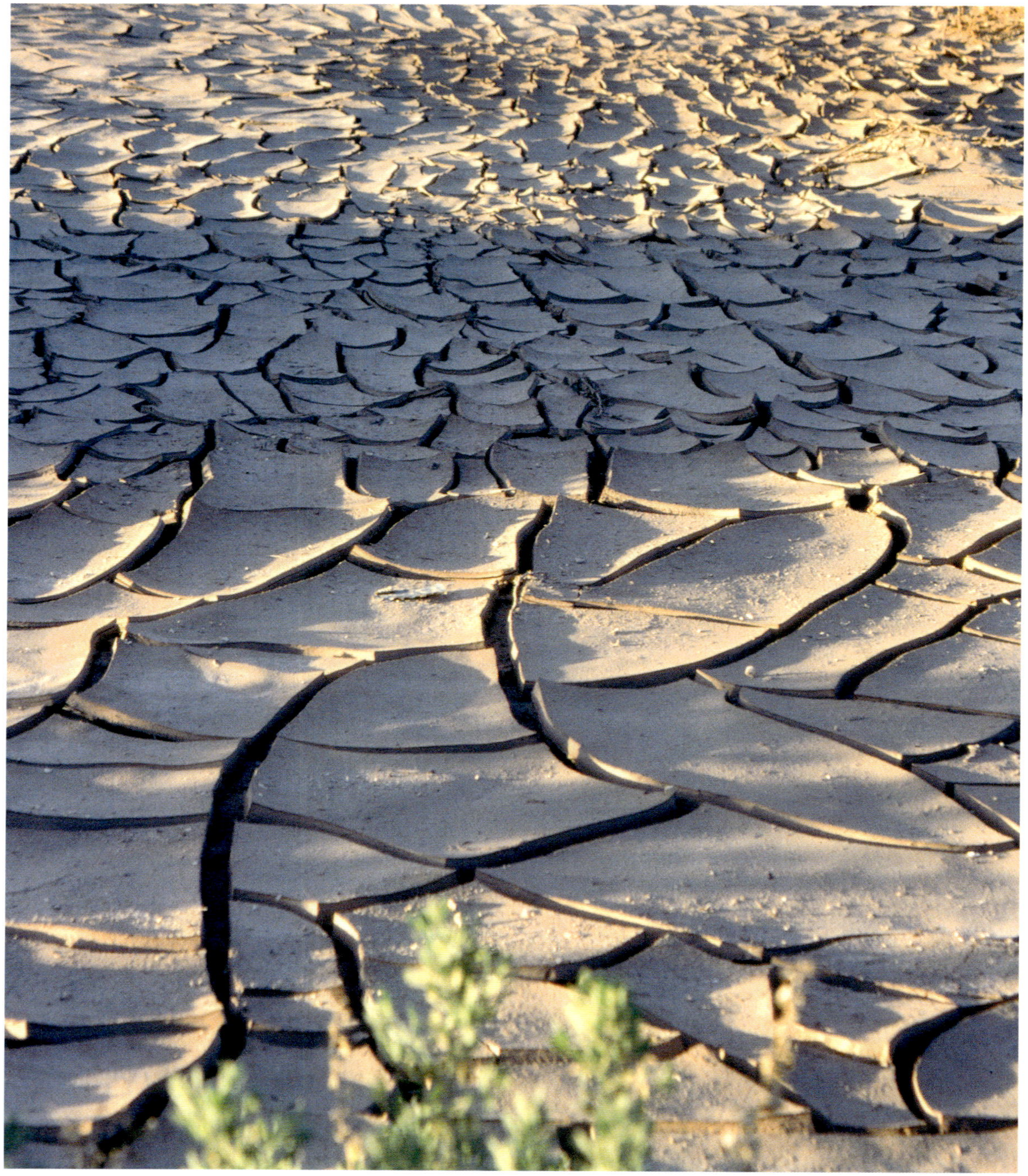

gather in the afternoon, but the rain evaporates before it reaches the ground. In the evenings, many visitors gather at Valle de la Luna near the village. The sinking sun lends a golden shimmer to the mountain peaks, creates shadow creatures on the layers of earth. We climb up a sand dune of about 50 m and settle down on the ridge. I enjoy the wonderful view of the other side of the valley and lose myself in the breathtaking landscape. Shadows have fallen on everything. The sun sinks lower behind the rocks, while the moon rises white and round in the sky.

On our way towards the Pacific, the temperature is at least 40° C in the shade and we meet almost no one else. A bus stop provides the only protection from the sun as far as the eye can see. I don't like the area much, the kilometre seem to stretch out like rubber. Finally in the late afternoon, we reach Iquique, a town at the foot of a dune with a height of 800 m and called "dragon hill". The port town saw its heyday between 1880 and 1920, because there were nitre mines on the

Left: The Desierto de Atacama in Chile's north is the world's driest desert

Page 61: The Valle de la Luna seems like a lunar landscape Atacama desert

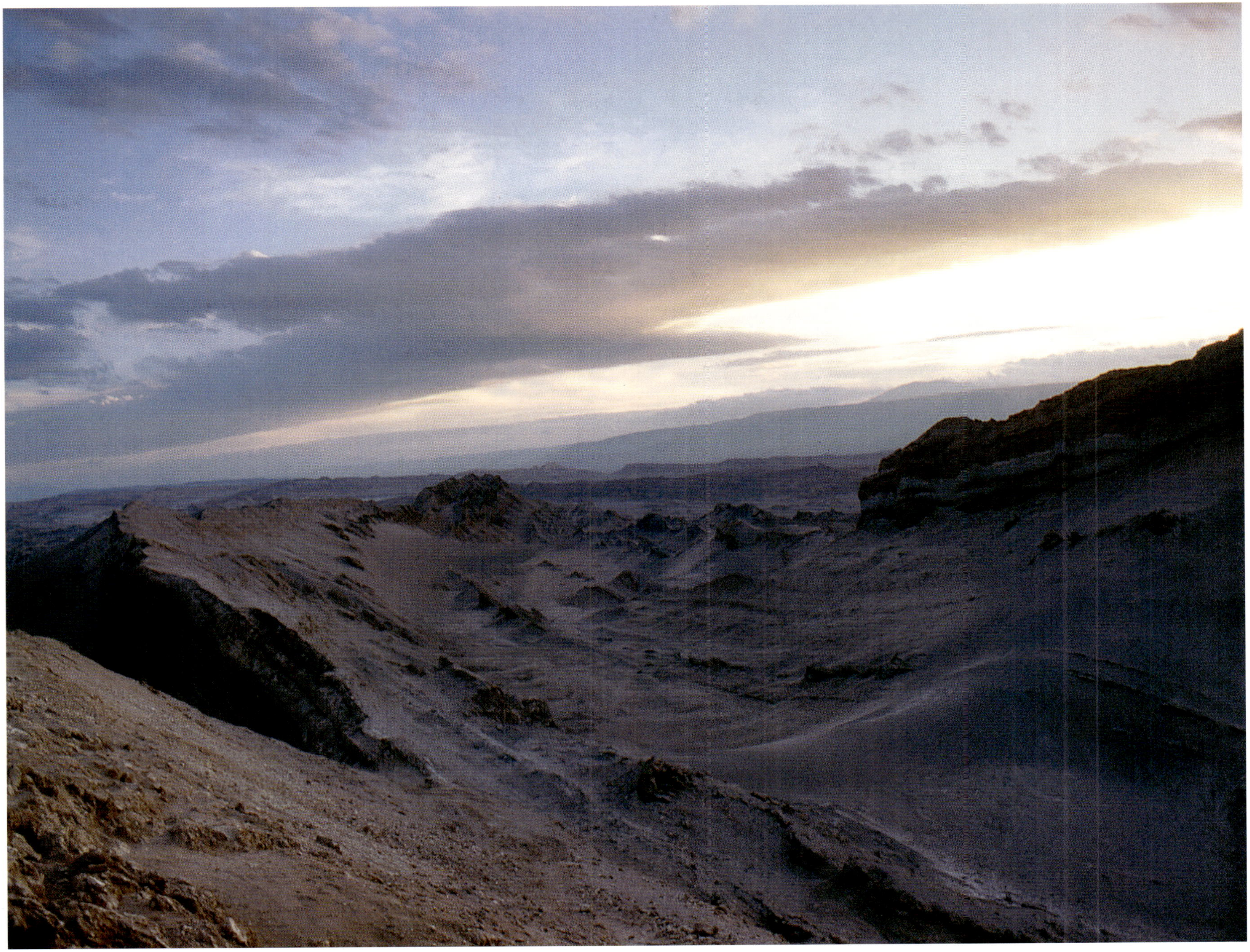

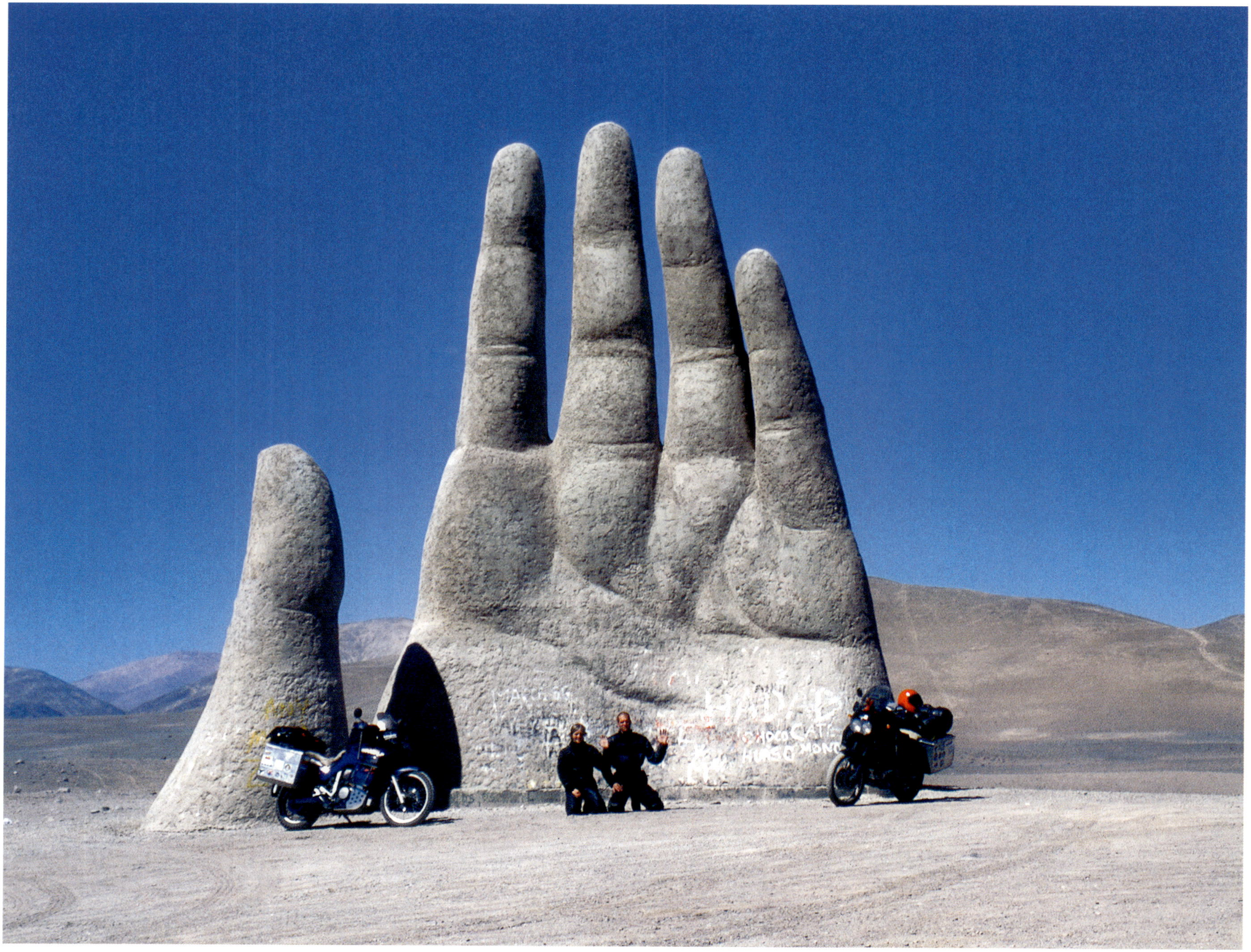

high plateau. The mine owners became rich. After the end of the nitre boom, the town gained importance again with the establishment of a free trade zone in the 1970s. At the height of afternoon rush hour, the one thing I have tried to avoid happens after all. We make a turn, before a traffic light Axel gets into the right-hand turn lane while I am perched with my rear tyre just barely on the line between the two lanes. An off-roader approaches from behind, honks, but I can't move further ahead. Instead of waiting – we have a red light, anyway – the driver tries to pass me and pushes me to the side. My bike jumps to the right and I almost lose my balance. Axel reacts right away and blocks the guy's way. Gesticulating wildly, I yell at him in Spanish , while Axel gives him a piece of his mind in German. The driver seems to be a little scared now and just sits quietly in his car. There is a lot of commotion around us. Meanwhile, the light has turned green and traffic is backed up to the intersection because we are blocking the entire road. Everybody is honking, because they all want to move on as quickly as possible. Nobody seems to want to meddle with us though. I climb off and have a look at my bike, which seems to be okay. However, the aluminium box has left a big scratch on the side of the car. It would be prudent to make tracks as fast as we can. I give Axel a signal that we should move on, because nothing happened, really. He understands right away and we get back on our bikes.

Page 62: The "Desert Hand" by artist Mario Irarrázabal is found in Chile's "Great North"

For hours we follow the new motorway southward through a huge sandbox with its adjoining paddling pool, the Pacific Ocean. A light breeze cools our hot heads under the helmets. From Antofagasta it isn't far to the Oficina Chacabuco. The road leading to the mine is easy to find. After a few metres we see a warning sign: "Danger! Mine fields!" Axel slams on the brake, unsure if the entire area is covered with landmines or just the part behind the barrier. Carefully, we make our way to the gate, it is locked. We peer through the bars, but there is nobody in sight. I call out. Nothing. Disappointed, we decide to go back when two men hurry towards us to open the gate and let us in. At first glance, I see derelict buildings, rusty equipment and a few vehicles standing a bit further along. It is a huge compound. Everything seems a little eerie. Then there is the shimmering heat, again topping 40° C. The two men, at the same time caretakers and security guards, greet us warmly and offer a tour. The nitre mine was open between 1924 and 1940. About 1,500 Chilean and foreign workers lived here with their families until the mine was closed down. Each Oficina was an independent little settlement. There was a

Bottom: North of Antofagasta, "La Portada" rises from the sea, a million-year old volcanic rock

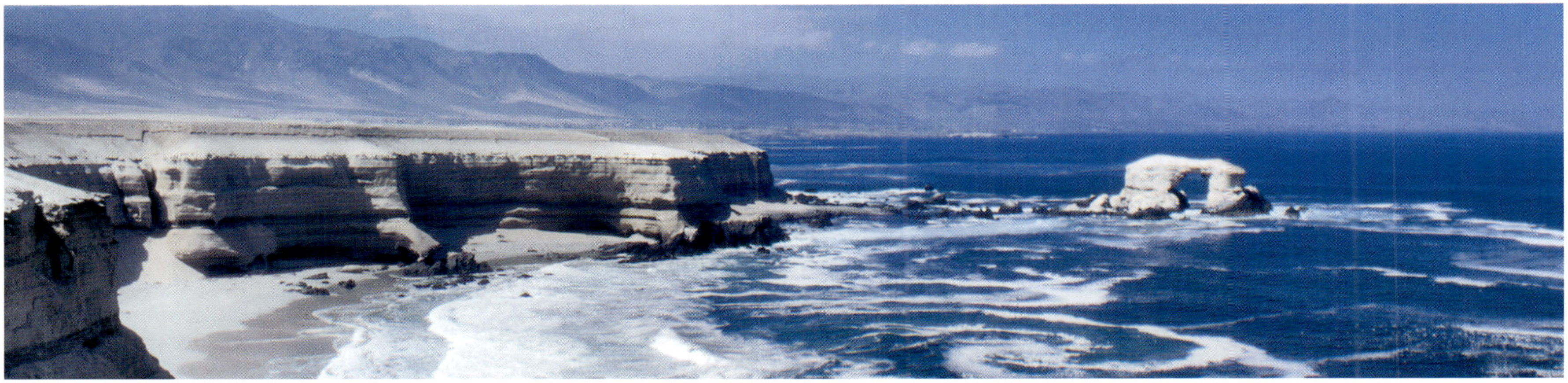

school, a hospital, sports grounds, a laundry, a grocery shop and a cemetery. Chacabuco also has its own political history. In 1971, President Salvador Allende named the mine as a national monument to honour the work of the nitre workers. When Augusto Pinochet came to power in 1973, he turned it into a concentration camp in order to destroy the glory of this monument in the "red north". Thousands of people were imprisoned and tortured here. The area was then mined to prevent escapes. Our guide shows us a tree trunk carved into a figure by a prisoner in 1974. It is a man whose head seems to rest on his right shoulder, while the arms seem to be tied to a branch above. All in all it looks like an exhausted and slumped body. Miraculously, the sculpture "survived" in the compound to serve as a silent witness and memorial for visitors. We fall silent. Until the 1980s, the Oficina was left to its own devices. Meanwhile, with the support of the Goethe Institute, the eventful history of the compound is documented in the former theatre, the only building restored at this point, and the entire compound has been turned into a museum.

From the motorway, we see two waving bikers at a rest stop near Los Vilos. On a whim, we brake on the side of the road and, defying all traffic regulations, turn back. They look at our aluminium suitcases and say, "You must be from Europe, because Europeans are the only people to travel with these things." Carlos and Maria Elena are from Santiago and ride a Suzuki DR 800 and a Honda AX-1. Finally, a Chilean woman on a bike, she is the first I have seen on this journey. And Maria explains to me that Chilean women do not usually ride motorbikes. They surprise us by wearing biker gear from German labels. Carlos is an expert in the market and imports clothes and accessories from Germany. The men start talking shop about bikes and tune-ups. The two Chileans invite us to Santiago where we have a good time with them.

The first snow is falling in the Andes, settling like a thin white blanket over the peaks in the distance. Autumn has arrived and it is time for us to say goodbye.

Page 65: In the mountains around Santiago de Chile

Bottom: Near Copiapó hot ají peppers dry in the sun

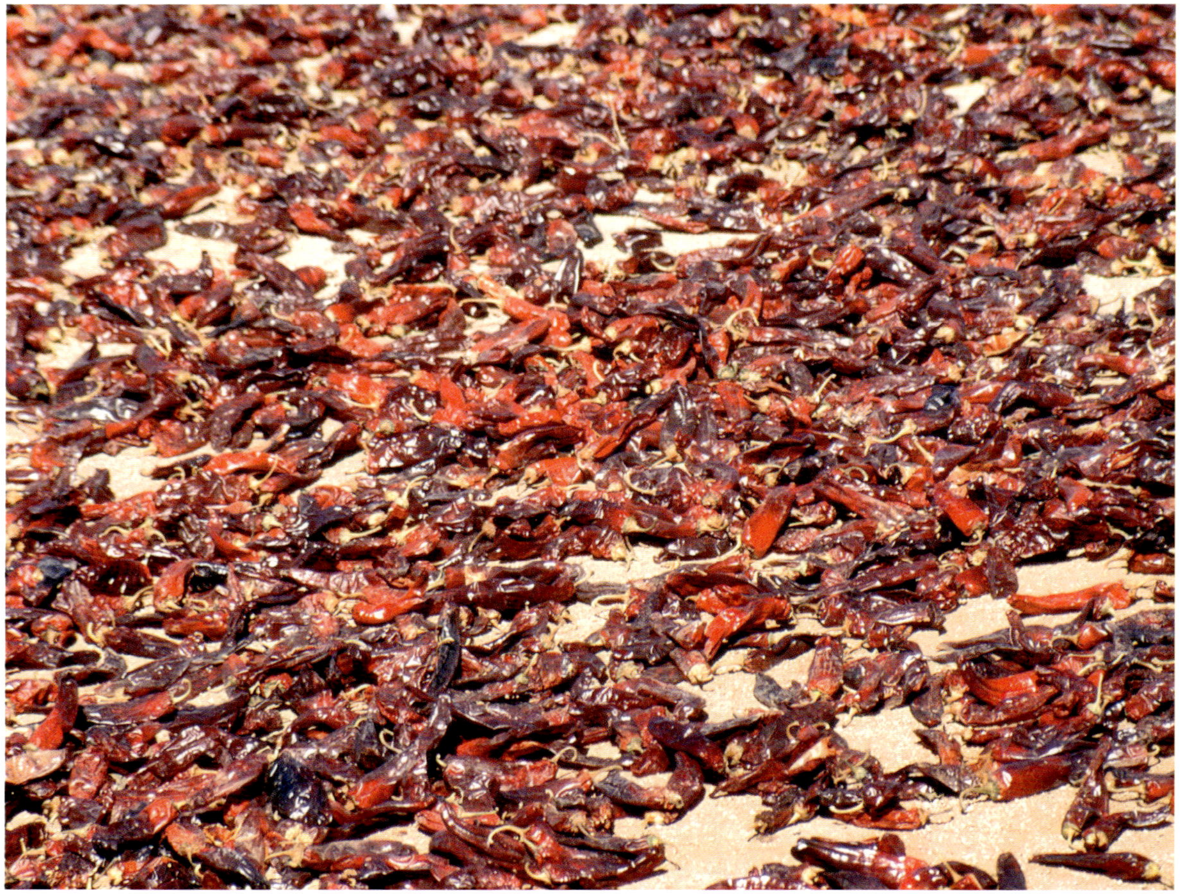

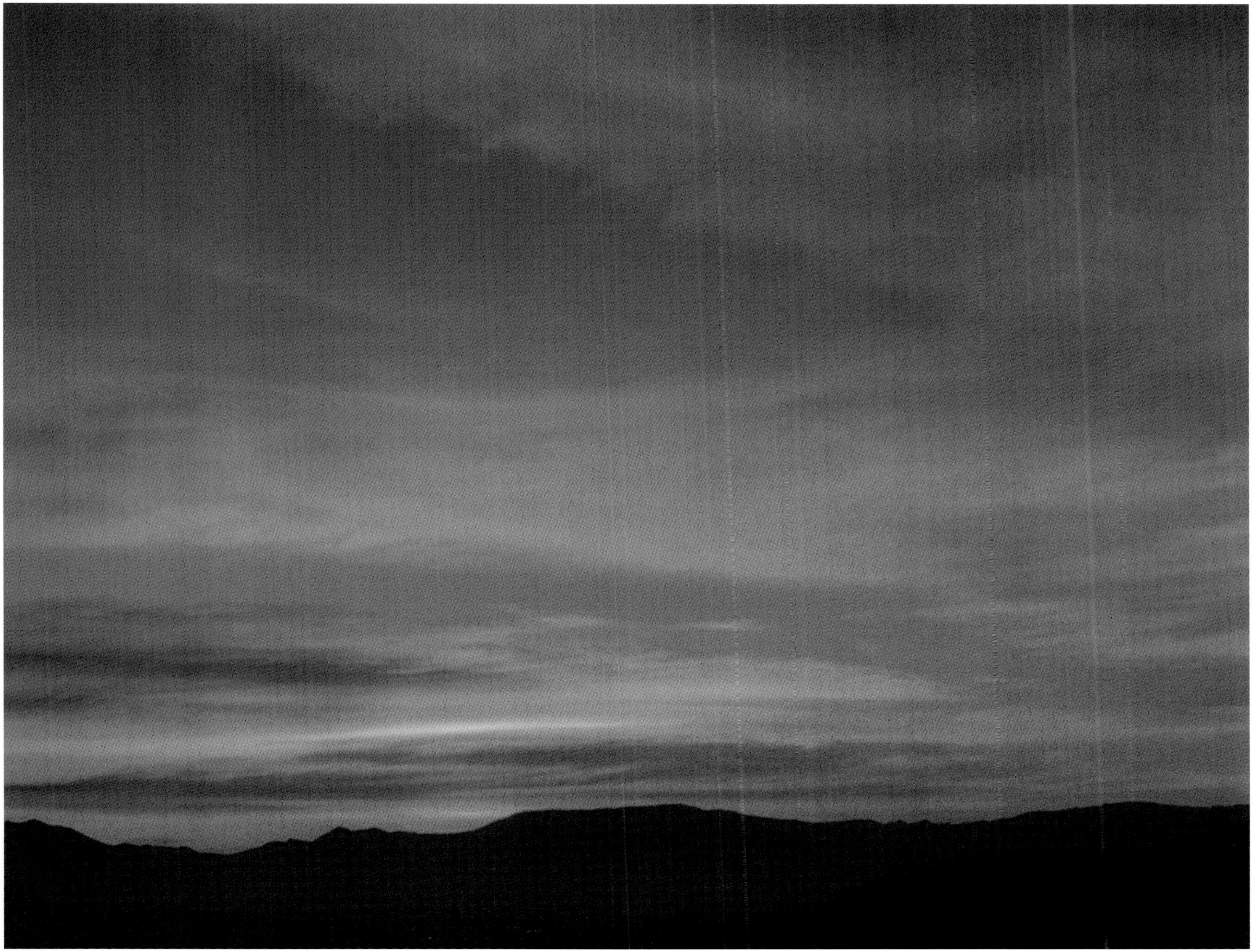

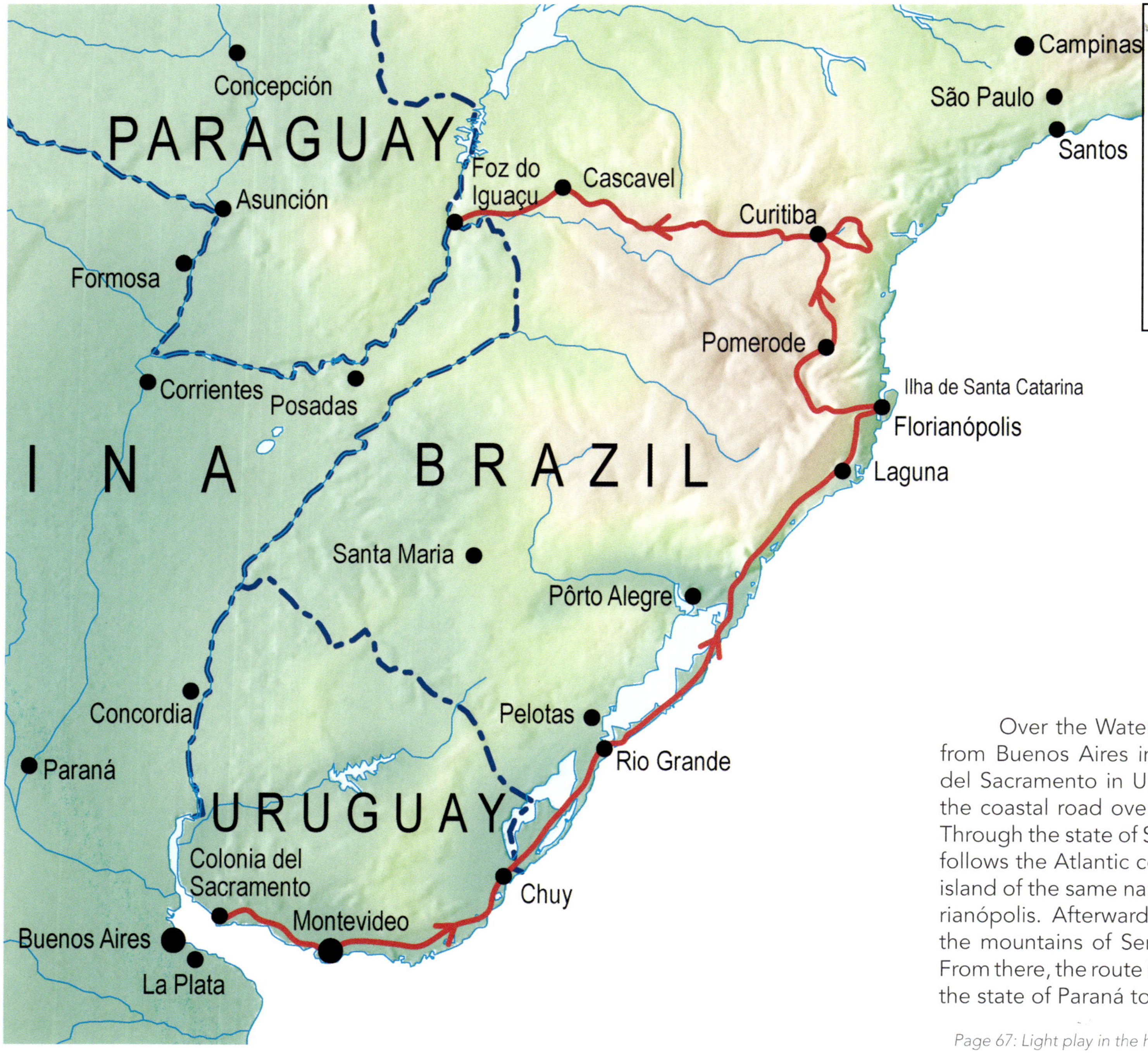

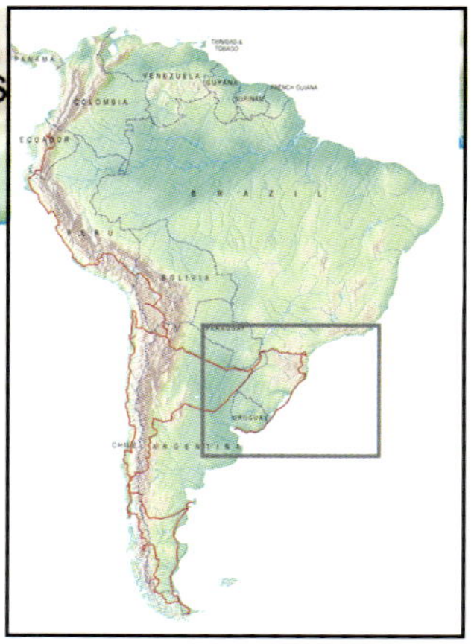

Over the Water Road, the route leads from Buenos Aires in Argentina to Colonia del Sacramento in Uruguay and then along the coastal road over Montevideo to Brazil. Through the state of Santa Catarina, the road follows the Atlantic coast until it reaches the island of the same name, and then on to Florianópolis. Afterwards, it proceeds through the mountains of Serra do Mar to Curitiba. From there, the route leads westward through the state of Paraná to the Iguaçu Waterfalls.

Page 67: Light play in the harbour of Rio de Janeiro, Brazil

URUGUAY – BRAZIL
DAVID AND GOLIATH

ON THE RIVER OF COLOURFUL BIRDS

Nothing but water all around us. Time enough to let my thoughts wander. People say that during a long journey on a ship one takes the soul along, and there is some truth to this. We have 35 long days to get in the mood for the second journey over time, are not thrown into a foreign culture within the space of one day of flying. A different clock begins to tick.

Along Brazil's coast we sail southward on the container ship: Salvador de Bahia, Rio de Janeiro, Vitória, Santos, until we finally reach Buenos Aires, our port of entry in Argentina. We take the opportunity to visit a couple of friends in the capital who we had met in Patagonia. The reunion is celebrated with a proper Asado. Skilfully we weave through the commuter traffic, cross the widest street in the world, the Avenida 9 de Julio, which car drivers happily expand to twice as many lanes as are actually marked, unharmed, and arrive at the ferry port on time. The customs formalities for Uruguay are taken care of quickly, and we have all the necessary papers together in just a few minutes. The catamaran brings us to the second smallest country in South America, into the harbour of Colonia del Sacramento. It seems a bit like being in the Netherlands. Flat hills, the highest "mountain" is around 500 m, pastures and farmland define the landscape. Supposedly there are more cattle than residents in the interior. Uruguay is a country for those who enjoy small things, not for people in search of adventure. Because of the low tide the ferry is lying rather deep and the crew cannot lower the ramp to the quay. Two narrow wooden planks are laid down as a provisional ramp, spaced to accommodate the width of a car. Everybody lands with a bit of momentum. This is the beautiful thing about South America – in special circumstances makeshift solutions are quickly found. In the port we are led through a trough of water to disinfect the vehicles under the stern eyes of a female customs official. Sniffer dogs inspect our baggage. At customs the motorbikes are given a one-year permit. A nice gesture, although it is unlikely that we will stay here so long. The city looks to me like a jewel where all is right with the world. Most of the streets in the centre are lined on both sides with old tall trees whose crowns join together in the middle like a roof, bushes and plants are in full bloom, the grass is cut short. Natural food shops, homeopathic practices and vegetar-

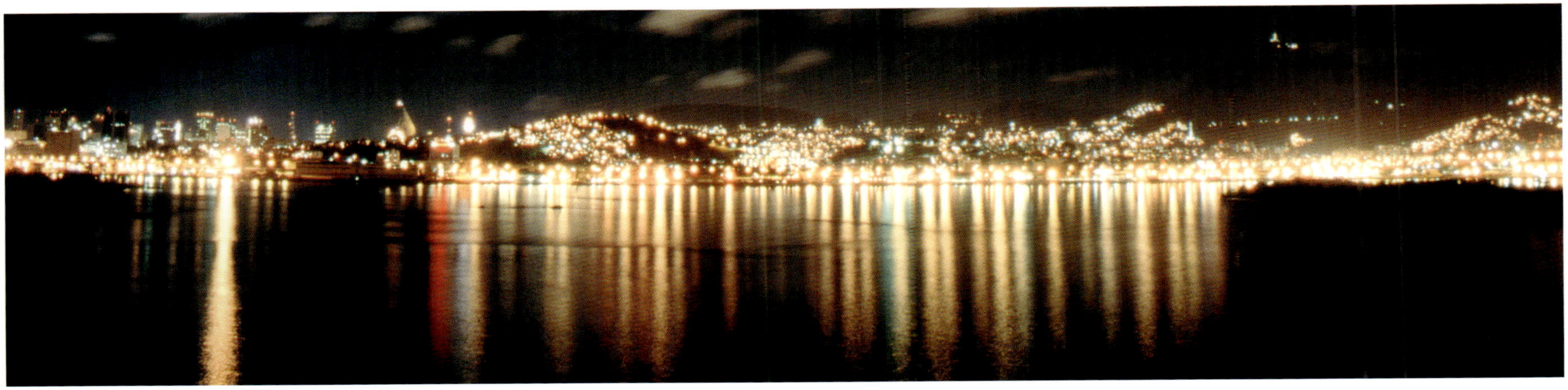

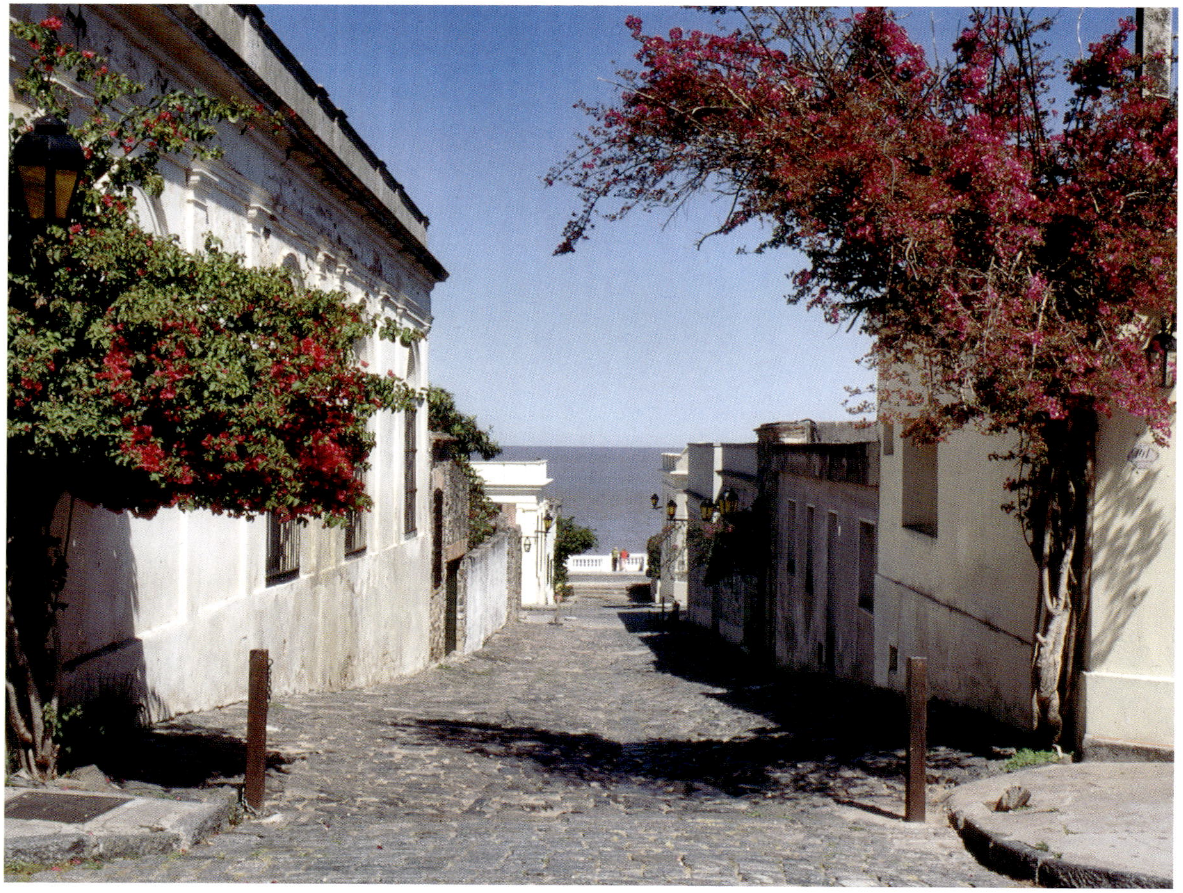

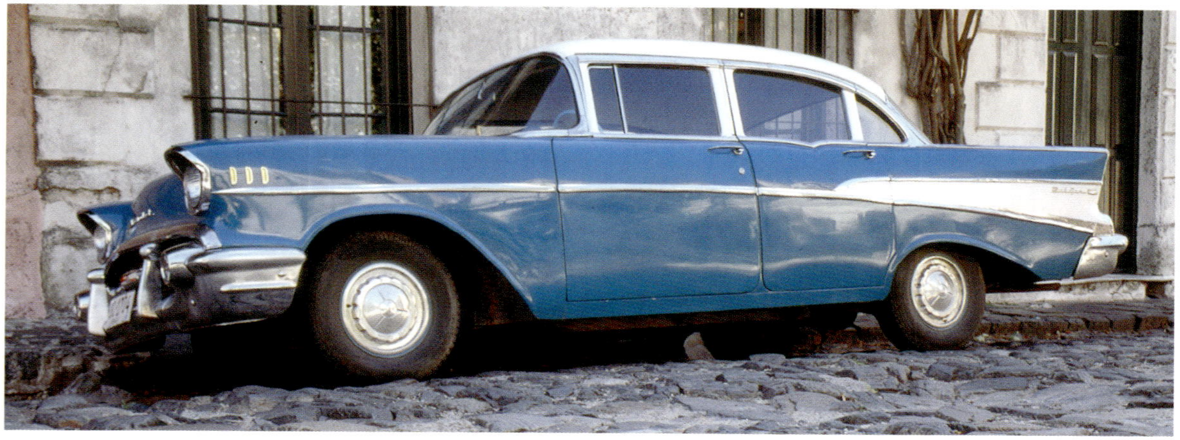

ian restaurants are located on almost every street corner. The cobblestone in the old city is swept, and well-kept old cars from the 1950s are parked on the roadside. Brightly painted house facades, colonial buildings and a whitewashed lighthouse round off the idyllic picture. Picnics on the weekend and fishing with the family in the bay of the Rio de la Plata provide an atmosphere of summer and holidays. Everything seems clean, orderly, tidy – almost uncanny for South America. Uncertain what I should make of it all, I have a sudden insight. In the search for a hotel I turn off the high street and drive over a solid double line. After five more metres, the shrill sound of a whistle reaches my ears through the helmet. Slamming on the brakes I come to a stop in front of the shoes of a traffic policewoman. I look surprised, not knowing what could have happened. She nods understandingly and explains the traffic regulations in Uruguay to me. Explains where I am allowed to drive and to make a turn, what solid lines mean, where motorbikes can be parked, what the small white arrows on

Top left: Old city centre of Colonia del Sacramento, Uruguay

Left: The oldtimer cult is very popular in Uruguay

Page 69: The lighthouse at the Plaza Mayor was built in 1857

the street signs mean – oh, if only she had crossed my way in Santiago de Chile! I thank her warmly for the clarification and assure her that this would not ever happen to me again, but that I had only just arrived in her country and still need to get my bearings. I therefore get off with a warning and the knowledge that it does not do to joke with the traffic police in Uruguay. Naturally, Axel has made his way according to the rules and is now waiting on a street corner a couple of blocks away from me; I can see the grin under his helmet even from a distance.

Along the picturesque coastal road passing one beach resort after the other, we drive in the direction of Montevideo two days later. A stiff breeze is blowing in from the ocean. Tower blocks come into view, like in Rio de Janeiro or Santos in Brazil the beachfront here is also built up and surrounded by a sea of concrete. Behind the container port, there are amusement parks and then villas with green front gardens. Actually we would prefer not to cross through this country so quickly, but before we know it we land in Chuy, the small town on the border to Brazil.

Once the Spaniards lost their supremacy in Argentina, they seized the narrow strip of land for themselves in the La Plata region. In 1814, the Spaniards were put down by the independence movement in Uruguay led by José Gervasio Artigas after several battles and sieges. A short time later Brazil occupied the east of the country as far as Montevideo and annexed Uruguay as a province in 1821. Despite various setbacks, the independence movement was finally able to lead the country to autonomy in 1825. Brazil recognized Uruguay as an independent state three years later. The insignificant had prevailed against those in power. In Chuy traces of this series of historical events can no longer be recognised. The 9,000 inhabitants live shoulder to shoulder in this village with the border crossing their Avenida which gives the high street a sense of internationality. The town is a free-trade zone and, as a result, one big supermarket. Both sides of the street are filled with duty-free shops. It is only through the language in the individual shops that it is possible to recognize whether one stands on Uruguayan or Brazilian territory. We overlooked the border posts on our way to the town centre looking for accommodations. We are not worried, we can still deal with the formalities first thing tomorrow. In the hotel the owner puts Axel in his guest register under the name of "Stadt Duisburg" after thoroughly studying his passport. Admittedly the name of the authority which had issued the passport is written confusingly under the passport photo. But he has been travelling incognito the whole time through South America in any case. Since the letter "ß" does not exist in Spanish or Portuguese, everyone calls him Señor "Heb". The next morning we drive back to the Uruguayan tollgate in order to officially leave the country. With the customs official in Brazil on the other side I try very hard to make myself understood with the bits of the language that I have learned, but I don't get very far. At some point we just smile at each other, neither of us able to understand a single word from the other. With gestures, a lot of patience and charm we manage to get all the papers filled out. The relaxed reception in Brazil puts us in a good mood.

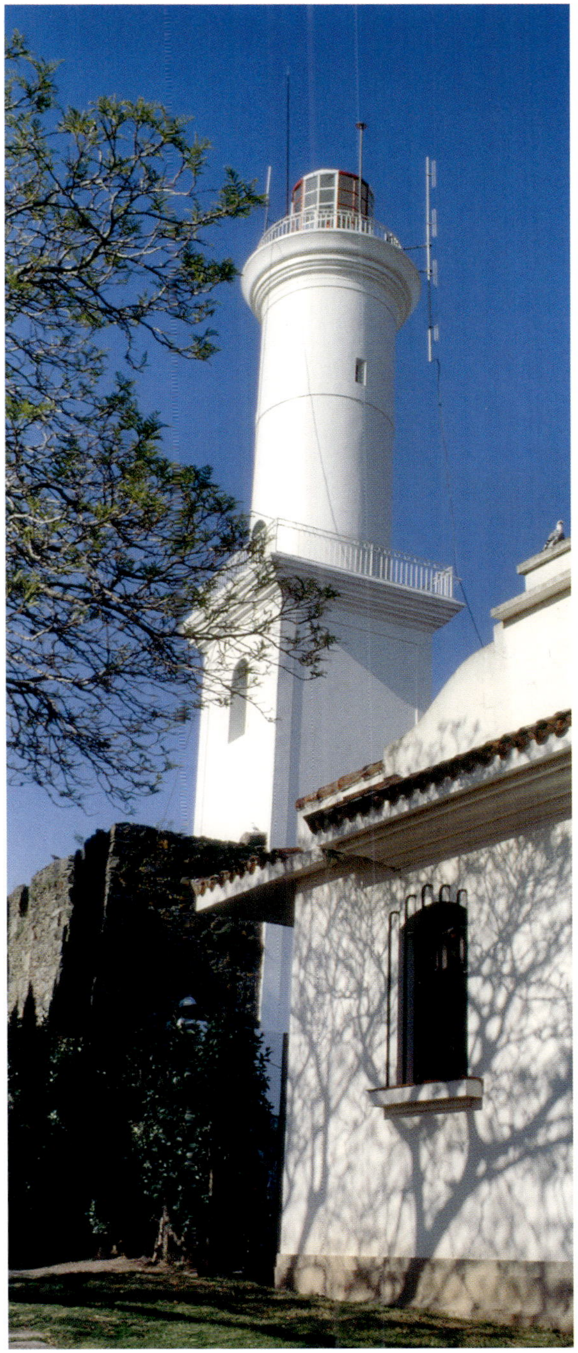

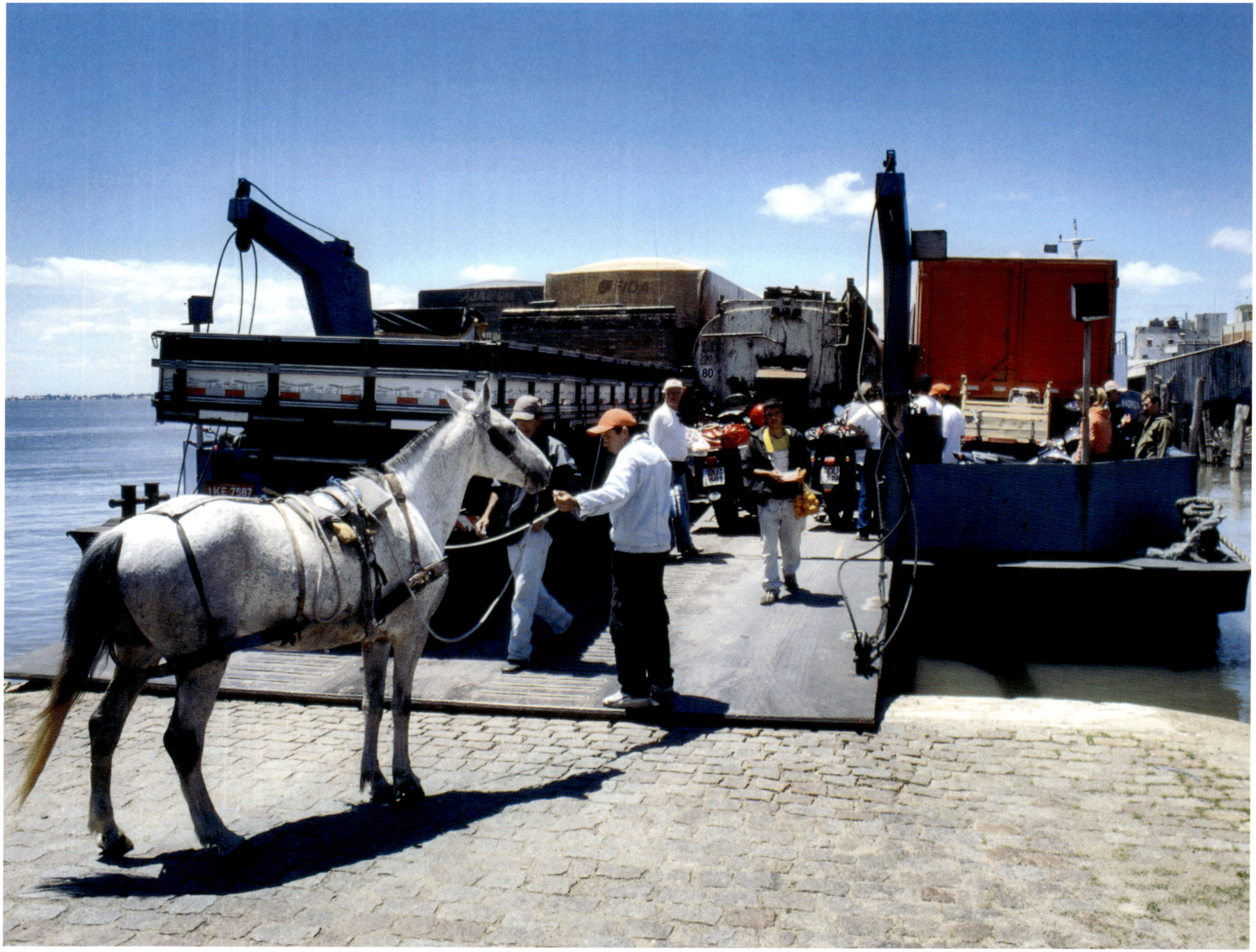
LKE 7587
80

THROUGH HELL INTO PARADISE

On the small ferry from Rio Grande to Sao José do Norte our motorbikes are squeezed in between trucks and a horse. The boat is so overloaded that the wheels of a van stick out over the open ramp. From a driving perspective, the last couple of days were not particularly demanding, but instead rather tedious as Uruguay's roads are in the best of conditions. There's no need for us to think about monotonous driving routes all day long after arriving in Sao José do Norte. After the small town of Estreito we go from the asphalt surface directly into soft sand. The tyres are digging in deep under the weight of the motorbikes, and we have to catch ourselves with both legs again and again. In contrast to the desert in whose expanse it is possible to select your own route, we struggle on the 6 m wide road against numerous tyre tracks. All-terrain vehicles, trucks and excavators with chain drive have left their traces behind and we constantly drive ourselves in solid. After one hour we have left those 6 km

Page 70: Ferry from Rio Grande to São José do Norte

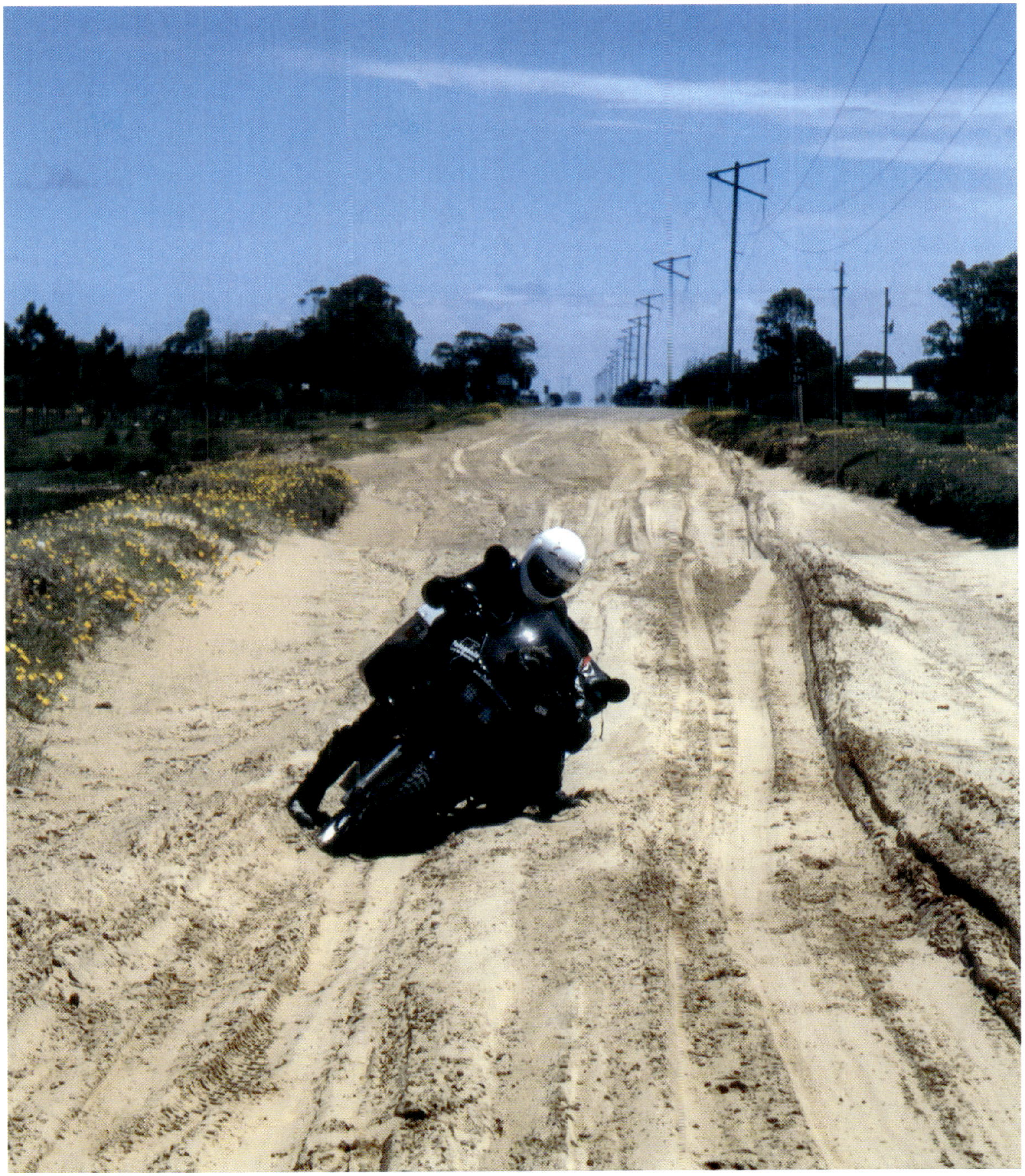

Rechts: The road outside of Estreito isn't easy

behind us, I have gone down four times, and with a temperature that has climbed to 32° C in the shade, the sweat is running down my back. As a result of the constant rainfall of the last few days, the next 30 km have been transformed into a mud track in which we regularly get stuck or slide on as if on soap. I can hardly move my shifting hand, and my shoulders and neck are totally tensed up. The high-splattering water and the churned-up mud collect in the boots. From solitary huts by the side of the road, inhabitants come walking out to look at us crazy people. No vehicles far and wide, only farmers on their horses smile about the two of us as they pass by. Then the Twin gets stuck completely and lies slightly slanted head first in the mud. Fuel leaks out of the tank. It is impossible to straighten it easily. With our boots we slip again and again, while the motorbike slides away to the side when we try to lift it. In order to lighten the weight, the luggage must be removed. Unfortunately we are not able to take off the left case, the heaviest with all our

Bottom and page 73: The Estrada do Inferno, leading along the lagoon Lagoa dos Patos in the south of Brazil from Estreito to Tavares, is a test of endurance for man and machine

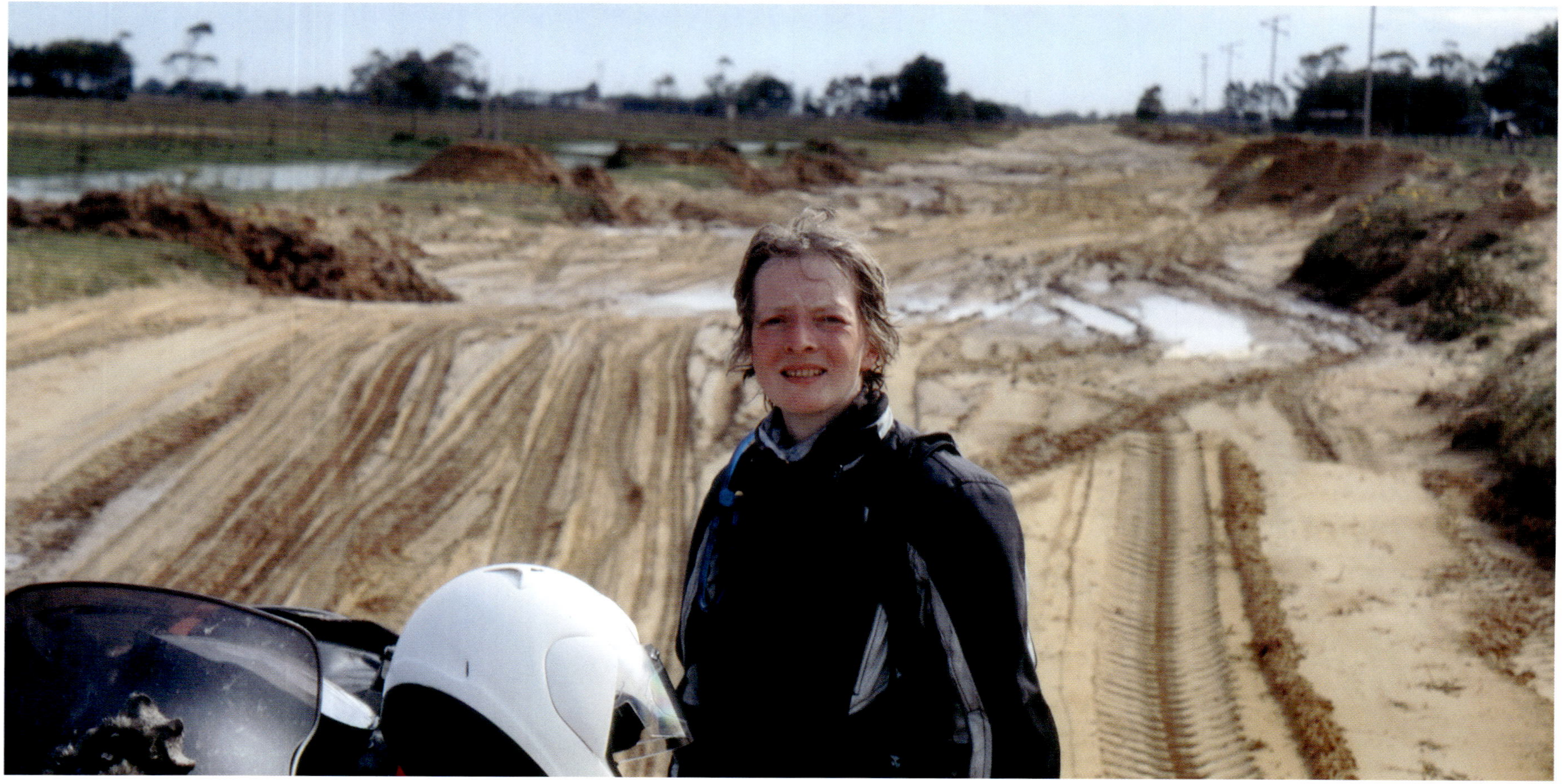

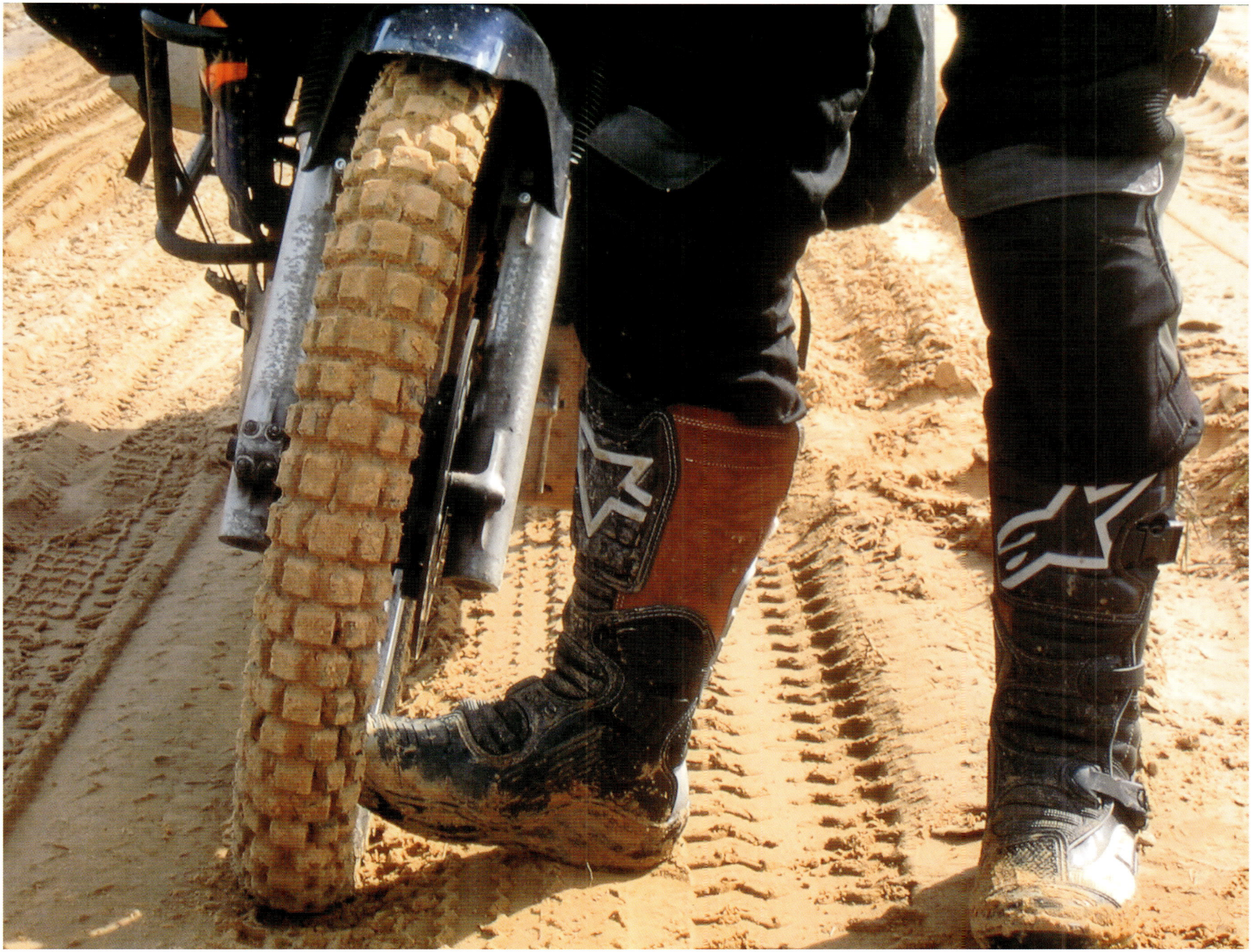

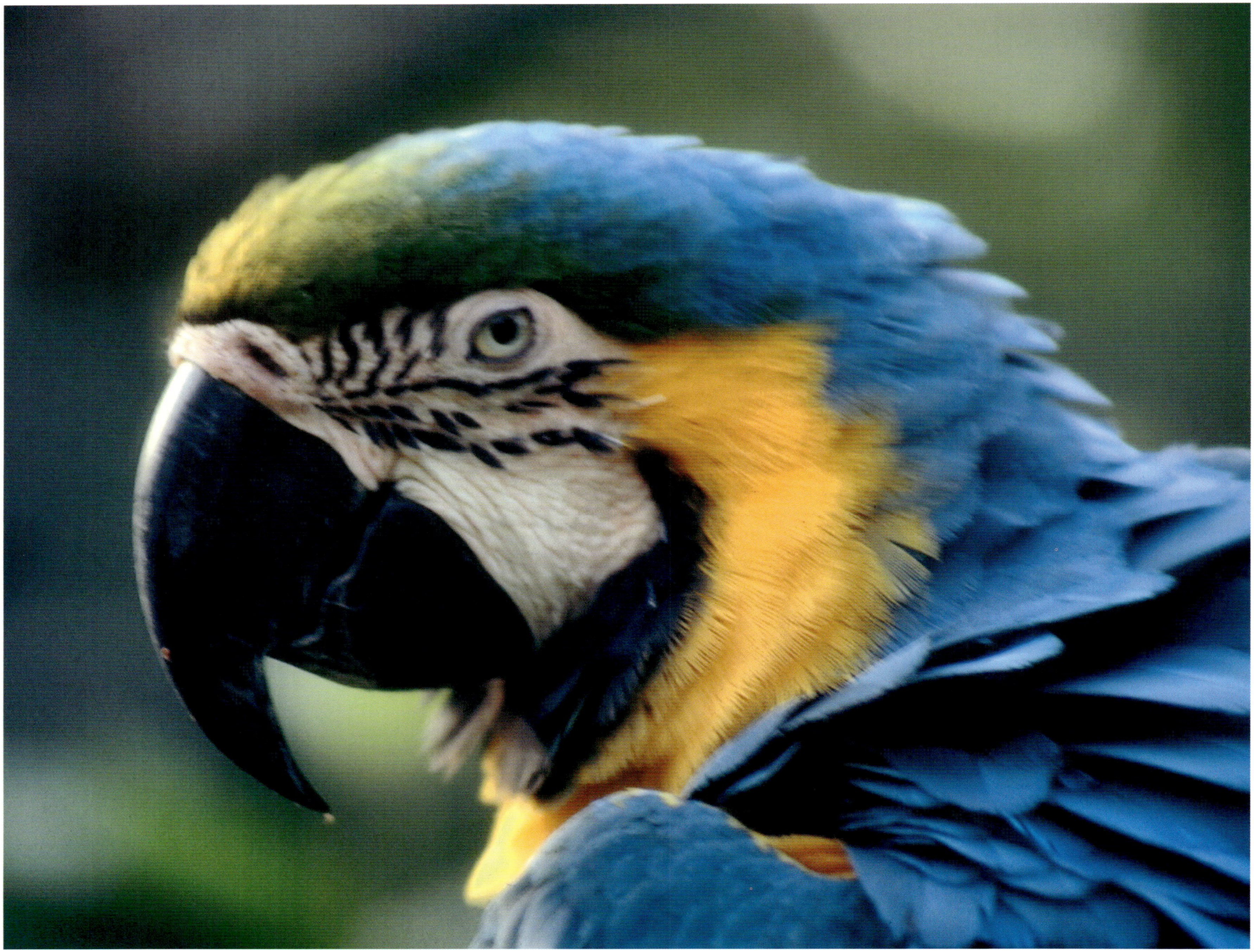

replacement parts and tools, because the bike is lying on it. I grab the handlebars, Axel the case carrier. Despite numerous attempts, we have no success hoisting it up. We only get it raised a little bit, so Axel kneels on all fours in the mud and pushes his entire body under the motorbike. With this kind of support beneath it we slowly manage to bring the bike to a vertical position again. Before we buckle on the luggage we allow ourselves a short breather. Finally, after a 5-hour struggle, the asphalt appears on the horizon. The Estrada do Inferno, Hell Road, as the local residents call it, is a true credit to its name.

Although we have only asphalt under the wheels the next day, we must now endure pouring rain. The weather god has no mercy on us. The motor cross boots are naturally not waterproof, and with every shift of gears a puddle sloshes from the front past the ankle and back again. With my toes I dabble in the pool of water in time to the melody that I hum to myself to put myself in a good mood. It does not help. During a break to refuel I shake the water out of the

Page 74: Embarrassment makes the ara blush

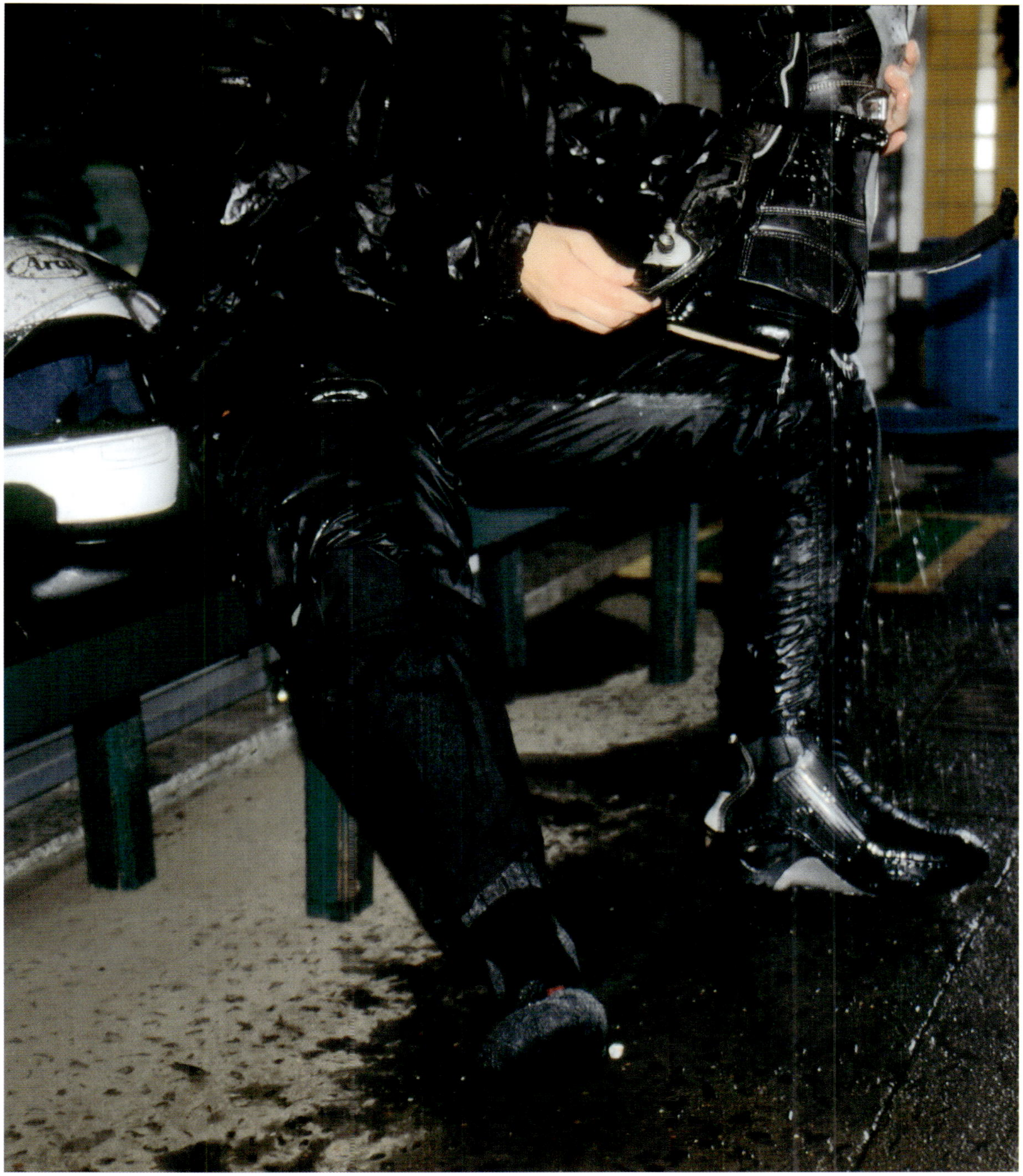

Right: Rain doesn't stop at boots

boots and wring out the socks. The soles are completely soaked. I stuff the boots with newspaper in the evening so that the wetness is soaked up. It takes quite an effort to get into the damp clothing the next morning. In the rain we work our way along the coastal road further towards the north until we reach the Ilha Santa Catarina. In 1503, the Portuguese discovered the island. It was first used as a hideaway by pirates, then banished prisoners were abandoned here. Rumour has it that this is still reflected in the character of many residents today. With about 424 km² the island is Brazil's largest. The north is quite overdeveloped, but in the south there are still wooded regions, small bays with secluded beaches, lagoons and waterfalls. In Costa do Dentro we land in Gerta's pousada, a small paradise.

Under the porch roof we lie in hammocks, wrapped in thick blankets, relaxing and watching the rain. And snakes. One morning the housemaid comes out of the breakfast room screaming loudly: "Uma

Bottom: Perfect camouflage for an unseen digestion break

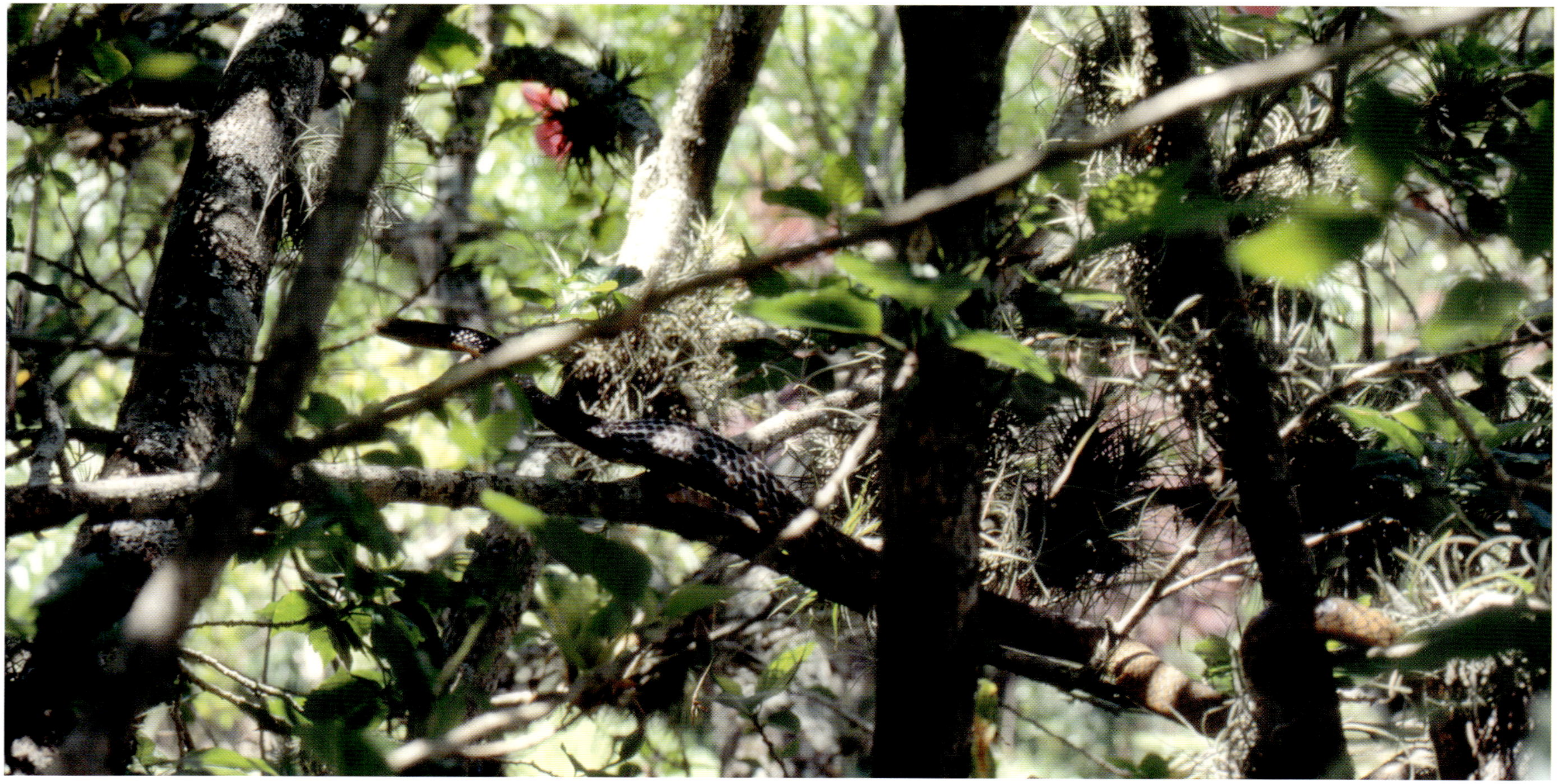

cobra!" I also cry out – because I don't have the camera on hand. I fetch it quickly and then Axel and I sneak in together with Gerta. Two dark blue glistening eyes look at us paralyzed with fear. They are attached to a long thin body of at least 2 m that has wrapped itself around multiple chair legs and a backrest. There is no question who is afraid of who here. We consider how the reptile can be freed from its unfortunate position. It has to find its way back to the window or the door. Gerta opens the screen and clears the way. The snake does not even twitch. Then very slowly, watching us, it moves its body, it must have noticed the breeze. In less than 2 seconds it has made its way to the door and disappears into the underbrush. A short time later we hear a miserable cry of pain, like that of an animal in mortal fear, from in front of the house. We go towards the noise and search the pond for a frog, but the sound comes from the tree above it. One last cry and then silence. One branch seems to be strangely bent and I have to take a second look to recognize that it is a snake. Its camouflage is perfect. Directly behind its head is a thick bulge that moves slowly through the

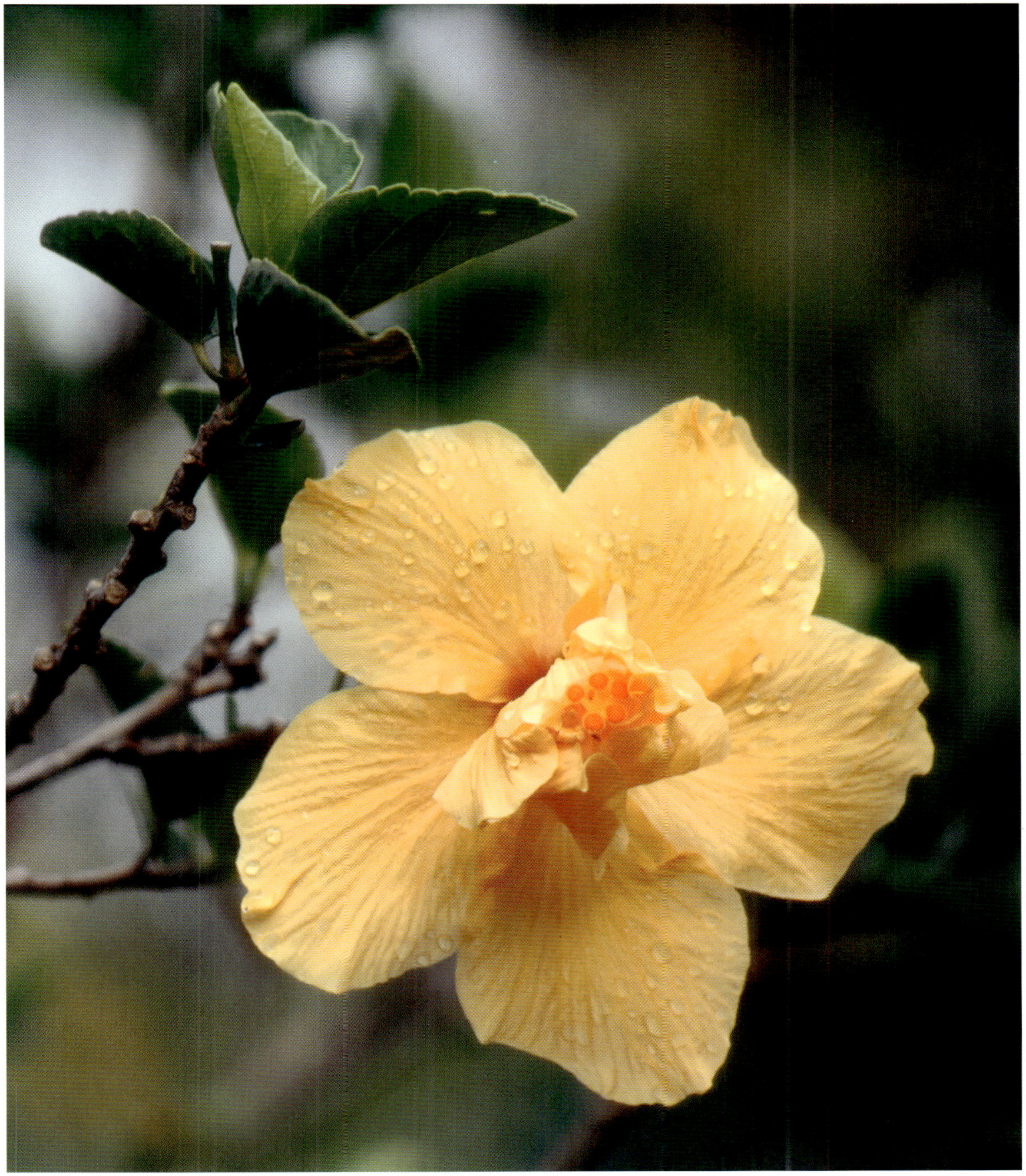

Right: Hibiscus blossom

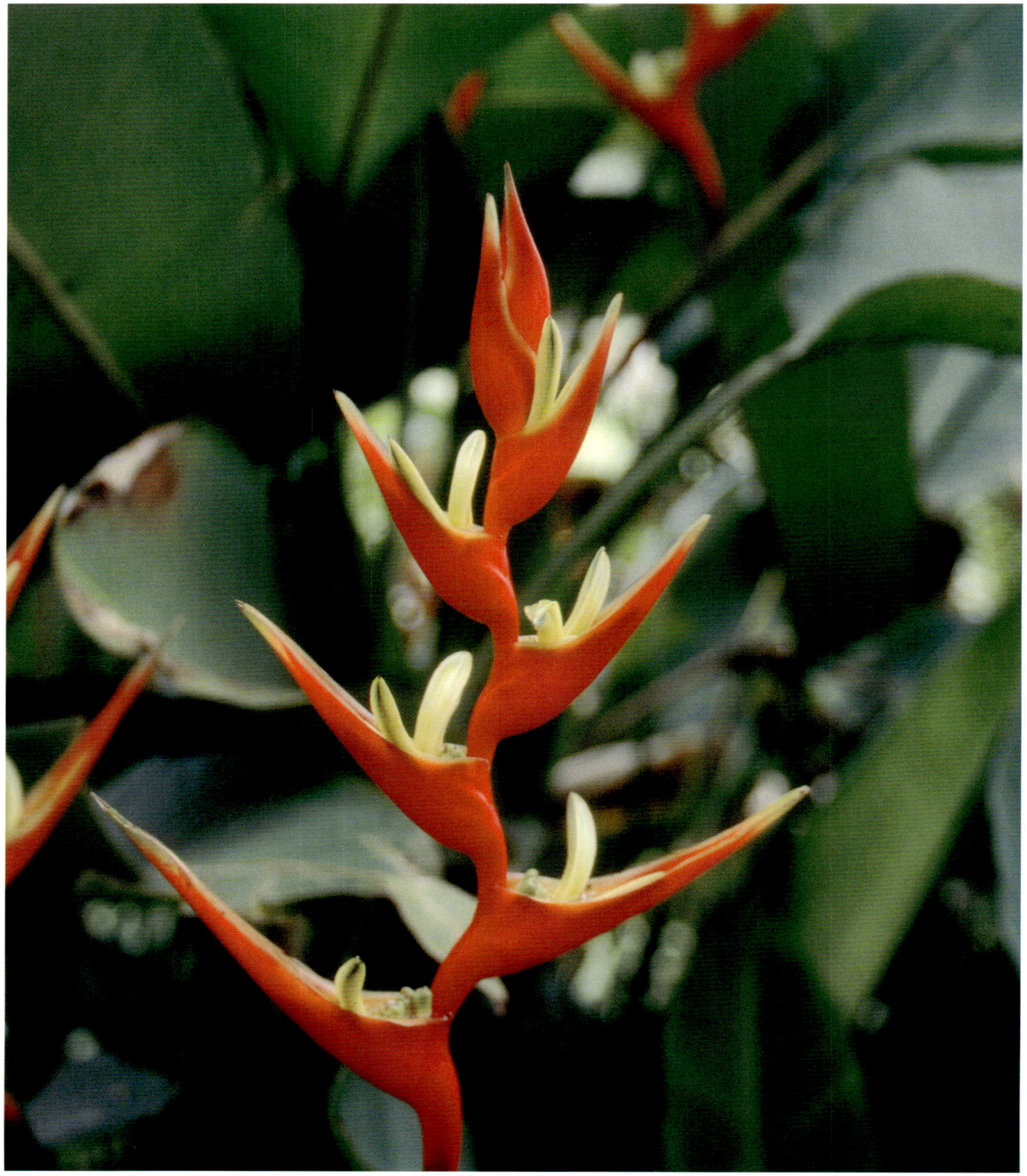

body. For the next days the snake will take an extended break for digestion, for a frog has breathed its last.

Gerta notes with a laugh that her guests usually leave earlier when the weather is bad, but it is for that reason that we stay here longer. Our perseverance is rewarded. After the clouds have cried themselves out a few days later, we go on a reconnaissance tour with the motorbikes. At a petrol station two Brazilian bikers talk to us and invite us to their table at a neighbouring café. For Brazilians, they drive big machines, a BMW 1150 GS and a BMW K 1100 LT. Thousands of smaller 125ers and 350ers flit about in the country, snake through the heavy traffic of the metropolises and fly over the tracks with their light weight. The "big ones" are only affordable for the wealthy people in the country, the elite, as Geronimo puts it. They organise themselves in motorbike clubs in order to indulge in their hobby. On a short weekend trip of 1,000 km they hardly leave their province, whereas at home we would cross almost half of Europe on such a trip.

Left: Heliconia

Page 79: Off-road fun on the Ilha (island) Santa Catarina in Brazil

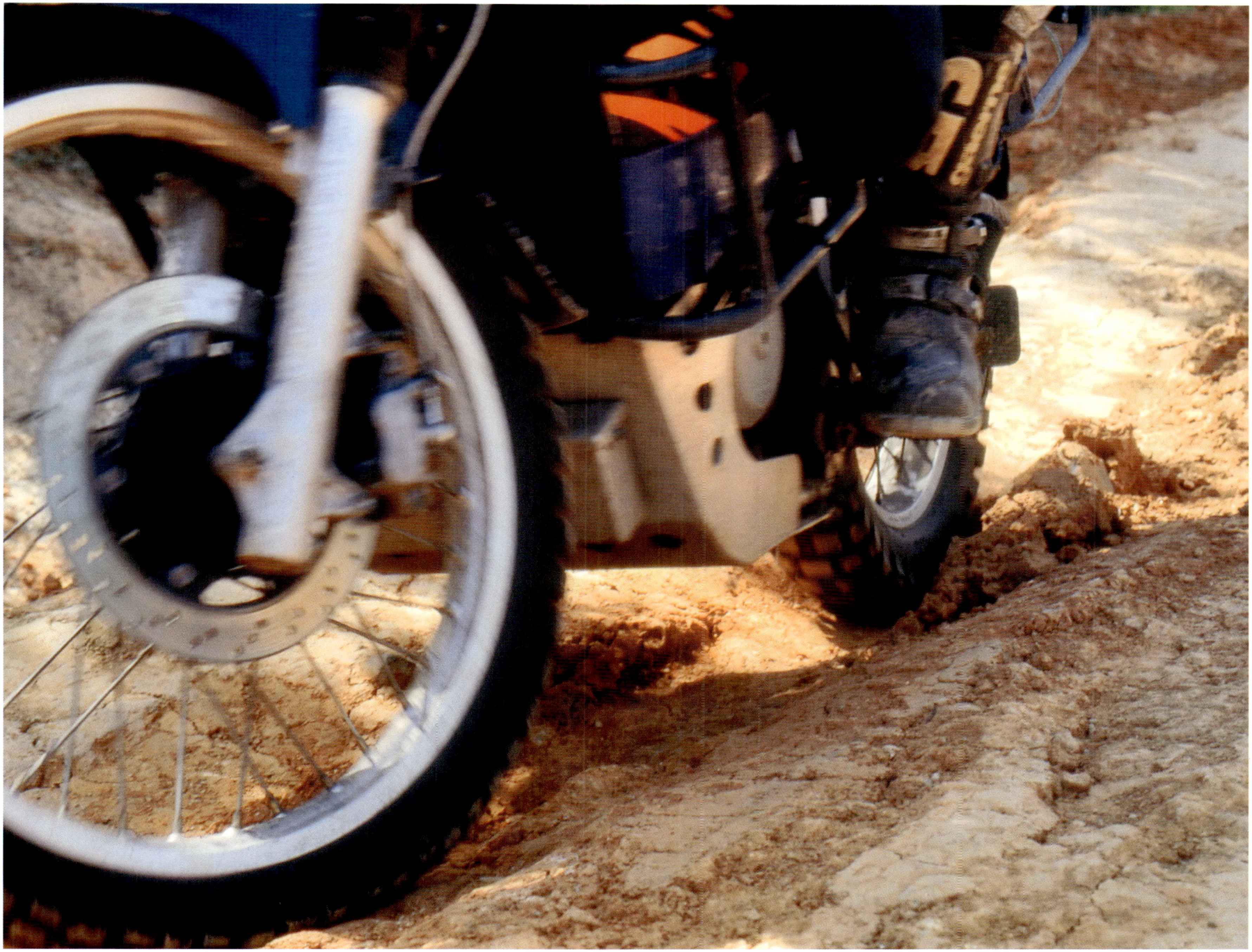

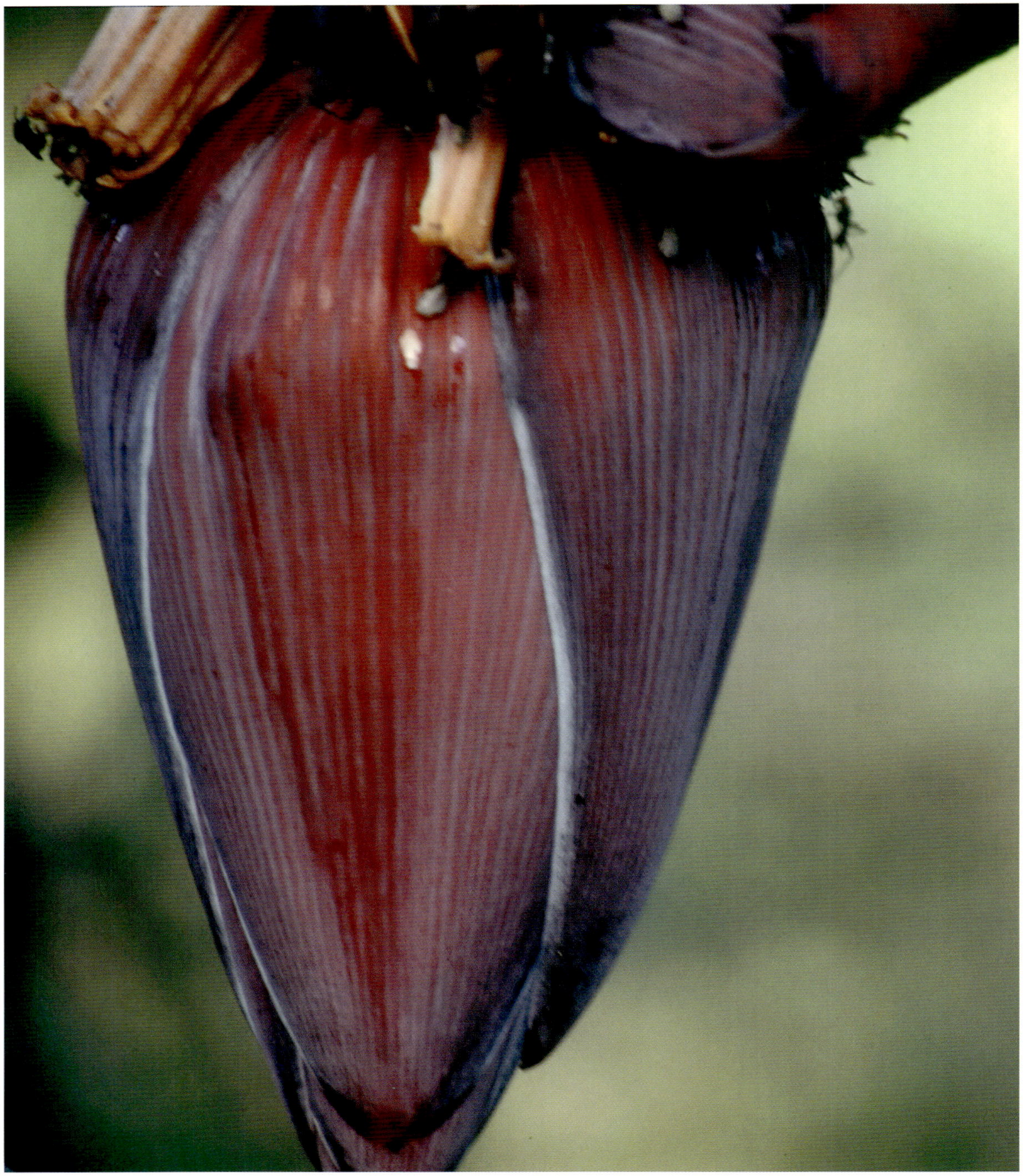

They immediately give us their telephone numbers in case we need help at some time on the road in this huge country.

Early the next morning the sun shines through the curtains again. It is not even 6 o'clock but nothing can keep me in bed any longer. I get dressed and take a walk with the two dogs that belong to the pousada. The atmosphere is amazing. The last raindrops from the night still hang on the flower petals; here and there I breathe in their scent, birds twitter, butterflies flutter around me, the grass is slowly drying under my feet. My gaze wanders down to the bay, white small cirrus clouds meander in the sky. With freshly baked bread, homemade jam and fruit from the fruit trees near the house we fortify ourselves for the day. We explore the south-west coast. In the villages the people live off oyster farming, the quays stretch out along the coast like wooden footbridges. The fishermen go out in their boats and haul in the "catch", which is then offered as a specialty in many small restaurants.

Left: Banana blossom

Page 81: On the south-west coast of Ilha (island) Santa Catarina oyster farming is very popular

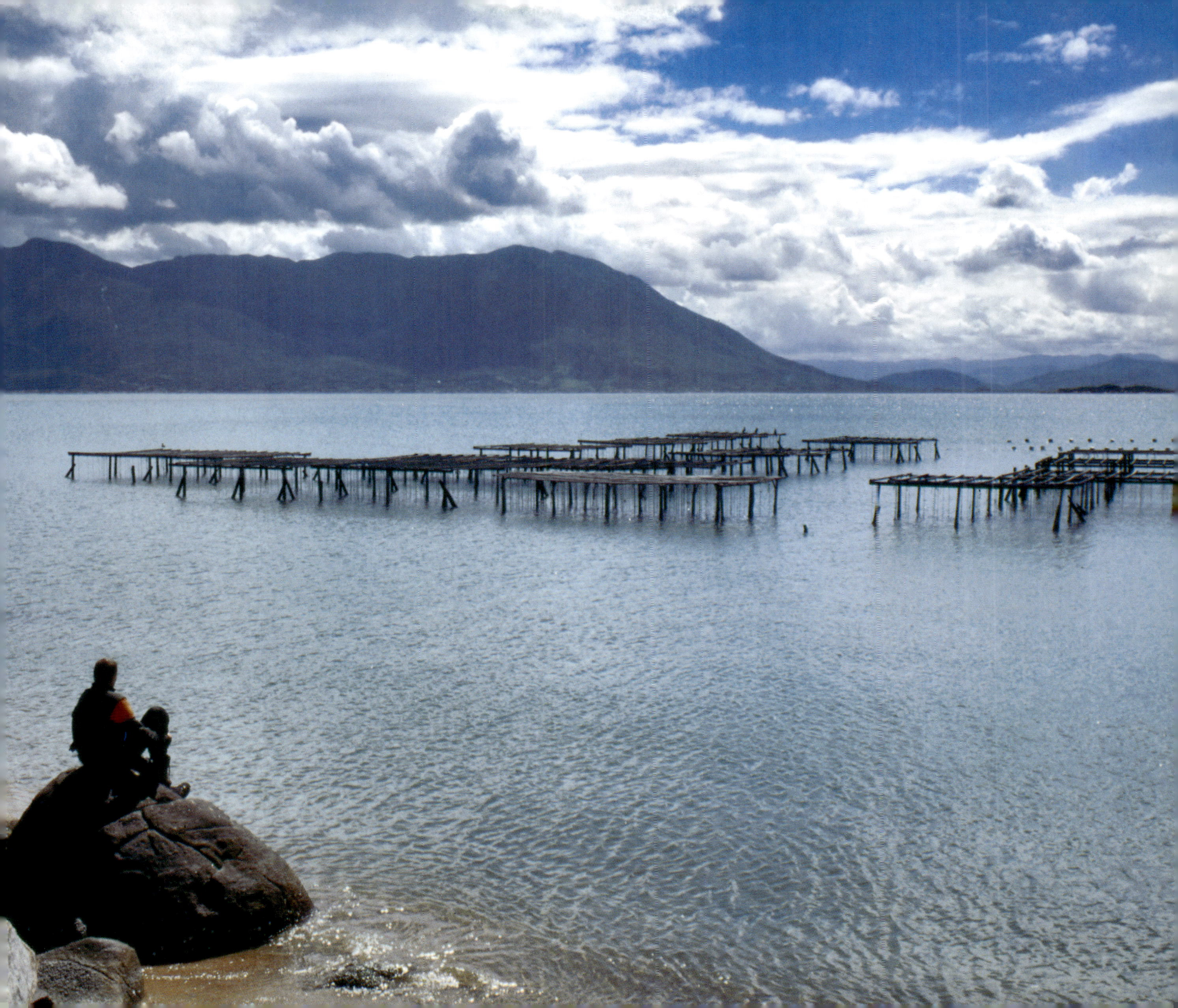

COLOURFUL MIX OF ETHNICITIES

We have stayed in Costa do Dentro longer than planned and it is now time to set off on our way again. Through the mountains we travel towards the north-west with the feeling that we are in the low mountain ranges of Germany, were it not for the high palms and banana trees everywhere along the road. Agriculture is very important here. We arrive at Pomerode, in the valley of the river Itajai. The small village is the most German in the region. Here in the south of Brazil there are many European roots, while the north is characterised by a black population. In the 19th century a decree was issued allowing foreigners to obtain land in Brazil. Settlement was advertised in Europe. From Italy, Germany, Portugal and Croatia came the first immigrants who were often farmers, charcoal burners and seasonal workers. However, they had to struggle with the local bureaucracy. Many moved out to the solitude of the forests in groups of families or clans

Page 83: In the district of Testo Alto in Pomerode German inspired half-timbered houses define the look

Page 84: Memorial for the Ukrainian immigrants in Curitiba, Brazil

Page 85: The architecture on the complex of the free Environmental University in Curitiba is inspired by the four elements of nature

Bottom: The house of the first German immigrants in Pomerode of 1898

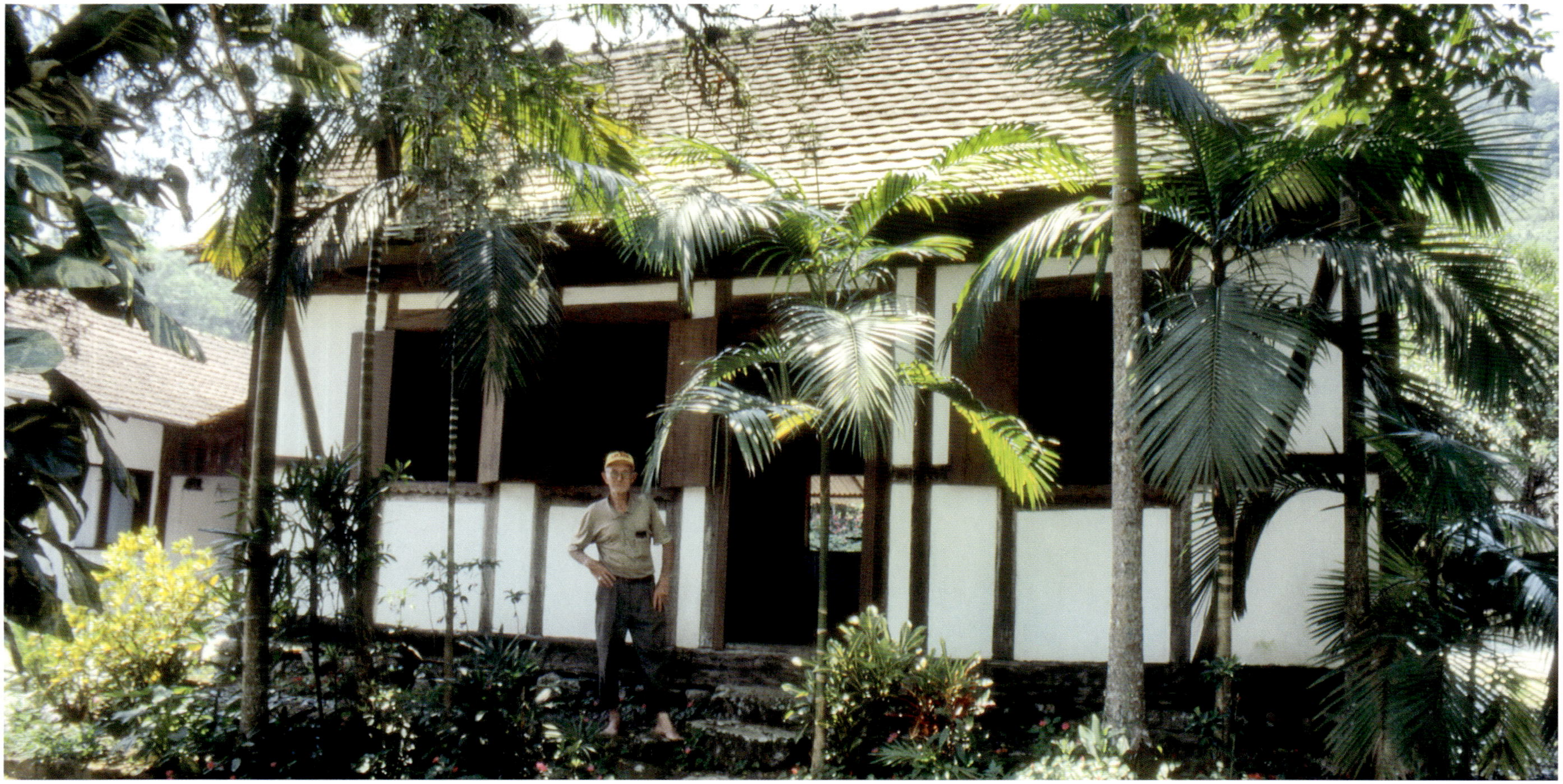

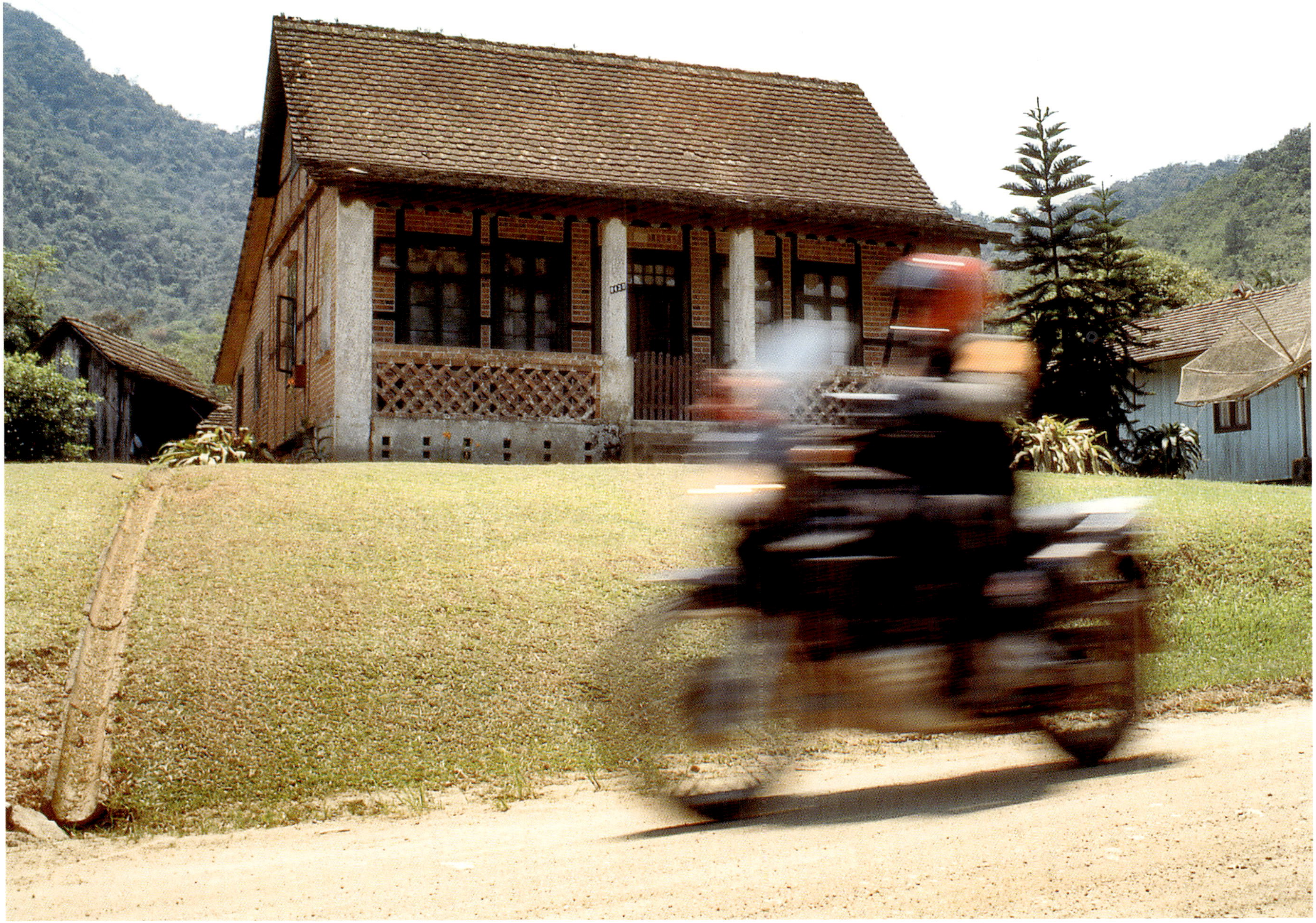

and created their own small worlds, retained their language and culture, and lived off agriculture and crafts. The first German families settled down in Pomerode in 1898. We visit one of their grandsons in the house of the founder. Until 16 years ago Herr Lümke still lived with his family in the timber-framed house of his ancestors before he built a modern one nearby. In an old German dialect, he tells us a bit about the history of his family. In the city district of Testo Alto everyone still speaks High German or Pomeranian Low German. During the war, in which Brazil became involved in 1942 under the dictatorship of president Getúlio Dornelles Vargas, pupils were forbidden, under corporal punishment, to speak German. Adults who conversed in their native language were arrested on the street. Many of them had never learned Portuguese which became a problem for them. It was a difficult time. Today the German language is openly cultivated, as are other traditions of the distant and foreign "homeland". The man at the reception desk of our accommodations is thrilled that he can speak German with us. He proudly shows me an illustrated book about the history of the settlers in Pomerode. His deepest desire is to spend a winter in the home of his grandparents. It is quite astounding how people are attached to a culture that they have never experienced themselves but know only from the stories told by their ancestors. The traditions are also apparent in the cuisine and in the architecture. In the neighbouring town of Blumenau, for example, the biggest Oktoberfest outside of Munich takes place every year. We make a short trip to visit the town. The timber-framed houses are spruced up and colourful, many names of businesses are of German origin. Everything seems clean and orderly. And the traffic police do their job diligently. On a parking lot for motorbikes we find the last space and stroll through the streets already decorated for Christmas. A man comes after us and asks whether the big black motorbike there belongs to us before announcing that we will be given a ticket immediately. We hurry back, afraid that they might tow it away. Alone on a wide space La Trochita stands by the side of the road. A slip of paper is stuck between the tank and the seat. Our parking space is marked with a no-stopping sign of all things. "That just can't be," I exclaim. Passers-by gather around us, discuss, smile and wait to see what happens. We let the ticket disappear into a pocket and want to make a quick getaway. At that moment a traffic policeman stops next to us, "What bad luck, it almost worked." But he just requests in a friendly manner that we drive away, since we are standing on a space reserved for armoured cars. I thank him for

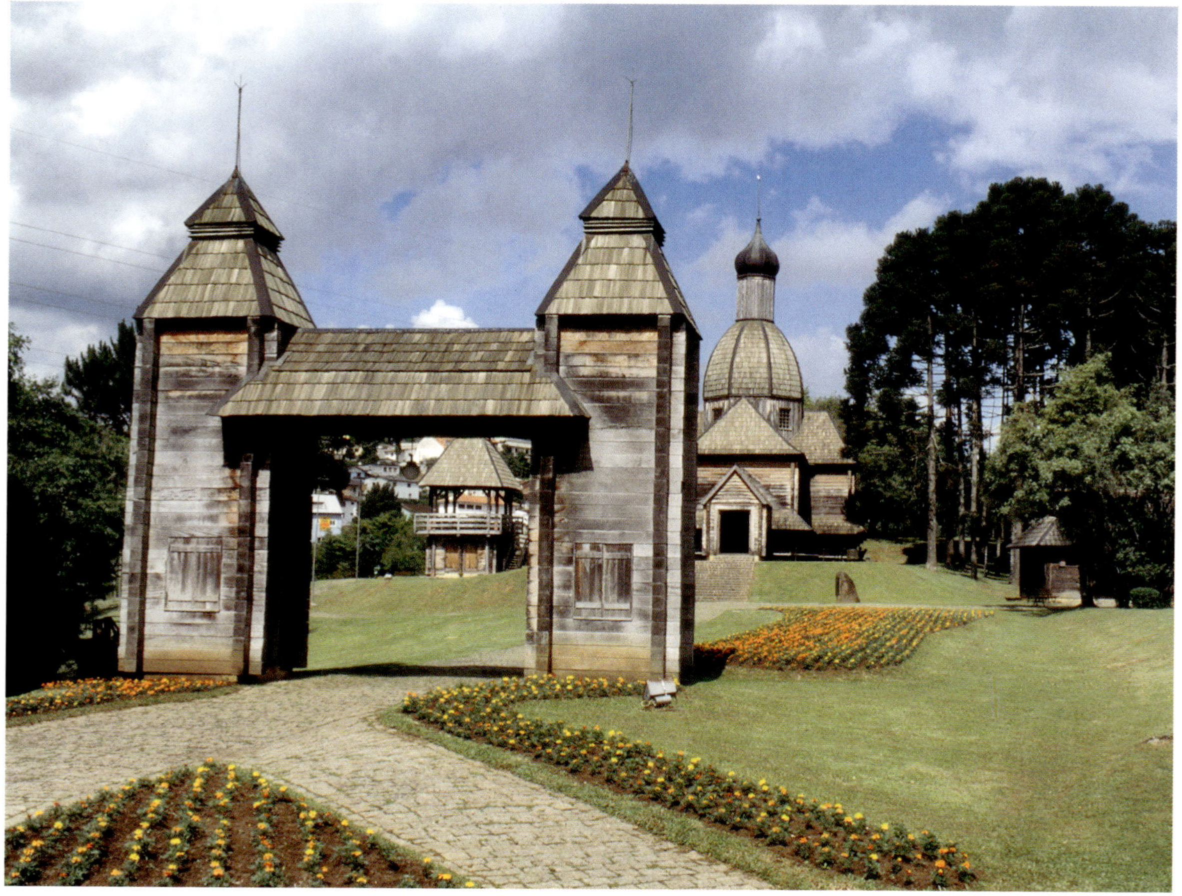

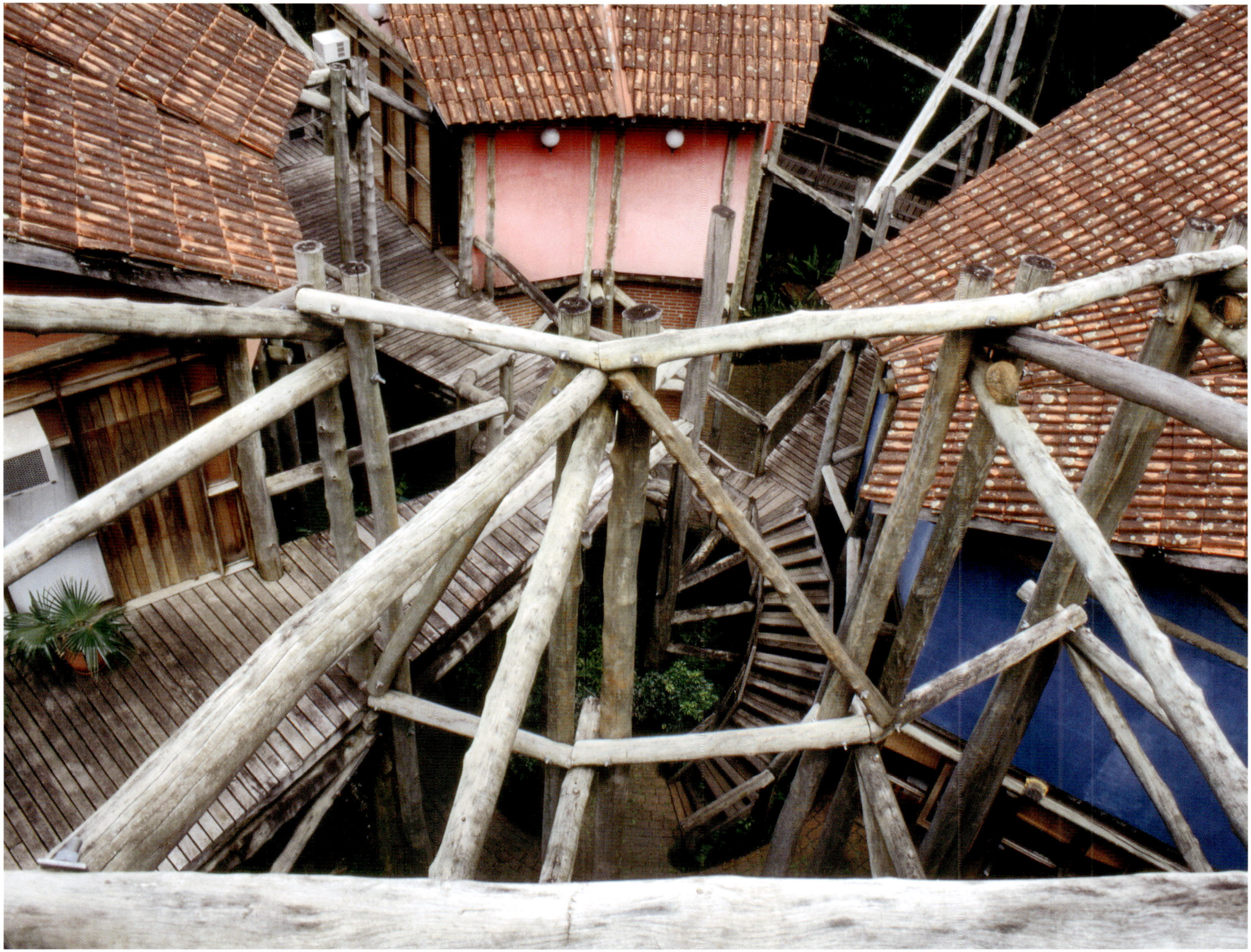

the information and answer that we had just been planning to drive away. We take the ticket with us as a souvenir.

Over beautiful serpentine stretches the road leads through the mountains to Curitiba. Until now we have rarely had as much fun driving along the way, apart from the fog that suddenly hangs low in the mountains after 40 km; the higher we climb, the more limited the visibility. We have to reduce our speed, which takes time and nerves. But what concerns us is not so much the fog as the Brazilian drivers, who often pay little attention to the traffic rules and speed limits. Even in this weather they drive "to win" and not to arrive safely. In narrow curves they overtake despite the very limited visibility. Only when they encounter bumps in the road, they literally push their cars over them, and they slam on the brakes at speed traps. Serious accidents happen again and again, but we are lucky enough to just pass them by. The ecological capital of Brazil Curitiba, earns its sobriquet not only for the 55 m² of

Page 87: "Flowergirl" on the flea market in Curitiba, Brazil

Bottom: Searching for the source of the river Iguaçu

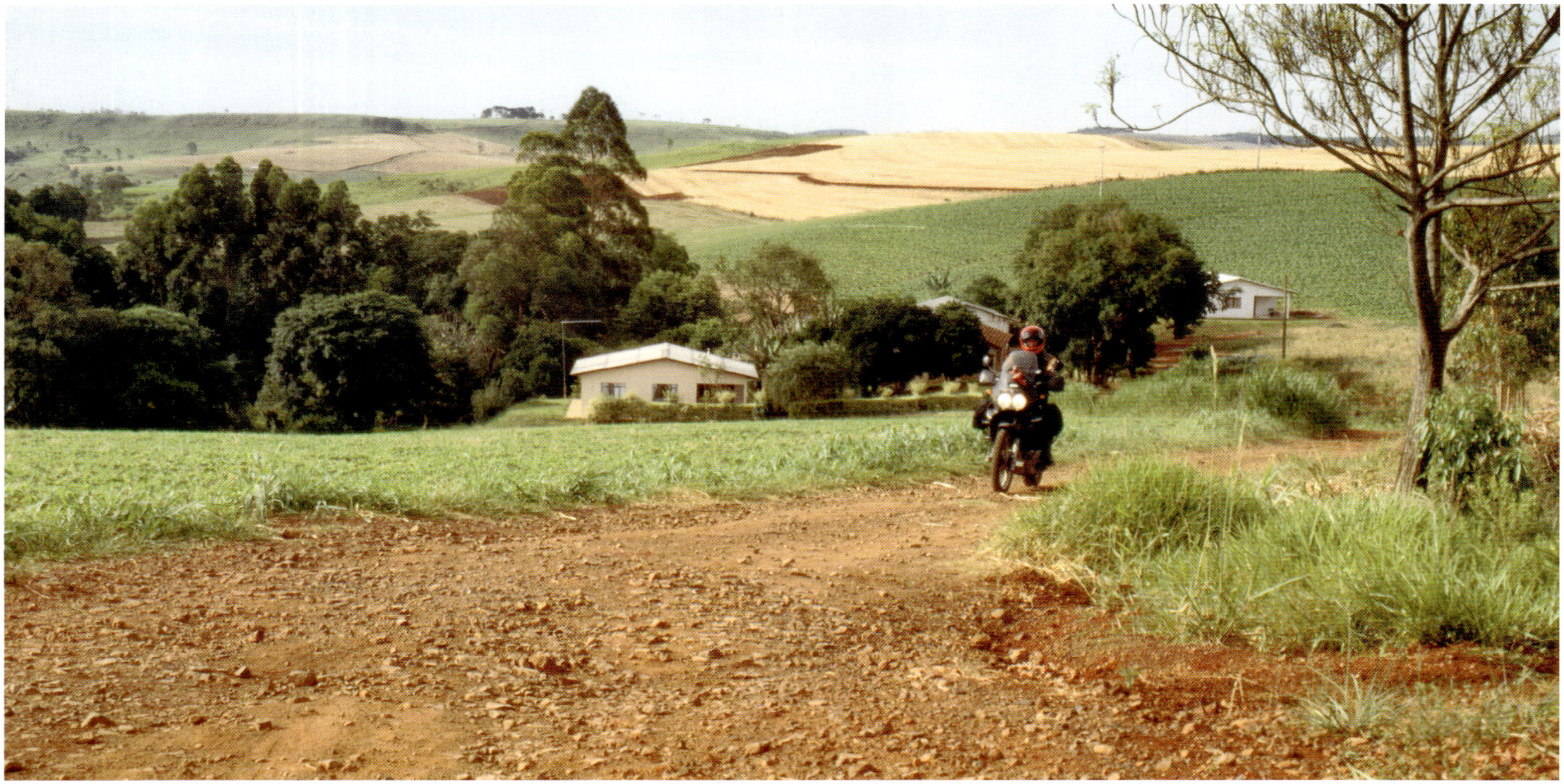

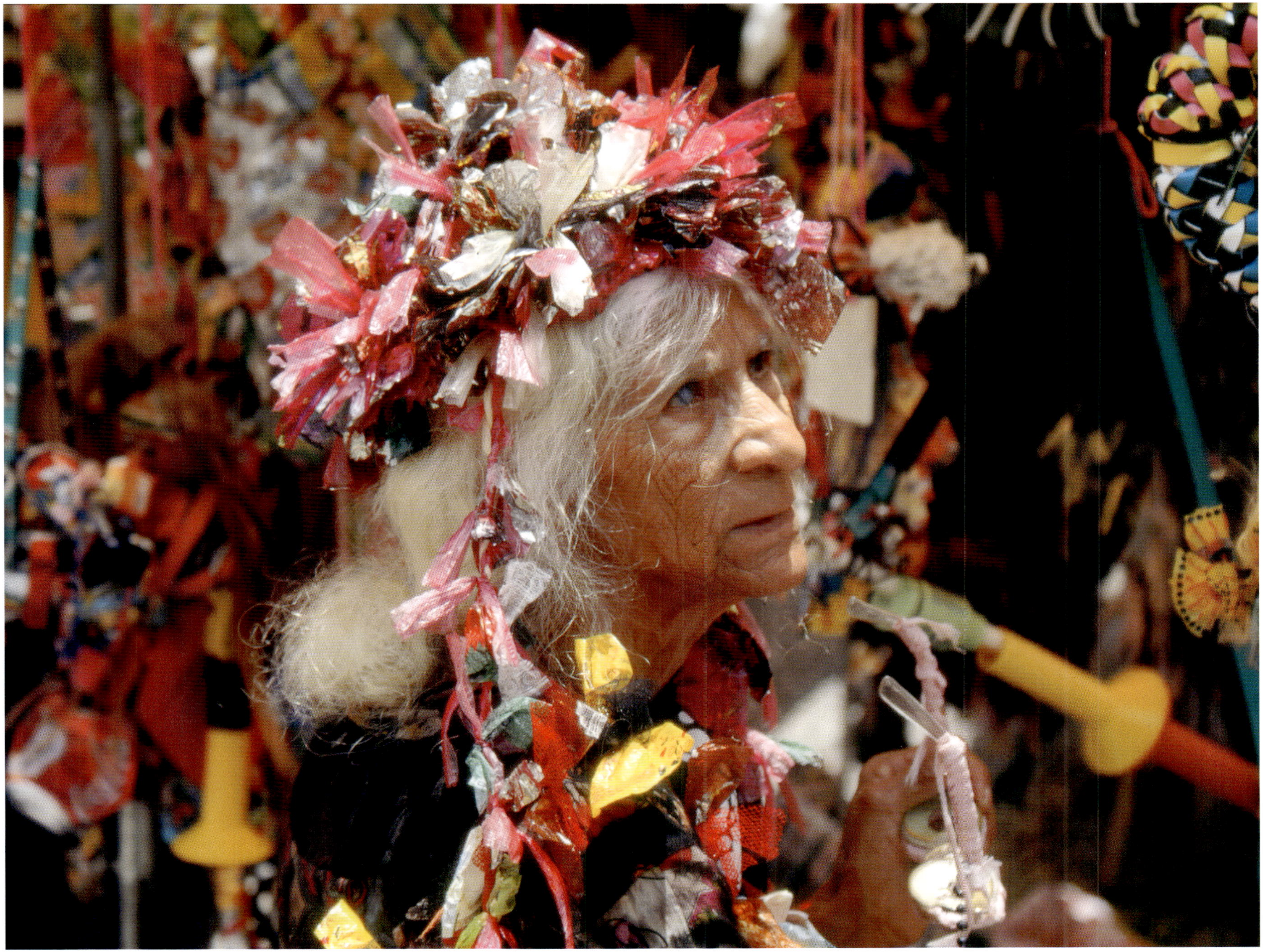

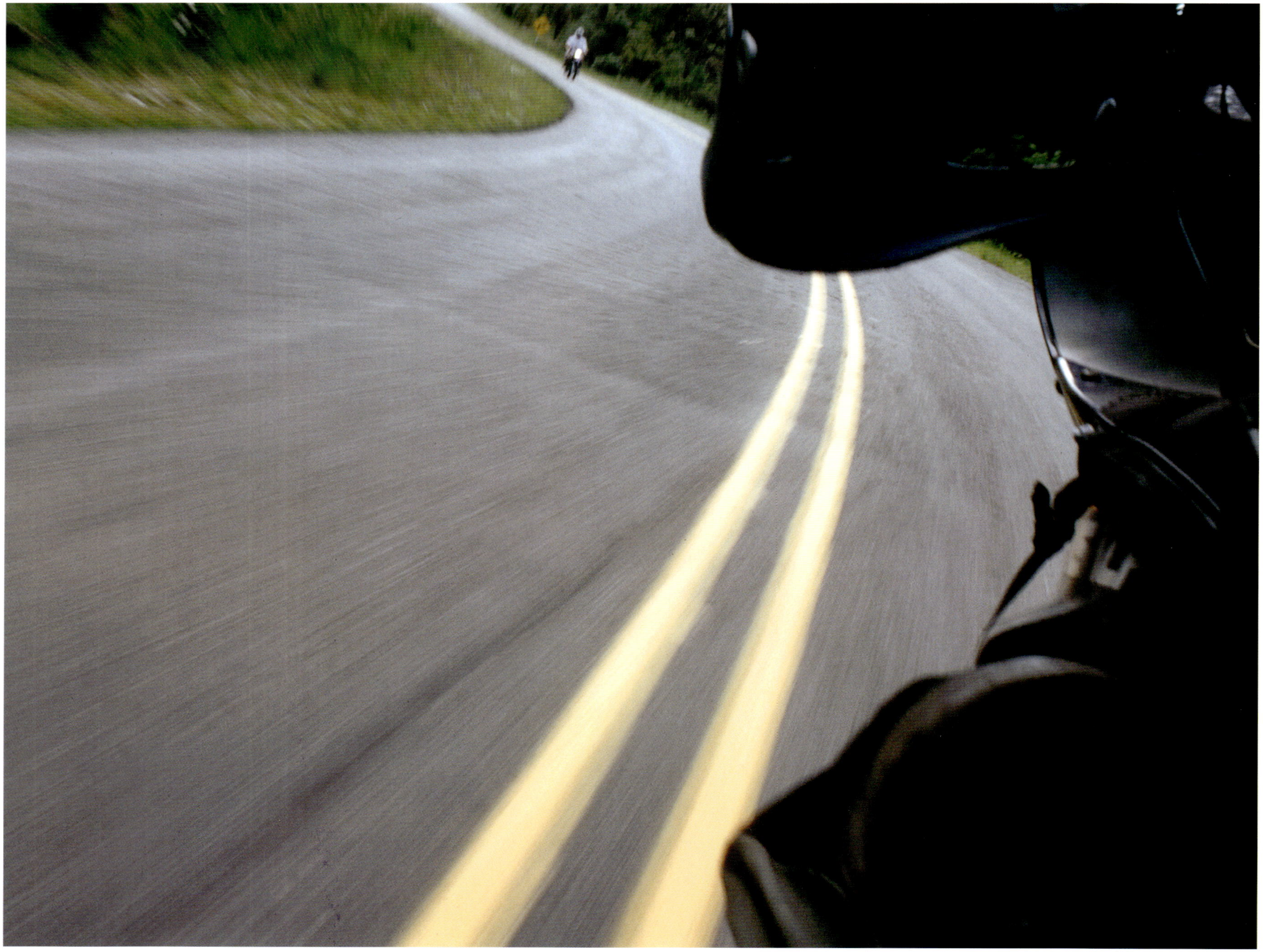

green space available to every resident and the sophisticated local public transit system, but also for the first environmental university in the world, which was established in 1991. Awards from UNESCO for the most innovative urban development and a nomination for the American Capital of Culture 2003 make the city a cultural, environmental and architectural centre. We switch from our bikes to a public bus for tourists that takes visitors to the most worthwhile sights in the city. The Universidade Livre do Meio Ambiente impresses me not only with its architecture that is inspired by the four elements of nature, but also with its program that explores complex ecological relationships scientifically but in a very practical manner, and implements its concepts in cooperation with the inhabitants.

Back in the hotel we meet a German biker who is travelling from Peru toward the south. We sit together to talk about our experiences and trade tips on routes, excursions and accommodations. It simply does us good every once in a while. City maps that are not needed anymore by the other one are swapped across the table. They help with getting one's bearings more easily when arriving in the larger cities. In the evening we happen upon a German bar in the old part of town and allow ourselves to be seduced into eating a thick bratwurst and a juicy slice of smoked pork chop. Actually we don't yet miss German food after travelling for such a short time, but at that exact moment our mouths are watering.

We take a short trip to the east coast and drive over Morretes along the Estrada Graciosa. Morretes is an extremely popular tourist destination. We get off the motorbikes and are instantly bathed in sweat in our protective clothing. Barely 70 km away from Curitiba there is a completely different, namely tropical, climate. After a brief look around the city we find a café and eat – what a coincidence – German chocolate cake. Despite the fans inside we yearn for a breeze that blows a bit of fresh air in our faces. The further we push into the interior of the country, the more extreme becomes the humidity, which is surely around 90 %. We travel

Page 88: "Estrada Graciosa" in Brazil's south-east

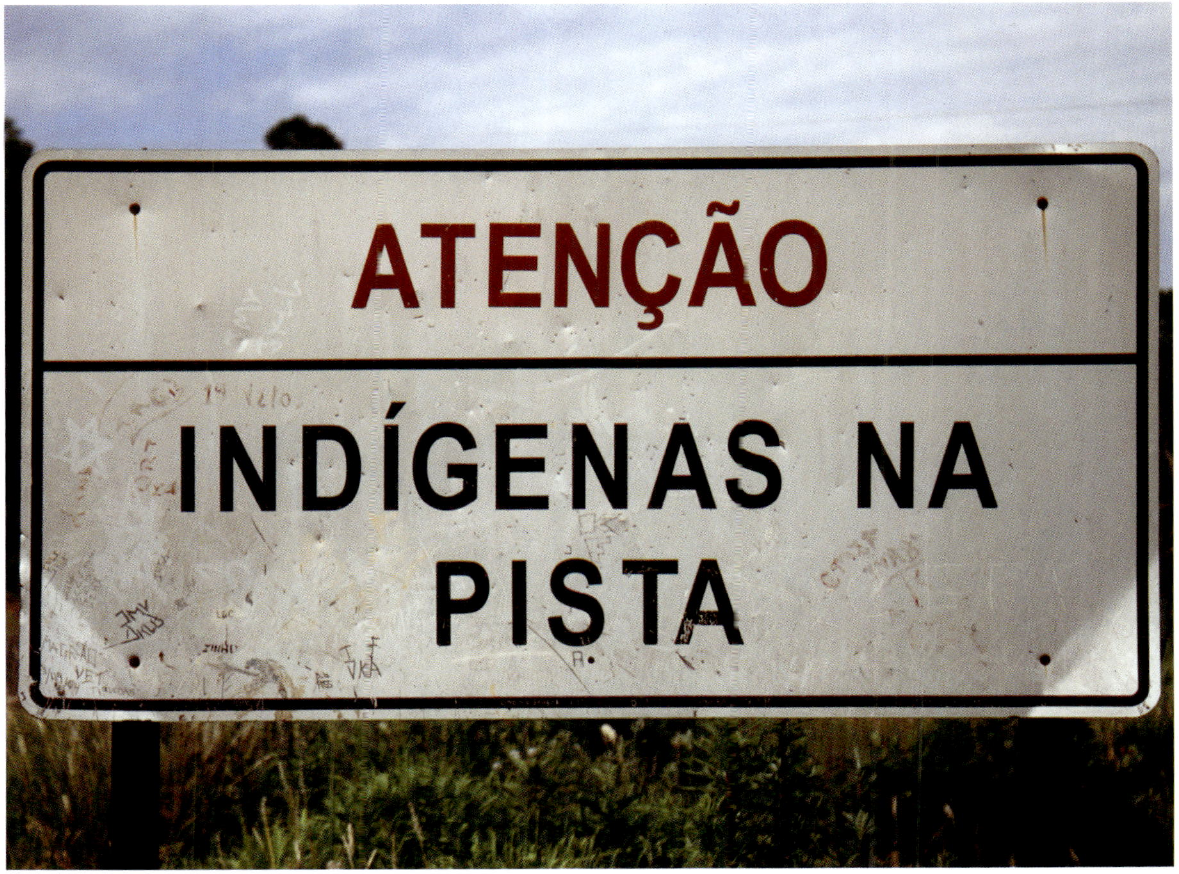

Right: Sign warning of indigenous people on the road near Laranjeiras do Sul, Brazil

through the Serra, past small waterfalls and ravines in which creeks babble down below. 10 km of curvy gravel road lead through a dense forest – a truly charming route.

As the indigenous inhabitants, the Guaraní have their own notion of the land. They call Brazil Parasil – big land. How right they are. After the thousands of kilometres of riding our bikes through the south of Brazil, we have the feeling that we have hardly moved at all. Even just the Serra Mar mountain range to the west of us stretches with its outermost foothills, the Corcovado and the Sugar Loaf Mountain, all the way to Rio de Janeiro. We could reel off the kilometres here for months but would only press forward towards the Amazon. However, we set this route aside for another journey.

South of Laranjeiras do Sul, the Rio Iguaçu, which will guide us from here, begins as a confluence of the Jordão and Iratim. We take the opportunity to drive to two native villages of the Caingangue and Guaraní. The river Rio das Cobras borders one of the regions. The indigenous peoples live on reservations today, having been relocated there provided that their tribes were not eradicated first. In the state of Paraná, about 9,000 people of the tribes of the Guaraní and Caingangue live in small village communities. The Caingangue sell colourful baskets as well as bows and arrows in plaited quivers from stands on the street. The Guaraní live in seclusion in the interior. A road sign that warns drivers of "indigenous people on the road" grabs the eye. What seems discriminatory appears to have a sadly practical reason: many indigenous people lose their lives in traffic accidents. In light of the driving behaviour of Brazilians the advice might be sensible, but that would be true for all pedestrians who venture onto the road. The sign leaves an unsavoury aftertaste, because the indigenous peoples seem to be placed on a level with animals crossing the road haphazardly.

We visit a school for the 1st to 4th grades in which about 150 children from the surrounding area are educated. Many of them are excited when they see us and the camera; others remain very reserved and shy. A couple of them immediately want to see themselves in the apparatus, but we don't have a digital camera with us. And, unfortunately, also no instant camera in order to leave behind a photo here for them to remember. One girl sits completely still on her chair, hardly participating in the crafts

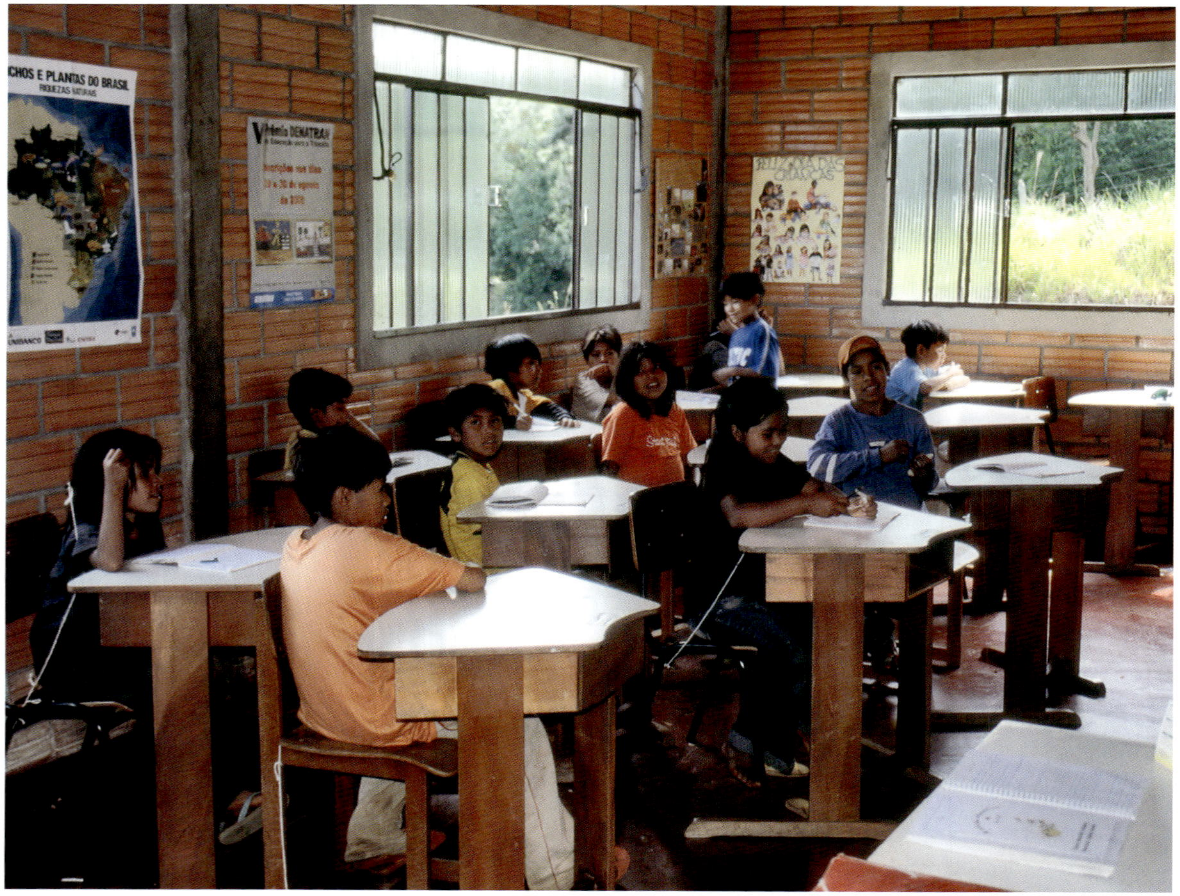

Left: School class in the indigenous reservation in the region Paraná, Brazil

Page 91: Caingangue boy in school

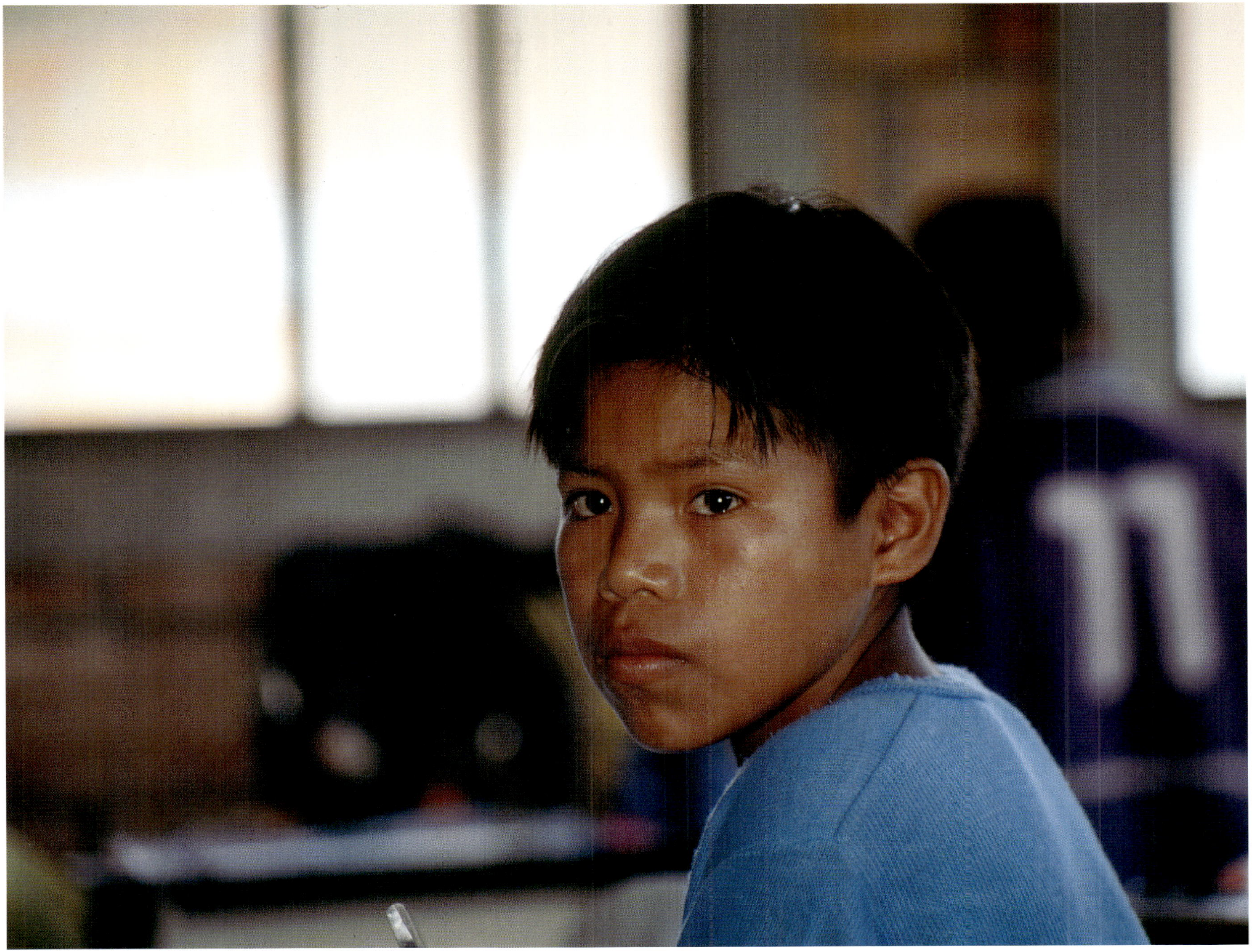

project the others are currently working on. The teacher explains to me that the girl is the only one in the class who speaks just the language of her tribe, which she, the teacher, doesn't know in turn. She therefore explains the subject of the lessons to her as clearly as possible in sign language. I imagine that this is very difficult, but perhaps she at least learns the basics of writing and arithmetic in this way. As a school project, a vegetable garden is being set up. Because the principal food consists of rice and beans, the school children and their parents learn to cultivate other herbs and vegetables and to feed themselves more nutritionally.

We leave the main road and stutter over a dusty track to a village of the Guaraní. The government has erected new houses for them with access to electricity and toilet huts. It is a form of compensation for their resettlement from their ancestral fertile lands to this region. One snag in the plan is that the majority of the families don't have enough money to buy themselves a wood stove. Many of them have therefore left their old wooden huts standing so that they can light a fire in the middle at which to warm themselves in the winter. Plastic bottles filled with water stand on the junction boxes on the electricity pylons, with which they hope to reduce the power consumption. Similar tricks are also known in Germany, when one hangs a damp cloth over the heating pipes and hopes to be able to influence the heating consumption gauge. Neither of these methods is very effective but the belief in them is crucial. We visit Sebastiane, the wife of the chief of the village, who is taking a siesta on the terrace with a friend. Next to

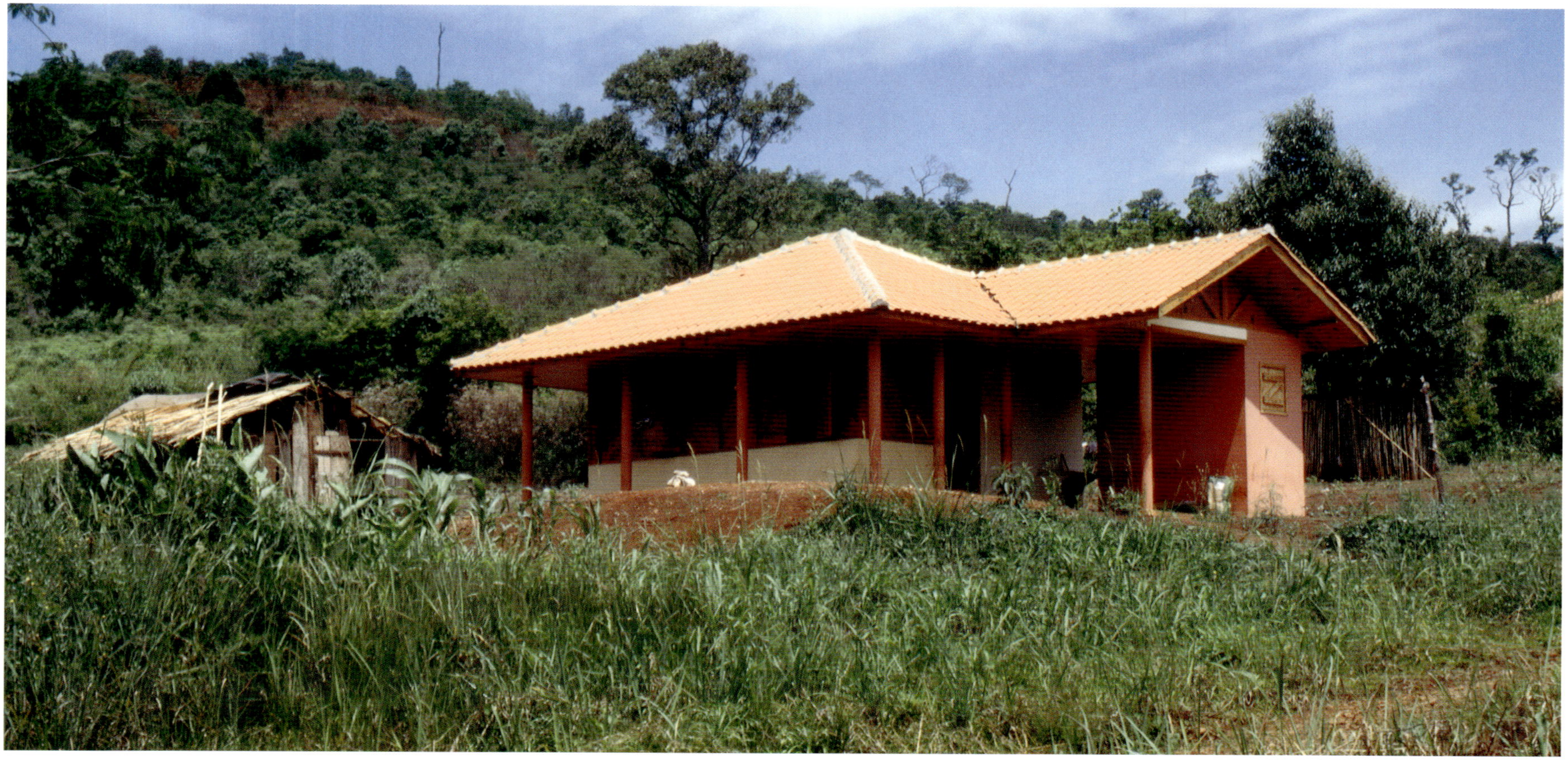

the wooden hut stands a large satellite dish. Technical progress with the advantages and disadvantages of "modern civilisation" has come to the villages. We chat for a while with the two women but the time is unfortunately too short to get a deeper insight into the lives of the indigenous peoples.

We follow the Iguaçu river toward the border to Argentina. Up to Cascarel we progress quickly, then at 4 p.m. on the dot, as forecast, the sky becomes black, a storm cloud follows us along the way and soon unburdens itself above us. Soaking wet we stop in front of a bus stop, want to push the motorbikes backward onto the verge, I lose my balance and am just able to catch the Transalp with my left leg. Axel wants to come and help me as a jeep brakes sharply next to him and he is no longer able to dismount. The right back door is ripped open, bangs against the tank of the Africa Twin, a blond tuft appears under a colourful umbrella and a strident voice says to us in German: "This is unbelievable, have you driven your motorbikes from Germany to here?" The woman showers us with a further torrent of words. They were on the way to Foz to see the waterfalls, and just now it decides to rain. Before we are able to get in a word, the door slams shut again and the car roars away. She leaves us standing like drowned poodles. Have I just dreamed the situation? Thanks to this unforeseen occurrence we are wet to the bone and scarper into refuge. It is not particularly comfortable to put on the rain suit over the wet things.

In Foz do Iguaçu a cute little pousada on the edge of the city will be our place to stay for the next days. There is a kitchen in which we can sizzle ourselves, and a pool in which to cool off. Paradisiacal conditions considering the 37° C temperature in the late evening. Familiar clattering noise wakes us up the next morning. It is no simple rain that beats on the windowpane but a thunderstorm that whips over the city. The wind whistles through the window chinks. Perhaps the motorbikes will be washed clean again, but this hope deceives, the dust only becomes smeared on the paint. In the last weeks the wretched weather conditions in south Brazil have led to flooding, and in the national park Iguaçu on the Argentine side the footbridges and the platform on the Devil's Throat have been torn away. With the field glass this can easily be seen. The last time we were able to walk there, but this time this is denied to us.

Page 92: New and old living quarters in the Guaraní reservation in the region Paraná, Brazil

Right: Inhabitant of a Guaraní village, region Paraná, Brazil

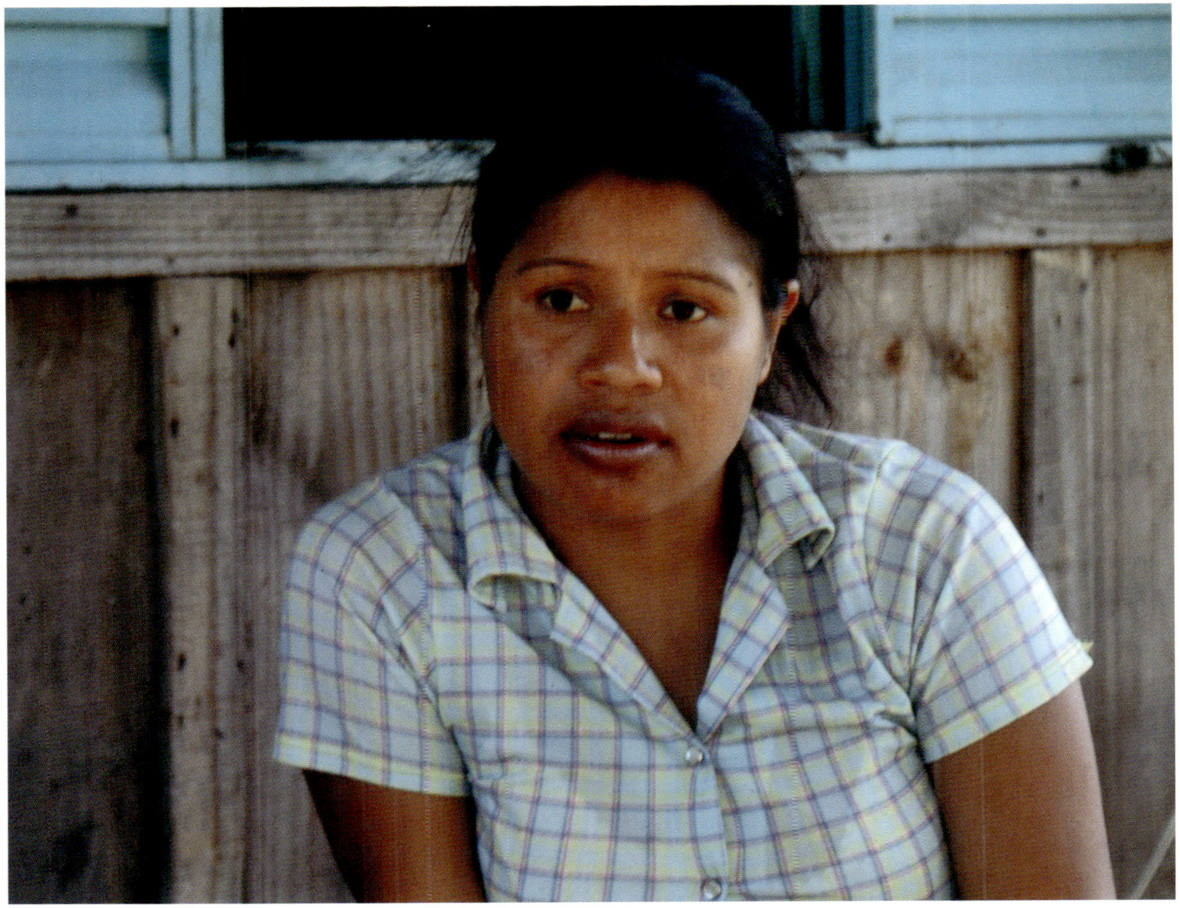

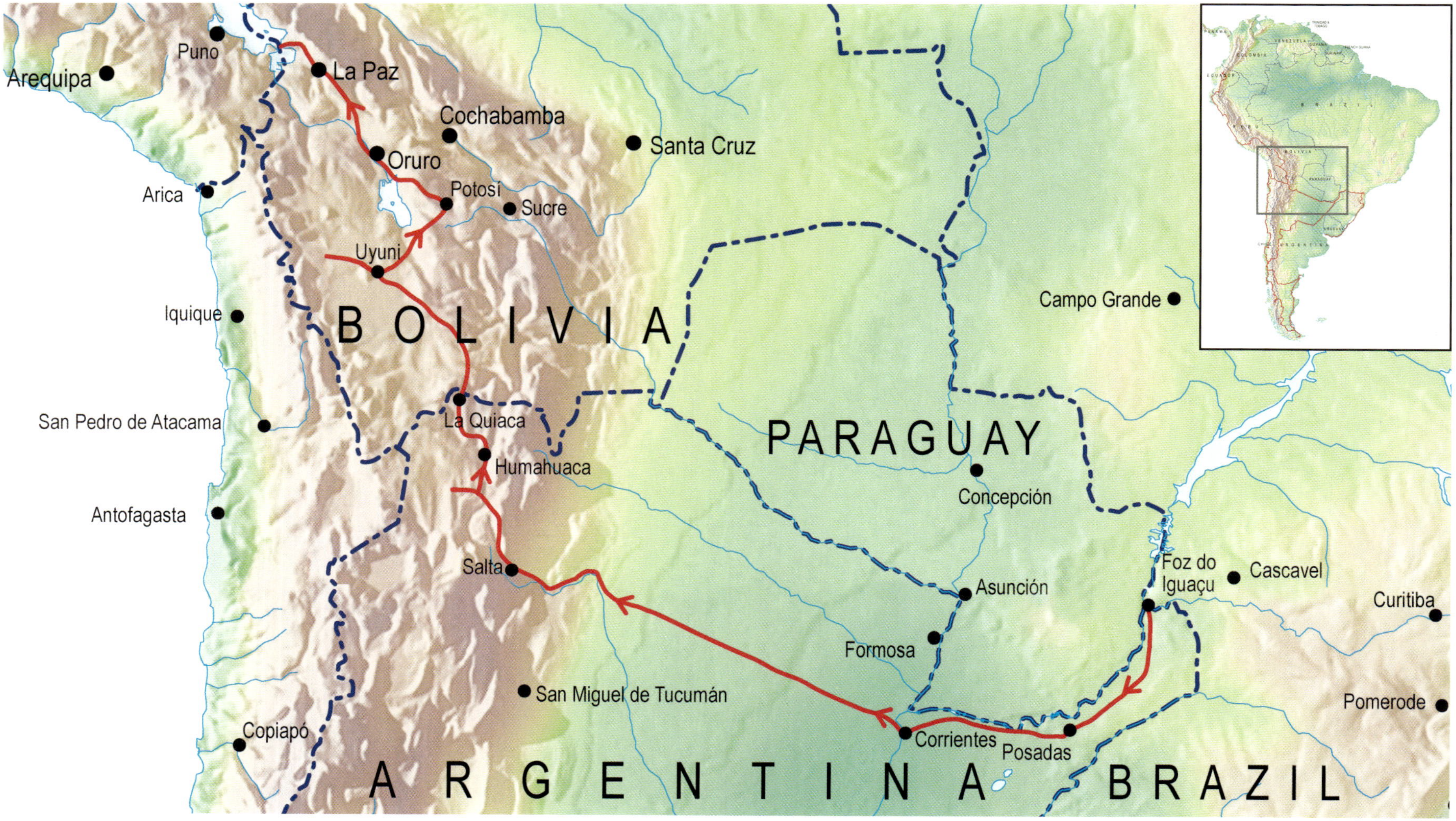

Memorial stone for Che Guevara in Caraguatay, Argentina

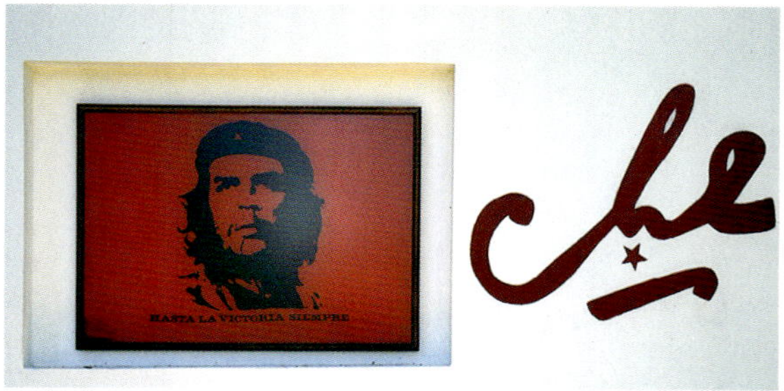

Starting from the Iguaçu Waterfalls, the route proceeds through the provinces of Misiones and Chaco into the Puna. With a short excursion to Purmamarca, the border to Bolivia is reached in La Quiaca. The trip continues through Tupiza to Salar de Uyuni and from there to Potosí and Oruro. Over El Alto, located above La Paz, the route leads to Lake Titicaca and then to Copacabana.

ARGENTINA – BOLIVIA
DIZZY HEIGHTS

Bottom: *In the region Misiones*

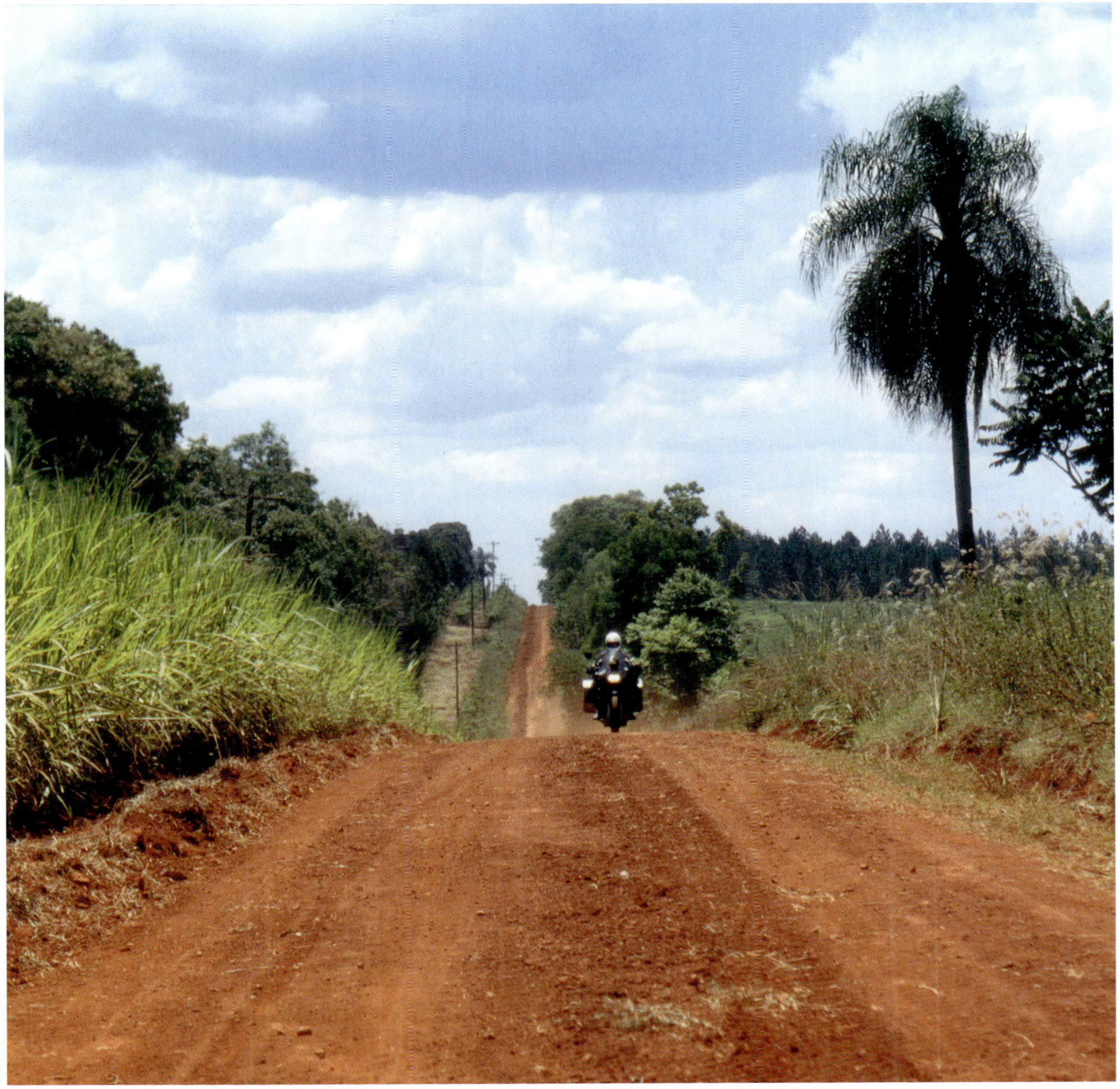

LAND OF RED EARTH

In the middle of the jungle, by the Paraná river, the "father of all South American rivers", Ernesto Guevara Lynch settled with his new wife Celia to cultivate mate. Soon, their son Ernesto Rafael Guevara de la Serna was born. Ernestito spent the first years of his life with his parents here in Caraguatay. Translated from Guaraní, the name means "sweet water of the wild pineapple". A few years later, the boy's asthma attacks forced the family to move to a drier climate, before little Ernestito became the great "Che". After his murder in Bolivia in 1967, his name was taboo in Argentina and other South American countries until the early 1980s. The property deteriorated. We hear this story from Miguel, one of the dedicated employees at the open-air museum that has been established on the property. We are standing on a clearing looking down on the river, which is one of the 30 longest rivers in the world and forms the border with Paraguay. There is not much left of the original building: a few stone heaps, a cistern with a water pipe leading to the house, plants and trees that were cultivated here. A poster shows a snapshot of Che in his hiding place in Bolivia, in the year of his assassination. He sits in a treetop, reading, a cigar in the corner of his mouth. A typical image: the asthmatic could breathe much easier up in the treetops than on the ground, says Miguél. He tells us that many school classes come here to learn more about the life of the outlaw. Times change. The museum staff does its best to pass on his political motivations, which were based on the firm conviction that all people have the same rights. On the road, Che Guevara becomes our fifth travel companion. Not only does his face look at us from mugs, tee-shirts, postcards, posters and caps everywhere, but the poor people also still worship him, which reflects their undying hope for a better and fairer life.

40 km before Posadas, the black cloud that has been floating in the sky for quite a while now catches up with us. We just manage to put on our rain gear at a toll booth when it begins to rain. We keep on riding, because it doesn't seem as if the rain will stop soon. After 1 km, Axel calls out to me that his bike isn't running anymore. He coasts to the verge of the road. In the pouring rain, he begins to look for the problem. Battery okay, fuses intact. It seems likely that the fuel pump isn't working anymore, but it

Bottom: Repairs at a very inconvenient moment

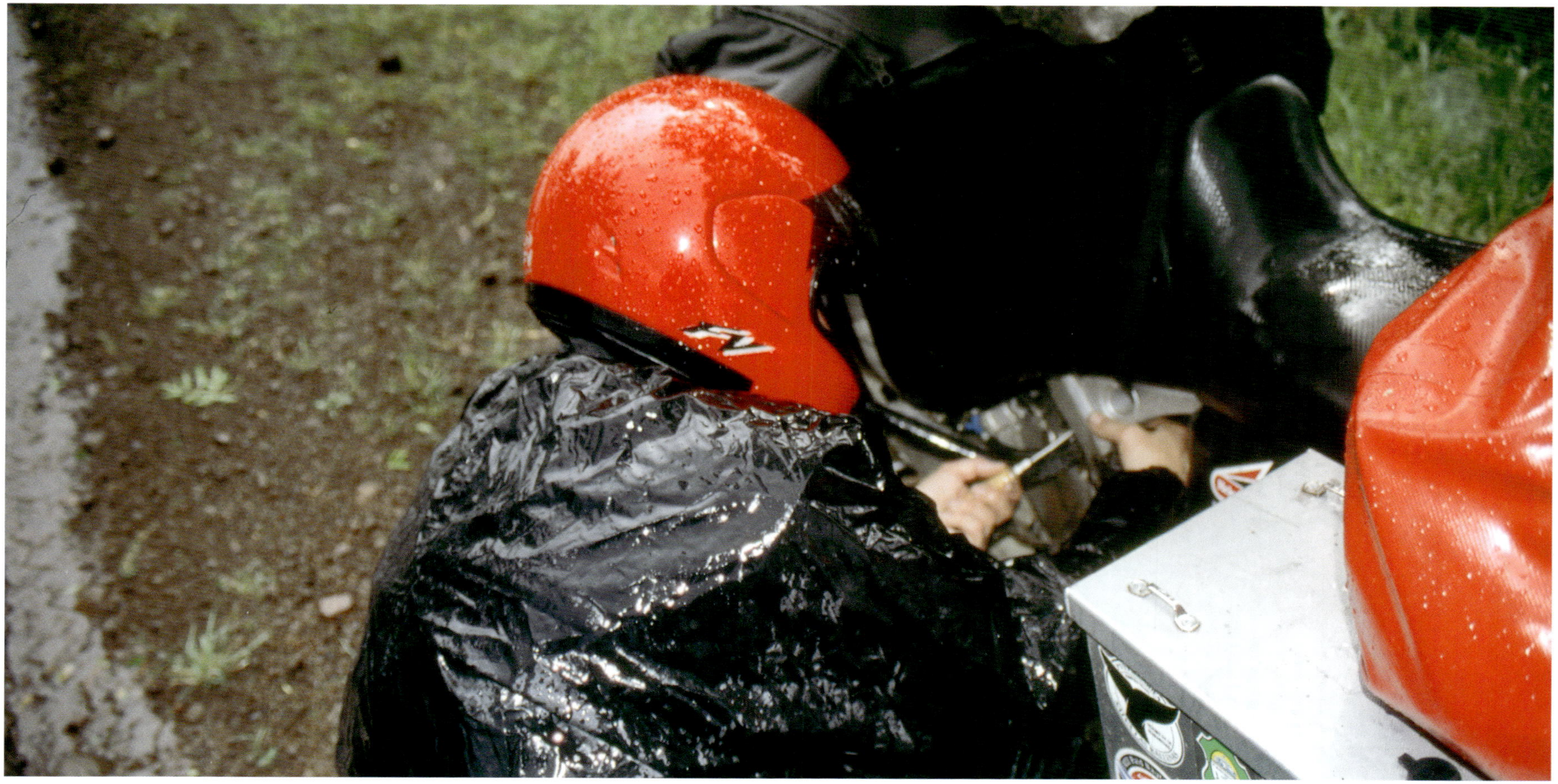

also turns out to be all right. When he opens the fuel tank cap, there is a loud bang. The Twin starts up again, and we can continue. After 10 km, the same thing happens again: we stop, Axel takes the tank cap off, the pressure equalizes and we can go on. after two more stops, we reach our destination for the day, Posadas. The sun burns down on us and there hasn't been a single drop of rain here. At our accommodation, we dismantle the tank; the ventilation hose is stuck. Small cause, big effect. Our stomachs growl, we haven't eaten all day. Looking for a snack, we stroll through the town. At the entrance of a pub, a guy is sunbathing on a chair, with his legs splayed wide. Casually, he lifts a hand, touches his cap with two fingers and calls out: "We have the coldest beer in town, people!"

In the meantime, we have become used to the constant police checkpoints on the way, even if I have to grin sometimes. They stand before us with a sombre face, greet us in a military manner and rattle off their questions: "Where from, where to, which nationality, documents". They don't like to talk to me because I am a woman. However, they still encounter a language barrier with Axel. Either they end up talking to me or, best case scenario, we can go on without having to answer questions, which has its benefits. Sometimes they just stop us out of boredom, to look at our bikes. We are making good time to Corrientes when three men stop us on the through road and wave us over to the side. There is a man with broad shoulders wearing plain clothes, a tall thin man with a stud in his ear, and a guy in a white shirt with a patch on his arm. Traffic check. They say that we have just driven through a red light, but that is ridiculous, because we had just been enjoying a lucky green phase through the city. The tall thin guy asks for our documents, the one with the broad shoulders writes out a ticket without a carbon copy. I am getting suspicious and refuse to take it. Allegedly, they work for the municipal authorities, so we ask to see their identification, which is a bad, laminated colour copy. The guy in the white shirt threatens to call the police to arrest us. We don't let them intimidate us because we haven't done anything. They say that they have caught us on film. I would like to see it but it has to be developed first. Fifteen minutes pass, a biker stops and tells us not to give them anything because they are not authorized. More minutes pass. The broad-shouldered man gives it another try. He will let us go if we give him US$ 50. I was waiting for a demand like this so we don't budge, pretending to have all the time in the world. The man with the stud in his ear turns away and makes a phone call. They are clearly at a loss. Finally, I've had enough: I announce that we will go to the town hall and discuss the matter with the mayor. The thin guy reaches for his mobile phone again. They talk among themselves and then offer to allow us to leave the town without paying a fine. Surprised, I insist that they destroy the ticket before our eyes. The man with the broad shoulders does it very thoroughly: he crosses out the information, tears up the paper, stuffs it in his mouth and wants to swallow it. We try very hard to suppress a grin and hurry on our way.

The 800 km of straight road to Salta are still in the same poor condition between Rio Muertos and Los Pirpintos as the last time. Chunks of asphalt have been ripped out and gaping holes open in front of us that were mere shadows moments before, so all we can do to keep us from falling in is to swerve to the gravel verge or to the other side of the road. The monotonous drive makes me inattentive and tired. We refuel and decide to take a few minutes' break when I lose the balance on my bike once again. Bending down to retrieve a glove, the bike tilts and I fall over. The aluminium suitcase bumps against the edge of a stone step, is gets dented considerably and pushes against its fixture. The lid sticks out a few centimetres and is not at all water-proof anymore. A few onlookers have gathered around us, so I don't want to unpack the stuff from the suitcase with the money and the papers and spread it all on the ground at the filling station. We leave town to repair the damage. The echo of the rubber mallet can be heard far and wide. Axel manages to straighten the box out reasonably well. I think that now, nothing else will happen on the last 100 km. At least I believe so for a short while... There is a construction site, with detour signs in place. There is mud for several kilometres. Instead of being able to choose my speed in order to get through this, it is determined by the driver of the heavy truck creeping along in front of us and churning up the mud. The road is too narrow to overtake him, so we follow his fresh tyre tracks through the mud. It almost drives me insane and I wish for this day to be over soon!

Up into the Puna, the Argentinean high plains, we follow the barren vegetation, once again enchanted by the shimmering colours of the mountains. We stay in Purmamarca, within sight of the "mountain of seven colours". The various colourful layers are the result of ocean, lake and river sediments and are due to the high content of various minerals deposited over several hundreds of million years. At a first glance, they look like mere rocks. But the intense brilliance of the rocks in the morning sun is incredible. The valley stretching out behind the village cemetery explodes in a firework of colours, while the mountain slopes form bizarre, abstract figures. According to the indigenous people, this riot of colours comes from "pachamama". "Mother Earth" enriched the ground with non-ferrous metals and lets the slopes and canyons blossom in colourful petroglyphs. Simón, a waiter at a restaurant, explains that in the language of the Quechua, "pacha" does not just mean "earth" but also stands for the universe, time and space. At the centre of the world dwells "Mother Earth". She is the central force, source of energy for all life and the divine symbol of fertility. She observes human actions and reacts to them. The inhabitants of the Andes show their deference and respect by pouring out a few drops of their beverages or by dropping a few crumbs of their meals. They worship her and offer sacrifices to appease her when they invade her realm by ploughing or cropping the soil.

Page 98-101: Around Purmamarca: Page 98 and 100: Quebrada; Page 99: "Mountain of seven colours"; Page 101: Crafts market

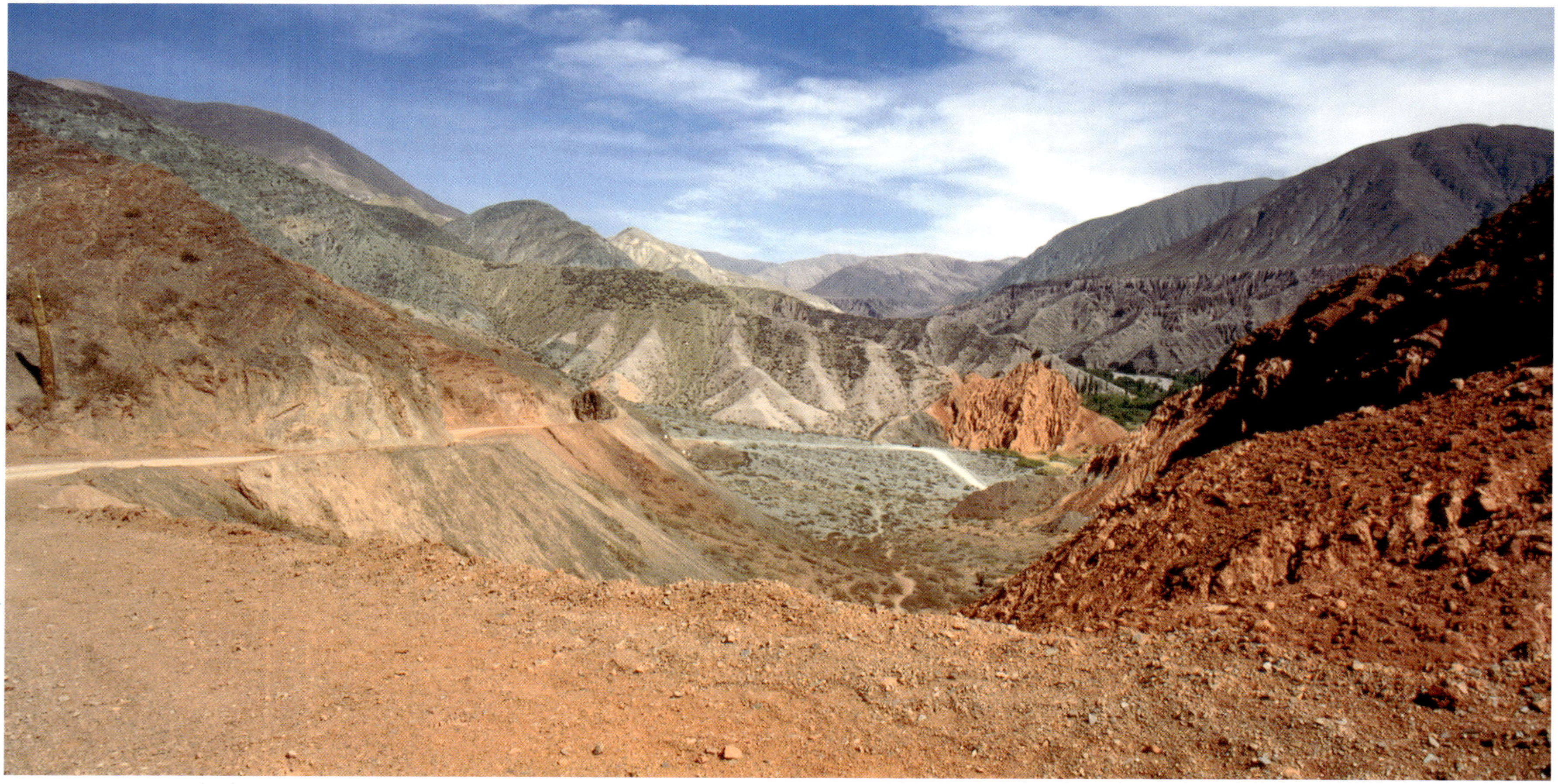

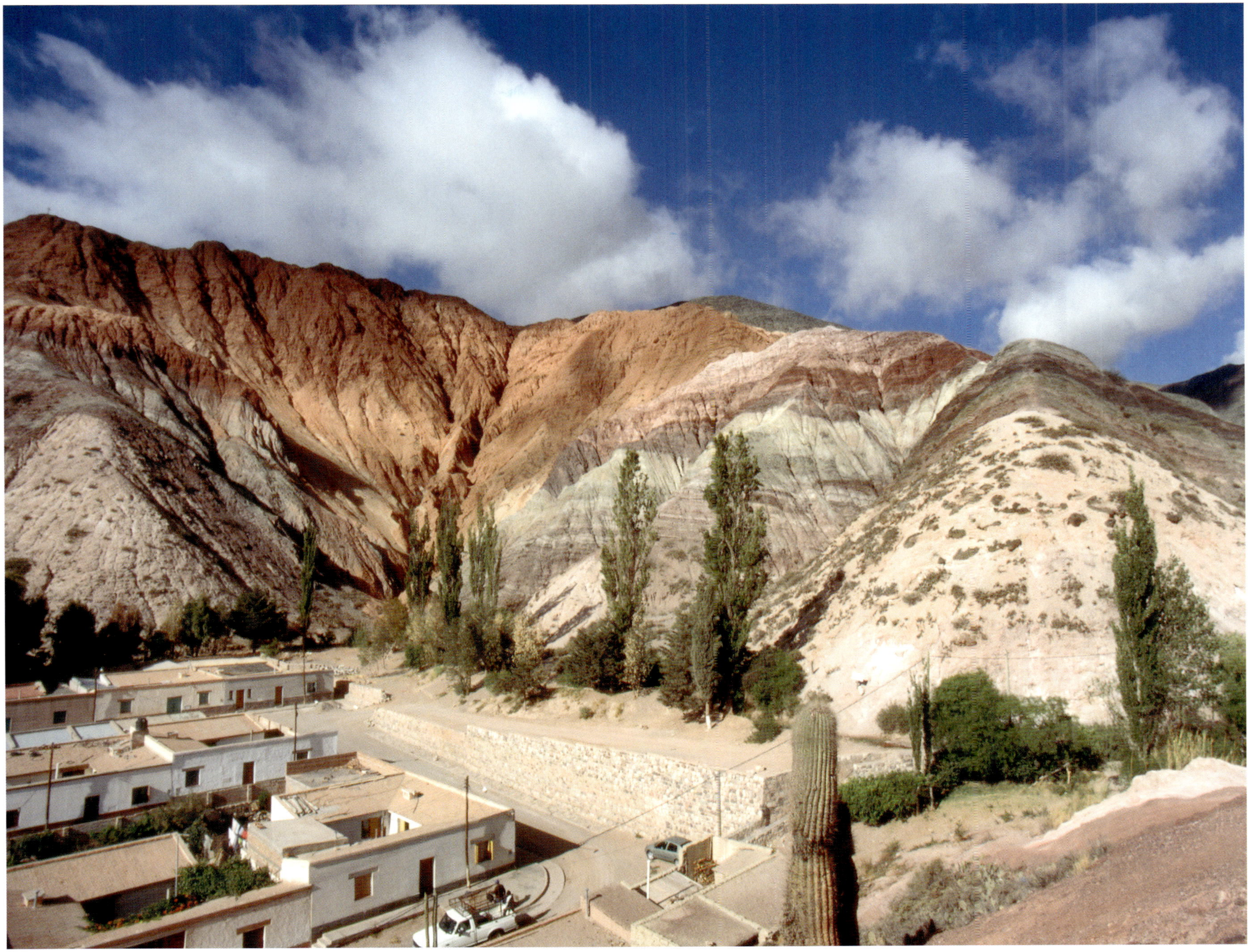

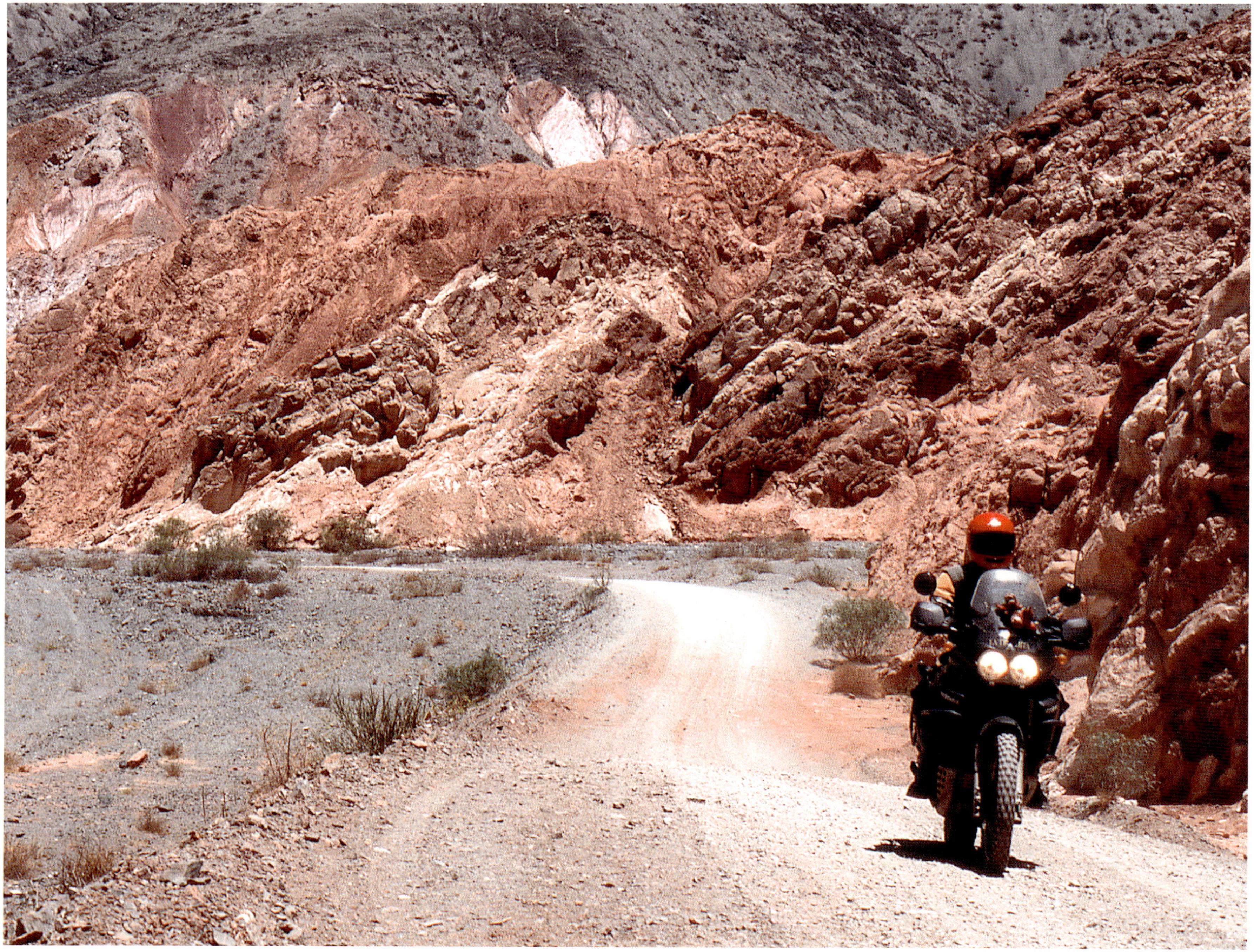

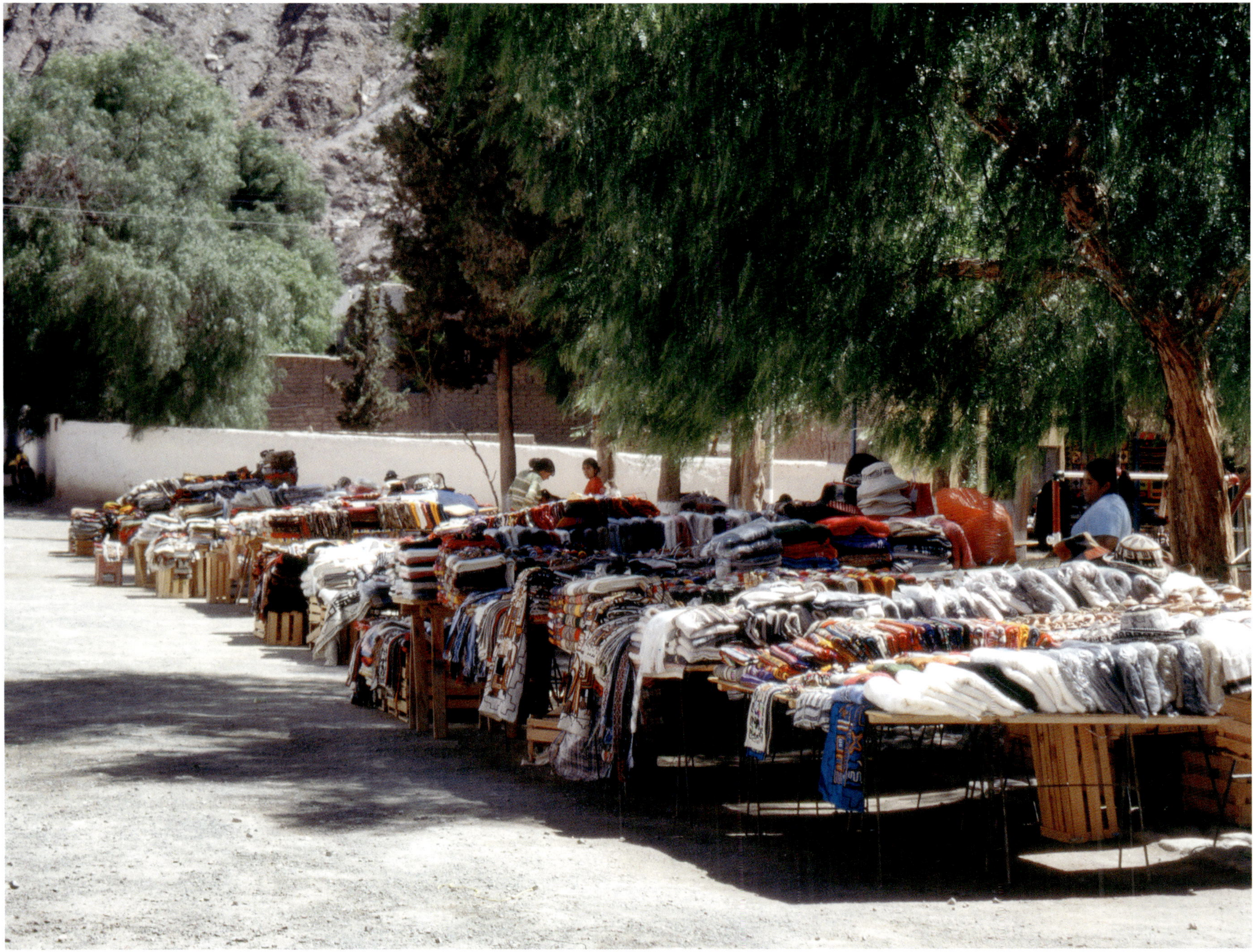

SAND AND SALT IN THE WORKS

On our way to La Quiaca, road blocks stop us in the Altiplano. Demonstrators use drums to draw attention to the bad job market and social cutbacks. After half an hour, one lane is cleared and we can go on. At the second road block, nothing is moving. They don't let any vehicles pass. The bus drivers are prepared for this. They let their passengers get off with all their possessions to pass the barricade and board another bus on the other side. I try to negotiate with the demonstrators by the side of the road so that they let us pass on the bikes. They refuse at first. A bus driver supports me. Briefly, I have my doubts. What if we get through this blockade but not through one of the next ones, and become unable to move on or to turn back. Not a pleasant thought. It is at least worth a try. Finally, they agree to let us pass if we push the bikes past the block. Great, pushing the heavy machines halfway down the hill

Page 103: No question who is the boss of the Llama herd here

Bottom: Roadblocks in Argentina's north make it impossible to pass

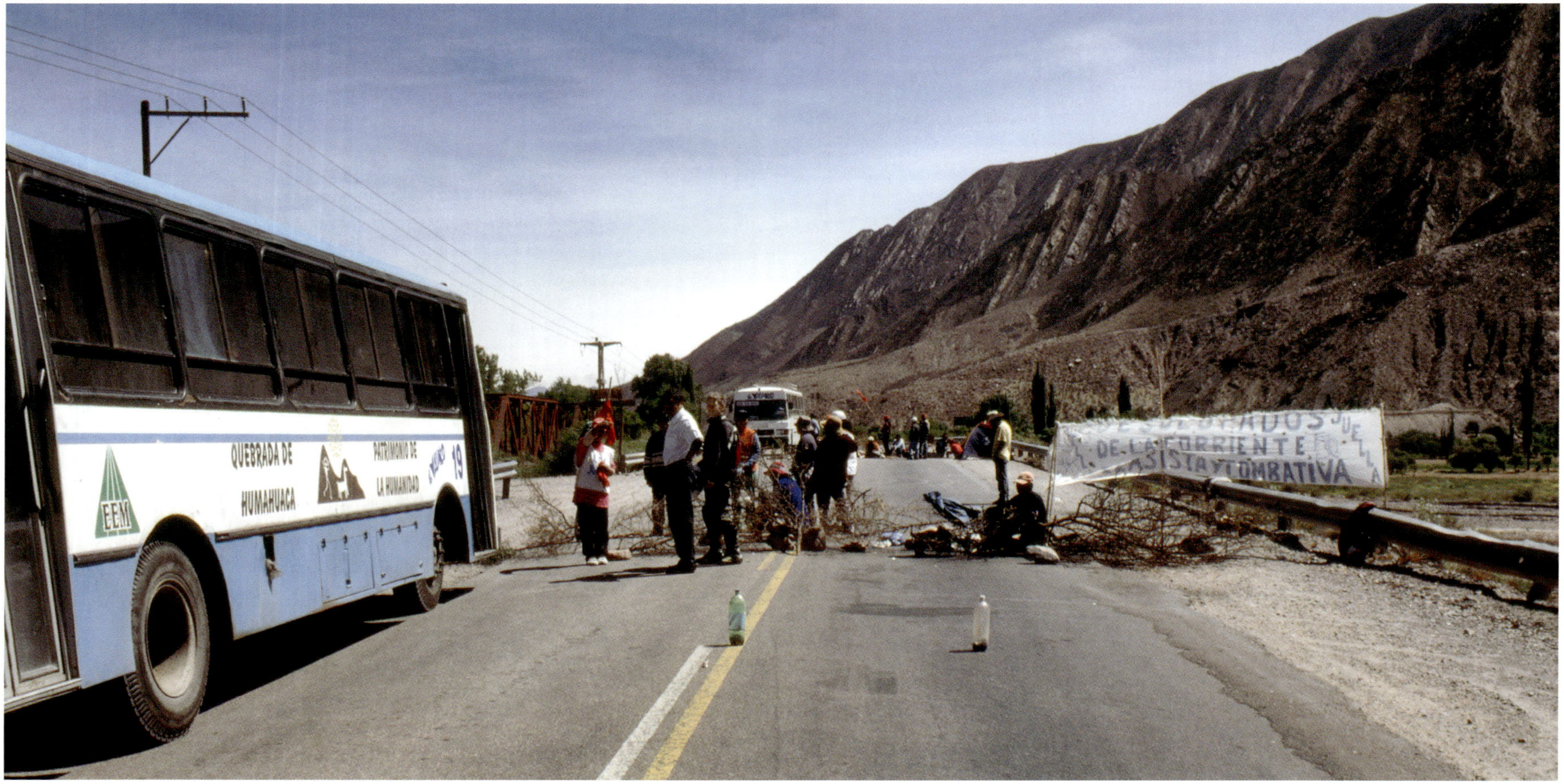

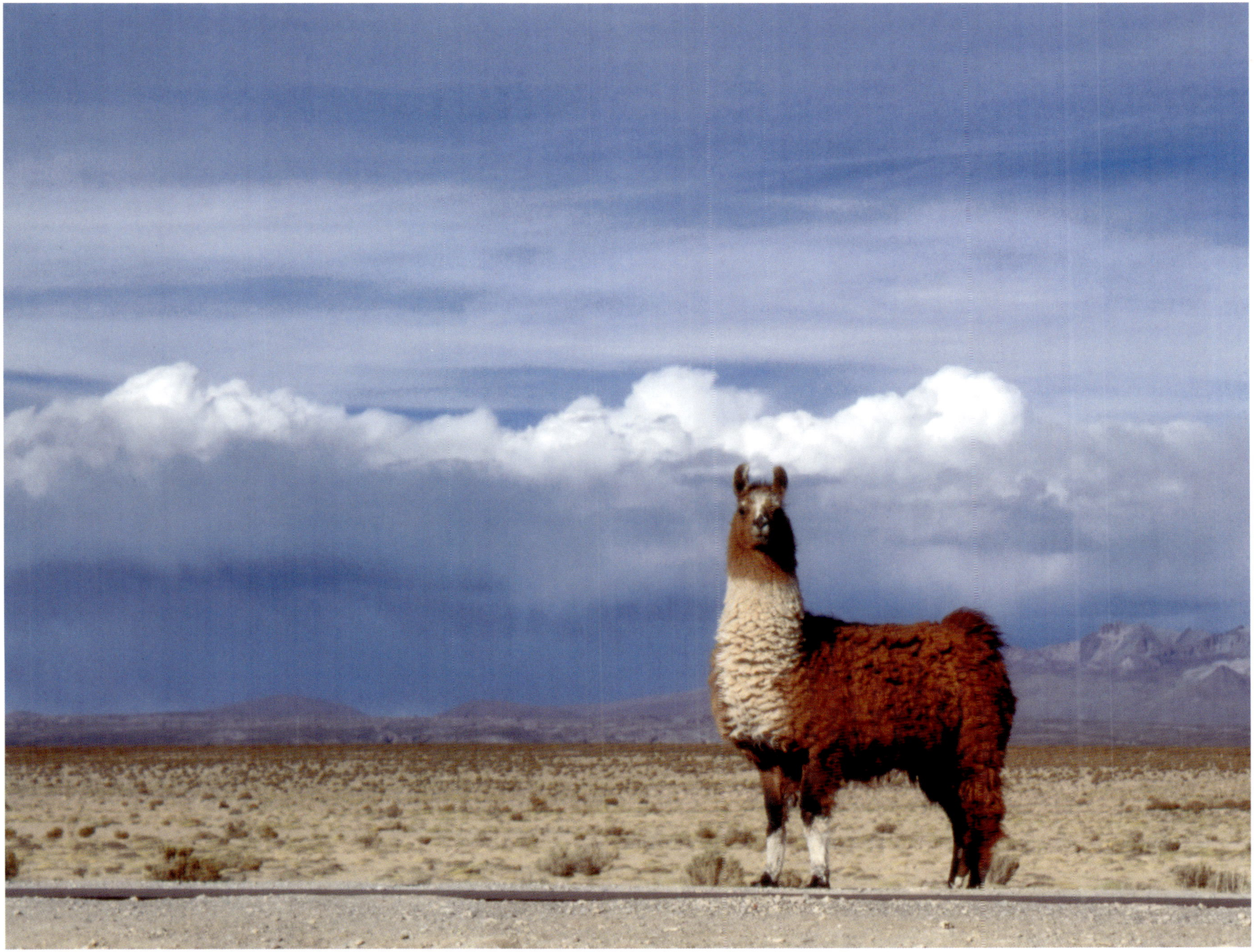

and up again. That will be difficult without the engine. My desperate looks help. The demonstrators remove a few bushes and rocks. We thank them profusely and push first the Transalp and then the Africa Twin through the barricade. The bus driver calls after us: "suerte" – "good luck!" The cars stay behind. Normally, bikers receive absolutely no consideration in traffic and are always at a disadvantage, but here it is a great advantage to move on two wheels.

On the Bolivian border, we just need time and patience; other than that, our papers go through smoothly. It is as if the customs officer knew that we would have trouble with the police when leaving Horrillas. We brake at a barrier where a policeman leans pompously in the doorframe of a wooden hut and waves us into his office. It is furnished with an old wooden table, a chair and a nail in the wall that holds his coat. The wind blows through the boards of the walls. The floor is covered with sand, blown in from the dry village road. A highly official document lies on the table before him, a book slightly worn with age from years of service. With neat, meticulous handwriting, he enters the information of all vehicles leaving the village. Instead of adding our names, however, he insists on a copy of our documents, which we, of course, don't have. I try to convince him that he could just copy the information from our originals into the book. He waves

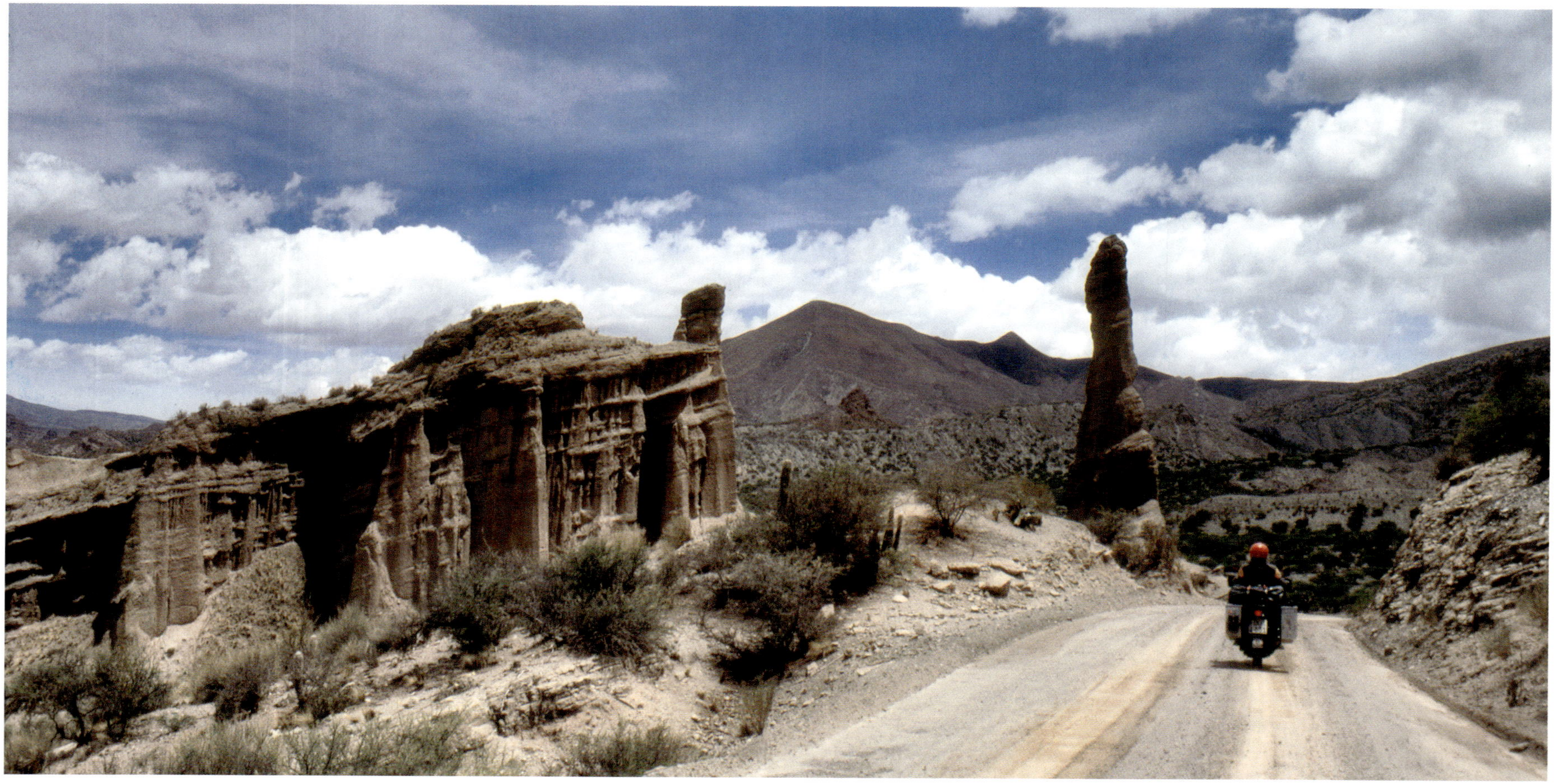

Page 104: Rock formation La Poronga near Tupiza in Bolivia

Page 106: Lost in the sand near Uyuni, Bolivia

Page 107: The Salar de Uyuni is the world's biggest salt lake

Bottom: Altiplano in Bolivia

copies of other vehicle licenses and says that everybody leaves copies here, everybody. I don't get it. However, there is no cure for his stubbornness. I keep trying, but to no avail. We return to the village and look for a copy shop. While the pages are being copied, the shop owner takes my hand, strokes the palm and asks if I ride with gloves. Thoughtlessly, I answer: "Of course, it is safer." She shows me her hands, which are covered with calluses and blisters, and says that she doesn't have any gloves and that without them, her hands hurt when she rides her bike over the gravel roads As we finally pass the checkpoint to prove our off-road skills once again, I'm wearing my extra pair of gloves.

The next 80 km lead over corrugated iron and sand. Covered in dust, we arrive at the next barrier. In the guardhouse they tell us that we have to pay a toll for this miserable road. Unbelievable. An old, toppled sign next to the hut lists prices and the relevant

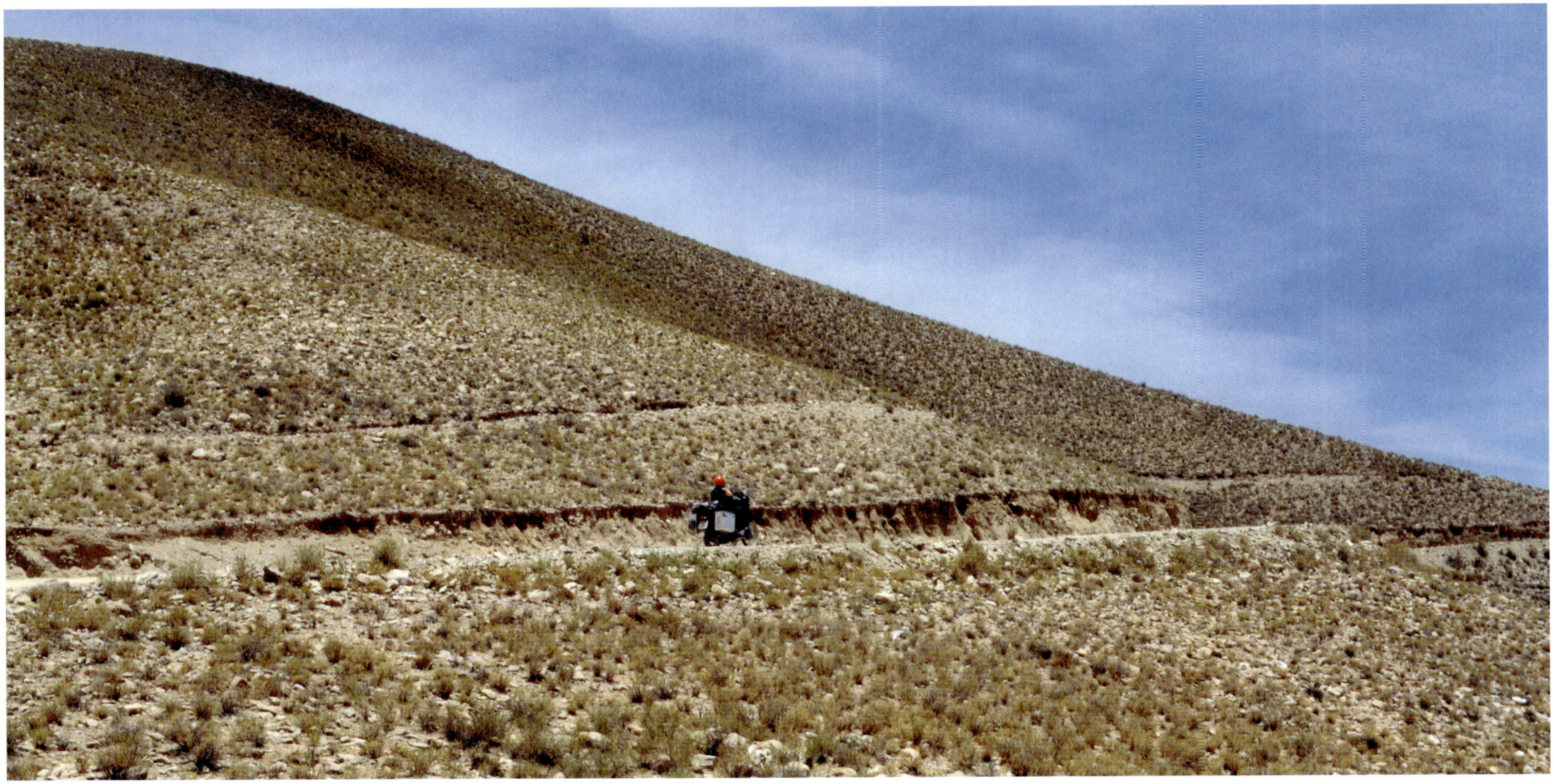

legal passage. In Bolivia, tolls are collected for all roads, and it seems as if the highest prices go with the worst, shortest roads. But not everybody pays the same. We leave our money, they lift the barrier. It starts to rain and the drops mix with the dust on our clothes and create a brown grease. Tupiza, a small village without a cashpoint, is not far. We scrape together the few bolivianos that we exchanged at the border in order to pay for our accommodation, which turns out to be rather comfortable, with a pool and a big, planted courtyard for the bikes. It costs € 13 including breakfast. While the scantily clad female guests enjoy the sunshine by the pool the next morning, we are dressed in full gear wearing cross boots and we lug our heavy cases past the pool to our bikes. Axel takes his sweet time…

We hurry to get to Uyuni as fast as we can. "Fast" is relative, however. In all of Bolivia, there are almost no signs for towns, streets or any other directions. Signs seem to be a valuable curiosity, maybe collectors' items? 215 km lead through a colourful mountain landscape. Suddenly, the road ends next to a wide, partially dry riverbed. There is a factory on the opposite slope, a dead end. Dozens of tracks wind through the wet sand. No people anywhere in sight. Axel goes on a test drive to see whether we will sink in or be able to drive on this ground. It seems to work. The GPS shows us a route through the river further north. What a strange feeling – I'm used to all kinds of unpaved surfaces and can also cross brooks, but it is a new experience to drive in a dry riverbed for many kilometres. It seems to take forever, but then we spot a village on our left. We climb up the bank hoping that we can find a way up into the mountains, but the roads just lead through the village. A local resident gives us a rough description of the route and the place we need to find in the river bed. Even with these directions, it is only by accident that we find the right road, where we cross small brooks, drive around sand hills and stutter across corrugated iron. The little village of Uyuni can't be far. "We are almost there, everything went pretty well" I hear myself say, but in the future, I will resist making remarks like that because it means that something truly unpleasant is going to happen. A bus veers off the route and takes a detour to the right; deep holes filled with soft sand gape in front of us. We slam on the brakes; no vehicle can pass through here. The bus leaves similarly impassable tracks, so we choose the left-hand side. Axel takes aim at a sandy slope, vanishes behind it and then comes to an abrupt halt, standing bolt upright. The rear tyre has sunk in and become stuck. Game over. We unload the

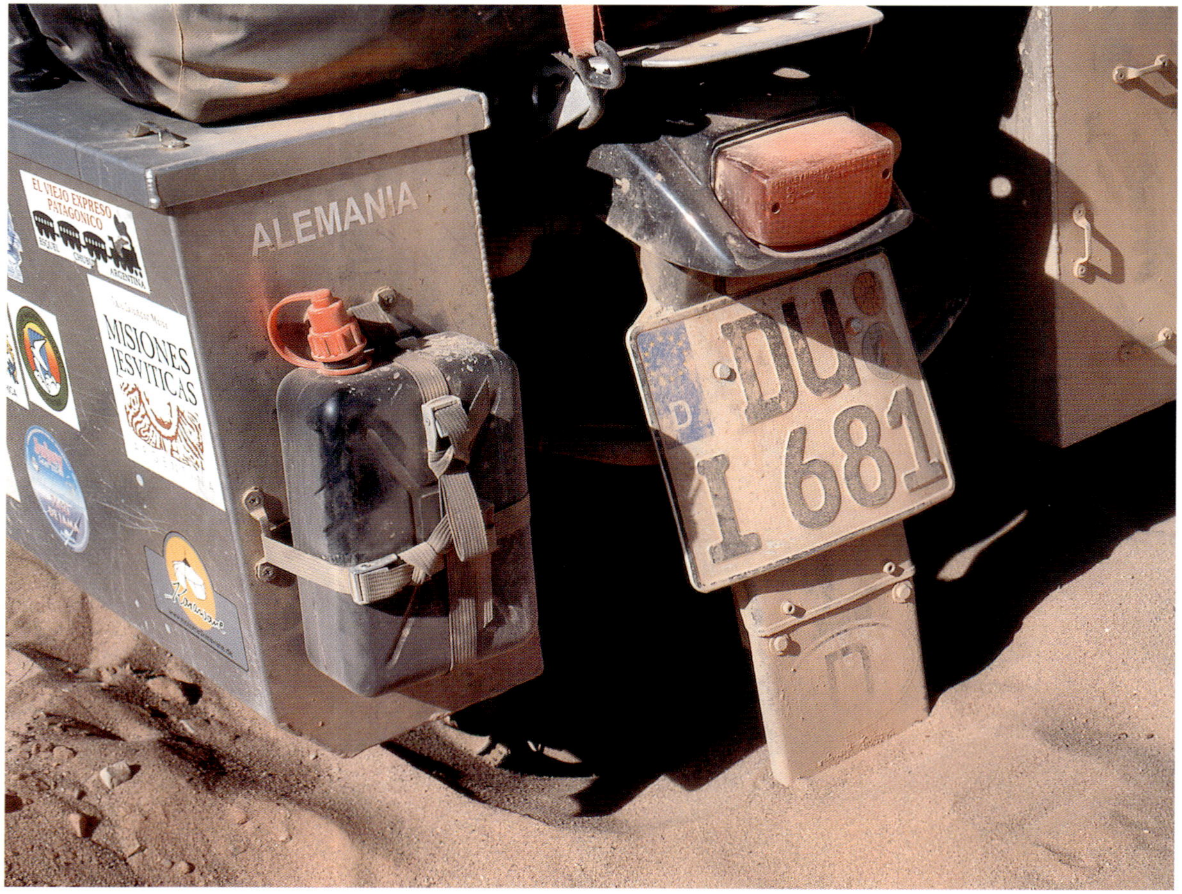

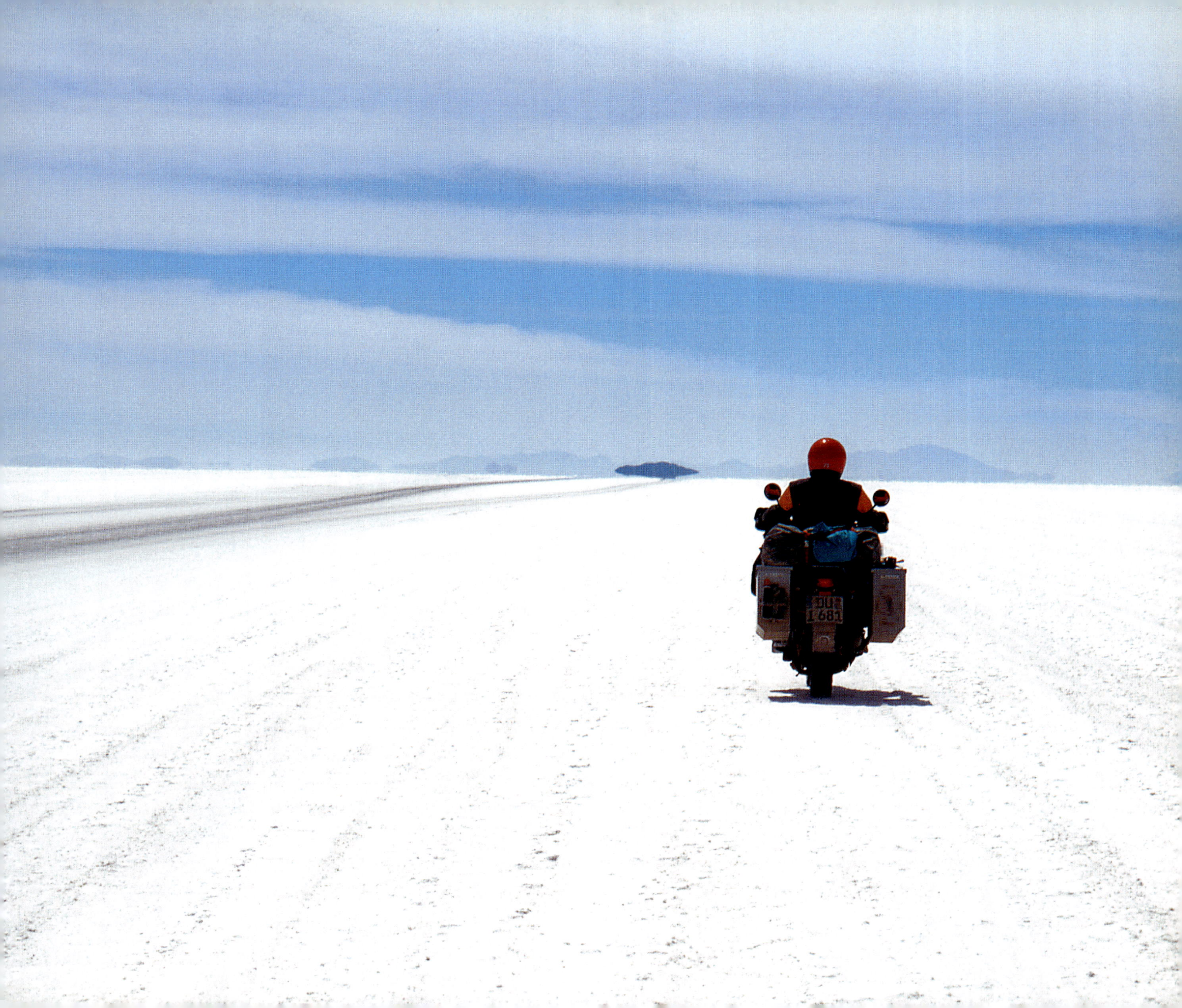
DU
1681
D

luggage and try to dig the machine out with our hands. We are sweating, but to no avail. After 30 long minutes, a jeep with five Bolivians inside passes us. I wave at them and persuade them to help us. Together they push while Axel plays with the gas and clutch. The spinning rear tyre is throwing up so much sand that our helpers are covered with dust. They still think it's huge fun. Thanks to their help, we reach Uyuni before sunset.

It gets very cold at night – no wonder at a height of 3,700 m. We snuggle up on our plank-beds under four woollen blankets, wearing long johns and socks; the room temperature is barely 3° Celsius. There is no heater. To make up for it, we get badly sunburnt during the day on the Salar de Uyuni, the world's largest salt lake. The shimmering salt crystals are so blinding that you cannot drive without sunglasses or a protective tinted visor. For the first time in Bolivia, we can put the bikes in fifth gear – what a feeling to shoot across the salt at 100 km/h, hear it crunching under the tyres, and I

Page 109: At the train cemetery on the edge of Uyuni

Bottom: The Isla Pescado on the Salar de Uyuni is a popular trip destination

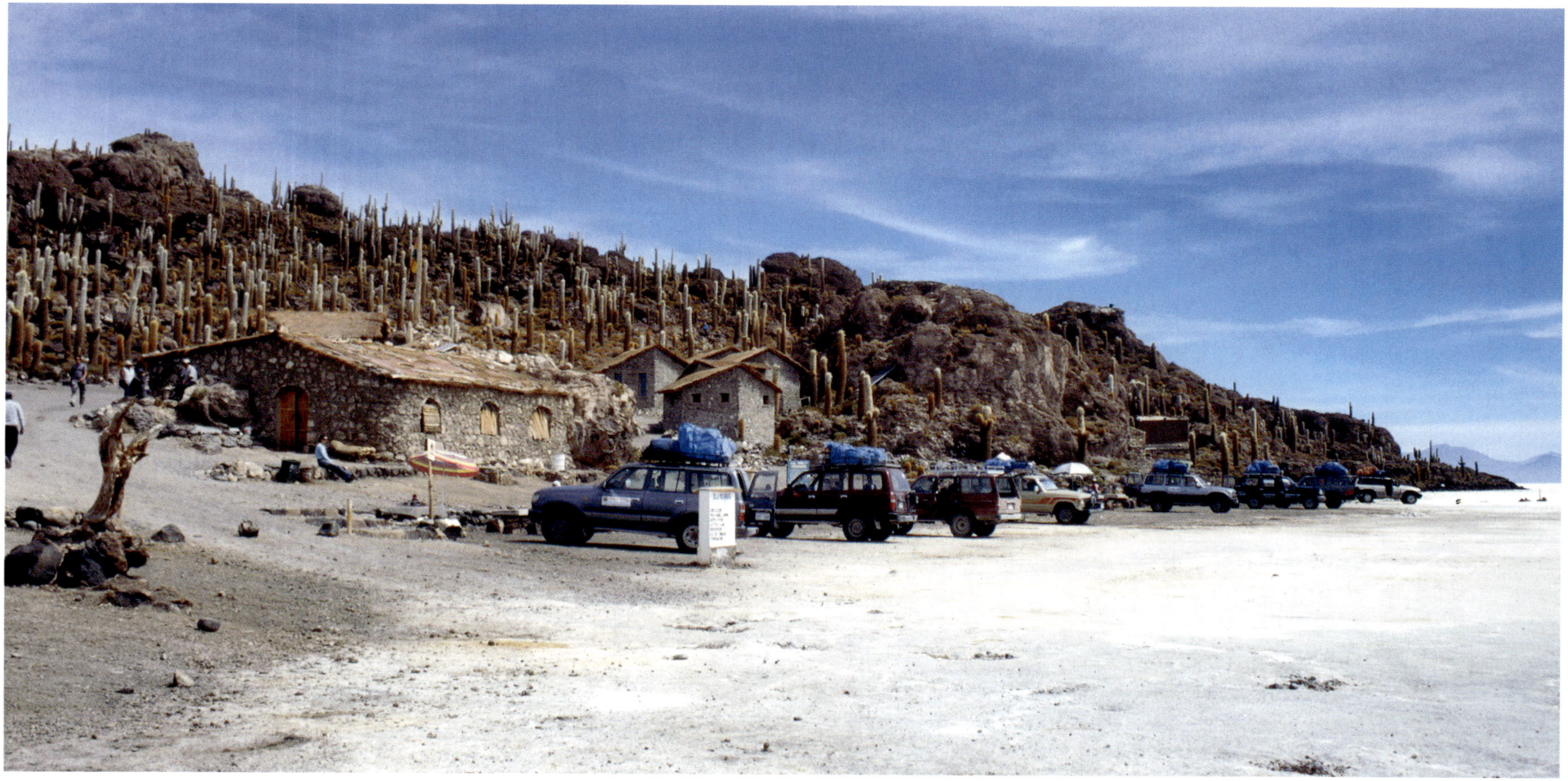

am inebriated by the experience. My gaze travels to the horizon and gets lost in infinity. I'm surrounded by the blinding whiteness that stands out against the blue sky. I feel almost dizzy. In the distance, hills and islands appear in a blur. We are alone in the salt universe and drive towards Isla Pescado, an island overgrown with cacti in the midst of this overwhelming sea of white. The prickly ancient plants rise up to 12 m high; being thick like tree trunks, they withstand all kinds of weather. There is nobody here. On the other side of the island, it is a different story. A few groups of day-trippers have come in jeeps for a picnic. The bikes with the luggage are becoming a popular snapshot motif. It is a little too much fuss, so we retreat into the loneliness of the salt lake.

Since we are too tired to take the bikes, let alone to walk, we take a comfortable taxi to go to the train cemetery that night. We learn that roads with potholes are much easier to tackle on a motorbike than in a shoddy four-wheel vehicle with broken shock absorbers. Realistically speaking, one could say that we are standing in front of an oversized trash dump of rusting iron and steel. Train fans, on the other hand, might not believe their luck when facing the dozens of engines and broken up carriages that look like a huge adventure playground. The scene has something almost archaic about it. The material, subjected to the forces of nature, disintegrates in the course of the decades. I am fascinated by these huge transitory skeletons in this barren landscape. Bathed

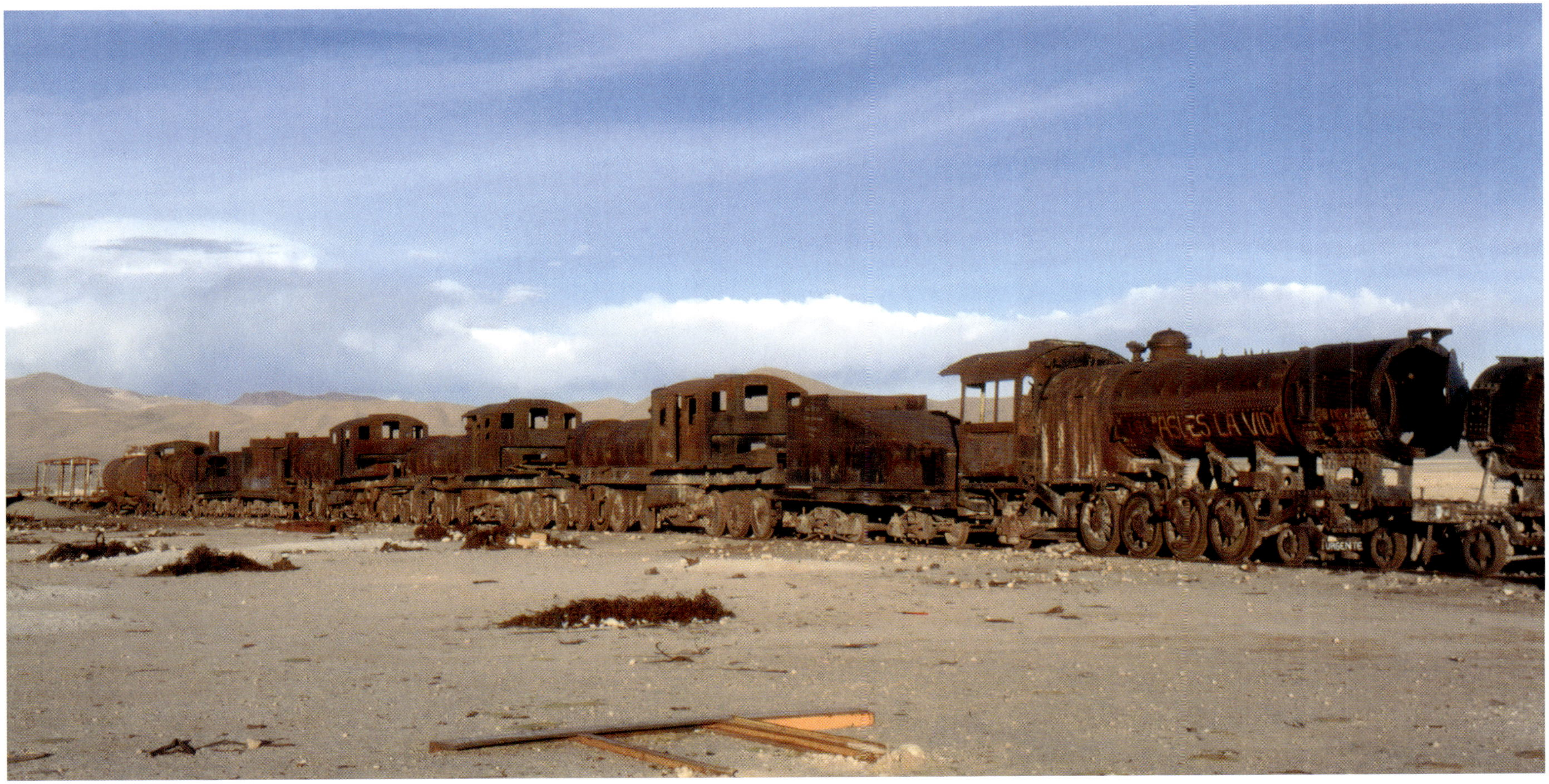

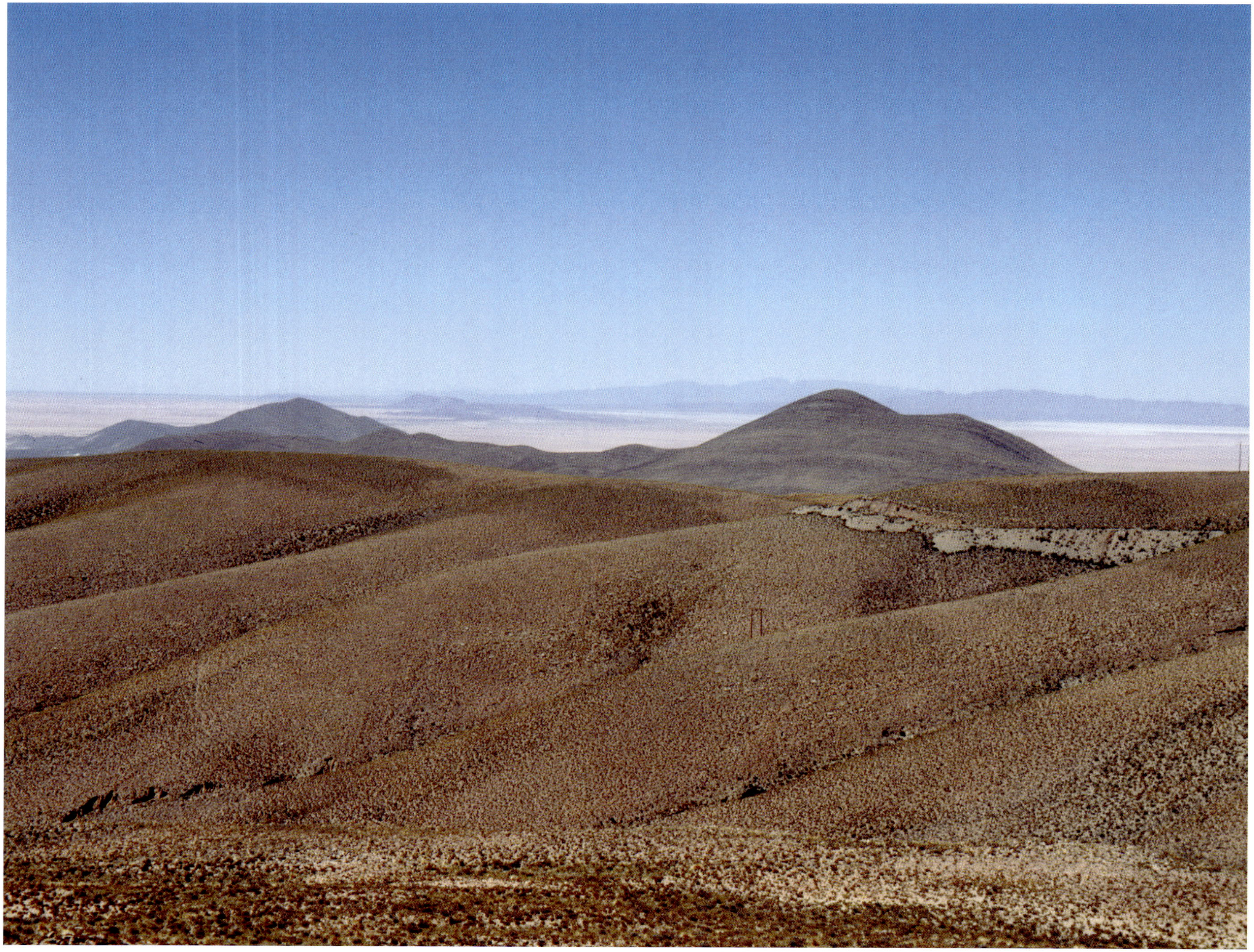

in the light of the setting sun, they tell their wordless story. If you listen carefully, you can almost hear the voices of passengers waiting on the platform and the sound of the steam whistle, you can watch a couple in love looking dreamily out on the plains, small children playing, racing up and down the corridor, and you feel the rattling of the wheels as the train pushes onward over the endless tracks of the Altiplano.

Page 110: View of the Salar de Uyuni in Bolivia

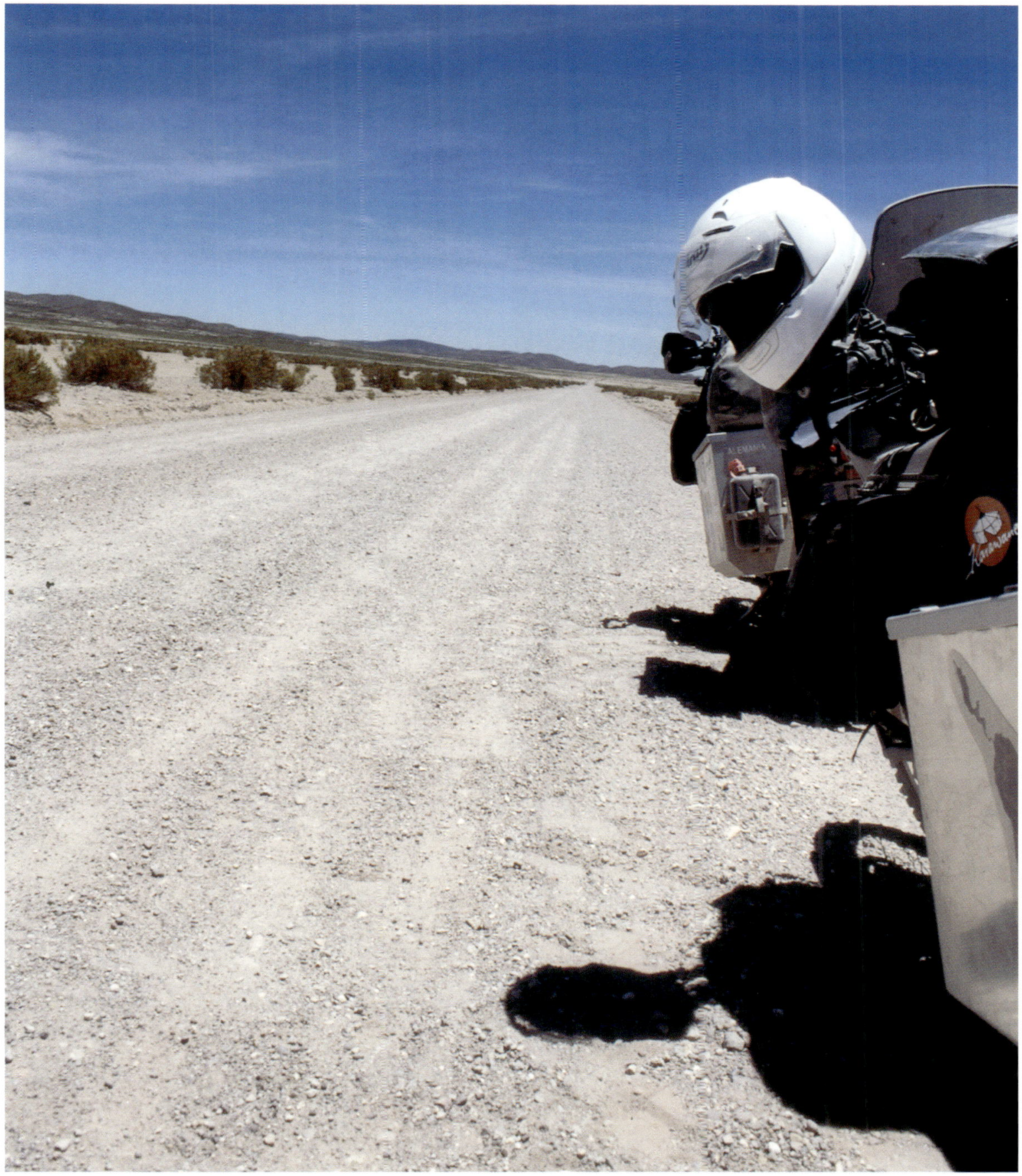

Right: Through the barren landscape, the road leads to Potosí

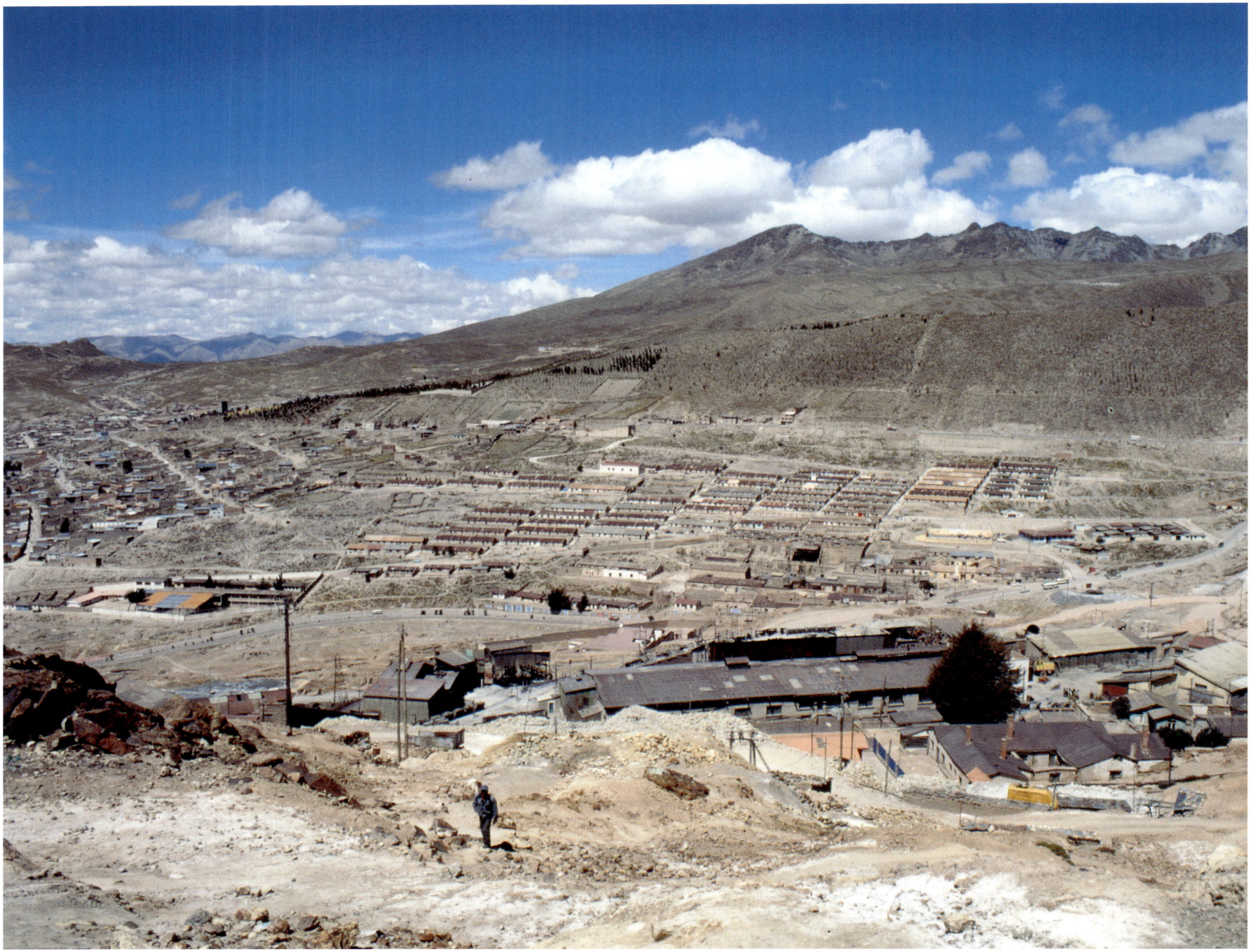

Page 112: The worker houses lie below the mine entrances of the Cerro Rico in Potosí, Bolivia

Bottom: Dark, narrow shafts lead deep into the Cerro Rico

THE "TIO" CULT

So far, we have done fairly well on the high plains. We are glad about this, even though the Bolivians smile indulgently when we tell them about Germany's highest mountain, the Zugspitze, with 2,962 m. They would have to hike down the mountain to reach that high, and many of the locals will never get to such low areas in their lives. It is 215 km to Potosí. At a height of 4,200 m, the Transalp flakes out, gets out of breath.

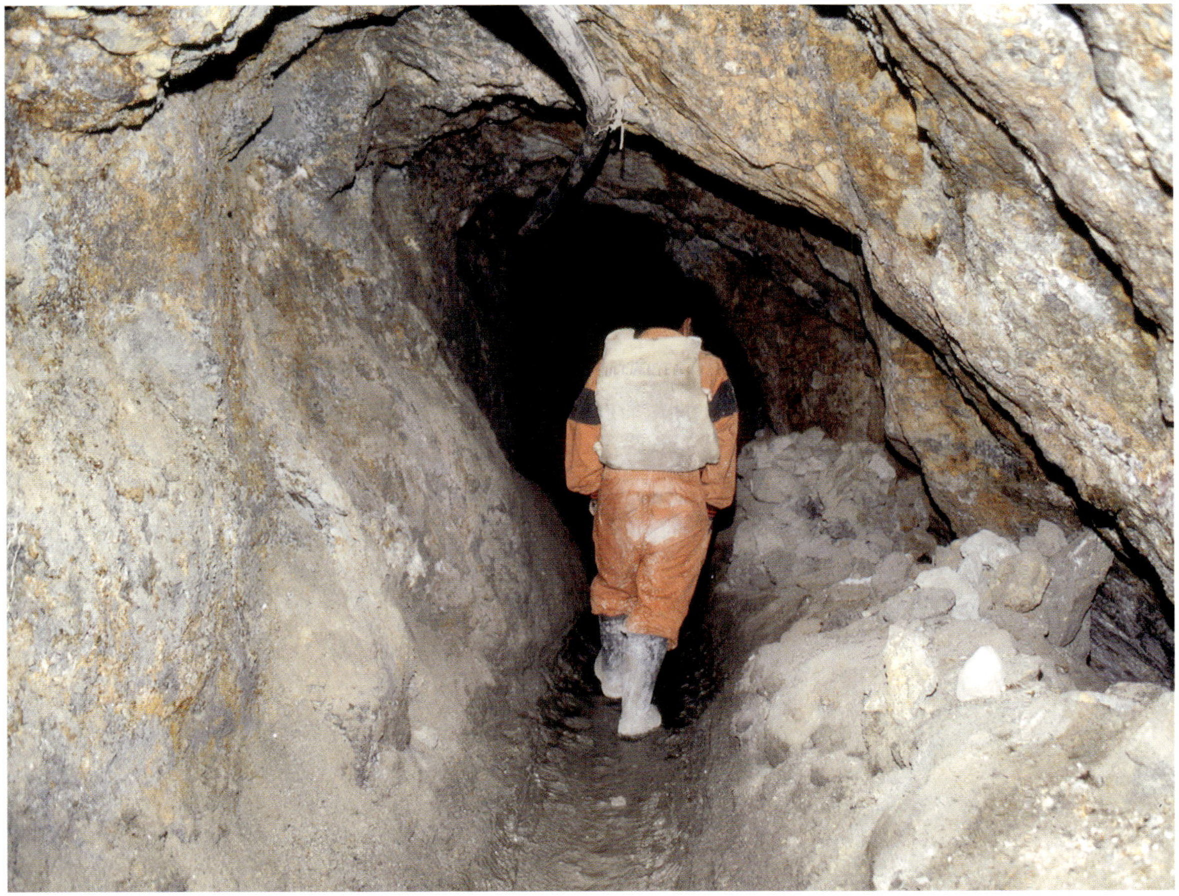

The bad fuel quality doesn't help: 75 octane are just not enough. It climbs the mountains laboriously, sputtering and wheezing, and it hurts me to watch. We stop at last and knock the air filter on a rock because it has caught a lot of dust. Now it can breathe easier, but it is time for it to get something better to drink. We will have to wait, however, until we get to Peru.

Even though the names are marked on the street map, Potosí itself does not have any street signs. So we just let the dense tide of traffic carry ourselves towards the centre. We stop at a plaza and don't know which way to go. With a counting-out rhyme, we pick one of the small alleys leading away from here – and arrive in a neighbourhood that actually offers accommodation. After swallowing lots of dust over the past few days, we use our bathtub to soak our biker gear in soapy water. It is unbelievable how dirty our things have become. We seem to have transported the sand of half of Bolivia's Altiplano; no wonder the jacket kept growing heavier.

With a small group of seven people, we start out into the Cerro Rico. At one time, the "rich mountain" made people incredibly wealthy. At least the Spanish immigrants. In the mid-16th century, Potosí had 160,000 inhabitants and was one of the world's biggest and wealthiest cities, bigger than Madrid, Paris or Rome. The reserves inside the mountain seemed to be inexhaustible, with pure silver in its depths. Today, Potosí's only claim to fame is that it is the world's highest city. The Cerro shines red, veined with the colours of the other ores: pink, crimson, ochre, grey, gold, brown. There is not

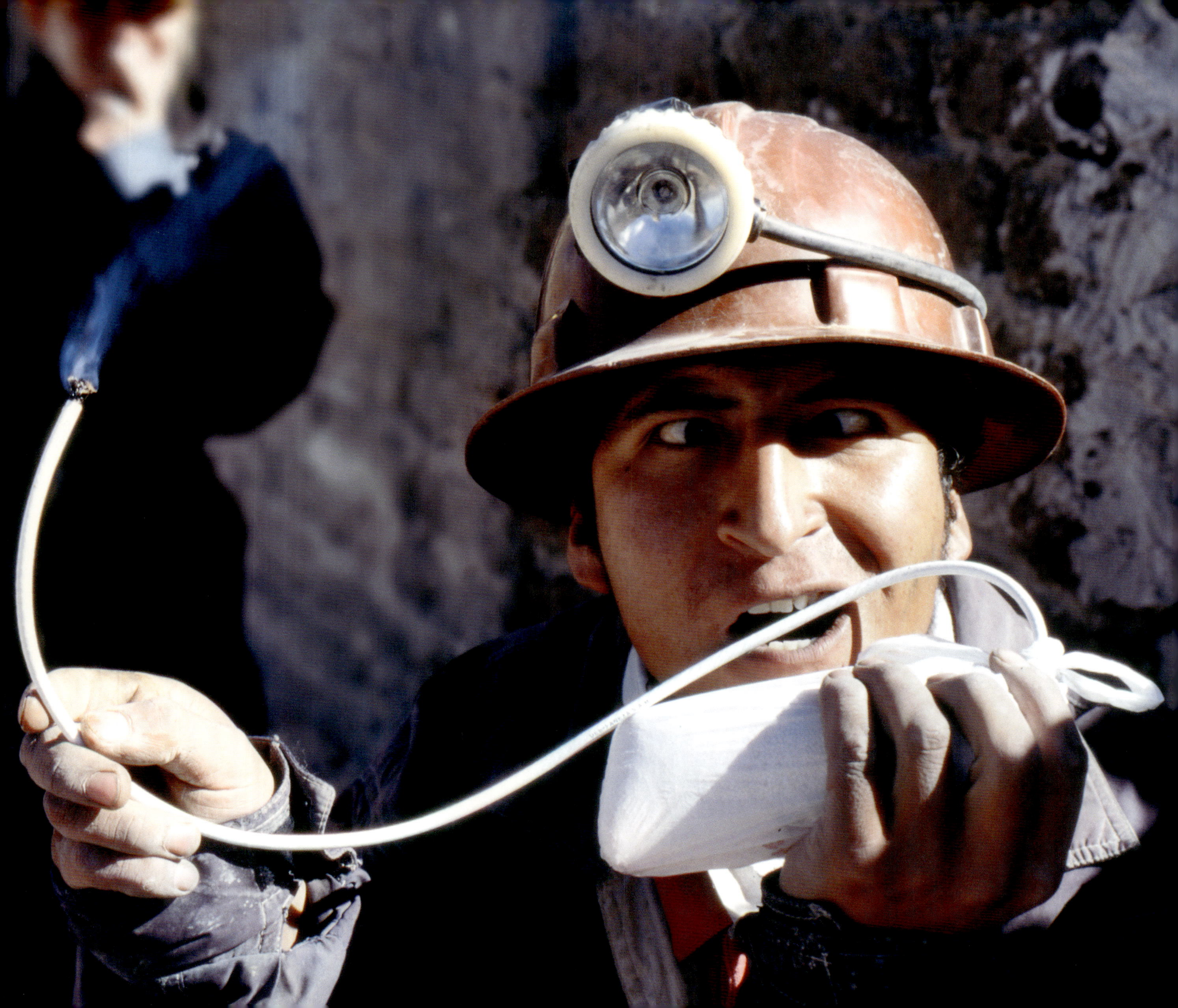

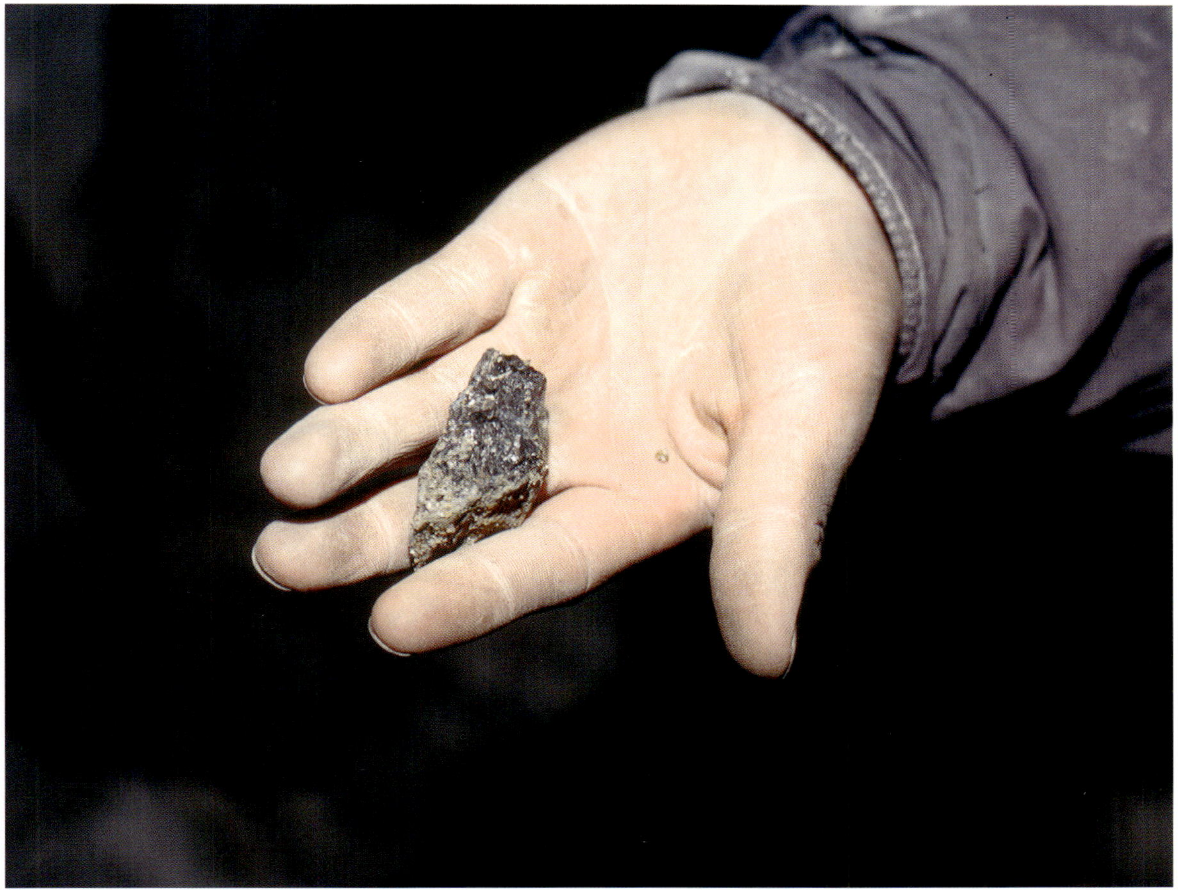

Top: A chuck of rock containing silver

Page 114: "Playing with dynamite", a daily risk for mine workers

much left of its treasures though. Potosí gave its riches to the world and is now reduced to poverty. That is the slightly wistful summary offered by Pedro, our tour guide. He tells us that the silver mountain is still the main source of income for the local inhabitants, even though the interior has more holes than a Swiss cheese. Driven by the hope of finding a good vein, the miners from the small cooperatives working in the government mines keep blasting new tunnels. Some of them are cool and narrow and you have to pass through them by crouching. Other shafts are wider and higher, but unbearably hot and stifling, the air mixed with poisonous gases. When one gallery is exploited, the next one is developed. In the bigger pits, a worker's average life expectancy is 40 years; his monthly wages are about 500 bolivianos, approximately € 60. In the smaller shafts, where Pedro's father works, the men make a lot less money but the work is not as dangerous – there is a relatively good chance that they live to see 50. 25 to 30 fatal accidents happen in the mines every year, caused by gas leaks or rocks loosened in blasts crashing down, weighing about 100 tons. Still, they go into the mines every day, even the children, hoping that it will yield enough to feed their families. When they were boys, Pedro and his brothers had already used their father's tools to play mineworkers, and they hoped that they would be able to follow him soon. Since he turned 14, Pedro has been working in the mines. Officially, the starting age is 18, but there are no serious controls. Some of the working children take the opportunity to catch up on school work after their shifts, which makes their days even harder. A shift is eight hours. In months with public holidays, they work up to 16 or 20 hours in order to make up for the lost time.

At the market, we buy gifts for the workers: sticks of dynamite, fuses, coca leaves and small bottles with 96 percent alcohol and the label "Bueno gusto" – pleasant taste. Well, cheers! We climb up a hill to the mine entrance. The tunnel is narrow and there are only a few places where it is possible to stand up straight. Workers pass us with wheelbarrows filled with rocks, which

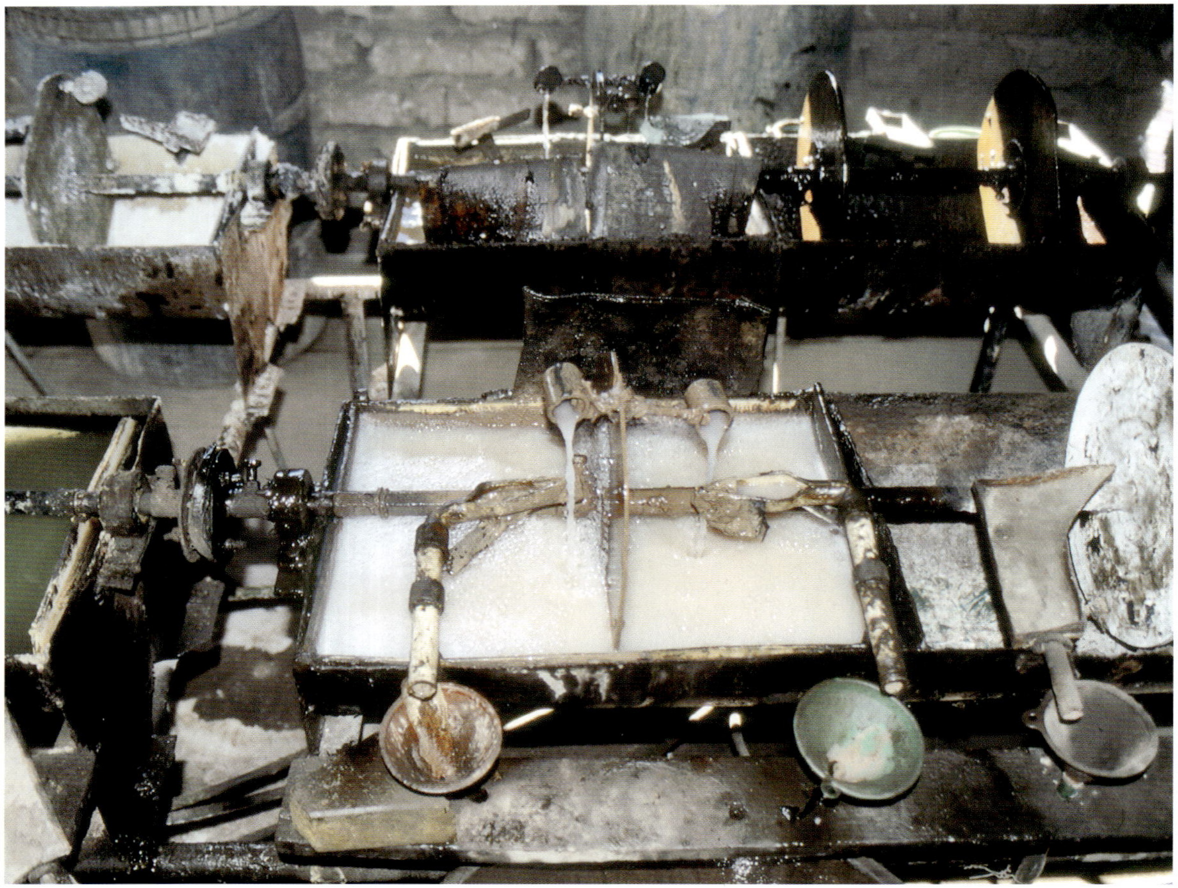

In the factory, rocks are treated with chemical substance ...

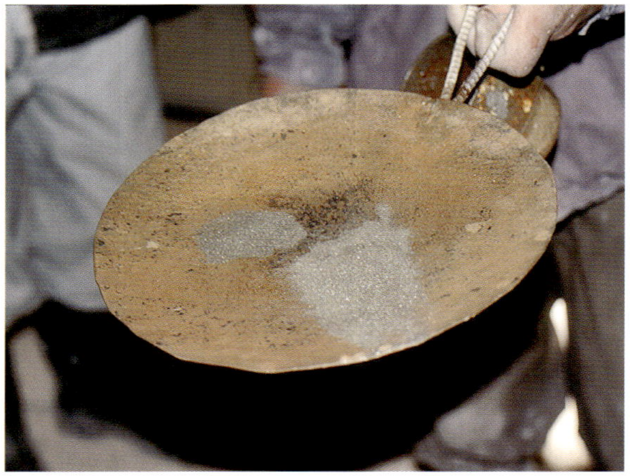

... until silver dust remains

they push through the shafts at high speed, their cheeks bulging with coca leaves. They are grateful for the brief rest and the gifts, some help in dealing with their day and the hard work. Without machines, they hack into the rockface with picks, the only light coming from a dim carbide headlamp. It is hard work. A small tunnel leads to the cave that is the home of the patron saint of mine workers. He takes on the shape of a devil. They worship and fear him. Huari was once worshipped by the Uru, but the tribe offered sacrifices to other gods as well. The god began a bitter fight against this humiliation, but he was defeated and retreated into the mountain, which he claimed for himself from that moment on. Up to this day, he lives there in seclusion. Thus it is he who owns the raw materials. As an act of submission and reverence, the workers, with their strong faith, take him into the family as an uncle, "tio". They gather here every Friday, bringing gifts such as cigarettes, coca leaves and alcohol. With a "Ch´alla", a sacrificial greeting, a few drops of the "pachamama" are dedicated, the uncle's bottle is replenished, and then the bottle of strong alcohol is passed around. Every worker takes a healthy sip. They thank him for the good production week or, if the yield was insufficient, ask him to release more ore from the mountain. Either way, the alcohol flows freely. We, too, take part in the ritual and taste the fine drink. I barely get my lips wet because it burns and almost sweeps me off my feet; it possibly could make you blind. The ritual is repeated. In the faith of the Quechua, everything exists in pairs, explains Pedro. Humans have two eyes, two ears, two hands and two legs. The "tío" has two sides, a good one and a bad one – just as day and night, sun and moon, woman and man, earthly and spiritual things are complementary parts of a whole. You always take coca leaves with both hands and the alcohol makes two rounds. They are very serious about this ritual with "tío" because in their minds, their work and even their survival in the mountain depends on it.

Outside, back in the fresh air, Pedro begins to build an explosive charge. He kneads dynamite mass in a small plastic bag, adds the fuse, seals it and lights the cord. Then he takes a leisurely stroll towards a slope. He seems to be utterly calm, but then he scrambles for cover. Anticipation rises. Nothing happens. All cameras point to one spot. The air is charged with tension. Any second now. Nothing. I focus again on the charge. Nothing. Suddenly, we are gripped by a strong shockwave that travels from our toes up to the tips of our hair, as if we were about to be lifted off the ground. Instinctively, I raise my arms. An ear-splitting explosion makes the whole area tremble and echoes from the opposite hill, the Huakajchi, the "mountain that cried". This tenth of a second seems like eternity. What would such a detonation do inside the mountain? The locals are used to it, none of them is even a little startled. The picture I have taken is blurred.

We watch the processing of the fragments of rock in the nearby factory, where the ground fragments are mixed drop by drop into chemicals in open tubs. The mud is washed and skimmed off several times until pure silver dust remains. The workers here are also only able to manage their shift with their cheeks stuffed. Saliva transforms the content of the coca leaves into a substance that has a stimulating effect and relieves pain, while reducing sensations of cold, hunger and thirst at the same time. The traces of cocaine disintegrate in the stomach acid and do not have an effect of the central nervous system, contrary to what many people say. For the local inhabitants, the leaves are a healing herb, a nutritious plant that contains oils, vitamins, minerals and trace elements, and is thus an important supplement to their diets, if not a replacement when other food is scarce. "La hoja de coca no es droga – The coca leaf is not a drug". With this advertisement, the country is fighting against the classification of the plant as an illegal drug. International conventions prohibit the trade of coca products abroad, even though products range from tea to soap, from toothpaste to lemonade. The coca bush is thousands of years old and was sacred to the Inca. In the mid-16th century, it was rejected by the Spanish as being harmful and useless, and the prejudice is still circulating in the public today. It all depends on what you do with it.

With rain and a sandstorm, we are blown towards Oruro, which at first glance doesn't seem to deserve a visit. The carnival, however, means an annual state of emergency for the town. Hundreds of dance groups wearing masks and costumes walk the streets. It is probably the only place in the world where the tío in the shape of a devil, the mascot of the mineworkers, is blessed in church. Countless masked tíos crawl on their knees along the centre aisle of the "Holy Socavón", Oruro's patron saint, in order to receive the blessing. Over the centuries, the faiths may have been blended, but the indigenous people are still more in awe of "pachamama" and the tío than of Jesus Christ. Rumour has it that people still place sacrifices under the foundation of a new building in order to appease "Mother Earth". And it appears that not all of them are animal sacrifices…

Bottom: An indigenous woman on the way to the market in Potosí, Bolivia

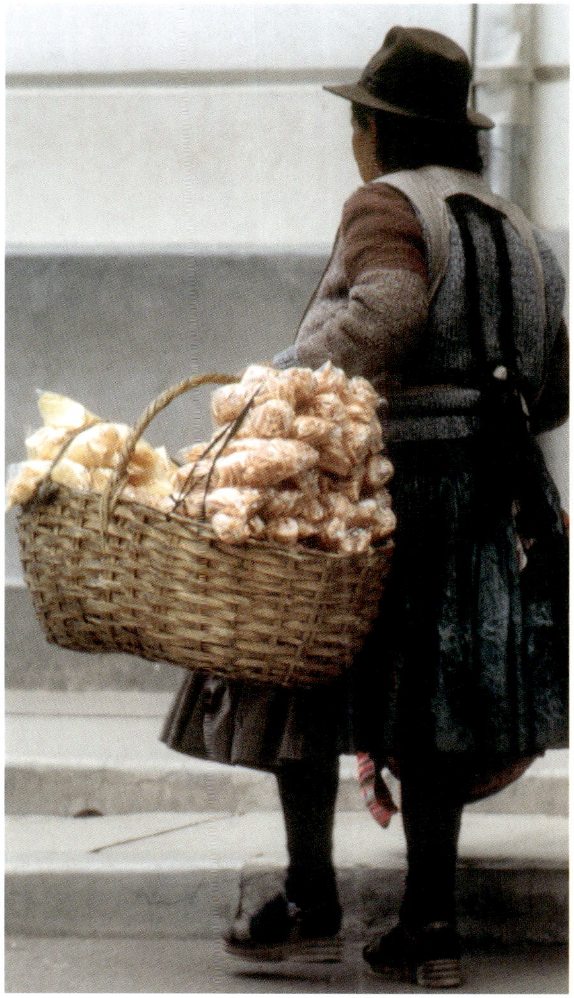

THE WEATHER GOD GOES CRAZY

In Oruro, we restore ourselves and the bikes. Axel needs to get treatment for his inflamed root of the tooth, while I recover with coca tee and antispasmodic medicine from a light bout of food poisoning. The clutch cable on the Transalp needs to be replaced before it snaps. That is a quick job. A new horn for me is much more important. It gave up because it was being overused, but in this country, it would be life-threatening not to have one. In towns, the right of way is given to the person who honks first at the intersection. The constant noise is nerve-shattering but helpful. The Oruros municipal administration banned honking horns for a while. But the number of accidents doubled because nobody knew who had the right of way anymore. Now they are all honking again. A pedestrian explains to me where the shops with the car parts are located – just around the corner, two blocks up the street. It turns out to be 15 long blocks until I finally reach the neighbourhood with the shops, but you can't take distances too seriously here. The important thing is that I get what I need. We still have a stick of dynamite left over from Potosí. I would really like to put it on a shelf at home as a souvenir. I add it to the things we want to send home in a parcel. But before we take the parcel to the post office, I have my doubts and take it out again. That is a wise decision, because it is not just the post office clerk in Oruro who checks the contents of the parcel; German customs will have a look inside as well, and then we would be in trouble…

We visit acquaintances who have been living in Oruro for many years. Ana works as a teacher at a German school. We would have loved to visit her class to talk to the children and show them that the German language is more than an annoying subject to study. Unfortunately, the Christmas break has already started. Instead, Lucío shows us the pewter factory where he works as an engineer. From the ore deliveries to the finished 25 kg bars, he explains every detail of the production process, a fascinating experi-

Page 119: "Chullpas", ruins of Uru huts near Oruro, Bolivia

Bottom: Mineral rock near Oruro, Bolivia

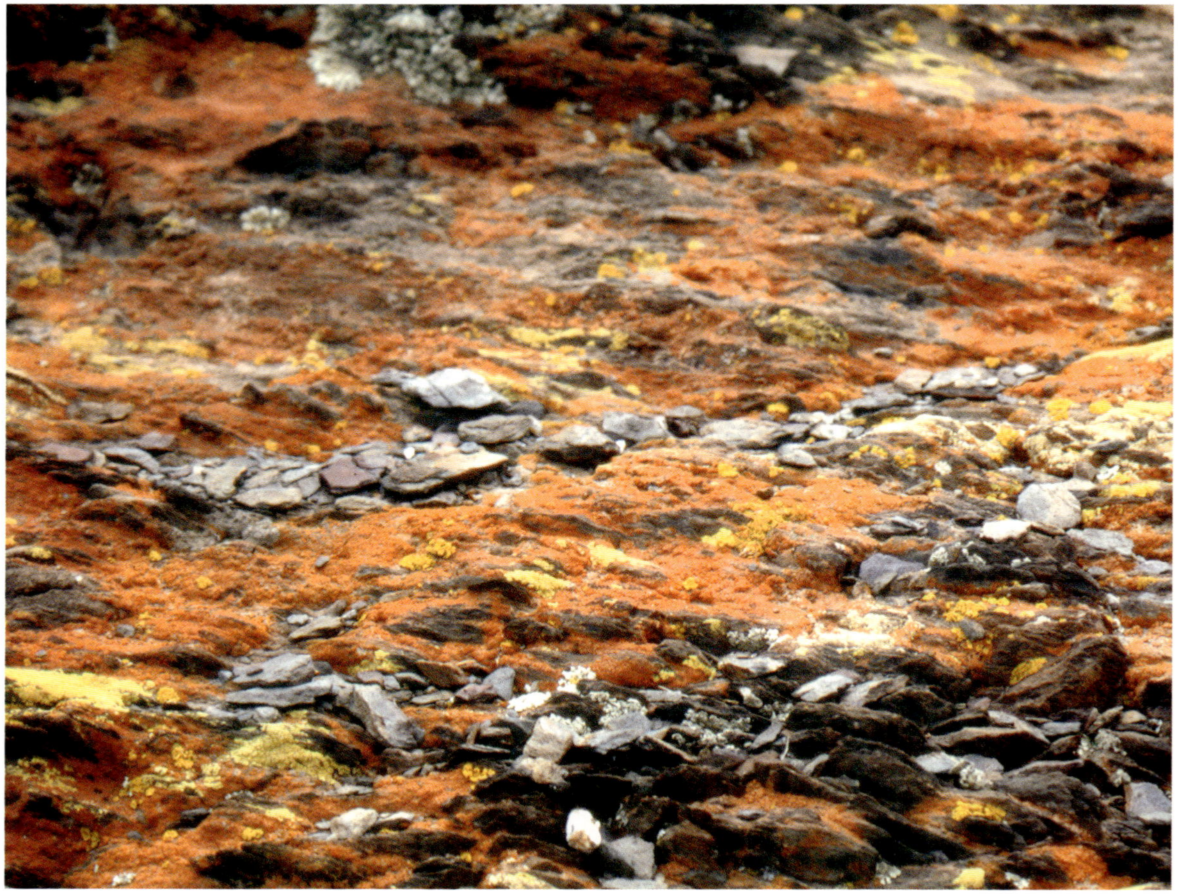

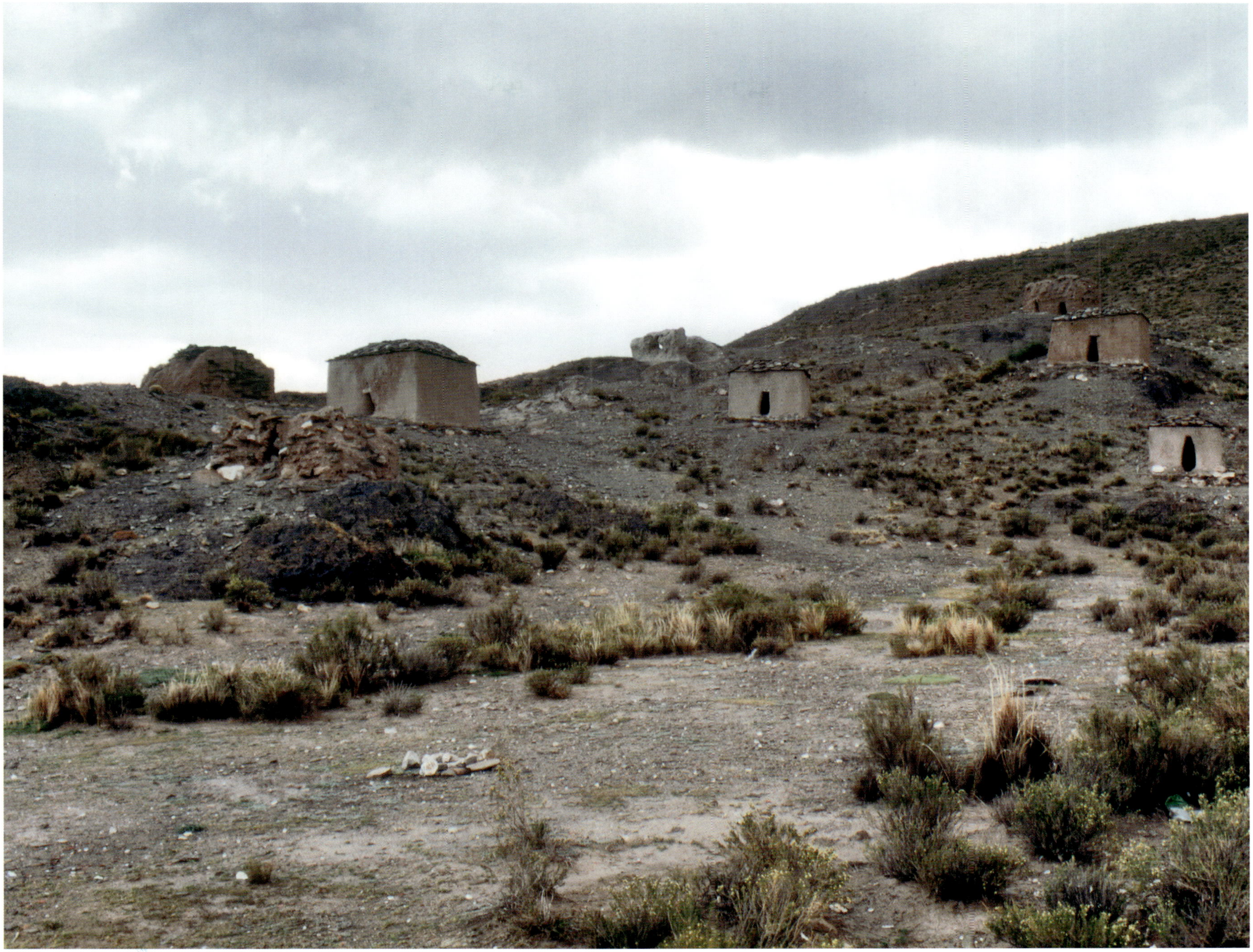

ence that we wouldn't have wanted to miss. The two of them recommend that we make a little excursion to the so-called chullpas located about 20 km outside of Oruro. It can be reached via a bumpy gravel road and a dried-out lake. Chullpas are the little huts of the Uru tribe that lived here before the age of the Inca. Due to the dry and thin air, bodies decomposed very slowly. The Urus positioned them in a crouch and kept them in the house, in the family circle. There is still a bone lying in one hut. The other mummies have been moved to the museum.

Bolivia is getting ready to elect a president, which means road blocks and unrest. We discuss several possible routes to the north with Ana and Lucío. On election day, there will be a ban on driving for all vehicles in order to prevent riots. We want to get to Copacabana on Lake Titicaca a day earlier. Road blocks on the Panamericana were removed with force by the police last night, so the road is passable again. The thought of having to drive through the traffic chaos of El Alto above La Paz does not thrill us. The alternative is another detour west, where we would have to enter Peru and then exit it again right away if we want to reach the town. So we decide to take the Panamericana in the direction of La Paz. Traffic is quiet, numerous herds of sheep, llamas and vicuña graze by the side of the road. The shepherd dogs are after us. Sometimes, only slamming the brakes saves us from colliding with them. In El Alto, we plunge into a huge traffic jam. For an hour, we fight with hundreds of minibuses competing for every millimetre and wedging us in from all sides. Traffic policemen are standing in the middle looking rathe lost with their whistles. Nobody takes them seriously. Even honking is no use anymore. I take a deep breath as we leave the chaos behind – I am relieved that we have covered these few kilometres without an accident, but we are both drenched in sweat. There is a feeling of having survived a rally.

A little later, the sky turns black, thunder and lightning all around. We wonder about the white layer covering the sheep by the side of the road. And the fields. A 2 cm layer of hailstones accumulates on the road. Cascades of brown mud flow down the slopes. For the next kilometres, we slide at a walking pace. The temperature is barely 4° Celsius at a height of 3,850 m. Our clothes are soaked and I begin to tremble like a leaf. Thirty minutes later, the storm goes away as quickly as it came. Blue sky, sunshine. Behind the next curve, the road slopes down to a small fishing village, and a ferry takes us to the opposite shore to get to Copacabana. "Ferry" is probably the wrong term – the boat looks more like a raft with sides. There is nobody

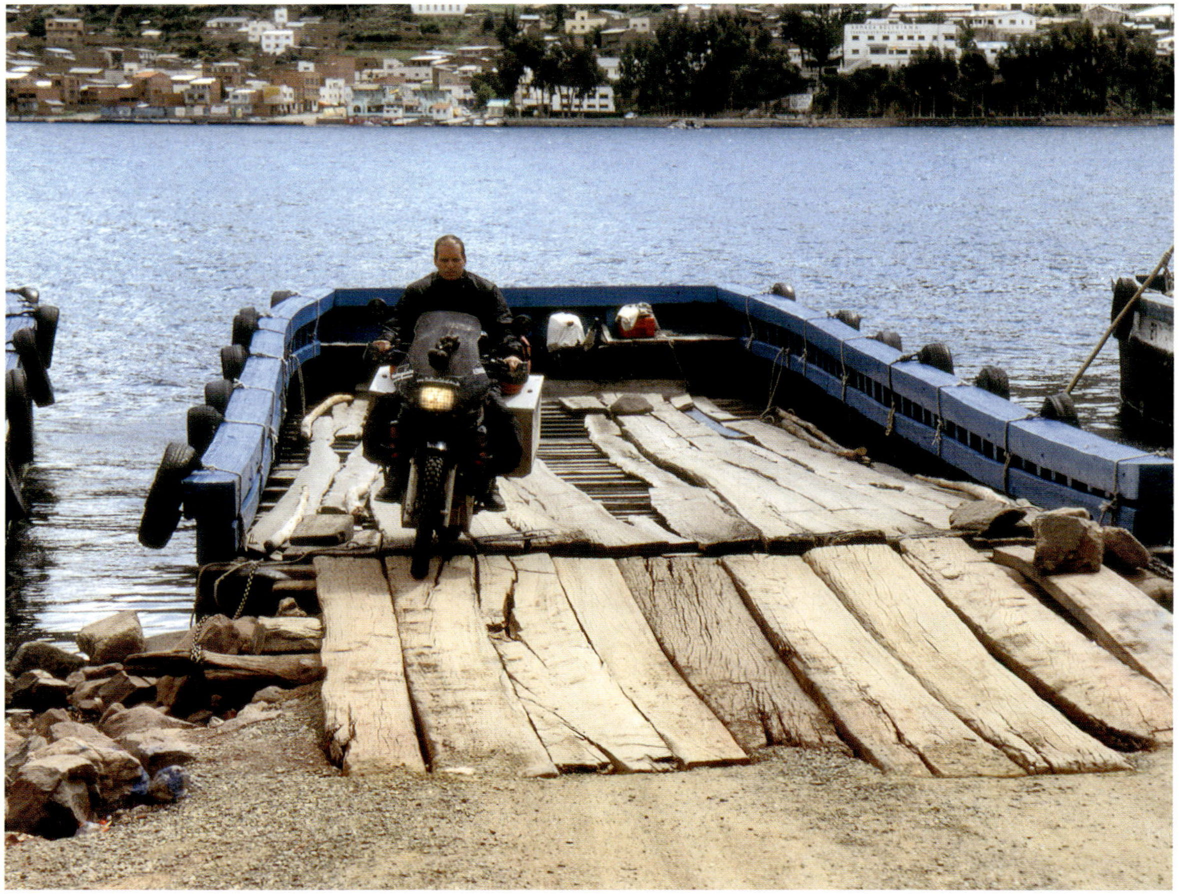

Page 120: Ferry on Lake Titicaca, the highest navigable lake in the world

Bottom: Farmland on the Isla de Sol in Lake Titicaca, Bolivia

except us. The ferryman indicates to us that he wants to wait for more passengers. The black clouds are back, swift and scary. Now what? Further discussions with the ferryman. He offers to take us alone for twice the fare. We agree even though we know that he is ripping us off. We steer both bikes backwards over the swaying plank onto the boat, which is easier said than done and takes some time. Just as the machines are secured as tightly as possible, they have to be unloaded again. A military bus is approaching and needs to get onto the ferry. To prevent us from sinking, the bus has to go on board first. We take two deep breaths; 21 … 22 … 23. The whole thing takes an hour, and then the ferry pushes off at last. Our reward at the other end is a wonderful serpentine road. The land surrounding the lake is exceptionally fertile and brings forth an abundance of potatoes, corn, quinoa and other vegetables. The origins of potato farming lie in the Bolivian and Peruvian Andes. Thousands of years ago, the tuber plant was already cultivated

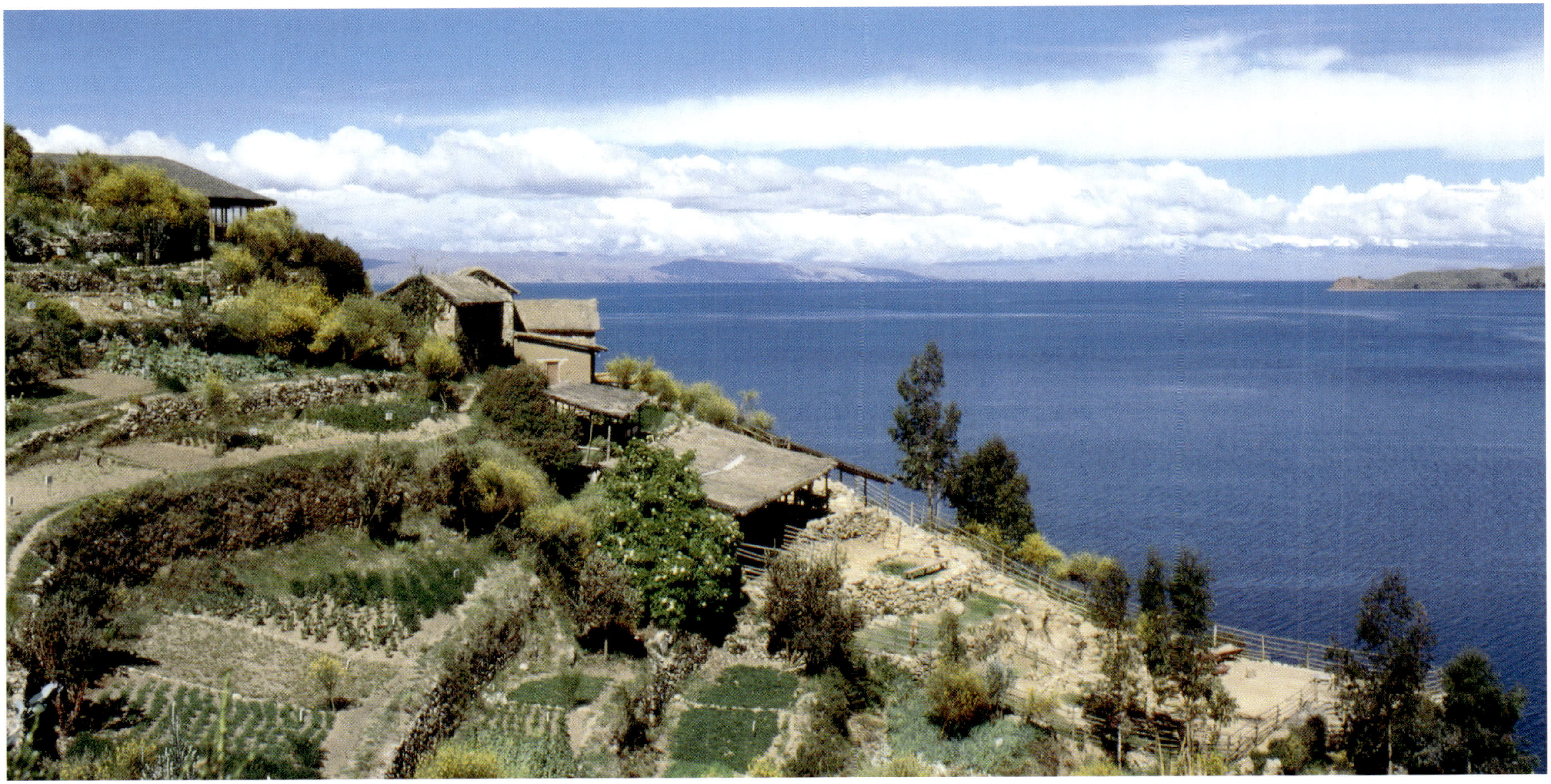

here, and there are more than 200 varieties nowadays. They have even bred a variety that can be preserved by means of a freezing and drying process to prevent famine in case of crop failure. In the late 16th century, the Spanish brought the potatoe to Europe. The agricultural areas and vegetable gardens are laid out in terraces. The lake shimmers blue in the sun and seems to be limitless. In the distance, one can just barely see the snow-topped six-thousand-metre mountains of the Cordillera Reál; the peaks melt into the white clouds that seem to be suspended behind them. I let my thoughts drift freely, and everything would be fine if it wasn't for the little shepherd boy standing in the middle of the road, trying to make us fall off our bikes with his whip...

The rainy season has us in its clutches; there is almost a guarantee that every day at noon, there is a storm and continuous rain until the next morning. We get settled in Copacabana, meet other travellers and use the time to read. I learn more about the myths surrounding Lake Titicaca. According to the Inca legends, the god Viracocha rose out of the lake and created the sun in the location of the Isla del Sol. It is thus the origin of the entire Inca realm. On the Isla de la Luna, Viracocha ordered the moon to rise into the sky. The lake became a holy place for the indigenous tribes. On both islands, temples were built in honour of the stars. With a passenger boat, we are ferried to the Island of the Sun. If the engines were actually running, we would be there relatively quickly,

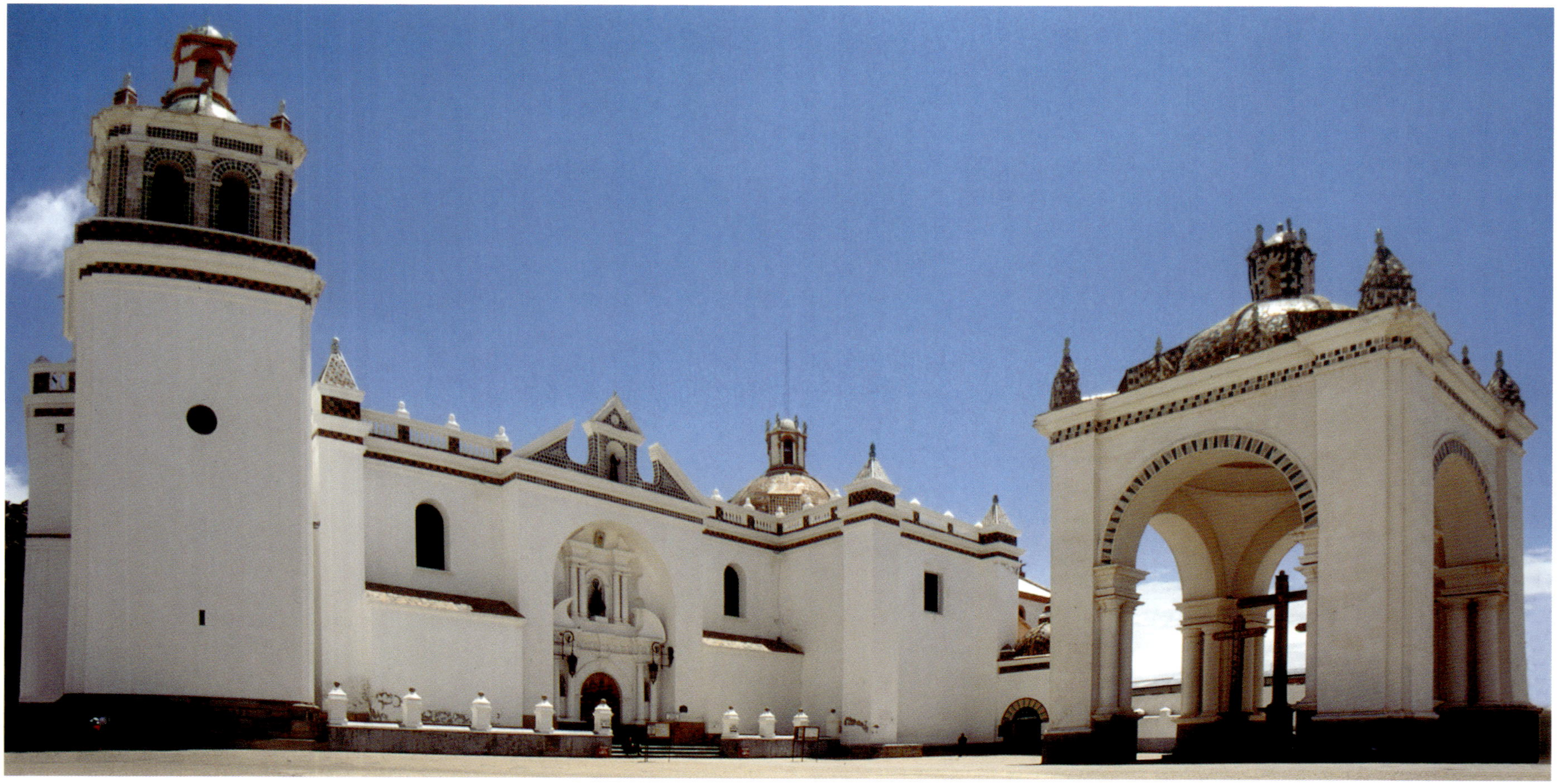

we would be able to take a walk around the island and go back on the last boat of the day. But that would be too simple – one of the engines breaks down. The helmsman tries to get it back to work but the boat stutters along at the speed of a pedal boat. The good thing is that we now have all the time in the world to enjoy the highest navigable lake on earth. The only drawback is that our time on the island melts away like butter in the sun. Once we finally reach the quay after two hours and climb up the Escalera de Inca, the Inca stairs – which is no mean feat at a height of 4,000 – we already have to think about going back. When I ask the skipper if he can repair the second engine, he gives me a disapproving look and says: "Claro, soy mecanico!" – "Of course, I am a mechanic". How could I doubt his skills? On the way back, it becomes evident what this means. The engine stalls again and we reach the port just before nightfall.

It is election day. Evo Morales, the people's man, is the clear winner with more than 52% of votes. In the near future, he wants to shake up traditional politics. In almost every country on our itinerary, there are presidential elections this year. Bolivia is not the only country where the left-wing parties can push through their programmes and thus give millions of people new hope for a better life. Let's also hope that long-term investments benefit education, health and the establishment of socially conscious economic developments. Nobody can say for sure whether the elections will lead to riots and thus to new road blocks. We prefer to leave. In front of the basilica "Virgen de la Candelaria", people can decorate their vehicles with plastic flowers and receive a blessing with holy water and incense, an old tradition that most of the locals and tourists follow. We, on the other hand, prefer to trust our driving skills, open eyes and ears and start off on our journey to Peru without the blessing of the church.

Page 122: Basilica "Virgen de la Candelaria" in Copacabana, Bolivia

Page 124: View of the town and Lake Titicaca from the Cerro Sancollani in Copacabana, Bolivia

Page 125: Storms over the lake occur often

Bottom: Inca stairs on the Isla de Sol, Bolivia

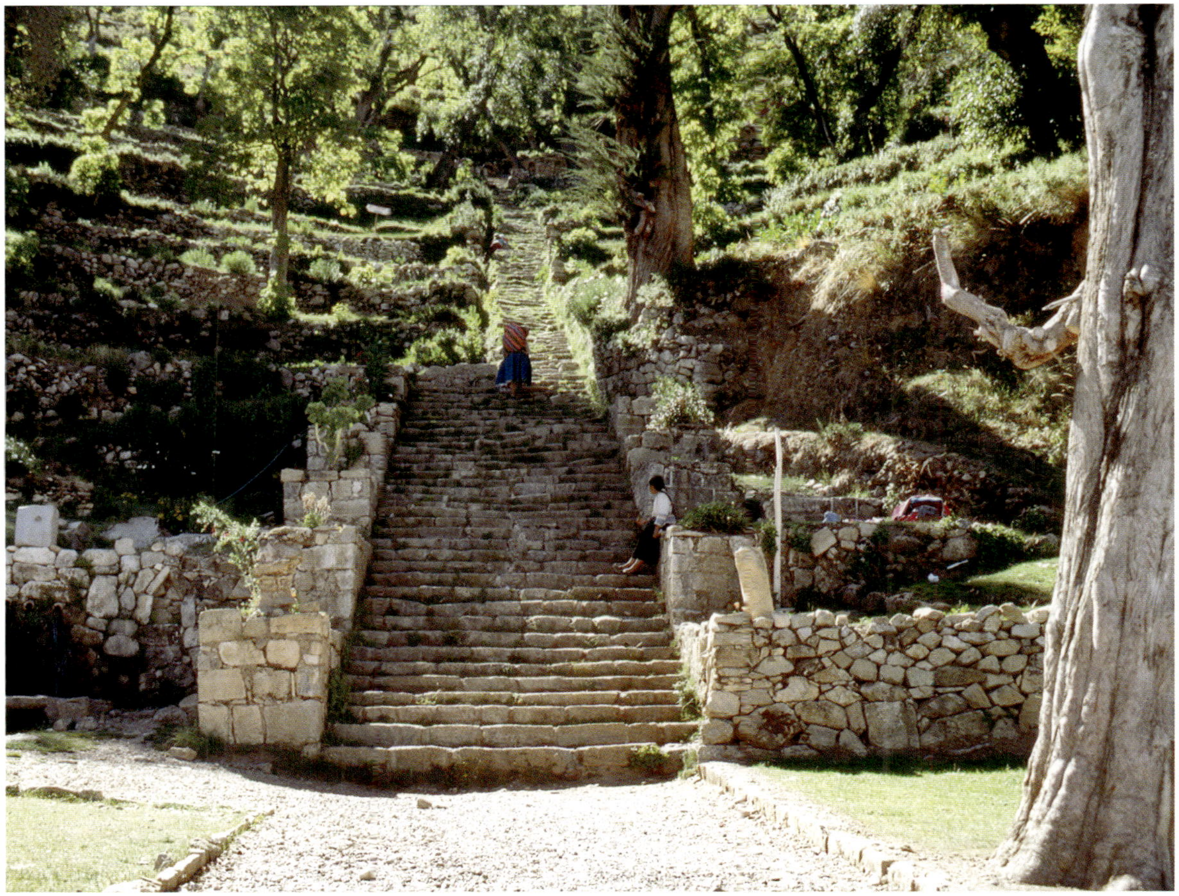

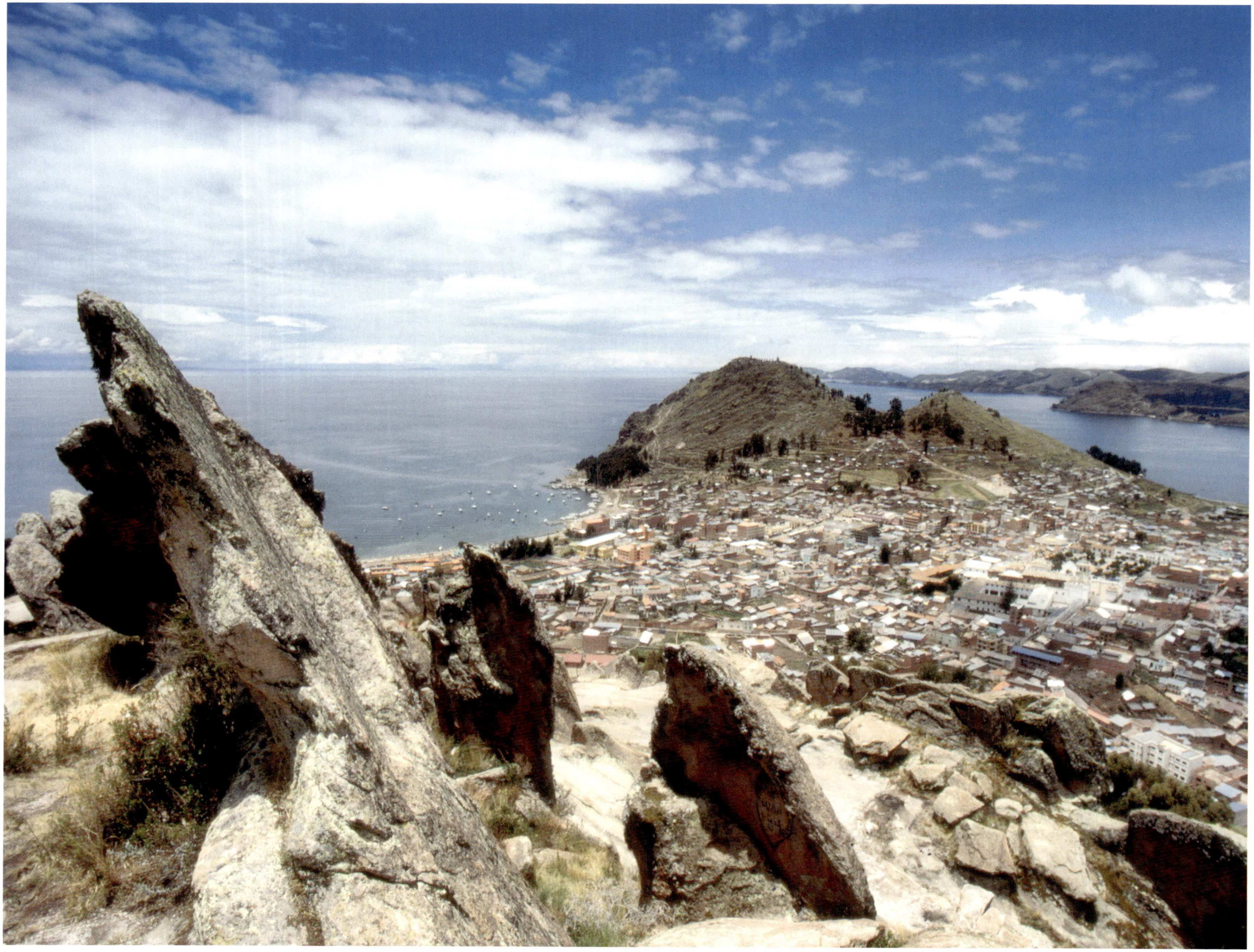

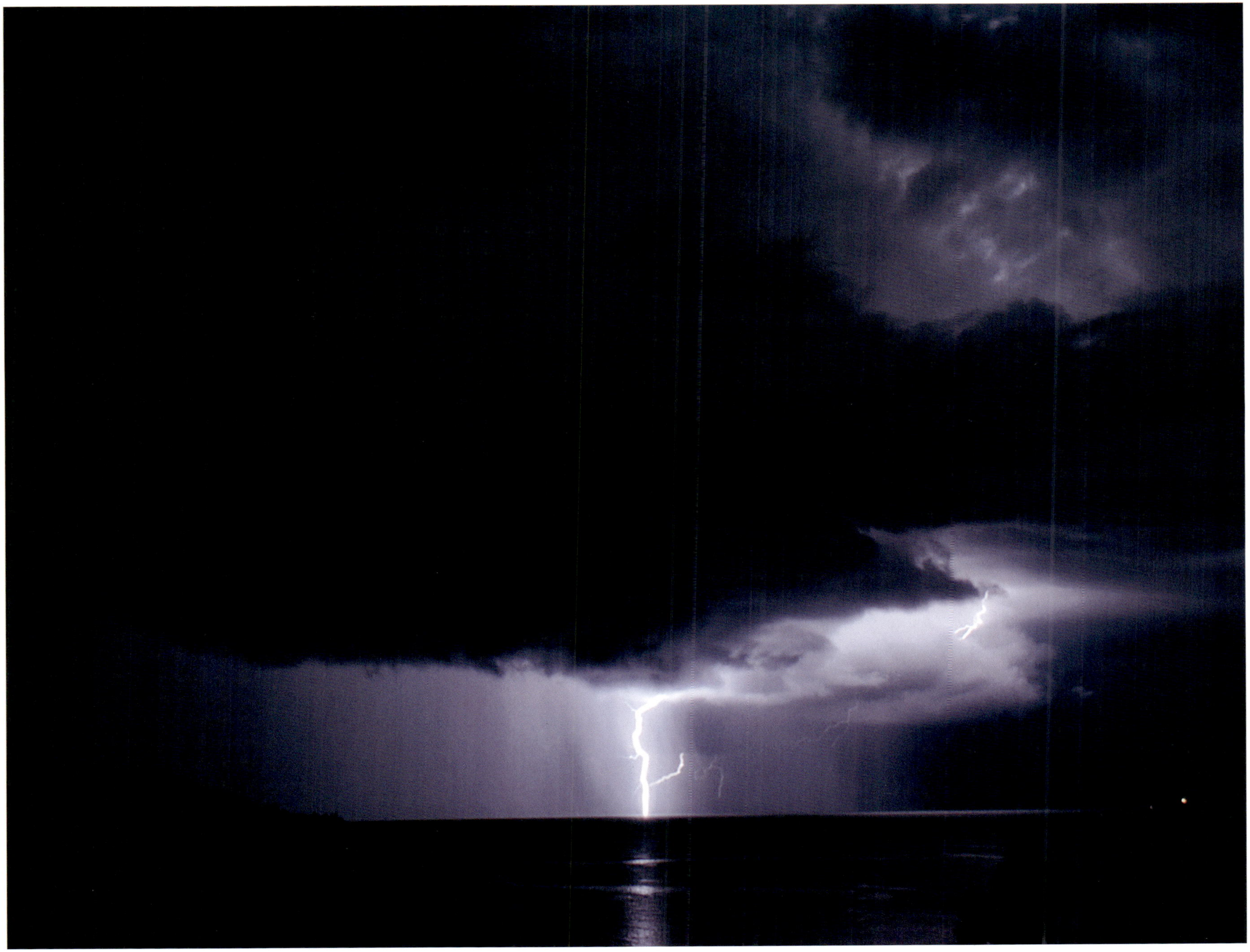

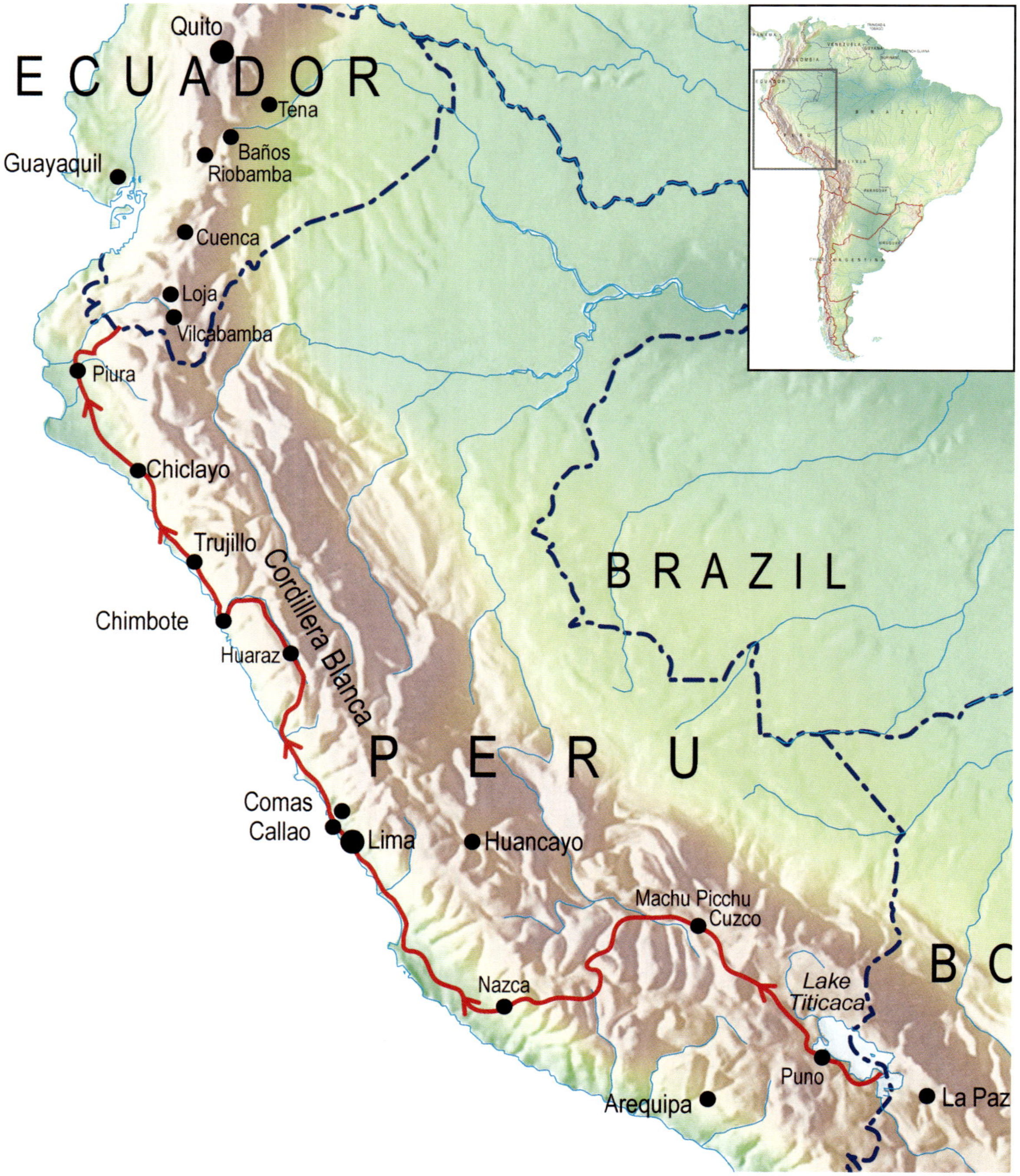

Puno on Lake Titicaca is the first stop in Peru. From there, the travel route leads to Cuzco and takes a round trip through the Valle Sagrado. The journey then leads to Aguas Calientes and the Inca site of Machu Picchu by train. From Cuzco, the route continues on through the mountains to Nazca, along the coastal road through Lima, and then again up into the mountains and to Huaráz. Along the Cordillera Blanca, the route proceeds again towards the coast, over Trujillo through the desert, in the mountains to Piura, and then towards the border to Ecuador.

PERU
IN THE INCA EMPIRE

OF ANCIENT PEOPLES

The border formalities are taken care of – I hardly need to mention it – in the rain. However, the landscape around Lake Titicaca makes up for the weather; everything glistens in a lush green. We quickly reach Puno on the high plateau of Collao. Finding appropriate accommodation, above all for the motorbikes, turns out to be far from easy. In a guesthouse, they want to move a sofa in the entrance area to the side so that we can park the bikes in front of the reception desk. This means, however, that all the guests would have to climb over the seats in order to get to their rooms. Although the owner would gladly rent us a room, the circumstances seem less than practical to me. Next door, they try to persuade us to push the bikes into a courtyard entrance just 70 cm wide, but even if all luggage was removed, we would still have to take off the handlebars. This also seems to make little sense. In another guesthouse, I ask about the price of a room and the manager answers: "That depends on how much you want to pay." I look rather puzzled; did I hear correctly? He explains that he lets his guests decide what the room is worth to them. An interesting approach, I have to admit. At the same time, it smells completely damp and mouldy, so I refuse his offer. Finally, we find a place and it even has a garage. We help to clear it out, shove old advertising billboards and a refrigerated counter to the side, stack boxes with tiles and stones and numerous bags of rubbish on top of each other, put a car onto the street and shove our motorbikes inside with the car parked behind them. The next days we go by foot.

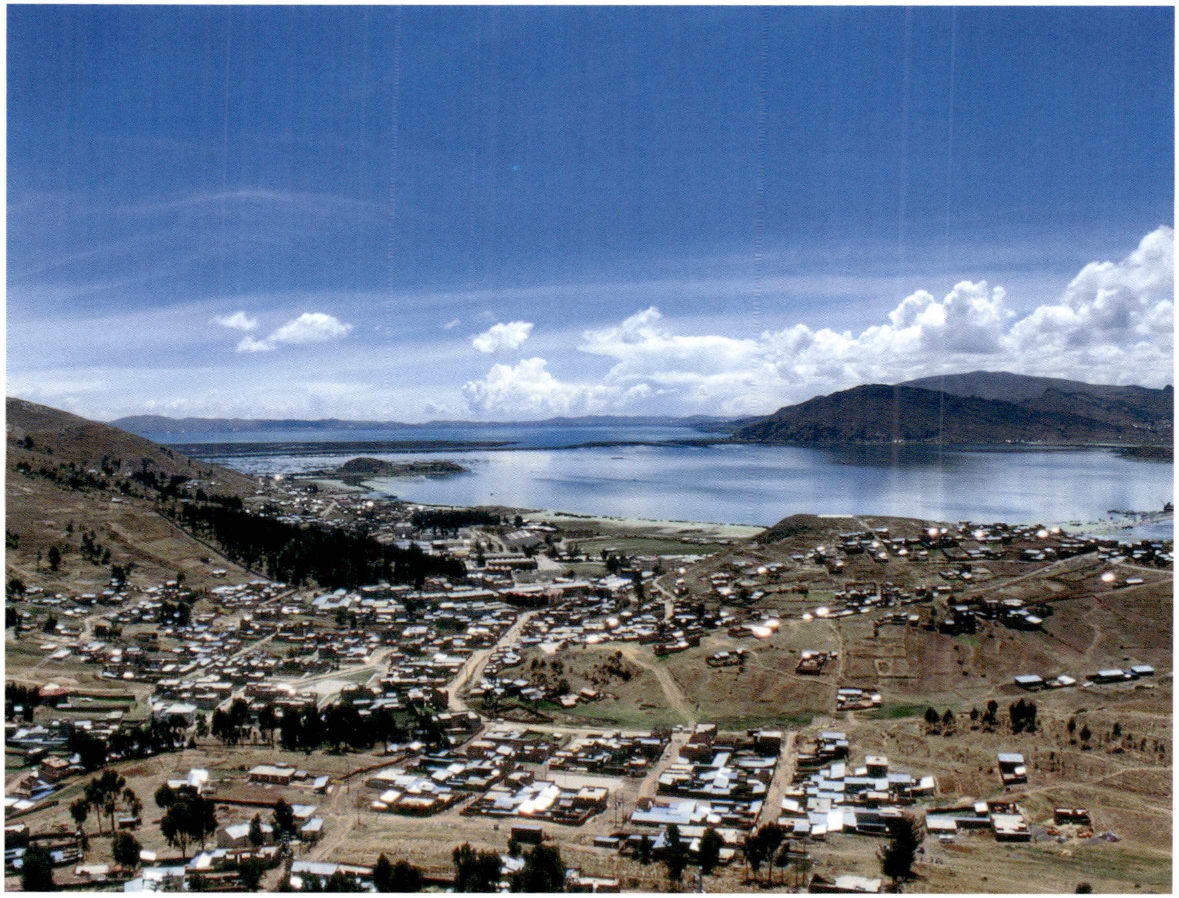

Right: Puno on the shore of Lake Titicaca

In the bay of Puno, the descendants of the Uru live on around 40 artificial islands made of totora reeds on Lake Titicaca. Building an island from this type of rushes takes about 6 months. On a bottom layer that consists of several square metres of roots, the so-called kili, the rushes are bound together into dense bundles and layered one over another until the surface reaches a draught of nearly 1 m. It is then stable enough to be built on. Every 6 months, the islands are heaped with new rushes because the material rots away over time. The Uru also produce their stable boats from totora. In addition, the freshly peeled stalks of the plant and the sweet white cores are a nutritious supplement to fish, poultry and guinea pig meat. The Uru people live in closely-knit social family structures, where the eldest, the head of the family, is an undisputed authority. We go over to the islands and visit a family. With my hiking boots, I sink into the soft surface with every step, an unfamiliar feeling. The inhabitants walk barefoot throughout the year, and many

Page 129 top: Stove

Page 129 bottom: Family life on a swimming island

Page 128: Swimming island of the Uru on Lake Titicaca

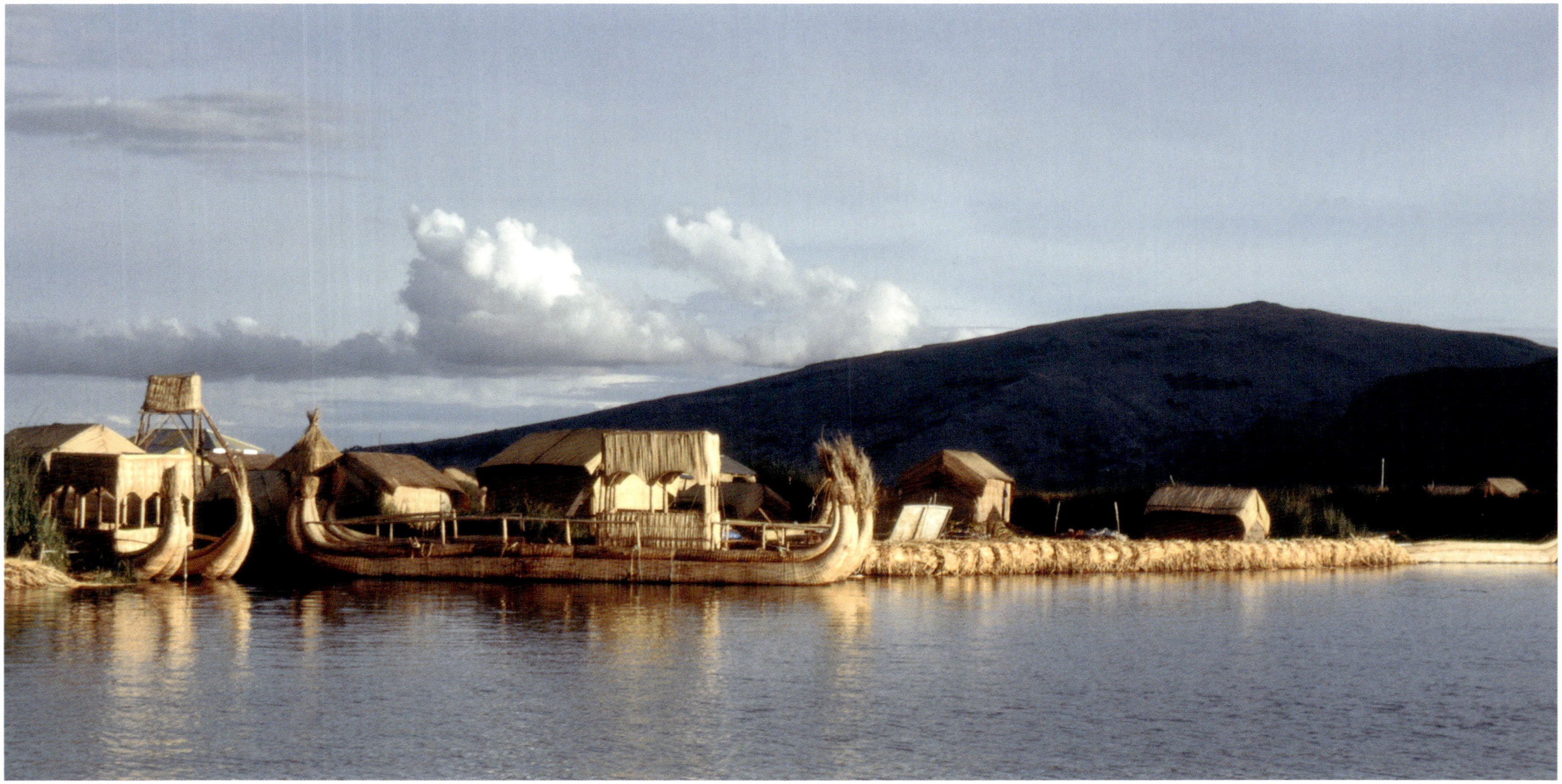

of the elderly have chronic joint pain. They speak Aymará among each other; however, a young girl perplexes me as she sings songs in several languages including Japanese, and apparently correctly because the Japanese woman in our group is utterly enraptured and sings along. I think I also hear "Alle meine Entchen", a German song for children. She has learned the melodies and texts from the tourists who come to the island daily.

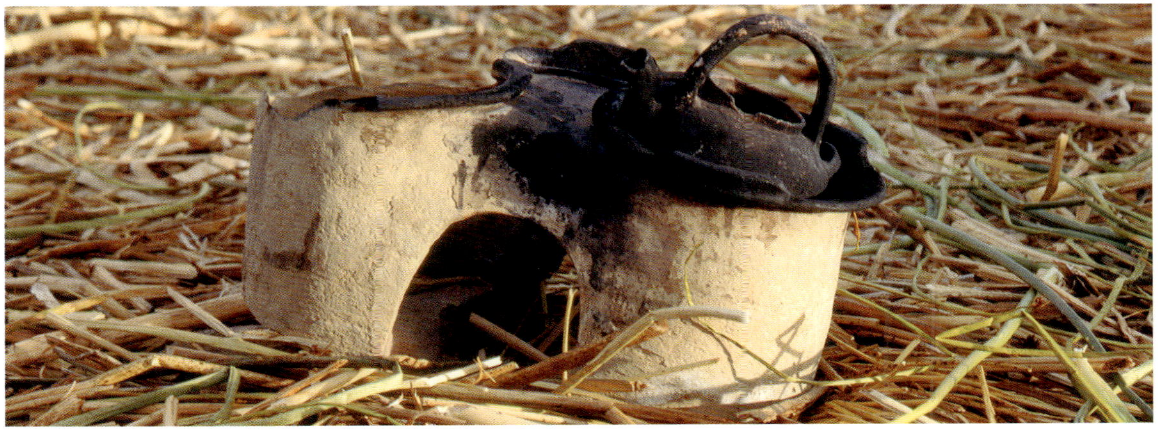

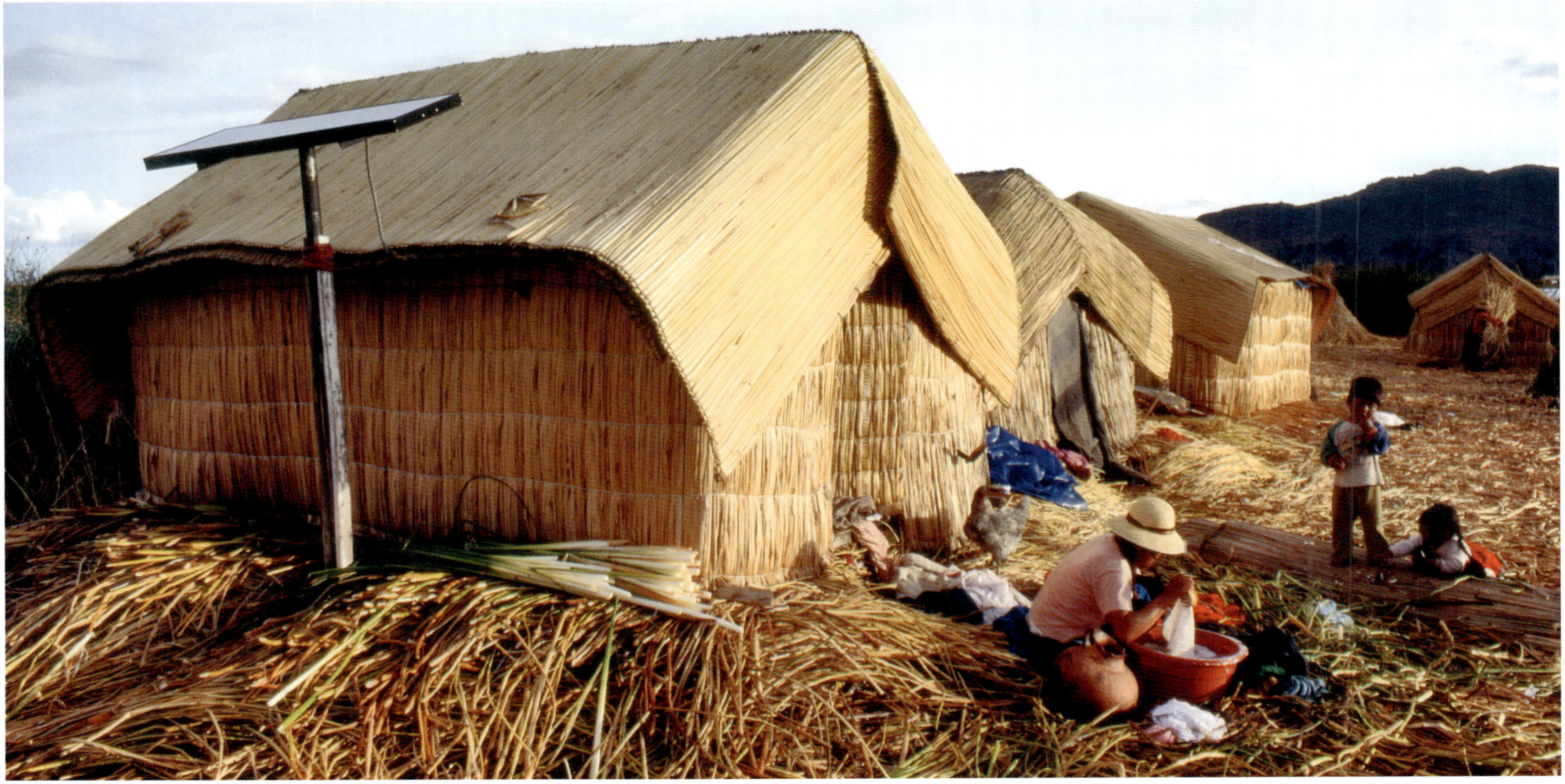

The better quality of fuel in Peru, between 80 and 90 octane, makes our bikes happy. While we encountered almost no motorbikes or mopeds in Bolivia, bicycle and motorbike taxis belong to the normal street scene in many of Peru's small cities. Before we know it, we are in the middle of the turmoil. Many call out a couple of questions to us and then race off with their passengers, while we manoeuvre our big machines through the heavy traffic. This is often easier said than done. All roads lead to Cusco, where constant chaos reigns the roads. It's not a problem when a driver stands at the traffic light in the left lane and wants to turn right – this only means that the minibus in the middle lane goes to the left and the taxi in the right turning lane drives straight ahead. With a bit of luck, 3 to 4 vehicles get through the crossing at each phase of the traffic lights; the other vehicles are tangled up with each other like a ball of wool, more lanes are created and the oncoming traffic pushes forward in the same way.

Page 131: The police sees everything

Bottom: Transporting gas cylinders in Puno

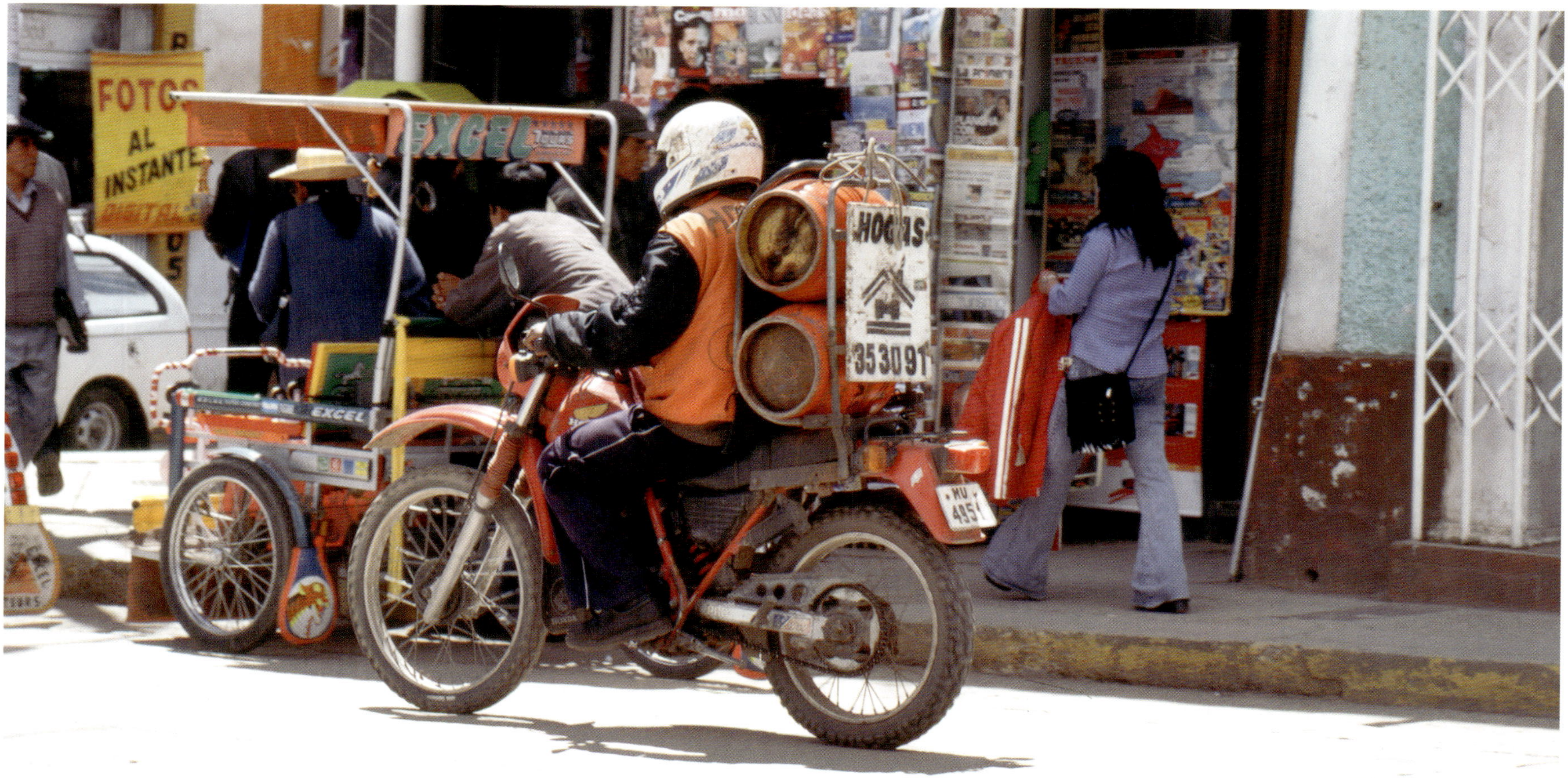

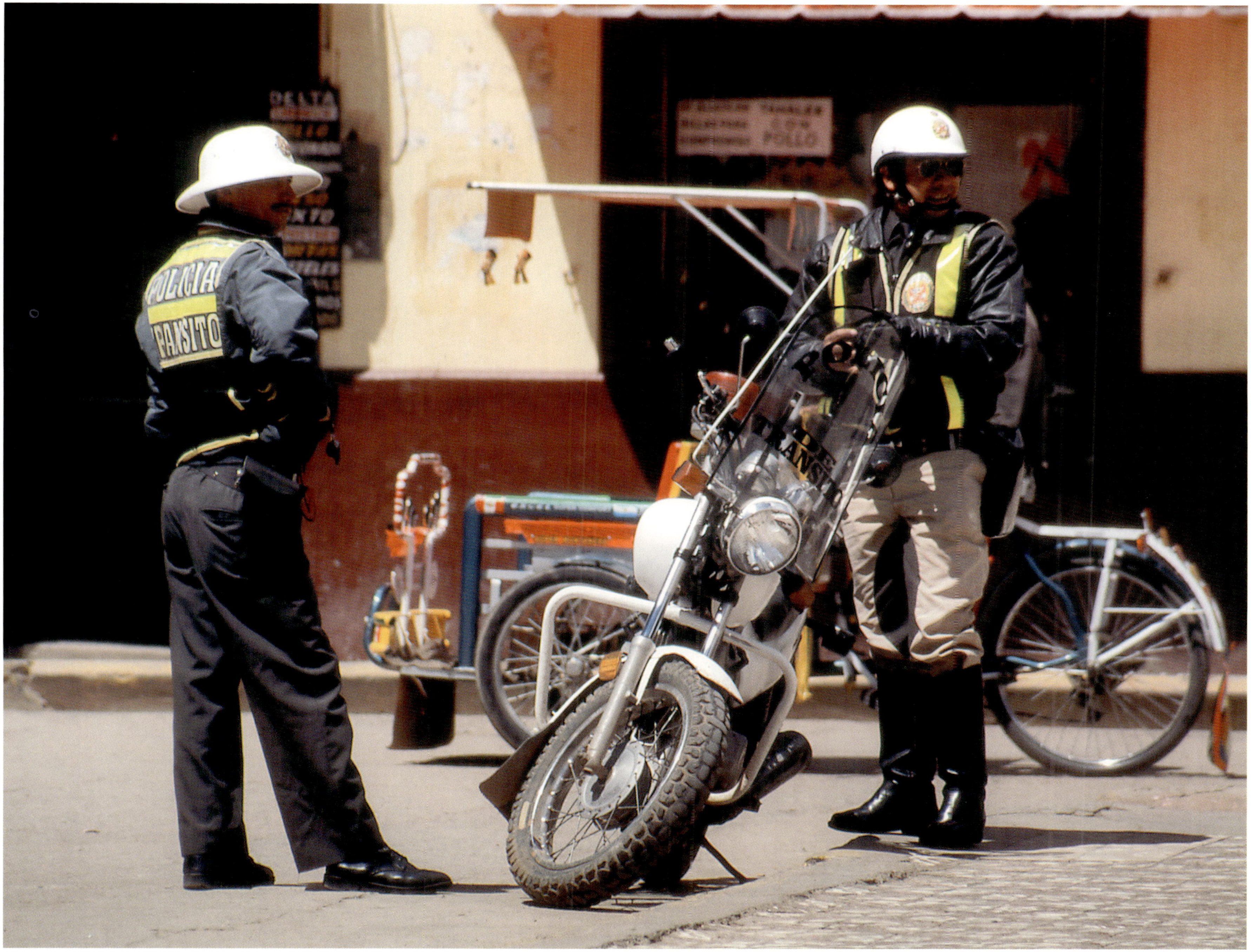
DELTA
POLICIA
POLLO

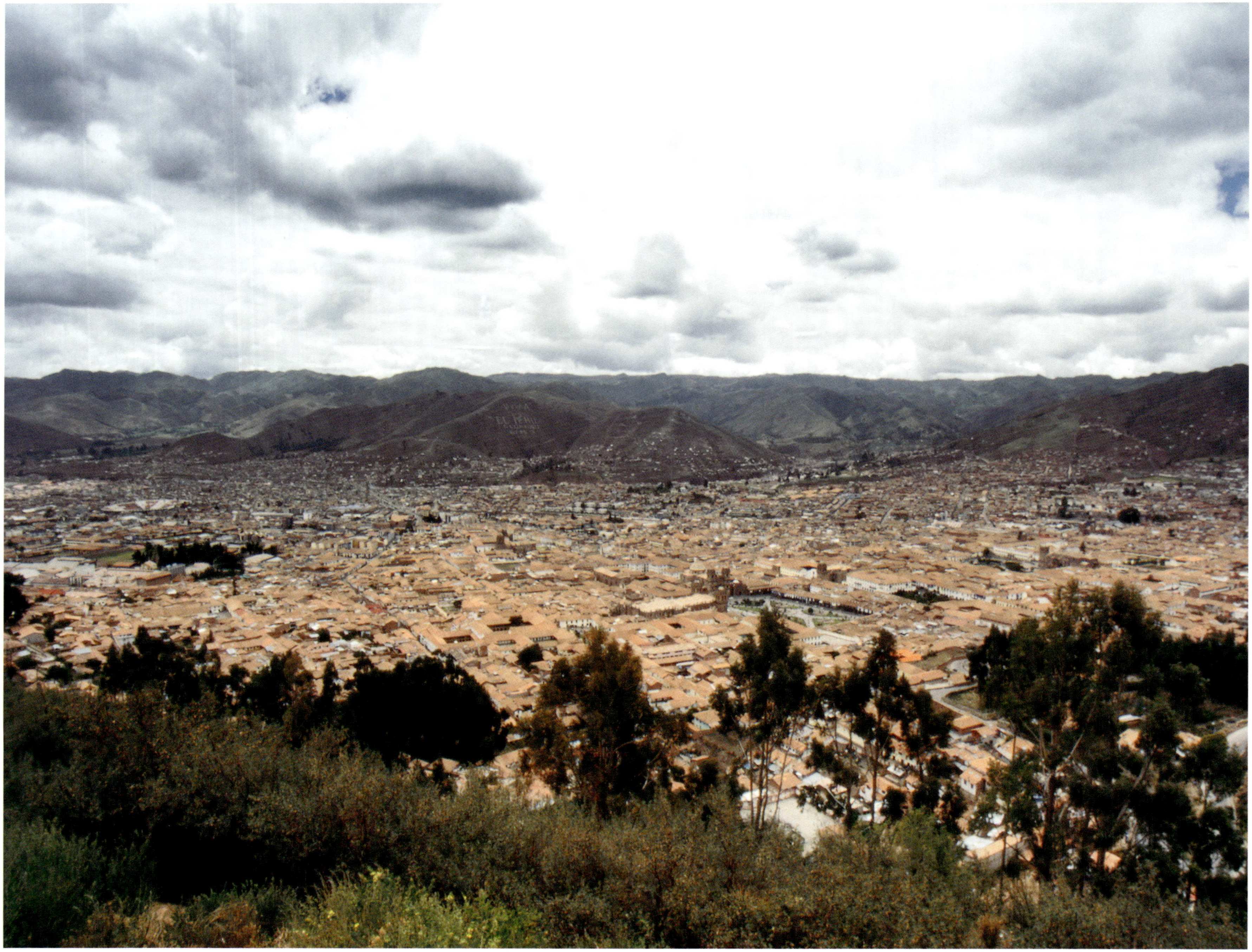

Page 132: Cuzco, the centre of the Inca realm

Bottom: The former Sun Temple in Cuzco

According to legends, it was in the "lowlands", as the name of the city is translated from the Quechua, where Manco Capac, the first Inca and son of the creator Viracocha, along with his sister or wife Mama Ocllo Huaca sunk his golden rod into the earth. Viracocha had told him to settle down where his rod remained in the ground and rule the people with justice, reason, forbearance and clemency. The cradle of Inca power developed in Cusco. Sinchi Manco Capac is the ancestor of the Inca. Every succeeding ruler followed his policy, left his relatives, gave up his right of succession, and built a new royal dwelling, a so-called cancha, to establish his own lordship. As a symbol of their political power, they wore the mascapaicha, a scarlet headband, around their temples. They were consecrated as an Intip Churin, as a son of the sun, by a high priest. In this way, they became an intermediary between the gods and the people. Between the late 14th and 15th century, the Inca created an empire that stretched over an area of more than 1

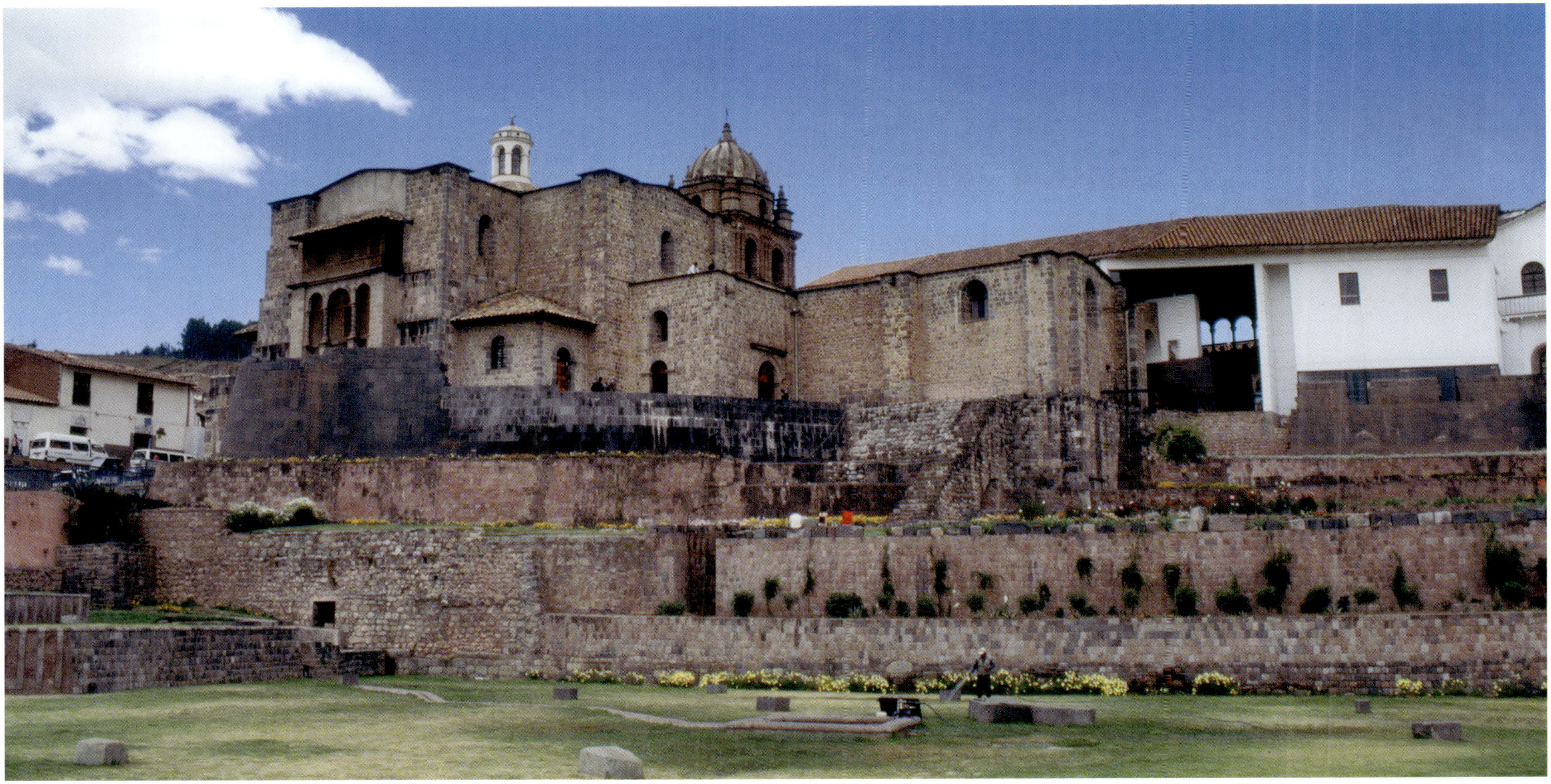

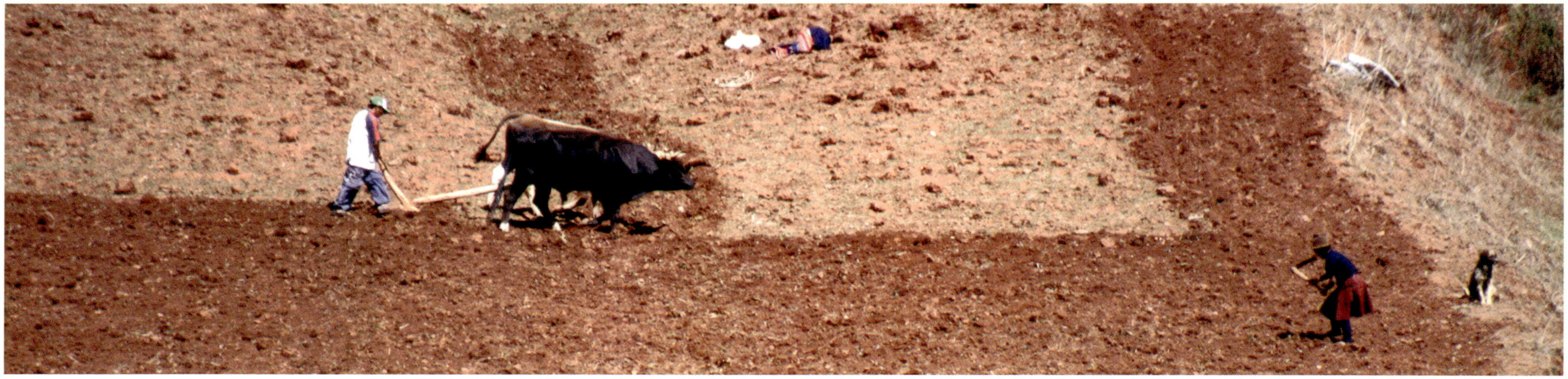

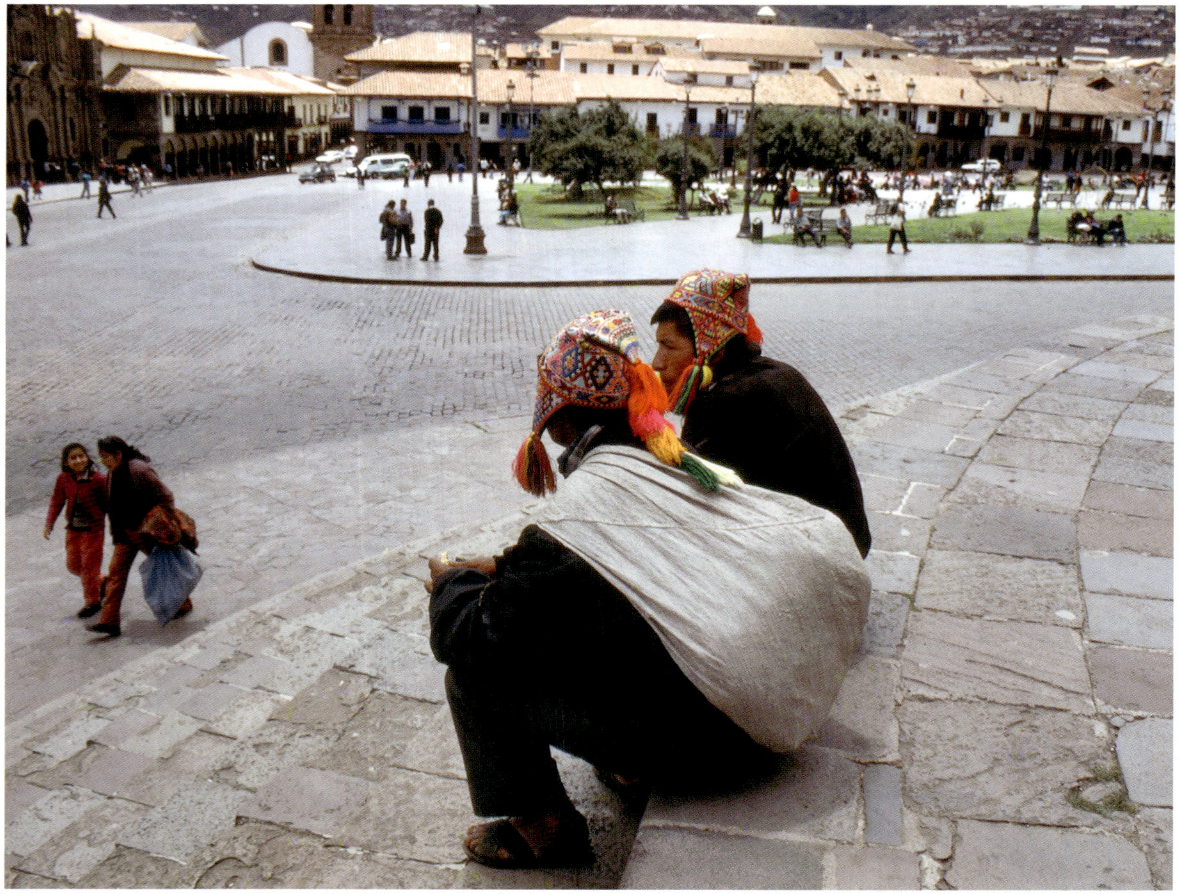

million km^2, from Quito in modern Ecuador to Curico in the south, where the region of the Araucanians, the original inhabitants of Patagonia, began. Many millions of people from various tribes were among the subjects during the heyday of the supremacy of the Inca Empire.

A trip through the Valle Sagrado de los Incas brings us to various impressive structures: Moray, Pisac, Saqsaywaman, Q'Enqo, Puca Pucara and Tambomachay. These are religious sites at which ceremonies were conducted and where the sun, moon, stars, water and light were worshiped. In Moray, the Inca constructed round terraces presumably as agricultural test areas. With the funnel-shaped stepped style of construction, the rays of the sun, and thus the differences in temperature of many degrees between the uppermost and lowermost levels, were

Top: Traditional farming in the Valle Sagrado

Left: Inhabitants of the Andes on the Plaza de Armas in Cuzco

Page 135: Inca site Moray

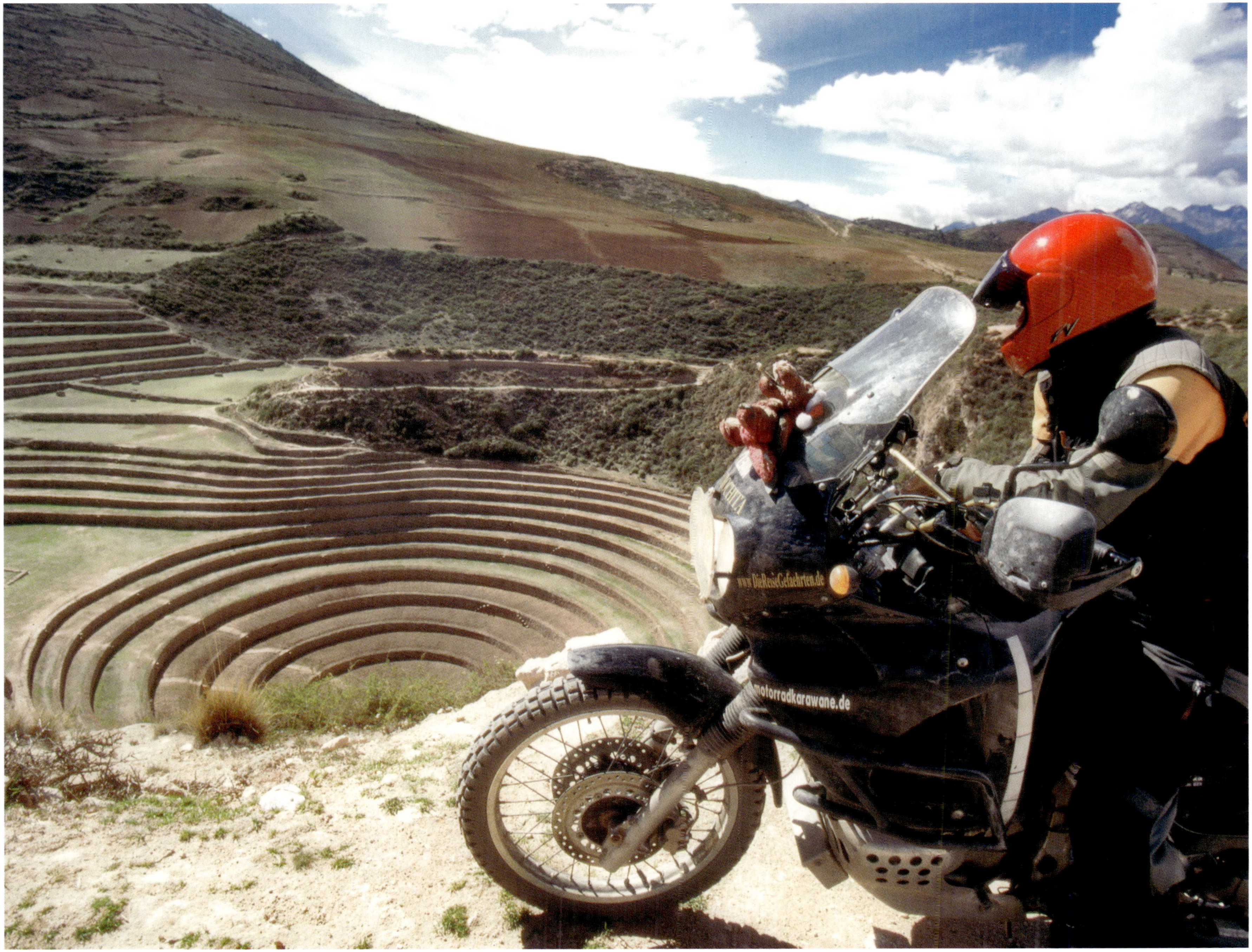
www.DieReiseGefaehrten.de
motorradkarawane.de

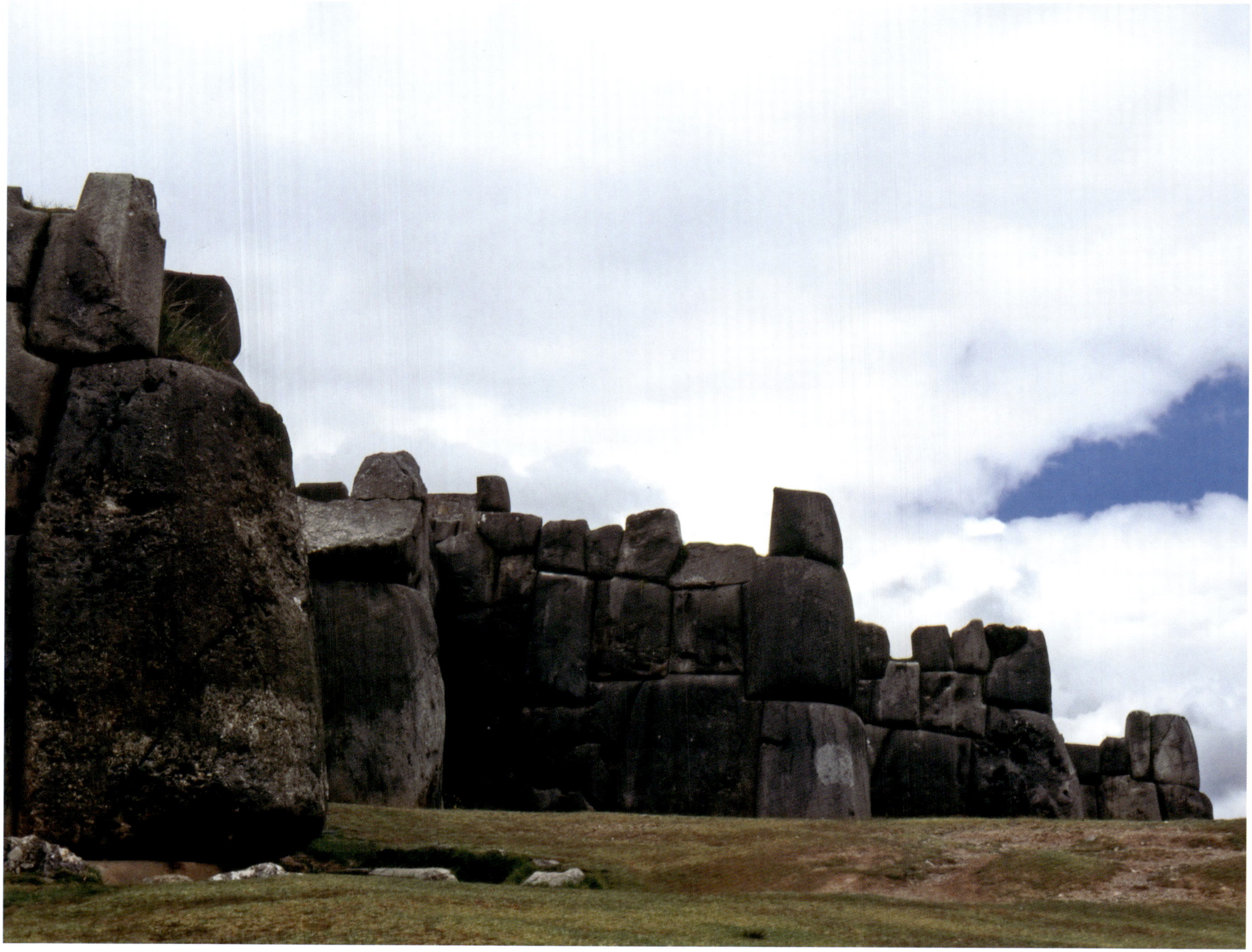

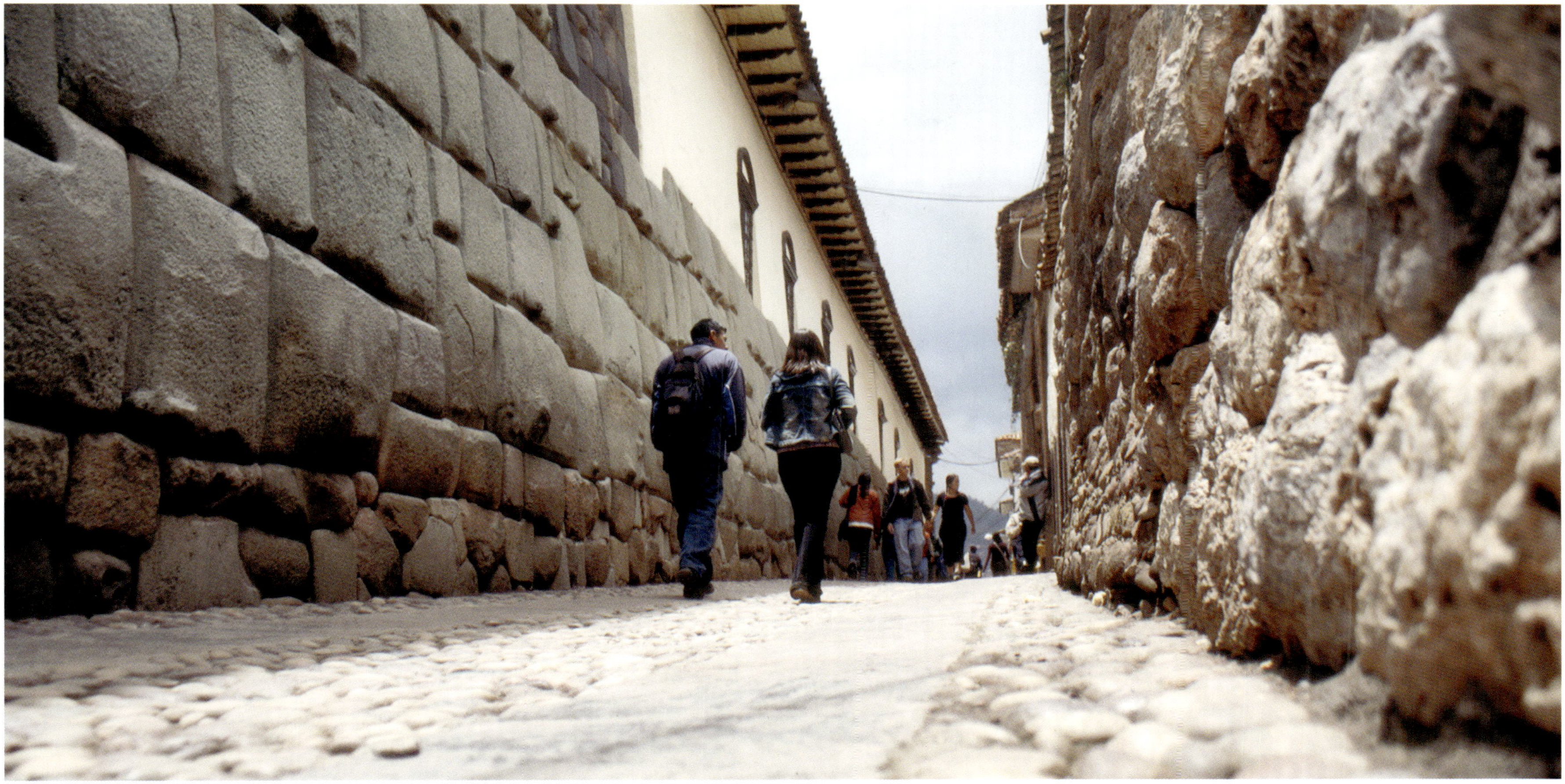

exploited. The fortress of Saqsaywaman, located 2 km outside of Cusco, served the Inca rulers as a place to which they could retreat in times of danger and it was virtually impregnable with three stone walls of 9, 10 and 5 m in height and nearly 3 km in length. Huge tall stones where transported to the site from stone quarries, with some of the monoliths purported to weigh up to 200 t. According to a specific system, the stones were cut, shaped and interlaced with each other without mortar or spackle until they fit exactly next to and over each other. It is hardly possible to slide a piece of paper between the joints, and I am not the first person who has tried to do so. It is unimaginable how it was possible to move these boulders and to work them in such a delicate manner.

Top: Calle Hatun Rumiyoc in Cuzco

Right: Mural detail, Inca architecture

Page 136: Sacsaywaman, the Inca fortress at Cuzco

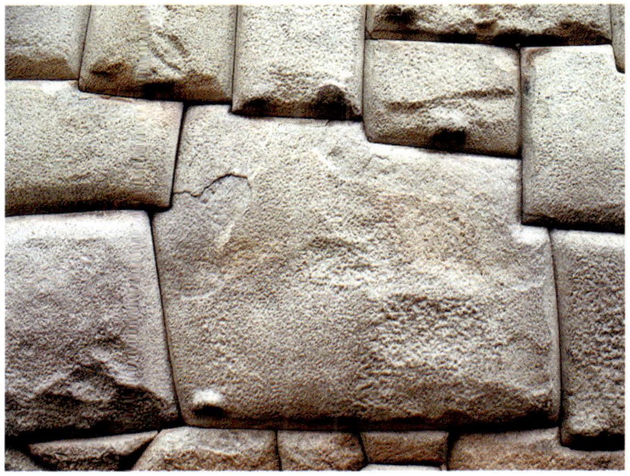

We spend Christmas in Machu Picchu, the "old peak". At an ungodly hour, we chug away from Cusco by train. During the first kilometres, the train snakes out of the city and up into the mountains on a zigzag course. There is hardly a metre of space between the waggons and the façades of the houses, where people live in miserable conditions. The train staggers and groans, drives into a cul-de-sac where the driver changes the switch, continues the route backwards to the next setting-back track and then again forwards until he reaches a high plateau. From there, we travel through dense rainforest, and after a short stopover in Ollantambo, we finally reach Aguas Calientes in the Urubamba Valley after four hours. There, we find accommodation in a small hospedaje. Santa Claus has come to the village and mothers and fathers are queuing up with their children. The girls can choose between purple coloured plastic doll dishes and large dolls with long blond hair and a fair complexion. Are they supposed to correspond to the ideal image of the Peruvians, or is it simply a question of goods imported from abroad? The boys receive gifts of footballs or toy cars, which they pull through the alleyways on long cords. No one envies the other because they all have the same things in their hands.

How could it be otherwise – in the afternoon it rains, heavily. After all, Machu Picchu lies in the dense cloud forest, and it is the rainy season. It's only that it would

Right: City gate Huaca Puncu

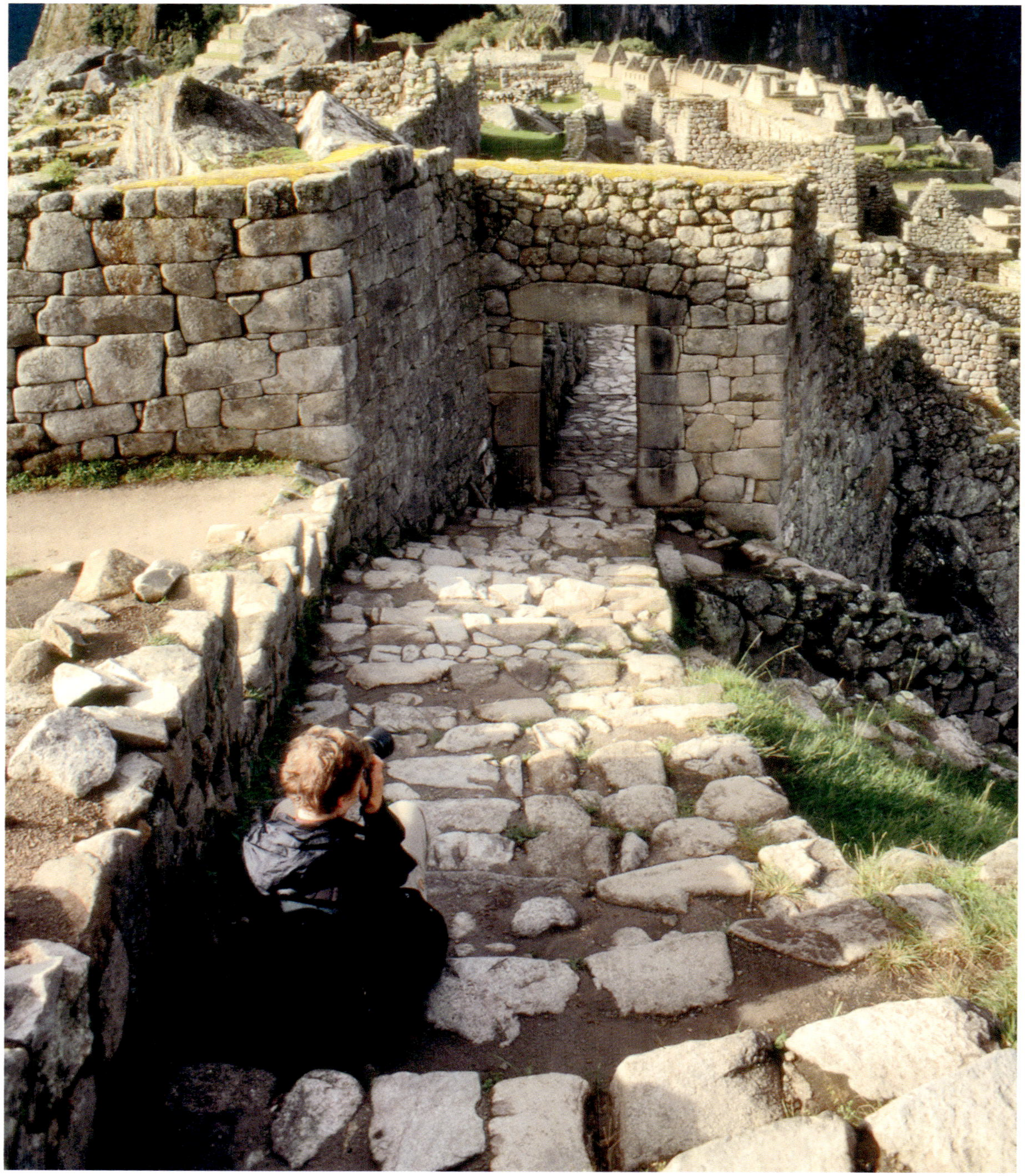

Page 139: Legendary Inca site Machu Picchu

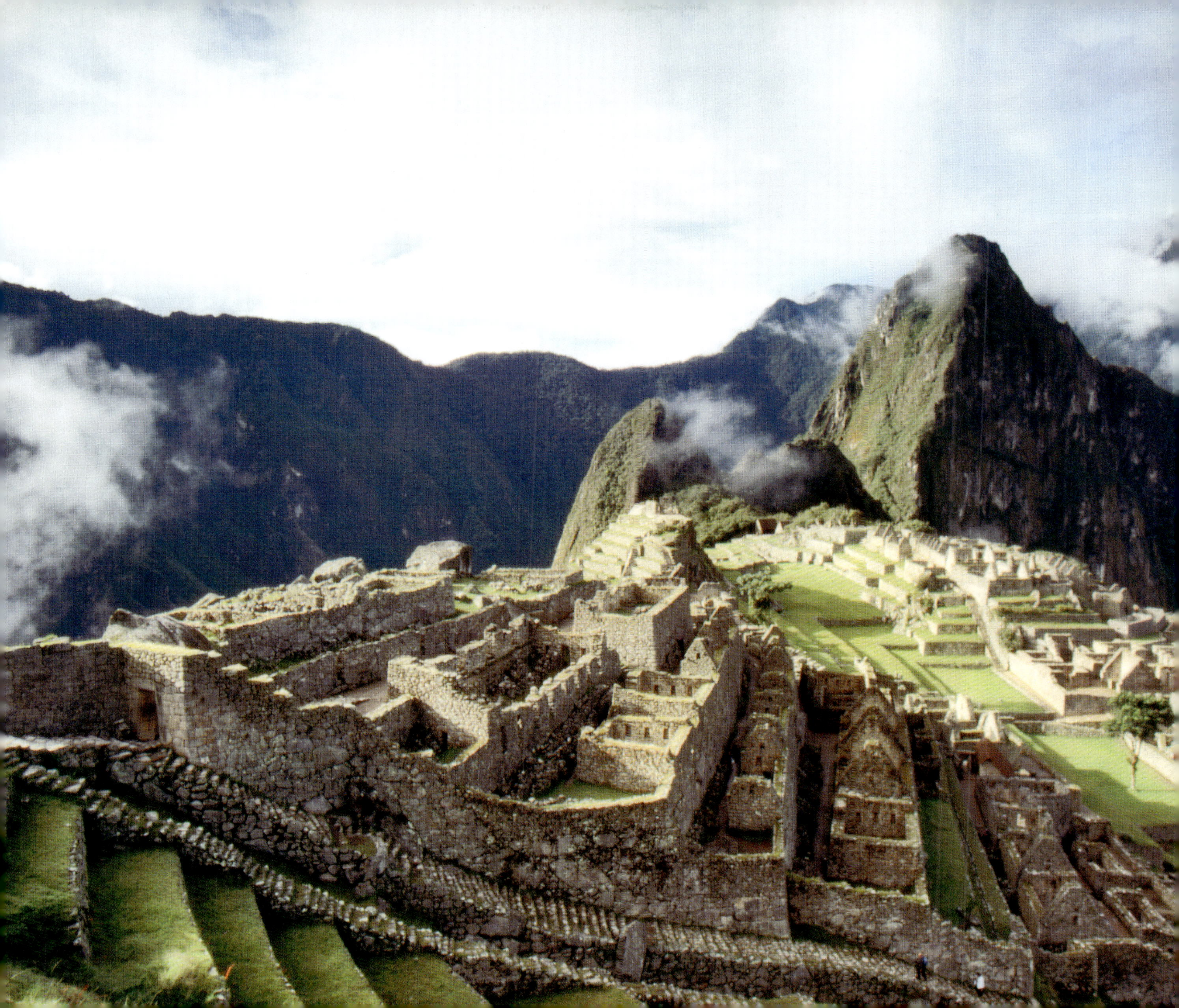

have been nice to see the Inca site when it was dry. Nonetheless, despite the showers, be they many or few, we are drawn to the holy site. We buy bus tickets and admission tickets. But we then learn that there are no more buses driving up to the entrance today. After a long discussion, we are refunded the price of the ticket at the bus station. The only possibility to still get to the Inca site today is a long steep ascent of 400 metres altitude. We have only just passed a bridge when a bus comes thundering up behind us. Spontaneously, we stick out our thumbs and the bus comes to a halt! With a grin, the driver says that he has to drive up anyway to bring down the day guests. At this time of day, he is not allowed to take any tourists up to the top anymore, but he would make an exception for us. We reach an agreement, a nice Christmas bonus, which I grant him and his family from my heart. Before one of the last curves, he lets us out and shows us a trail that leads us to the top. Mission accomplished. The next hurdle awaits us at the entrance, where we learn that the compound will close in one hour. This means that we don't have much time.

Not all of the secrets surrounding Machu Picchu will ever be lifted. Above all the question of the circumstances under which the Inca gave up this site and why it was neglected for many centuries. There are more than 200 buildings on the site, agricultural terraces with irrigation canals, temples, palaces and squares that are important from

Bottom: Today's inhabitants, Machu Picchu

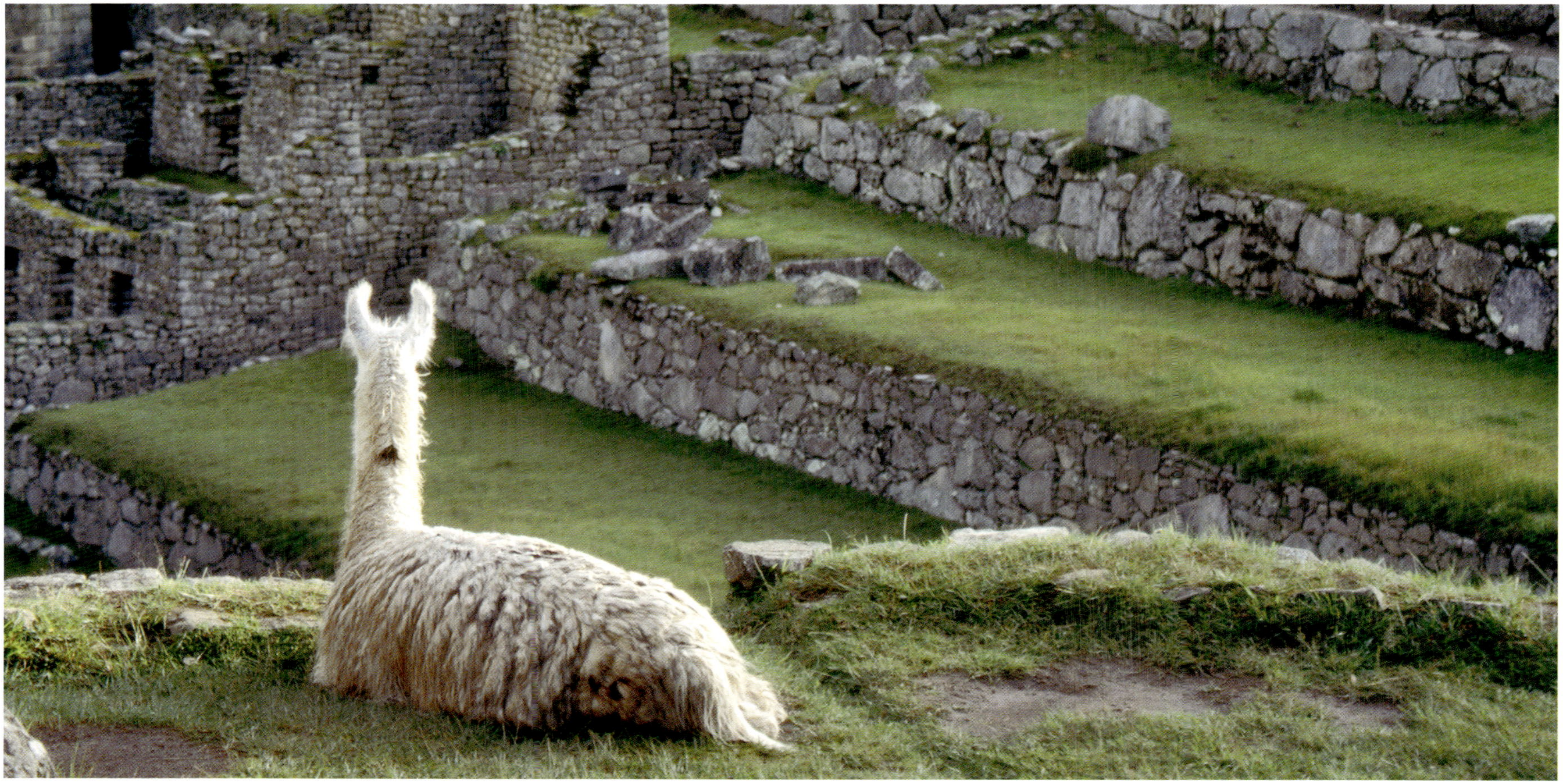

an astronomical perspective because they were aligned with the sun and the moon. The Inca were able to exist at this location in a politically, culturally and economically autonomous manner. On a plateau situated at a hight of 2,470 m, three sides of the site fall off steeply over craggy rocks and into the river valley of the Urubamba. The fourth side was easy to overlook and guard, and narrow paths lead to a city gate made of thick stone, the Huaca Puncu. We follow the steep steps along the city wall, walk past the city gate to the Puesto de Vigilencia, and something wonderful happens. The sky opens up, the fog lifts, and the sun casts a fantastic light on Machu Picchu. I have already seen so many pictures, but as I stand here myself looking down on the ruins, the scene is so overwhelming that it takes my breath away. We are almost alone at this hour and a mystical atmosphere unfolds. I mentally immerse myself in the holy site at which the Inca studied the constellations of the stars and worshiped their gods. In the atmospheric light of the setting sun, a peaceful stillness spreads.

Axel is thrown back into hard reality the next morning as he wants to climb Huayna Picchu, the "young peak", which rises majestically in the background of the Inca site. I don't go with him because for the last couple of days, I have been a little short of breath to go scrambling around at this hight. After a short time, he meets a couple that has been on the way for an hour and is not exactly well equipped for this climbing tour. They nonetheless want to climb up to the peak and ask Axel if he will accompany them. Narrow treads of high steps lead the way almost vertically upwards – a fitness challenge. Behind a ruin, the trek becomes even more demanding. On narrow stairs, they squeeze against the rock face and climb over ladders where the abyss lurks on both sides – one misstep means a certain plunge into the deep. On all fours, they climb through a tunnel and ascend through a crevice to reach the trail again. When they finally arrive at the top, the two are so exhausted that they cannot go another step. Axel starts his way back to get help. He follows the only arrow, which however has nothing else written on it, believing that it indicates the way back. Instead, it leads down the other side of the mountain into the valley and back up again. By the time he notices this detour, it is too late to turn back. The path takes him to the "Door of the Moon", a route that he would not have taken otherwise. He hurries forwards, rather exhausting himself, bearing in mind all the time that the two up on the peak are waiting and that he is already late to meet me to go on a guided tour. Shortly before the hut where everyone climbing the Huayna Picchu has to register, he meets the two again. Another hiker had brought them down with him. All's well that ends well. Only Axel's legs doesn't want to obey him any more. Exhausted, he sits down on a stone at the Sacred Rock Complex. We do indeed go on the official sightseeing tour of the site, but Axel drags himself from one ruin to the next as the last in the group. He only hears half of the guide's explanations although he tells us interesting stories about a time when there was vibrant life here. The area is still populated now, but by hundreds of visitors from around the world. Just as the daily rain begins, we reach the train back to Cusco in Agua Calientes.

Over a cup of coco tea one afternoon, our host Franco gives me in-depth information about the meaning of the condor, which had a special religious significance at the time of the Inca and which is still important for the inhabitants of the Andes. The condor is worshipped as a divine creature, and a temple dedicated to it was erected in Machu Picchu. On its wings, the condor brings the souls of the deceased from the earth to the Sun God in the afterworld. In the small mountain village of Catacambas on the Altiplano, the inhabitants celebrate a festival to honour the god condor once a year on the 28th of July. A small group of men treks into the mountains beforehand, sacrifices a horse and waits for a bird to approach, which is attracted by the carrion. They are not successful every year, but sometimes they get lucky. When the bird settles down, they surround it so that it is not able to spread its wings and fly away. They bind its legs together and transport it to the village. It is then the focal point of the festival. To honour it, they hold a service and bring it sacrificial offerings. Then the men, who are already slightly drunk, begin a bullfight, a "type of sport" imported by the Spaniards, on the village square. The peak of the festival is the duel between the condor and the bull. For this, they tightly bind the bird, which has a red piece of cloth tied around it, onto the back of the bull. This is an ordeal for both of the animals and they both become aggressive. The bull bucks in order to evade the claws and painful bite of the vulture, and the bird with its enormous wings panics on the bucking back of the bull. This spectacle has a highly symbolic significance for the inhabitants of the Andes. For them,

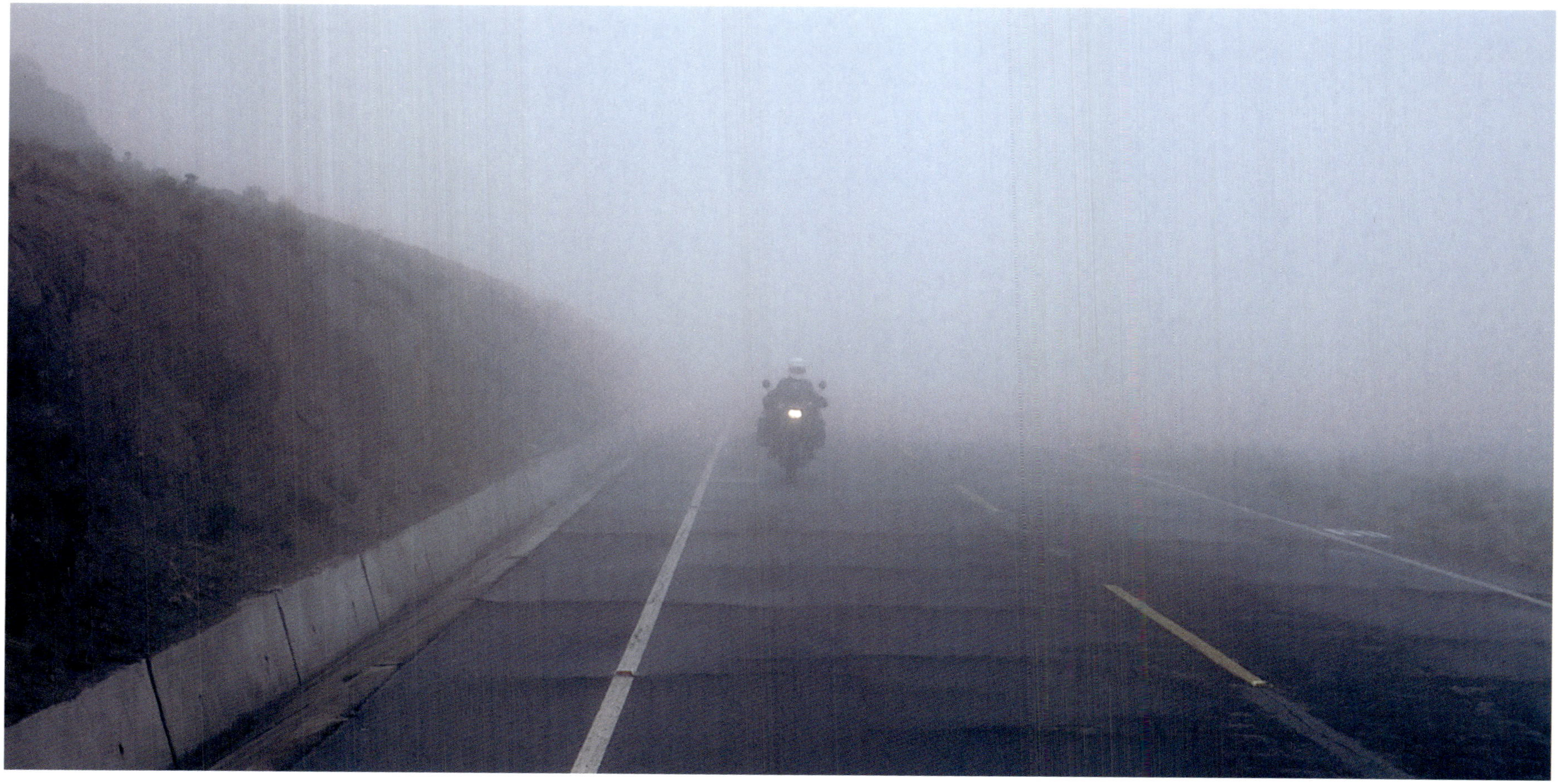

it symbolises the fight between the Inca and the Spanish conquistadores, who are represented by the bull. The battle is not fought out to the bitter death of one of the animals because the two of them are separated from each other before this can happen.However, the condor has managed to inflict serious injuries on the bull and thus symbolically triumphs over the Spaniards. The bird is taken on both wings and led through the village as a hero before it is brought to the edge of a cliff. There, it can spread its wings, use the thermal lift of the ascending wind, and fly back to freedom.

While Axel is packing the motorbikes in front of the hospedaje, his rain jacket and trousers are stolen from the side pockets of the rucksack on the tank. This is annoying because the weather shows no sign of improving. Although a security man was on patrol, someone took advantage of an unobserved moment. No one is prepared to do anything. An older woman points vaguely down the street and says that a small boy disappeared with the goods into one of the houses. We can't find out anything, but whoever has the things should at least be happy with them. The road leads in serpentines up and down the mountain between 4,000 m and 1,800 m. It is a pleasure to drive, but we are not covering much distance and we will no longer be able to reach the coast today. On the next mountain stage, we initially make good progress and travel along a river, but then the road once again climbs into a foggy area and the temperature sinks to 2°

Celsius. Solitude surrounds us, and in the distance, the snow-covered mountains of the Cordillera de Huanzo are outlined against a grey sky. We have to stop in order to transfer fuel into the Transalp because I ignored the petrol pump in the last village. A storm is brewing and a rough wind is gusting. A short time later, we can hardly see our hands in front of our faces. The road winds in narrow curves down the mountain. For 30 km, we run almost on vapours, anxious not to fall down the hillside at the next hairpin bend. The drive seems to last an interminably long time until we come to a deeper-lying region and are washed into the next village along with rain showers. At least there is a petrol station, even though it has no roofing. Because Axel left his waterproof things in Cusco, he is soaking wet in just a few seconds. We lean over the tank with the fuel hose so that the petrol is not thinned with too much water. The only street in Puquio that isn't paved is the through street, which has deep potholes that are filled with puddles and chips of stone. Torrents of water carrying clay and soil along with them search for a way towards the valley, and we slip on this surface like on soft soap. The whole village gives the impression of being a miserable grey-brown creature. Suddenly, a dog comes rushing from the side of the road and tries to bite the front tyre of the Transalp. In doing so, it hits the aluminium case and receives a hard knock in its ribs. Whining loudly, it limps to the side, writhing. I step on the gas in order to escape becoming involved in any kind of trouble and hope that the dog is not injured too badly. Curve after curve we advance through the fog. With chattering teeth I put the kilometres behind me. Suddenly the road plunges down. It is as if someone has drawn a curtain and opened up a new landscape. The rainy grey sky changes to brilliant blue, and the wet road with sparse vegetation turns into a bizarre desert landscape. The road descends to 500 m like on a slalom. The last 60 km to Nazca, I steer the motorbike listlessly, hardly able to hold myself upright. If I had to stop now, I would collapse under my own weight. In front of my eyes, traffic signs move like figures, hallucinations. Whirling sand sweeps over the surface. It is hot. But I am so chilled to the bone that the heat runs only slowly through my body. It is only much later on the campsite that I finally take off the thick motorbike clothing.

Page 142: Thick mist demands circumspection

Bottom: In the Cordillera de Huanzo, the mobile fuel station is needed

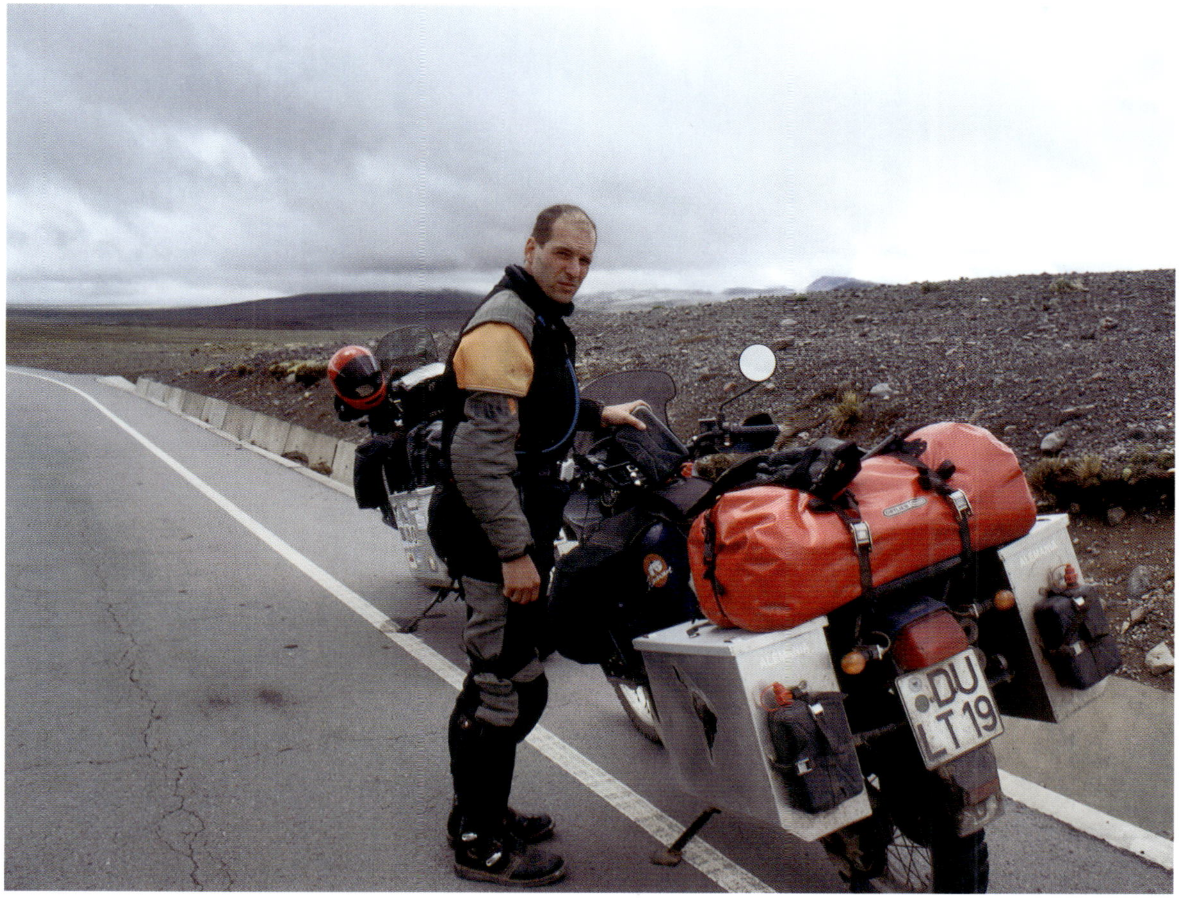

AMAZING LINES IN THE DESERT

From the ground they are hard to make out: hundreds of lines stretching over hills, some of them forming dead-straight paths. Others create geometric forms or animals and plants. In the 1920s, they were classified as the remains of old Inca pathways. It was only in 1941 that they were given more attention when the American professor Paul Kosok and the German Dr. Maria Reiche began with their scientific research. For Maria Reiche, this became a life's work, which she pursued until her death at the age of 95. Although it was initially assumed that the lines were created between 200 and 600 AD, researchers have since then come to the conclusion that they were made as early as the Paracas period between 800 BC and 200 AD. Based on Reiche's theory, the lines are considered to be the largest astronomical calendar in the world. In her opinion, there is an obvious connection between the figures and the constellations of stars, solstices and lunar cycles. With those lines, their creators passed on their knowledge about the constantly changing heavens and constellations to generations to follow and used them as an agricultural calendar with which to determine the times for sowing and harvesting. They thought it was possible to influence the gods responsible for the crops through sacrifices and worship. Many forms therefore have a ritual significance, above all those that refer to the element of water, the most important element required to survive in the desert. They immortalised their knowledge in a place where it would endure for a long time – in the pampas. This theory has not actually been proven, however, and neither has the much more bizarre theory that the lines are supposed to represent landing strips and signs from extraterrestrials. The geoglyphs were appointed a World Heritage Site by UNESCO in 1994. How were they created? The Nazca had to remove the uppermost layer of stone and cut grooves of about 30 cm depth into the earth. The ground contains gypsum, it is quite hard, and the whole area lies deep in a valley of the Andes over which the north-south wind is blowing – this is why hardly any sand or stones have become lodged in the grooves and they have thus remained in existence until today. The people build underground water canals to bring the water from the Andes mountain chain to the sea. Spiral-shaped "breathing holes" keep the water pure. The aqueducts are still used by the inhabitants today to irrigate their fields and to secure their water supply.

It is only possible to recognise the message in the sand on a sight-seeing flight over the desert. Axel overcomes his fear of flying and boards a Cessna with me. Before we take off, the pilot shows us a map to explain the series of figures over which he will fly. He encourages everyone to take pictures the minute he pulls the steering to the side and heads toward the lines. "Condor on the left side, condor on the left side – now!" Click. "Monkey on the right side – now!" Click again. This way, we get condors, hummingbirds, apes/monkeys, spirals, plants and geometric planes in front of our lenses and are thrilled, even when our stomachs flip with each turnaround. This flight is not for the faint-hearted. A young woman in the co-pilot seat doesn't take a single photo but instead holds a bag in front of her mouth. Back on the ground, we first of all jump into the pool at the campsite to settle our stomachs before having breakfast.

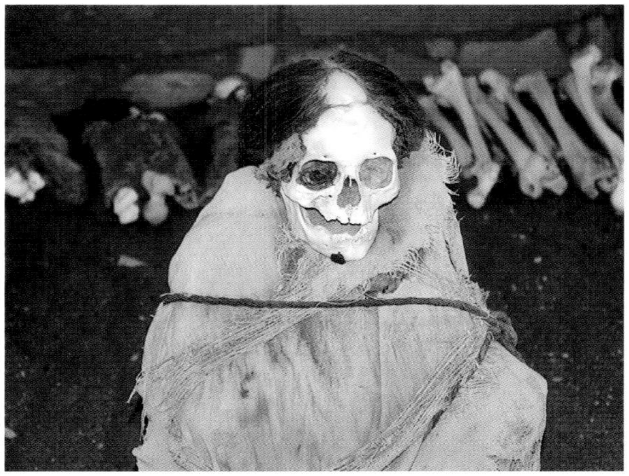

Shortly before sunset, we drive out on a desolate sand track to the Nazca graveyard, the Cementerio de Chauchilla. Far and wide, there is not a person to be seen. I feel a bit queasy out here. As we approach the first open grave, I flinch: a white skull is "looking" back at me, the pate covered with hair. It is crouched on the ground and the mummified body is wrapped in clothes, as if it is just taking a short rest. In other graves, there are feather ornaments, bones and burial objects next to the skeletons. Everywhere, waking eyes seem to be observing us, as if they want to say that we should go away now so that their peace is no longer disturbed. We obey this silent request and search in the darkness for the right track to bring us back to the main road.

Left: At the cemetery Cementerio de Chauchilla, the dead are still very present.

Page 145: Nazca lines have the form of a Kolibri

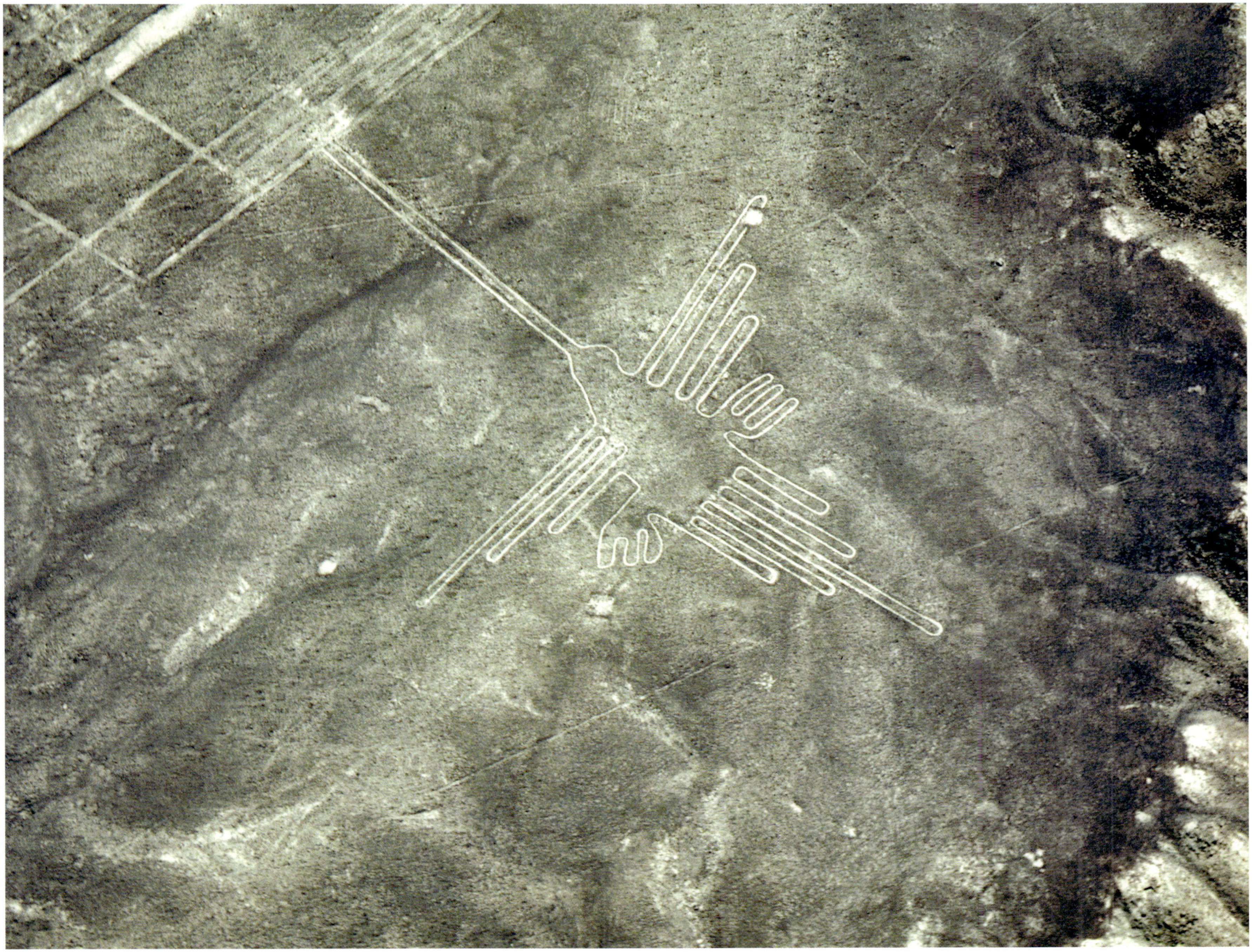

HOT AND COLD

A long way through the desert lies before us. A warm wind blows gusts of sand across the road. The silhouettes of the oncoming vehicles seem like a fata morgana, and the heat shimmers over the asphalt. Trucks thunder past us at high speed. Suddenly, a car peels away from the shadow of a truck, pulls onto our lane, comes swiftly closer, flashes its headlamps quickly two times and heads straight for us. I feel the draught of air on my sleeves as he shoots past us – not a hallucination, but instead very real! I am just able to pull the motorbike onto the sandy side of the road, a close call. Heart pounding, I breathe deeply and bring my racing pulse back to a normal rhythm while I drive on.

Driving via Ica and Pisco, we manage to reach Mala that day. A car mechanic from the capital, who is staying with his family in the guestroom next to us, gives us valuable tips for the continuation of our trip. We tell him that we want to go back up into the mountains, this time to the Cordillera Blanca, despite the cold and the rain. He telephones his friends, all enthusiastic bikers, to find out the most beautiful routes for us to take. When we say our goodbyes, his wife advises us not to stop at any lights or in traffic when we travel through Lima. Gangs of young men at crossings specialise in slicing open luggage with knives and if necessary, they will also go for the throats of drivers. We should always keep moving, but how is this supposed to work in traffic? At first, we are

Page 146: "windswept"

able to keep up well with the heavy traffic in the metropolis and orientate ourselves using the signs for the Panamericana Norte. This works until we reach a construction detour where the sign posting ends. We try to keep ourselves moving north but the layout of the streets takes us in a completely different direction, away from the wide through streets and into a district that doesn't seem to inspire much confidence. Shortly after, we are standing at a red light, worriedly on the lookout for gangs of youths about to pull out their knives. Nothing happens. It's only that we can't find anything out here, no sign to be seen. Finally, we stop at a street crossing in front of a police car. A man in uniform immediately gets out and says that we should leave the area as he cannot guarantee our safety here. If he can't, then who can? In a few words, he tells us which direction to take and then drives away. Somewhat by instinct, we find our way back to the main street and are relieved to see that there are once again signs for the Panamericana.

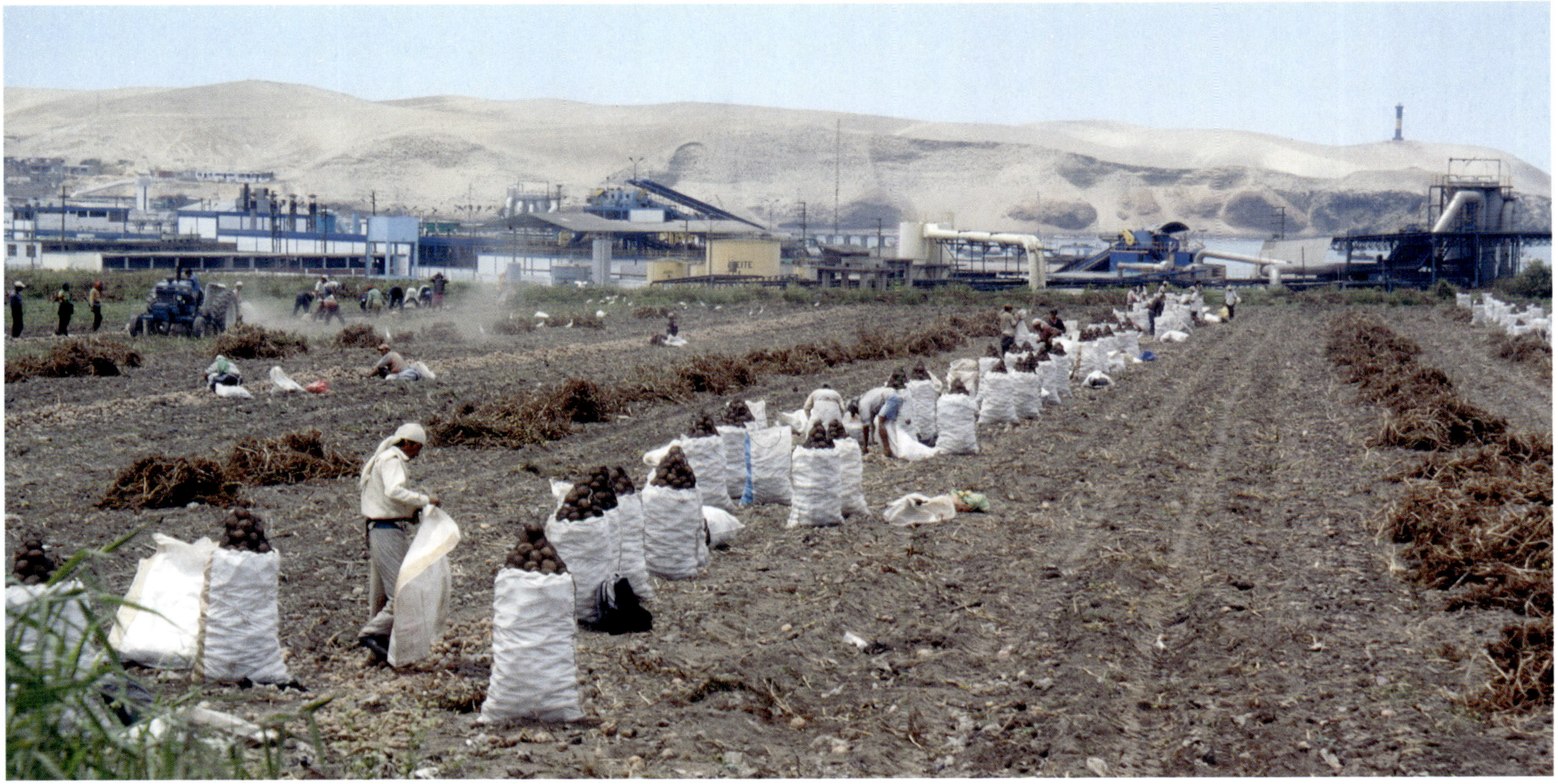

Bottom: Potato harvest near Pisco

Through small villages, lying in the desert as green oases, we drive along the coast, but soon get away from the stink of fish that hangs in the air and take a turn towards the interior near Paramonga. We follow the Rio Fortaleza. It is becoming cold and foggy. From behind, a small coach comes speeding up. Suddenly, 4 goats appear on the road in my field of vision and I have to brake sharply. Axel comes to a stop immediately behind me and, with screeching tyres, the coach whooshes almost directly into us. The driver definitely would not have braked for the goats, but I had no other choice because I would have fallen over with my bike. As we go over the pass near Coñococha, drizzle accompanies us on the rest of the distance to Huaráz. The city serves as the base for hikes lasting up to several days. Here we finally have some kind of chance to obtain a new rain gear for Axel. Because he wears quite a large size, this is not exactly easy. We end up in a shop for work clothes. Orange-coloured coveralls seem to be the solution, but they are quite large to pack and the trousers are too tight. In the end, he has to put a lot of money on the table in a trekking shop in

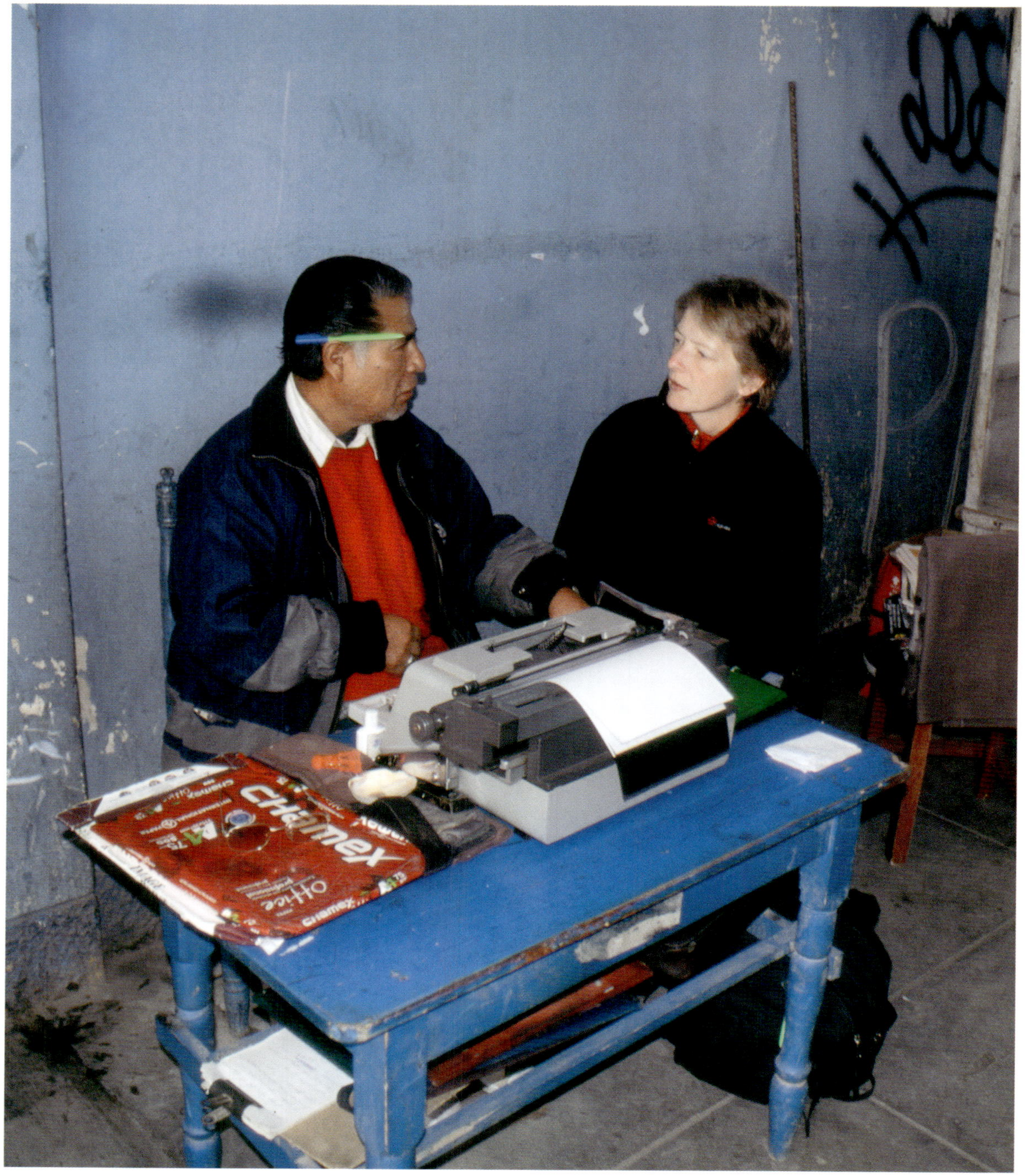

Right: In Huaráz, "writers" write the correspondence for the illiterate

Page 149: Covered in a thick blanket of snow, the 6,000 m mountains of the Cordillera Blanca

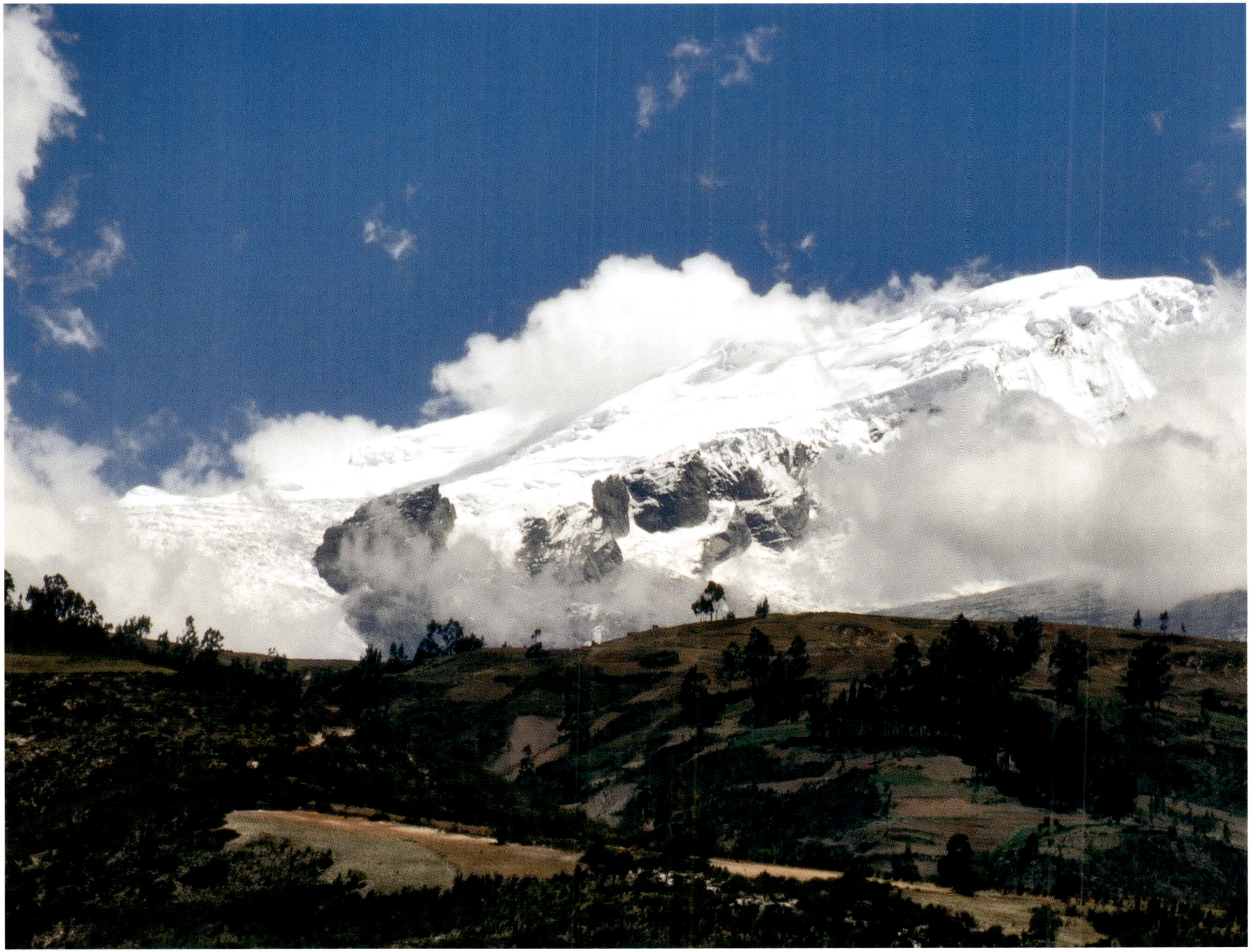

order to buy the appropriate clothing. In an alley, my attention is grabbed by a number of tables where men are sitting in front of typewriters. There is a brisk rush of people and speedy fingers hit the keys industriously. The melodic ring before the end of the line and the whirring noise of the carriage returning awake childhood memories. I start a conversation with one of the men, and he explains to me that many people in the city can't read or write. The men earn some money by helping people with their correspondence with the authorities, but also by typing private letters. Franco in Cusco had already told me about this. Particularly in the countryside and in the mountains, there are still many people who never go to school. There is a lack of infrastructure and teachers, schools are often located many hours away, or there is no money for school uniforms and learning material. Often the children already have to help in the fields and tend to the animals when they are quite young.

Page 151: Dirt road impression in the Cordillera Negra

Bottom: The lagoon Chinancotcha in the Cordillera Blanca

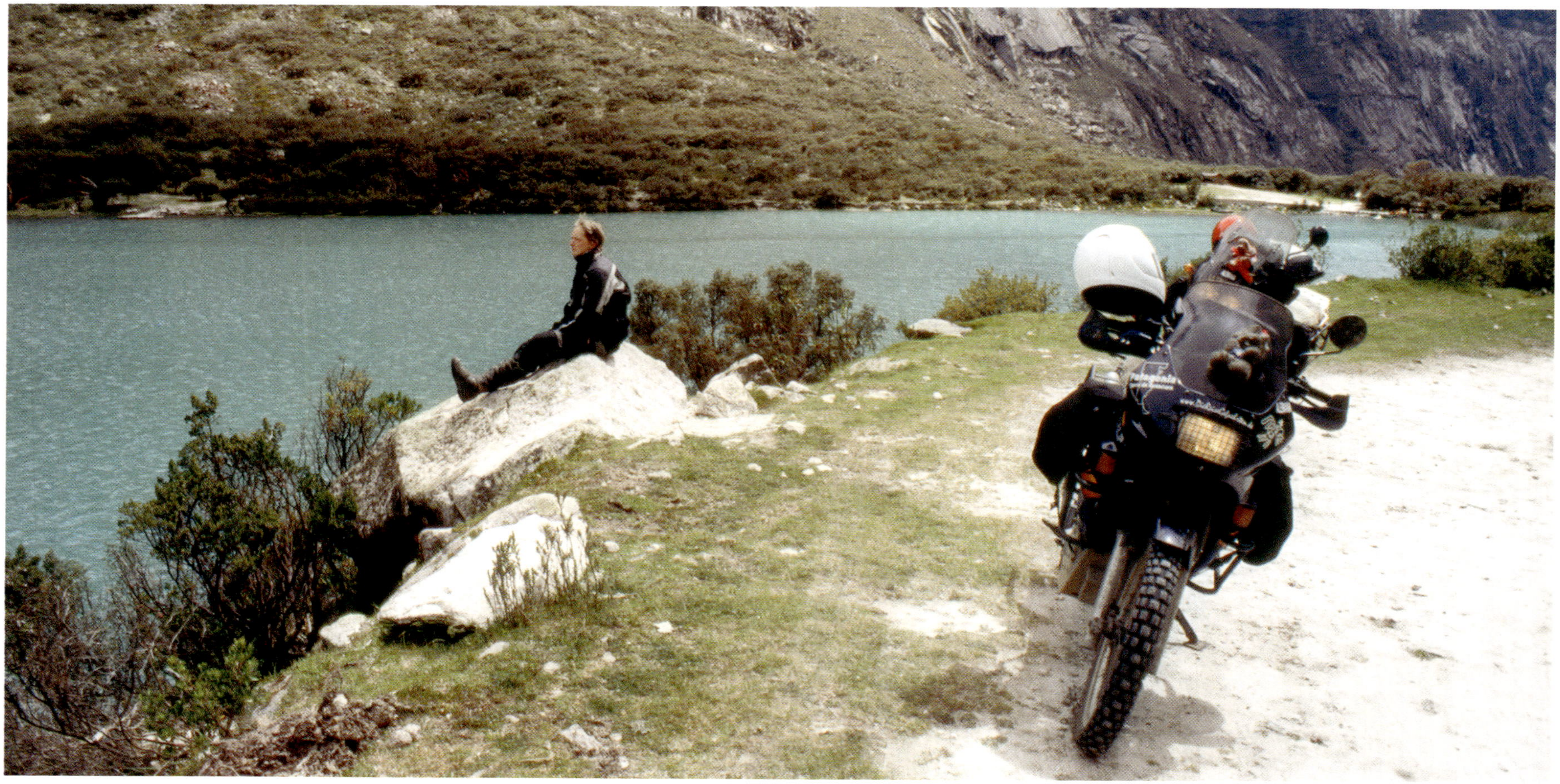

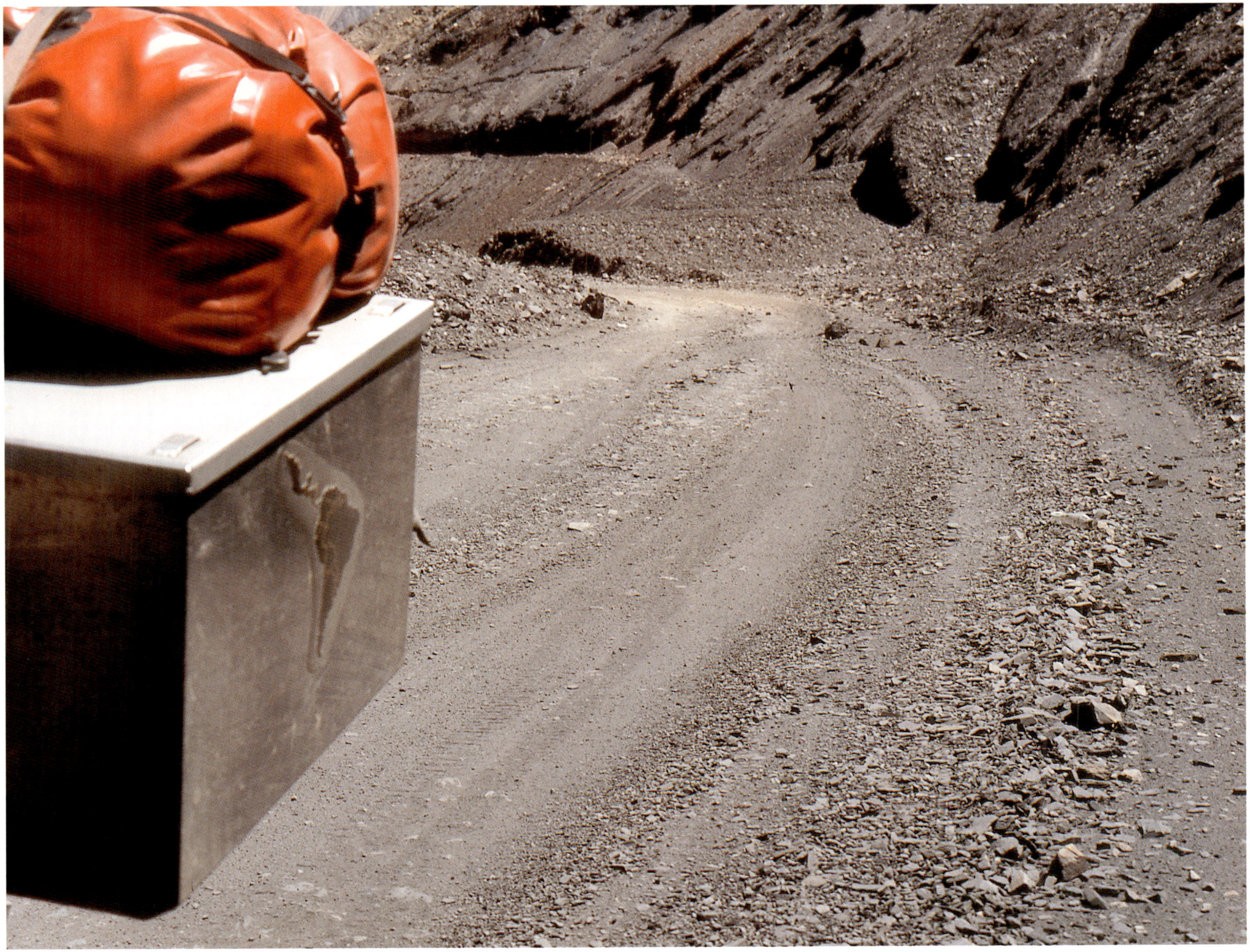

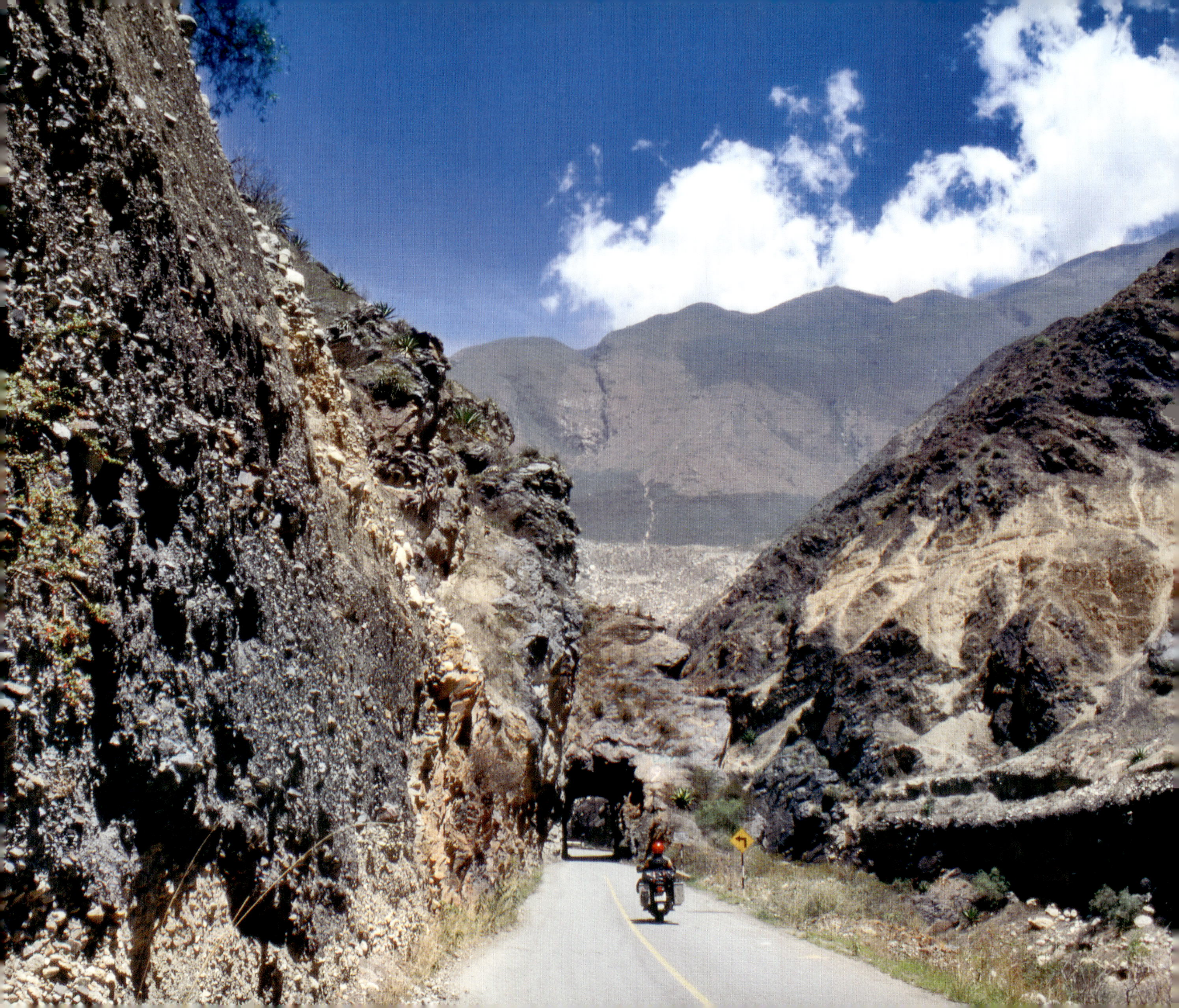

Page 152: Along the mountains of the Cordillera Negra

Bottom: Water and rubble in the way

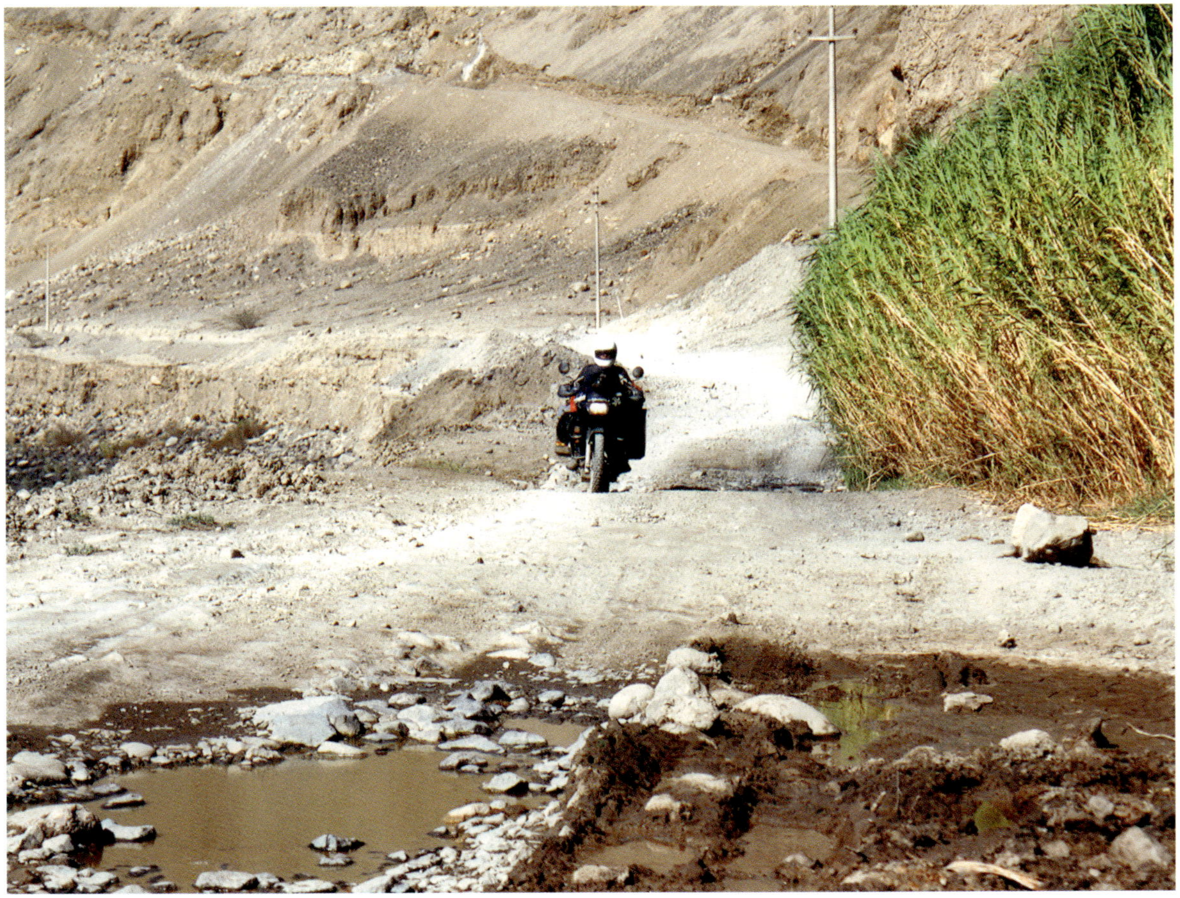

The Chinancotcha and Orcocotcha lagoons are the destination of our excursion one sunny afternoon. The road winds through mountains and small villages. It is strenuous to watch for the numerous stray dogs that constantly come running from the brush and follow us yapping wildly. As soon as we brake, they retreat, however, with their tails between their legs. We have to be just as alert to the young boys who make a sport of throwing stones at us. Even when luckily nothing actually happens and they only hit the back wheel, I find it not at all funny. Axel collects a few stones in order to "fire back", and astounded by this, the boys let us in peace. At the gate of the nature reservation, we come across a car with a flat tyre. The occupants have been waiting for help for hours as they don't have the correct spanner to loosen the nuts. Axel unpacks his on-board tool kit and the tyre is changed as fast as the wind. How practical that we always have a couple of spanners in our luggage. On the way back, my bike suddenly makes a loud crack and the back wheel blocks. I take a look at the problem: the extension of the mudguard on the back wheel is bent in and has become stuck in the tread! We have to bend it back, but on the bumpy road it gets stuck again. In order to prevent it from breaking off completely, we stabilise the mudguard with a rubber band. As long as I don't go faster than 20 km/h downhill and avoid all potholes, I advance undamaged. Back in the hostel, our hosts clear out their garage so that we can do the repairs where it is warm and lighted. The mounting of the mudguard is broken and the screw is slowly boring through the number plate. We stabilise the cracked plastic with 2 large flat washers and hope that it doesn't crack any further.

On the way back to the coast, we follow the river Santa for 96 km over scree and sand through 36 long and pitch-black tunnels, some of which are quite long. Luckily only a single car approaches from the opposite direction and there are no buses or trucks. If that happened, we would have to turn around and drive back to the next wider area. Apart from that, the one-lane road leads through a gorgeous wild landscape with craggy mountains to the left and a steep descent to the river on the right. A gaffe or an inattentive second would bring us threateningly close to the slope. Fragments of stone break off the incline and drop onto the road, and a fresh wind is blowing. During long kilometres of solitude, there are only rarely huts half-hidden in the mountains. Near Chuquicara, the road is once again paved with asphalt. When I'm no more than 1 m away, I brake – and lay my bike on the gravel.

The drive has sapped quite a bit of my energy. On the way, I have doubts about whether I can manage the heavy motorbike on another slope. When I get stuck in mud somewhere or jolt over fragments of stone and the bike skids, when the route drags on for kilometres, I have to clench my teeth in order not to give up. Then it is only the will to somehow put it behind me that keeps me going, because at this moment, there is no alternative. Yet, what a feeling of joy washes over me when I have succeeded, as if I could master anything, no matter what happens!

Page 155: In the adobe town Chan Chan

Bottom: Plaza Major in Trujillo

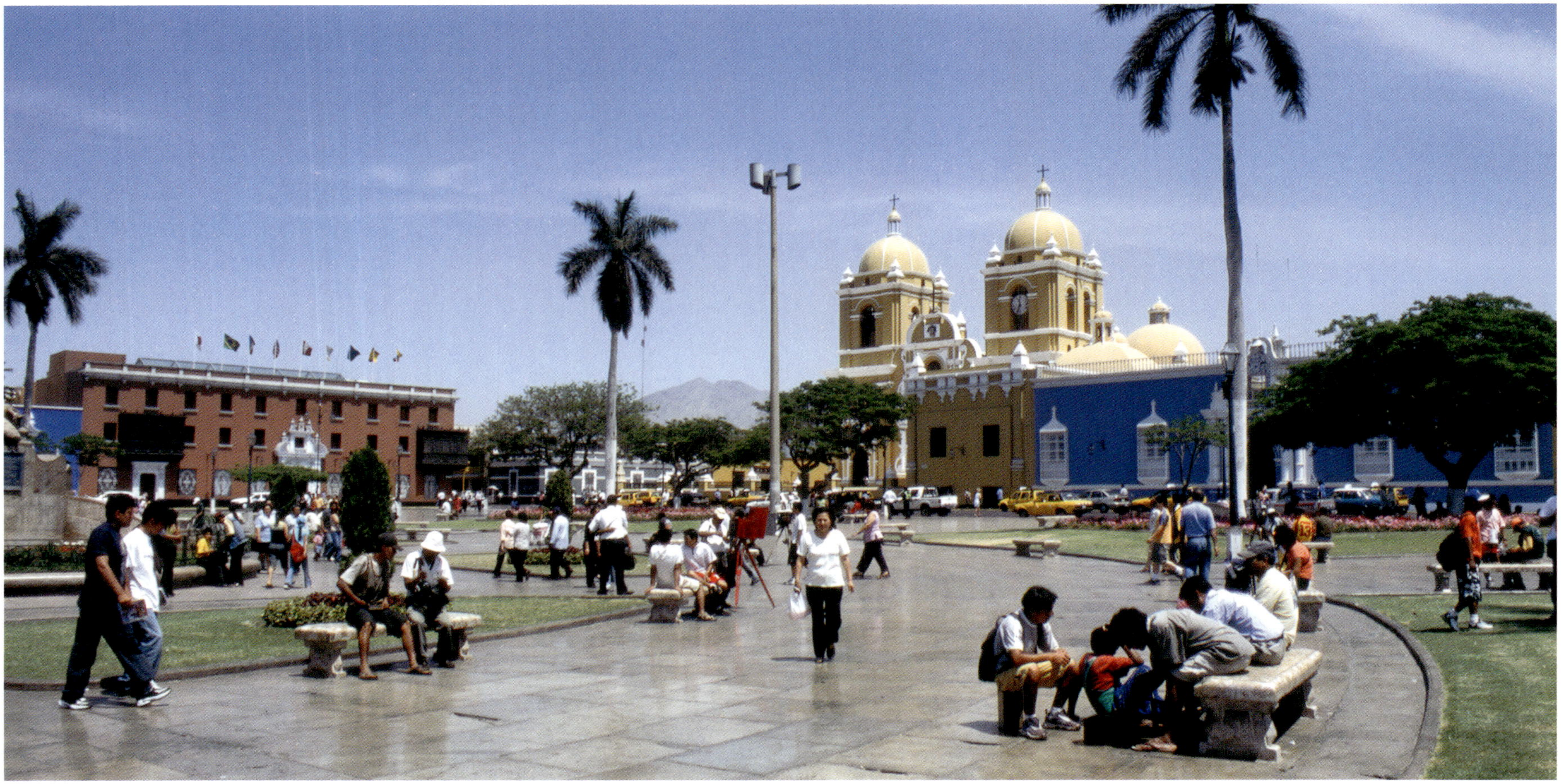

It is time to fuel up again. In Chuquicara, there is a small petrol station. The man asks me how many gallons I need because he only has a little petrol left. One gallon should be enough to get me to the coast. Instead of taking the hose, he walks away and comes back with a canister, which hopefully contains about that amount. Although twilight is slowly falling, we drive the coastal road up to Trujillo. As we arrive at the edge of the city, it is already dark. Near the plaza, we find suitable accommodation. I am just discussing with the night watchman about the best place to put the motorbikes on the car park so that the 3 currish rottweilers can see them as I notice 2 young lads engaging Axel in a conversation on the badly lit street from the corner of my eye. I start to get a bad feeling. One of the lads creeps around the motorbikes while the other one talks to Axel. Suddenly, one of them sticks his hand in his trouser pocket. I want to walk over to him but at that moment, a man from the hotel opposite calls out and blows on his whistle. The two bolt and we work on getting our things into the hotel.

Trujillo shines with colonial architecture. Many windows are furnished with rich, squiggly, white painted lattice work, which stands out from the colourful façades. In the middle of the plaza, there is a memorial dedicated to Peru's declaration of independence in 1820. A man in a navy uniform draws my attention to the fact that the figures, which are meant to describe the path to autonomy, were produced by a German sculptor and have European instead of Peruvian facial features, and that in their fight against the Spaniards, the soldiers wear hats in a Napoleonic style, which doesn't really fit into the factual context.

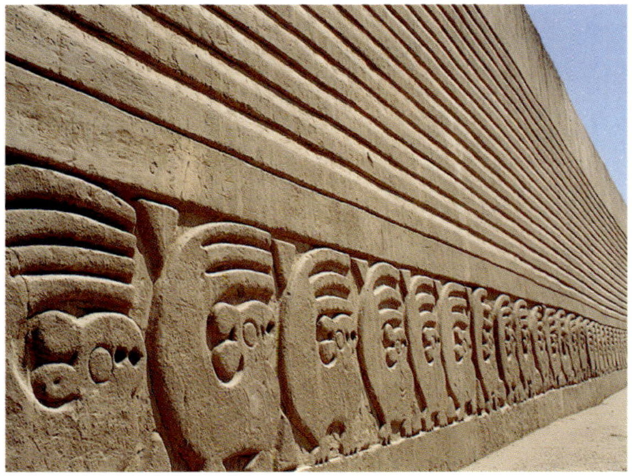

Outside of the city lies the former political centre of the Chimú kingdom, which existed from about 900 to 1470 AD until it was conquered by the Inca and integrated into their empire. For around 500 years, the Chimú expanded their territory in northern Peru by means of an organised army, and built up an influential kingdom. The site of Chan Chan is the largest surviving adobe city in the world. The estimates of the number of people who lived and worked in the 24 km^2 large area vary quite a bit, but it was probably between 20,000 and 30,000. Inside of the walls, there is a total of 9 palaces with various ceremonial sites. Many walls are decorated with delicate geometric patterns or images of animals such as fish and pelicans. They point in various directions and symbolise the high and low tides of the sea. The Chimú paid homage above all to the water, the moon, the stars and fertility. They built water canals and cultivated many sorts of vegetables and fruits on their farms. They also lived from catching fish, hunting and breeding livestock. In addition, they were masters in working with silver, gold and copper. The site is situated in the middle of the desert, which means that there are no shadows to be seen far and wide. Nonetheless, the simplicity and beauty of the adobe buildings is so impressive that I block out the heat. At least we have hats with us. Otherwise we would surely have already become sunburnt.

We urgently have to take care of getting a completely different type of headgear. The padding in Axel's helmet is slowly falling apart. It is crumbling and the small fibres make his scalp itch. For half a day, we walk through the city looking for foam until we land in a small shop that sells nothing else. We decide on a 2 cm thick yellow pad from which he produces some provisional patching and attaches it with superglue. It does not only smell terrible, it also doesn't hold. Double-sided tape serves the purpose better, and now the new padding will just need time to adapt to the shape of his head.

Our last night in Peru, we spend in Piura. We find a small hostel with a garden, located in a quiet residential district. It is again astounding that so many of the streets in the larger cities are watched by private security guards, just as the streets here. One of the guards stops us immediately and asks whether we were looking for something in particular. As we point to the entrance of the courtyard on the opposite side of the street, he stops the cars on the street so that we can turn, and then looks at the motorbikes with great interest. This means that this time, we can even leave the bikes on the street with the luggage attached. The courtyard in which we park is not guarded by Rottweilers as in Trujillo, but instead by a few turkeys, who immediately flock around the bikes with curiosity. It gets interesting the next morning as we want to pay our room. The boss is not in the building and the employee doesn't have any change. He therefore asks us if we don't want to pay for 2 nights. I am a bit taken aback because we have already buckled on the luggage and are ready to start. "Actually, we want to leave", I respond. He told me with a straight face that I could maybe pay for 2 overnight stays anyway. With a friendly smile, I persuade him to get change somewhere in the neighbourhood. The next border crossing is already waiting for us.

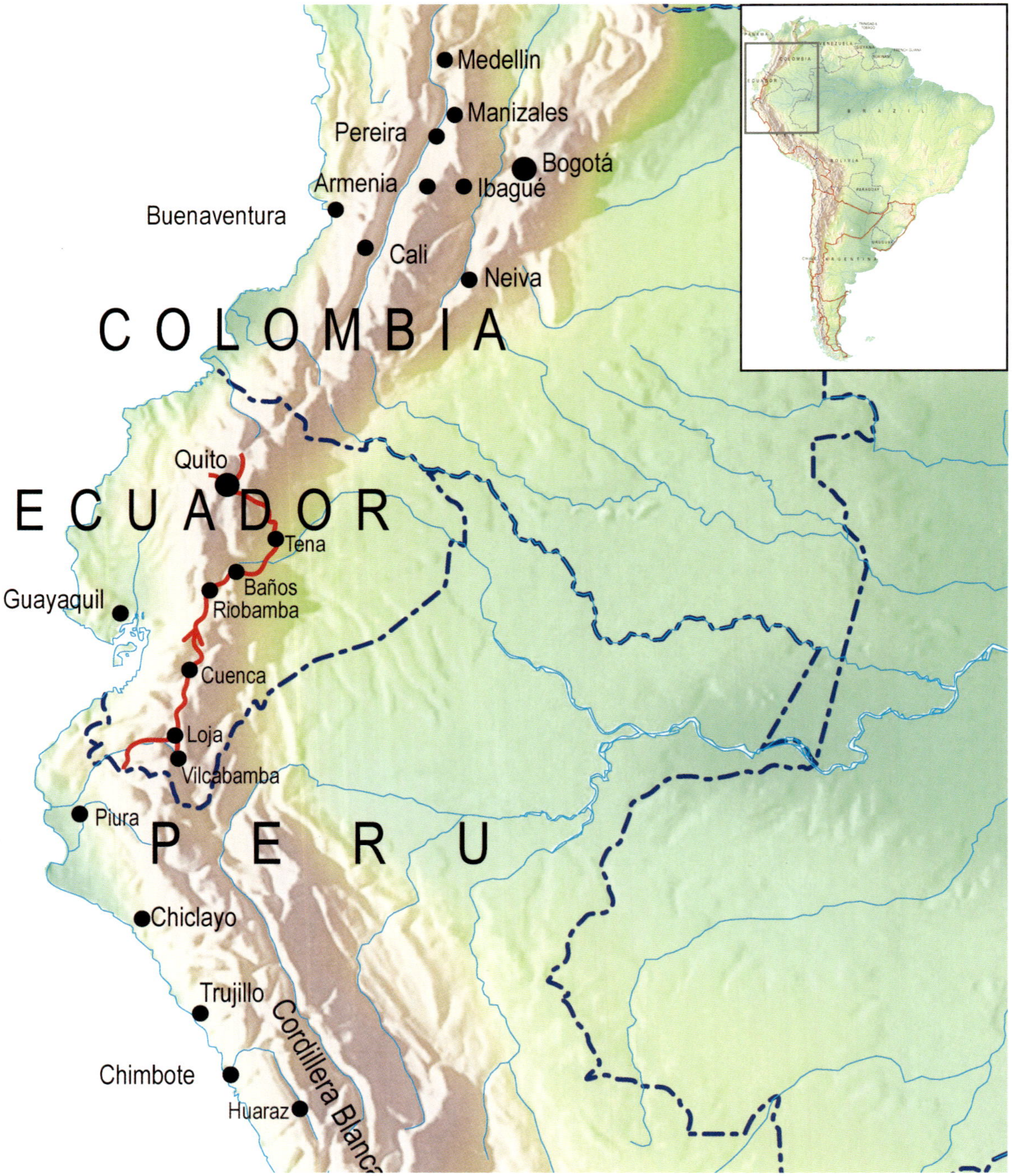

From the border town of Macará, the route initially proceeds over Loja to Vilcabamba and then northward to Cuenca. From there, the road leads over Riobamba to Baños. The route continues on to Puyo and Tena in the rainforest. Turning northward, the route finally goes over Baeza to Quito. The journey through South America ends with a short trip to the "equator line" and into the further surroundings of Quito.

ECUADOR
IN THE MIDDLE OF THE WORLD

OLD HATS

First I need fuel. Unfortunately, petrol stations in Ecuador take a break at lunchtime. It's not that they are closed, you can have coffee or a snack, wash your car, it's just the pumps that are blocked, and the reason eludes us. Once again, I rely on the mobile petrol station and we make good time through the mountains. In the afternoon, on well marked country roads, we reach the small village of Vilcabamba south of Loja. The "sacred valley", as the Inca called it, is famous for its long-lived inhabitants. In the 1970s, scientists

Bottom: In the valley of "old people", Vilcabamba

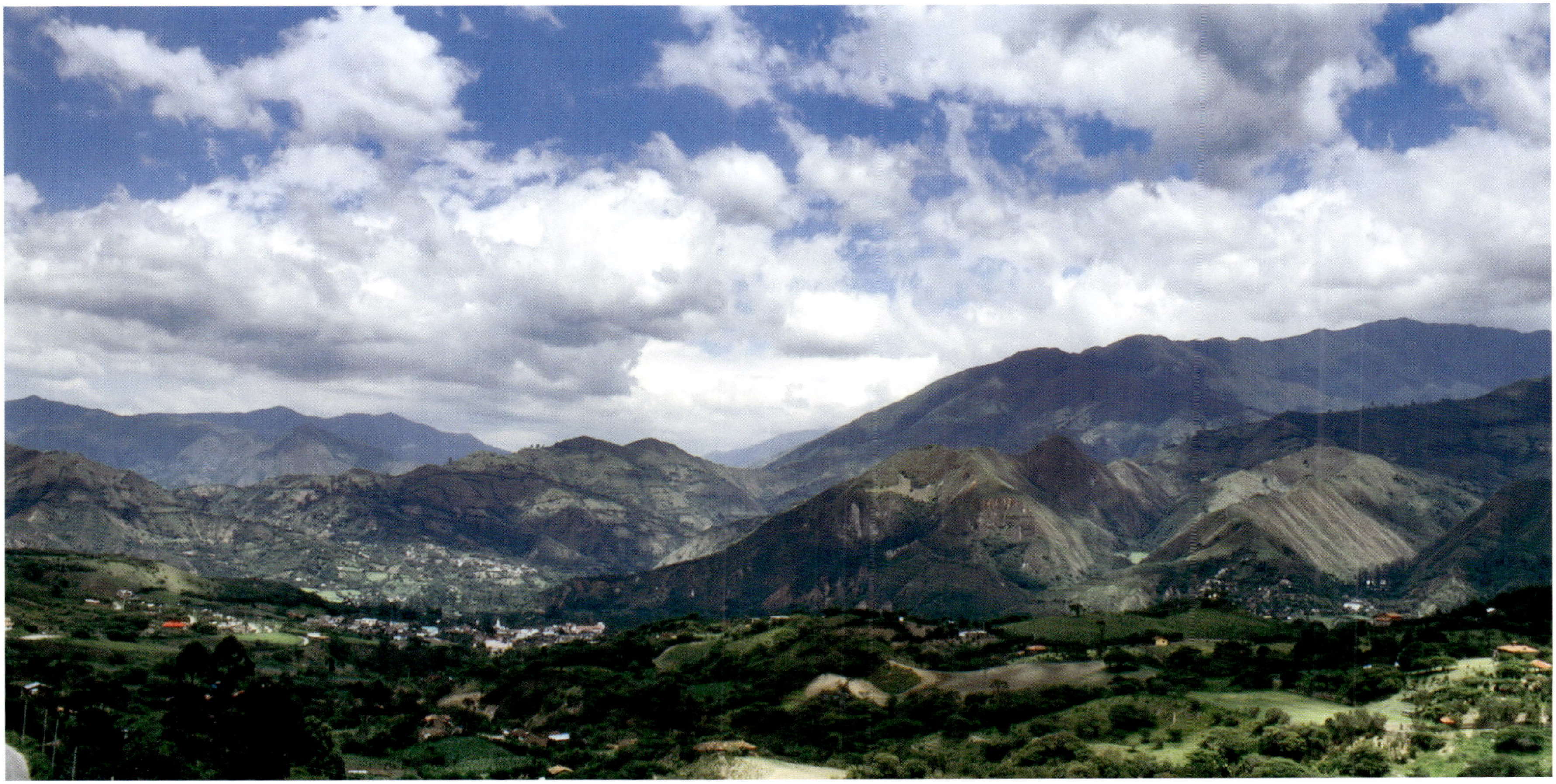

claimed to have found out why people here live to be 100 years on average: they traced the phenomenon back to the fact that the air is charged with negative ions, the water is supposed to be particularly balanced with minerals, and the climate is spring-like all year long. Of course we stay a few days to drink from the fountain of youth and extend our lifespan, which the bus drivers on the road always want to shorten. Opposite the local mountain Mandango, we come to rest on Izhcayluma, the "two hills" – a true understatement. In order to get to the village proper, we borrow bicycles. We coast downhill to the little plaza at 50 km/h, but I have to give up soon when pedalling uphill again. At an incline of 16%, I run out of breath despite the many tours we have made and the heights we have climbed so far. I get off and push. After about half the way, a pick-up taxi rescues us, we put the bikes on the loading area and sit down next to them, the wind blowing in my face.

Negotiating the curves to Cuenca is great fun as we are able to step on the gas.

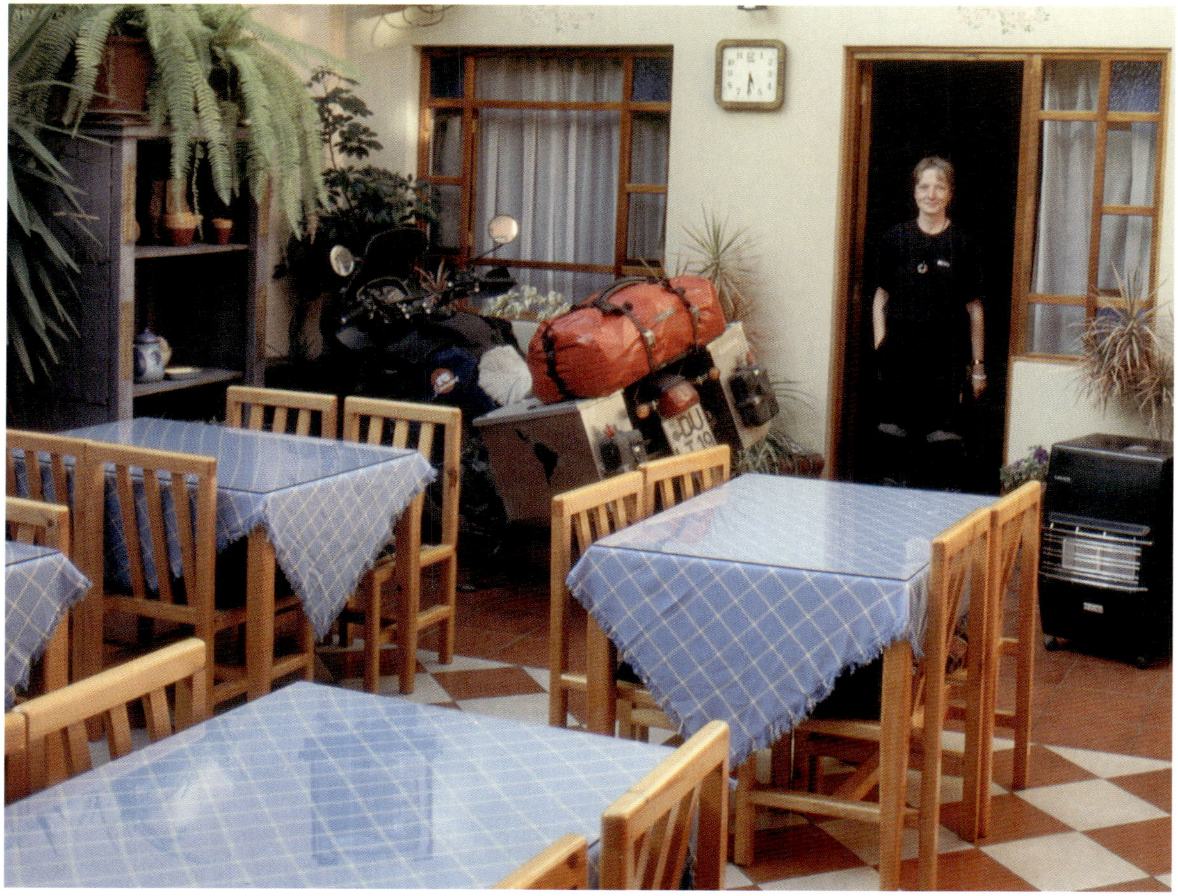

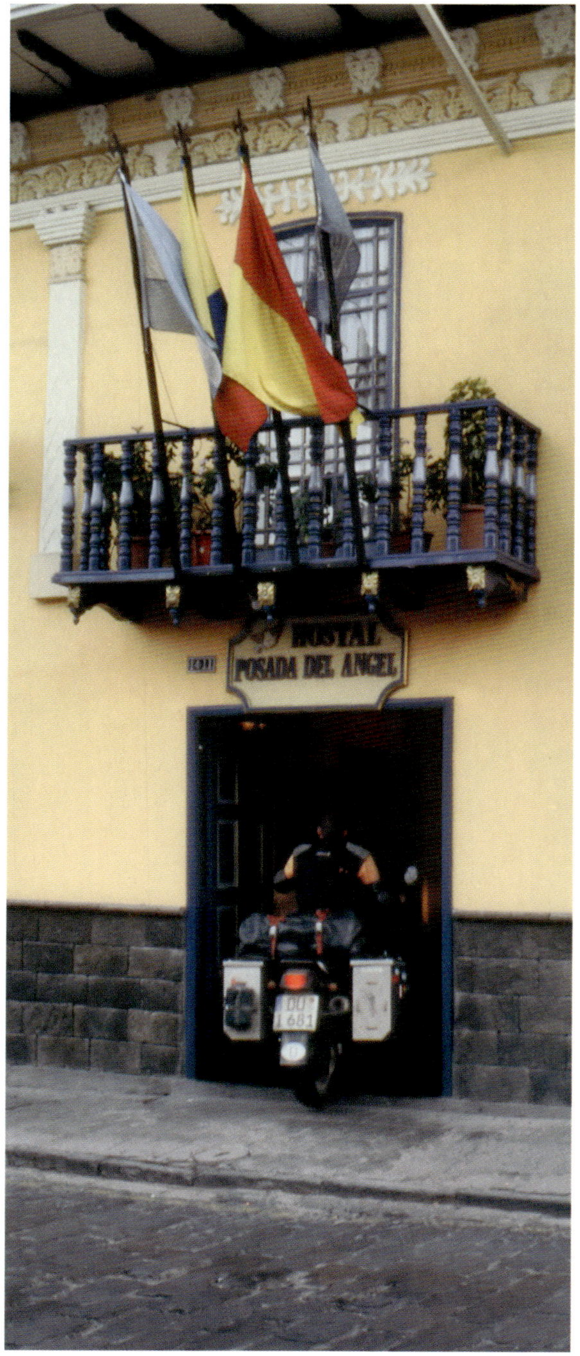

Suddenly, a bus appears in my rear-view mirror and the driver attempts to overtake me in an uphill right-hand bend. He doesn't see the oncoming traffic. He can't. Although I don't like to admit to myself that a bus driver manages to pass me, I still let him go because a race would be pointless. A local tells me later that the drivers get a commission if they get to their destination ahead of schedule, something which apparently none of them wants to miss out. In Ecuador's third-largest city, there is no affordable accommodation with a garage, so we push the bikes through the door of a boarding house into the foyer. I park mine in the dining room, while Axel's finds a spot under the tall palm trees next to the reception desk. In the course of the evening, the owner becomes unsure due to his own lack of knowledge. He fears that the tank might leak and that a careless smoker might blow everything up. He therefore suggests we put the bikes in an empty shop around the corner. We take a look at the room. A 40 cm step at the entrance presents an insurmountable barrier. Since he doesn't have a piece of wood or anything else that would serve as a ramp, he suggests that we lift the bikes. I reply that I won't stop him if he wants to go ahead and lift them across. Another glance at La Trochita convinces him that the heavy colossus will not fit. So, for the next two nights, the bikes are allowed to stay where they are.

Cuenca is the centre for the production of Panama hats, and the most important exporters are located here. In a house that is a museum, factory and shop at the same time, I learn about the steps involved in their production. Fronds are taken from the Paja Toquilla plant. It grows in only a few regions of Ecuador. The indigenous women cut off the leaves and boil them to kill the insects. Then they are bound into bundles, dried and pulled apart into thin fibres. If desired, the fibres are dyed with a variety of chemical or natural dyes. The finer the fibres are, the longer and more difficult is the production, which can take up to 2 months. They begin with the middle part, which is pulled over a

Page 158 left and right: The motorbikes find a generous space in the guesthouse

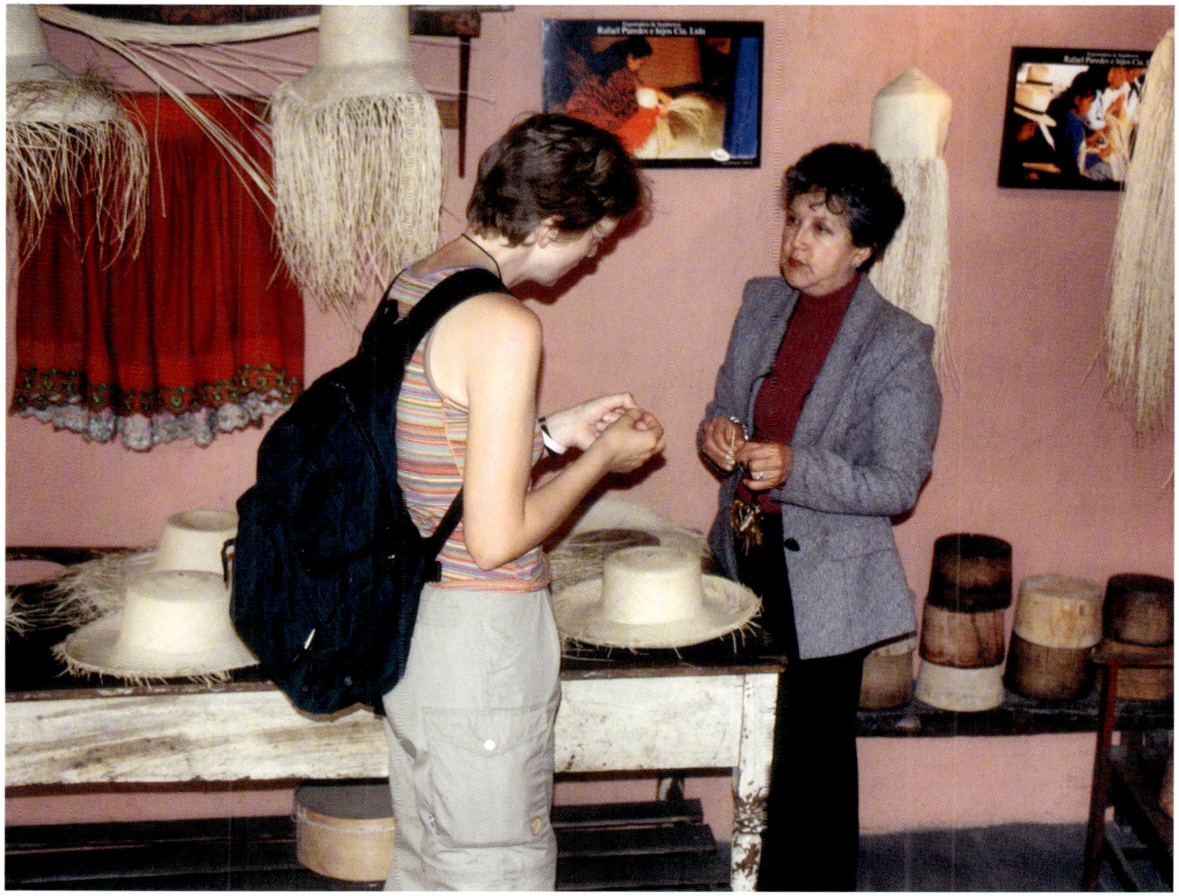

Right: Production of the Panama hat step by step

big block of wood to get the typical rounded shape. Then the hats are woven to the brim. At that point, the half-finished hats are sold to manufactures where they are finished. In the last step, they are put on a block of wood and then placed in an old-fashioned machine, covered with leather and pressed with hot steam four times for 15 seconds. Thus the hat receives its final shape. I wonder where the name originated because the hats are manufactured exclusively in Ecuador. There are many legends about its origin. The manager of the factory tells me that all hats used to be shipped to Panama to be exported around the world. The destination on the label said: Puerto Panama. As a short version, the term Panama Hat was coined, which is still used today. The plant and the know-how involved in the production of these hats, which have been made since 1630, mean that the hats are a true Ecuadorian product.

Page 161: Children's carnival in Cuenca

Bottom: Showroom of a Panama hat manufacture in Cuenca

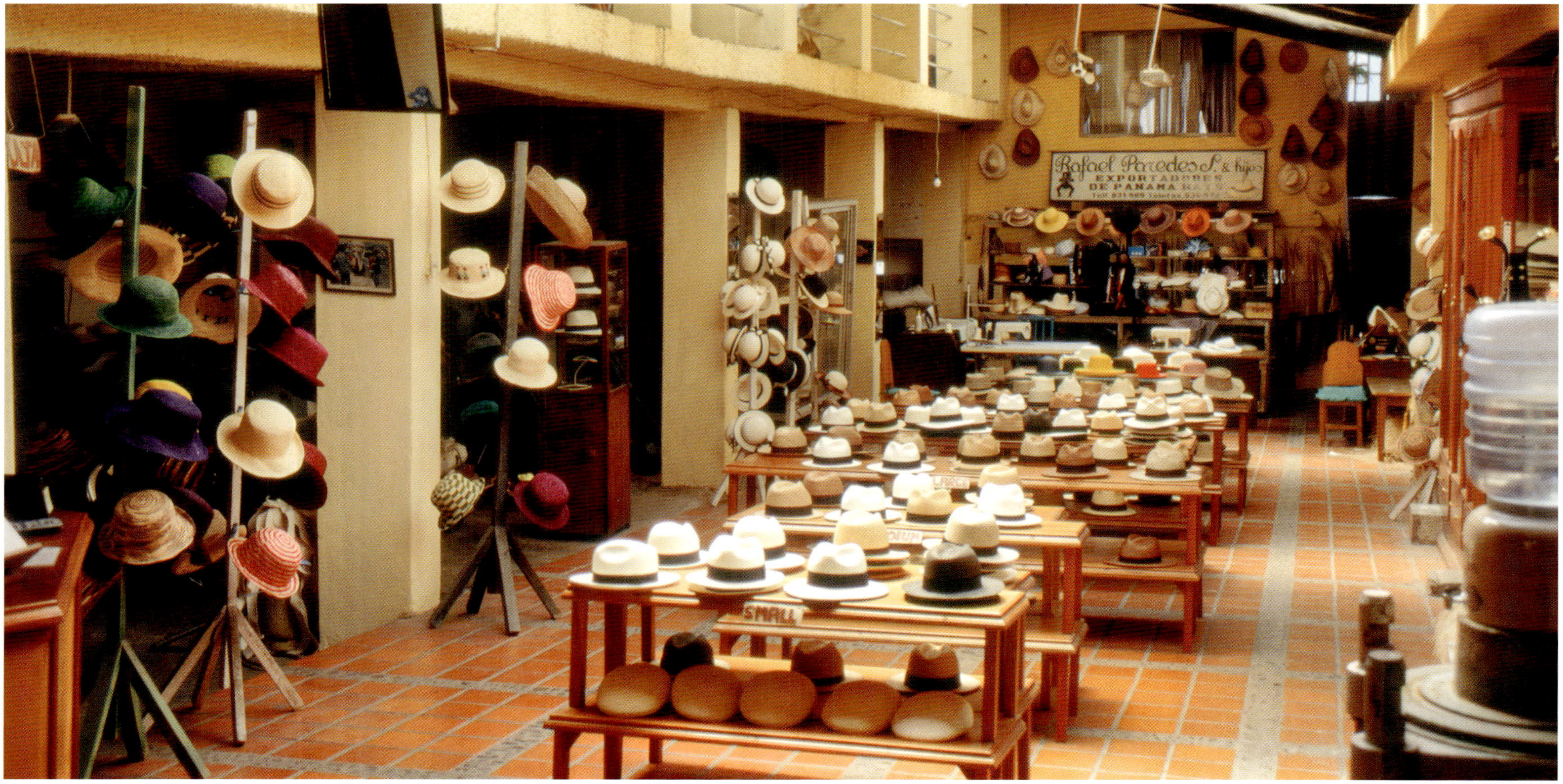

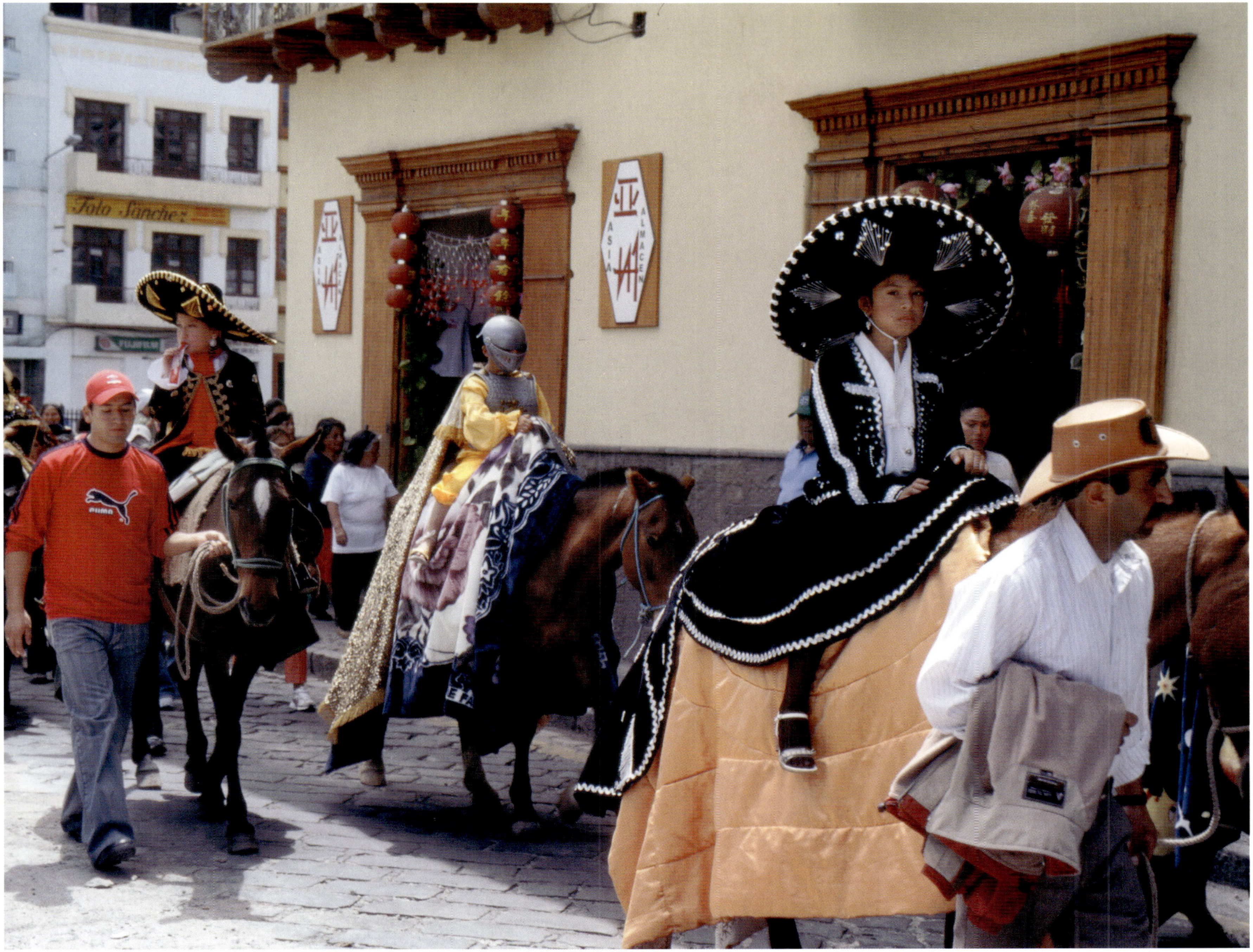
Foto Sánchez
ASIA
ALMACEN

PLUNGE INTO THE JUNGLE

Sun and blue sky make me feel confident as we depart. After a short while, however, rain and mist become our companions again. More than 50 km/h are impossible. Soon, gloves and gear are soaking wet. I could say that I'm used to showering on the bike after so many months and that it is now a real treat. But that would not be the whole truth. Maybe I should have new gloves made with more room for the webbing between my fingers. The other part of the truth is that the weather is not good for our disposition and the driving is exhausting. The mountain road is so narrow that we can't stop anywhere. It is only during the next fuel stop that we are able to get out our rain gear. Although it is rather sultry, I pull on the dry winter gloves. The ground is covered with dozens of finger-sized winged beetles, run over. It seems as if an army of them had invaded here, staggered in the petrol fumes and gone down. Their shells are hard and crackle when we step on them, which can't be avoided since they are everywhere.

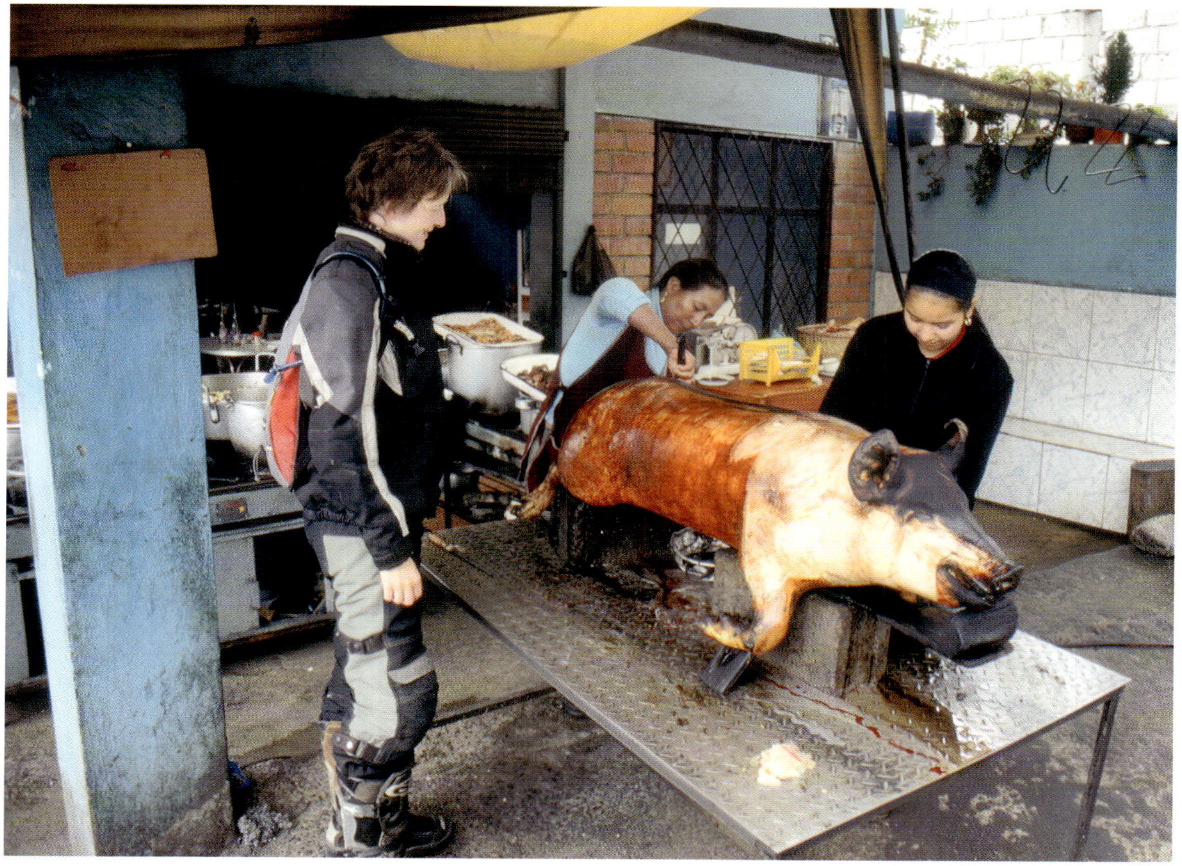

We make our way carefully up into the mountains, on detour routes and through mud. To Riobamba and then onward towards Baños de Agua Santa, where we come to the volcanic area of the Eastern Cordillera of the Andes. The active Tungurahua (5,023 m) buried much of the area when it erupted in 1999. The main road of Riobamba leading into the small pilgrims' village has still only been temporarily repaired after it had been completely impassable for a while. Instead of a bridge, two narrow steel sheets cross the brook without any rails and an abyss of 10 m in the middle and on each side. The daily bus from the provincial capital to Puyo is just passing us at top speed. We use the opportunity and let him guide us on a safe route, because it is not always clearly distinguishable from the parts that end in lava rubble. Only a few places have been asphalted yet, and most of the time we drive around construction sites on volcano ash. Then the bus gets stuck in a riverbed, and the driver is only able to get it free with great efforts. I gather momentum for the crossing and

Left: Typical street grill in Ecuador

Page 163 top: Murals in Baños

Page 163 bottom: Green parking space

make it in one piece to the other side even though my rear tyre slips. After that, the temporary bridges with metal sheets can't scare me anymore. In a small side road of the bleak village of Baños, we find a lovely spot for ourselves and the bikes in the middle of a garden with birds and a macaw. The boss of the house, Christian, sets it onto my shoulder. We get along well from the start and he eats out of my hand. The best thing about the boarding house is the spa area in the winter garden. There, we relax our tired bones and meet Christine and Fredi, 2 Germans on a tour through Ecuador. We sit next to each other in wooden sauna boxes, with just the head protruding. Fresh eucalyptus branches lie on the floor. Hot steam is blown into the boxes through nozzles and it slowly enters all pores. I manage to hang on for 10 minutes, and then take a shower with ice-cold spring water – what a stimulation for the circulation! In the evening, we meet up with people from Canada and Germany to go for a French dinner. What a luxury after all the strenuous efforts and spartan life on the road.

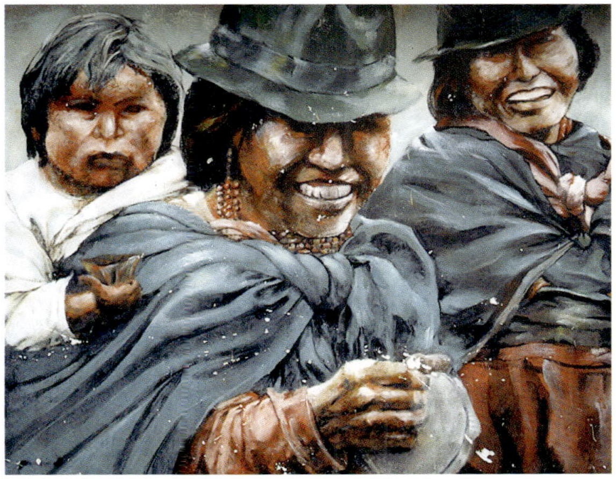

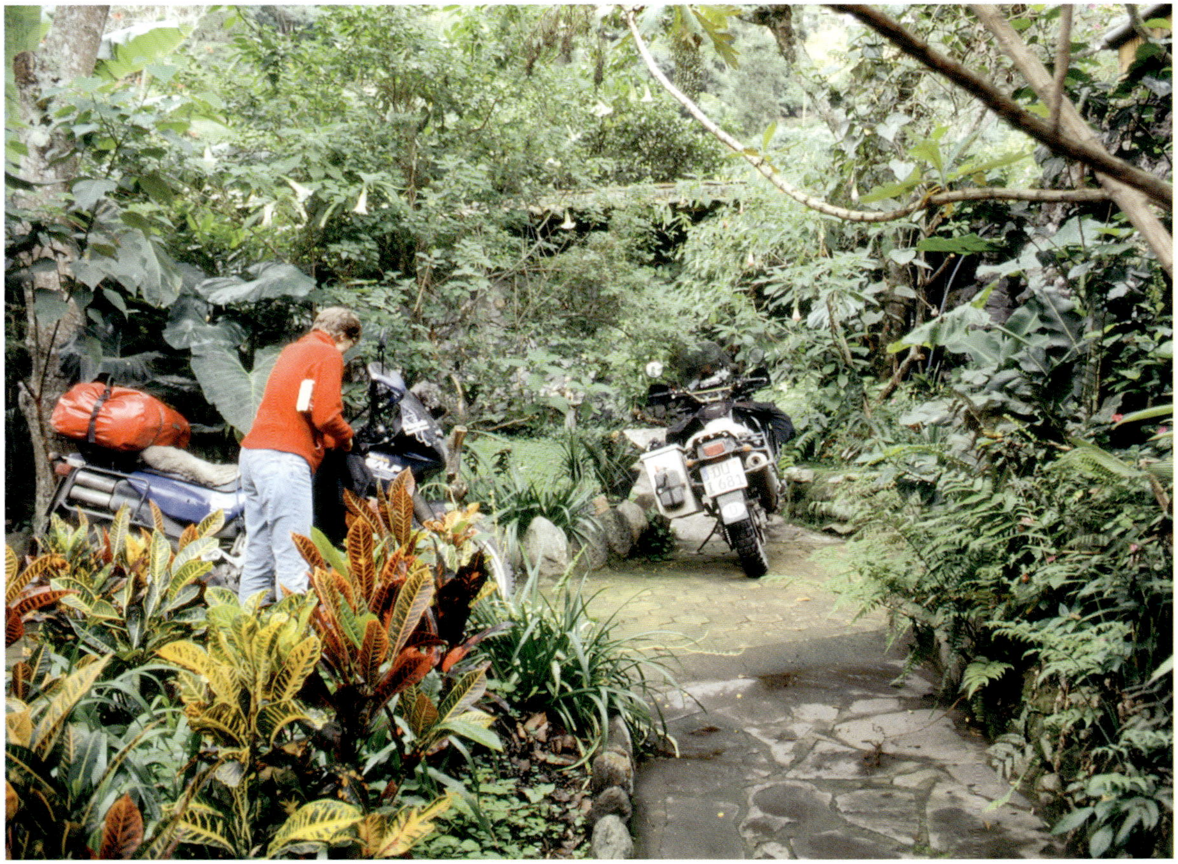

Baños is just about 8 km away from the volcano, which is closed off for climbers because it erupts frequently. Unfortunately, I can't get a clear view of the volcano from the distance even once because it is hiding in the mist. The village is marked by many signs with evacuation routes. The current alert level, yellow, allows the locals to live their lives fairly peacefully. The basilica features paintings depicting miracles from several centuries: people who saw the Señora del Agua Santa during eruptions and who were saved from life-threatening situations by her. Christian tells us about the most recent evacuation in 1999, when the residents had to leave their homes because a new eruption was imminent. Clouds of ash rose about 10,000 m high and mudslides destroyed the road, but nobody was killed. However, the locals had to literally recapture their village because the soldiers who had come to protect the deserted village from pillagers were stealing other people's possessions. Tungurahua is still not at peace and remains an unpredictable force of nature.

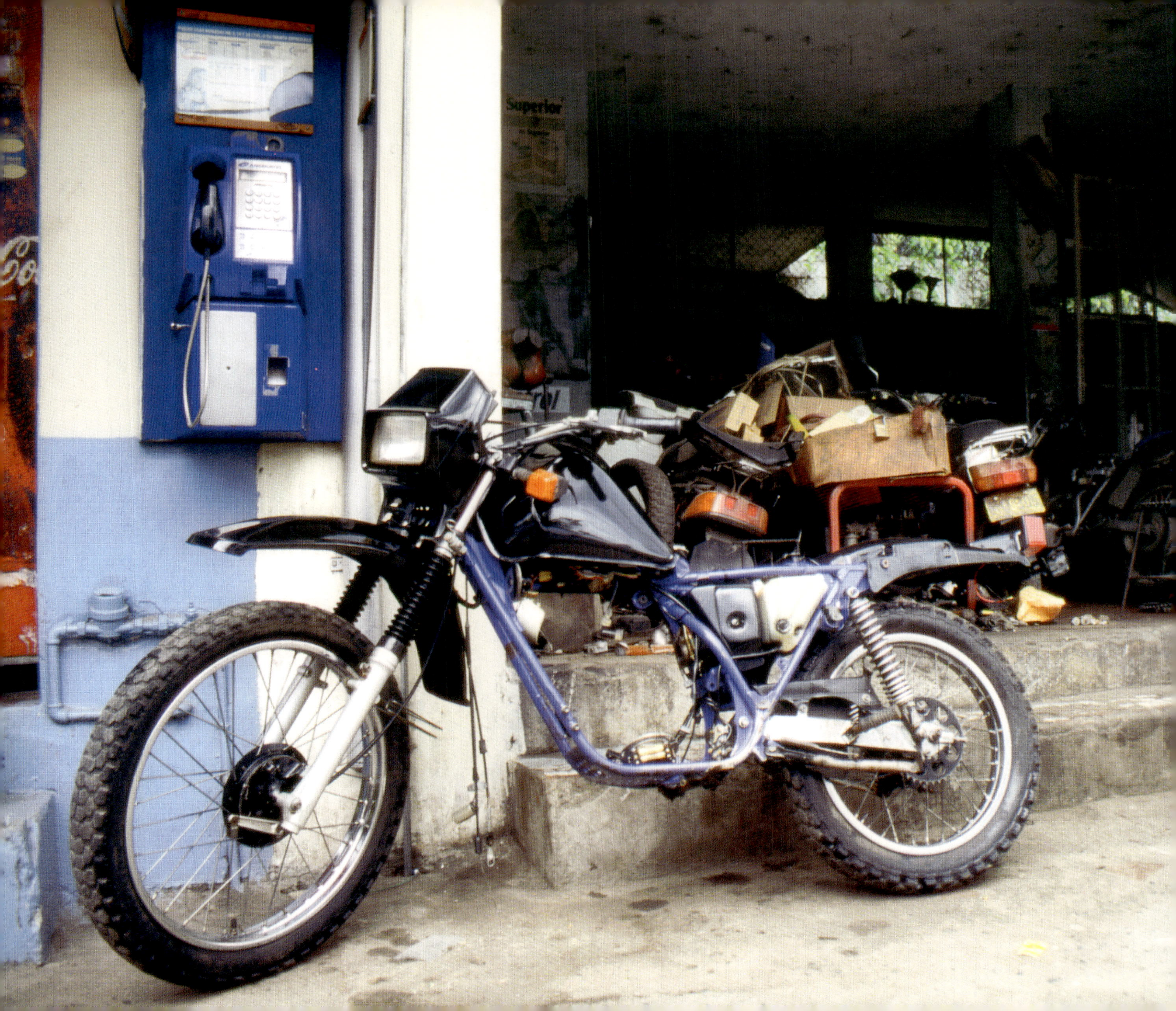
Superior

Page 164: Nothing tops an organized workroom

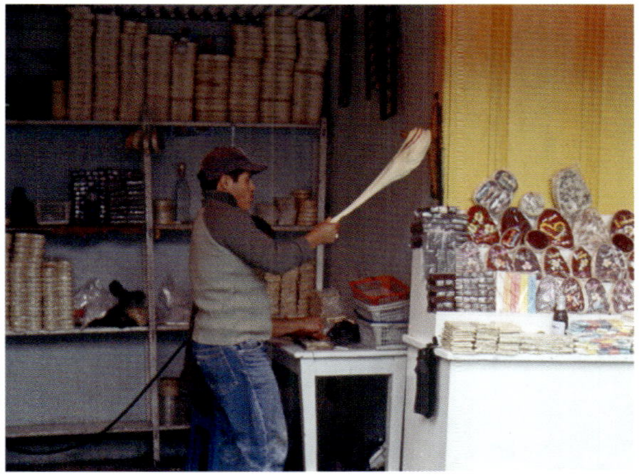

Right: Alfeñique, sweet speciality

Bottom: Friends and helpers in Tena

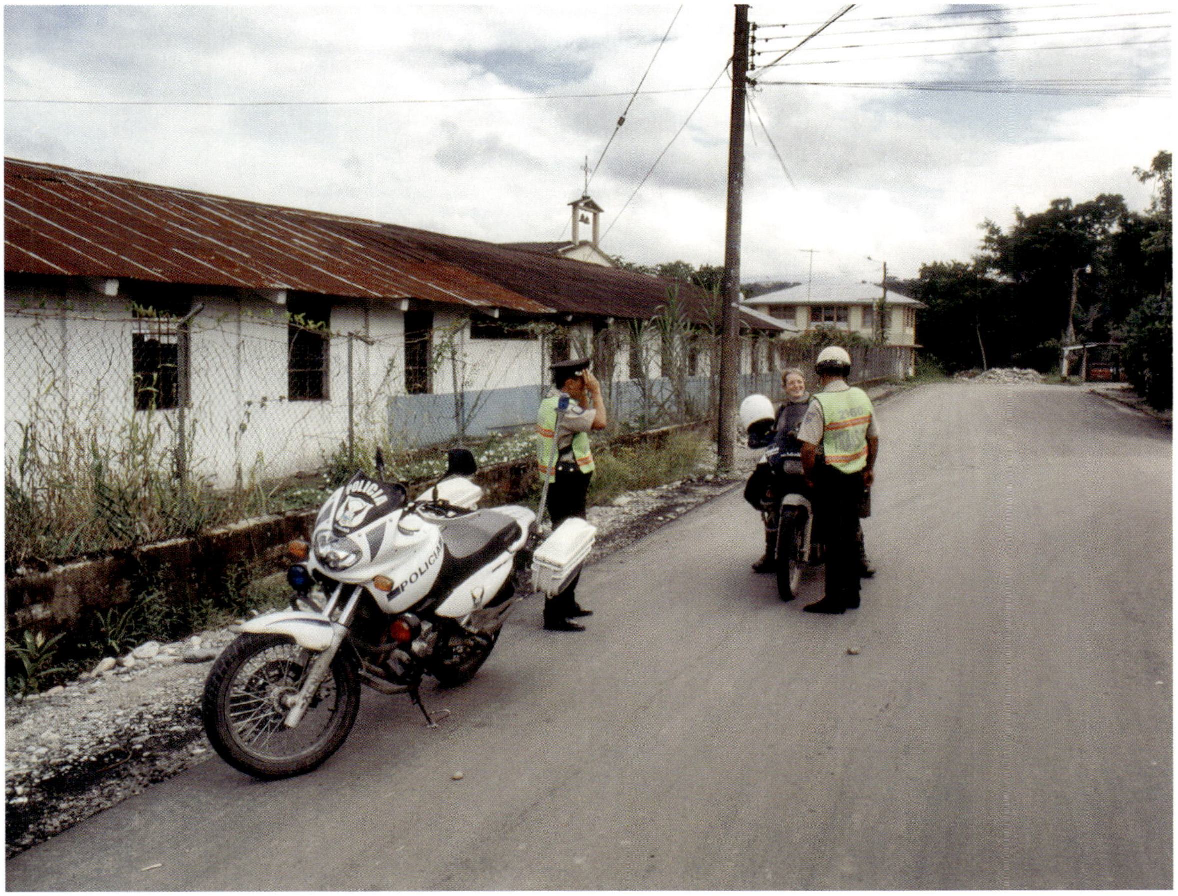

Every morning, we are woken up at 7:30 a.m. by military marches from the neighbouring school. The children line up in rows of two in their school uniforms to sing the anthem. After that, the director gives a 10-minute speech in which he reminds all students earnestly of their duties and tasks. The children are educated strictly and with a lot of respect for authorities. Can they resist the sweet enjoyment of Alfeñique? I can't. The sweet, sugary dough clings like rubber to a stick and is available in some shop doorways. The "melcocheros" pull and beat the dough constantly. Cut into pieces, the energy-rich little bars are shaped in rectangular wrappers and sold as candy.

Over muddy clay roads, we follow the call of the rainforest and have a date with Fredi and Christine in Tena a few days later. We look for their boarding house but can't find it. The taxi drivers on the market don't know it either, even though they should know their way around. Two motorbike cops on a moped stop next to us and radio in a bulletin to their colleagues. We are supposed to follow them as one of them is on a hot trail. They take us through the town to a country road and describe the way to a distant village, because there is a boarding house with the same name Fredi and Christine gave us. We are a little doubtful because we wanted to meet in a place in the centre, but it's worth a try. It is a 50 km drive, and back again, but we have no success. Back at the taxi stand we are greeted like old friends. There is a voice in the background – Christine, what a coincidence! She brings us to her boarding house right away, which has a very different name from the one on Fredi's key chain. We would have looked a long time. Unfortunately, they don't have rooms anymore, but there is a guesthouse next door that still has space for us.

For 2 days, we go on an excursion into the rainforest. It is not what we had imagined, but we make the best of it. Instead of walking into an indigenous village and gaining an insight into life there, we pile a few children, two men, and an elderly woman onto the loading area and they accompany us to a bamboo hut. They are our temporary villagers. The two nonetheless prove to be very knowledgeable advisors and explain what the forest has to offer in medicinal plants, nutritious food and animals. We kindly decline from taking a taste of small ants that are supposed to taste like lemon and refuse a white grub that is supposed to be great delicacy when grilled. They take our frowns with amusement and dare to put their arms into an ant nest on a tree so that hundreds of the little animals crawl over their skin. They are actually very useful because they heal wounds and remove poison from open wounds – e.g. mosquito bites. The shaman comes to the hut at night. From the days of the Inca until today, they have been responsible for spiritual and physical welfare, but also for the moral balance in a community. He shows us the secrets of his healing arts. He brews a hallucinogenic drink from which we are allowed to take a little nip. In the middle of the room, we sit in a line and are ritually „cleansed". For a real treatment, a patient is laid on the floor, the shaman frees him from the evil in a ceremony and sucks the diseased spot out of the body with his mouth. With healing herbs, he can alleviate or cure symptoms because he knows everything about the herbs' effects. Often people who could not be helped by traditional medicine come to him. I describe my chronic stomach problems, which nobody has been able to cure. He looks for several herbs in the forest and mixes a brew. I drink it and am impressed because I feel much better after a short time. The mixture also helps in the long term. It is no coincidence that international pharmaceutical companies have a strong interest in the medicinal plants and recipes of the indigenous people, which they would like to patent.

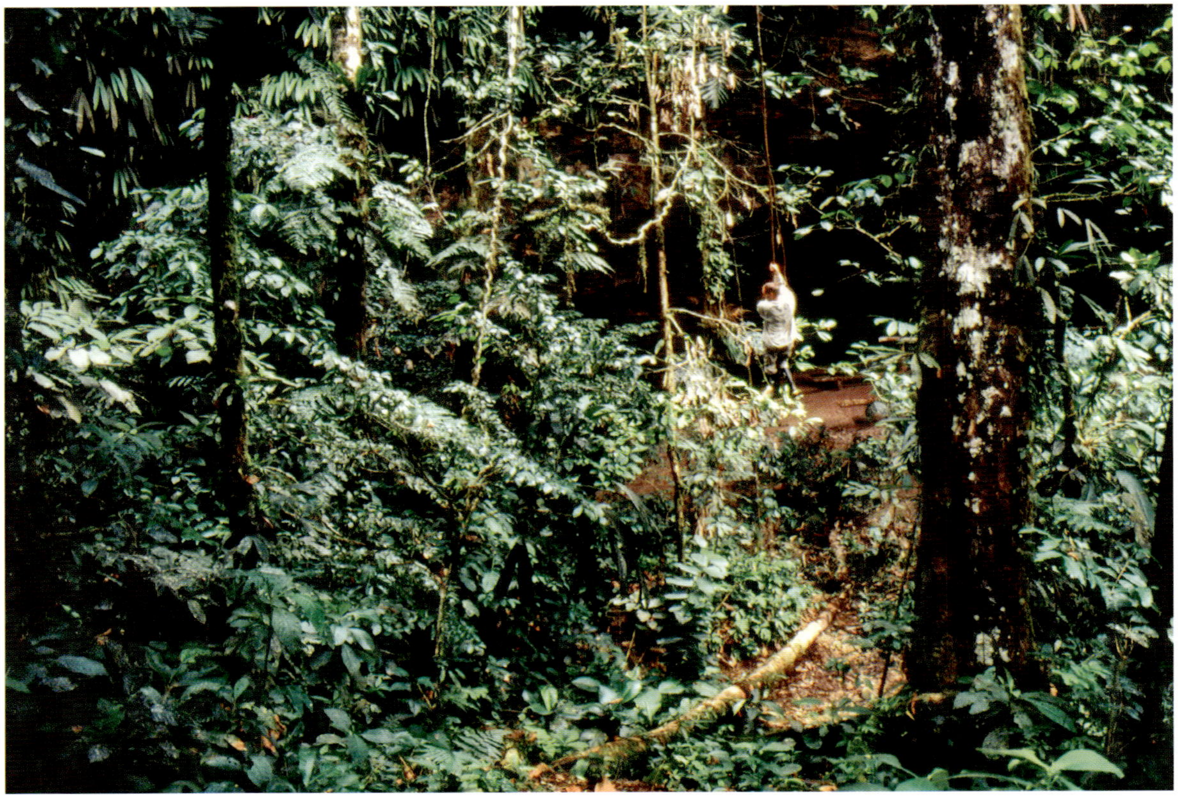

Left: With a liana through the jungle

Page 167 all pictures: Jungle excursion with indigenous people

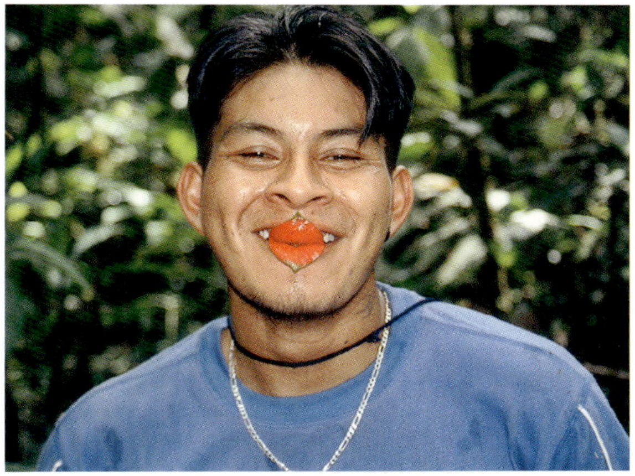
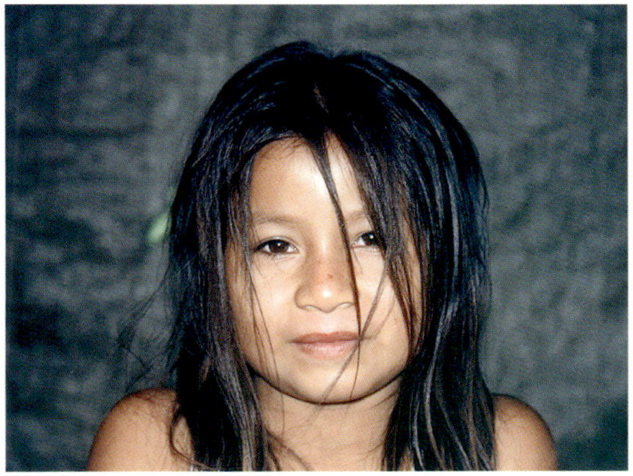
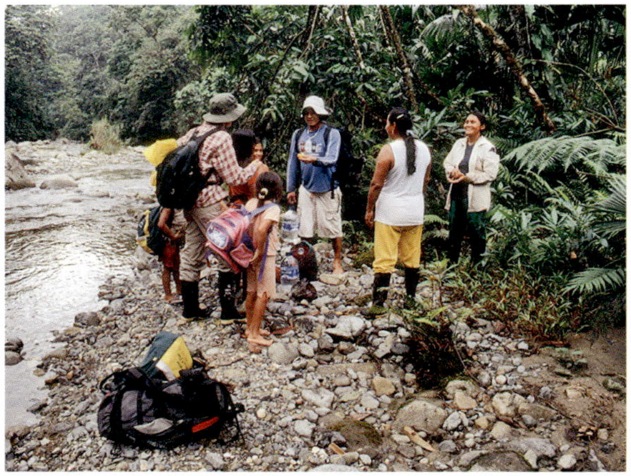
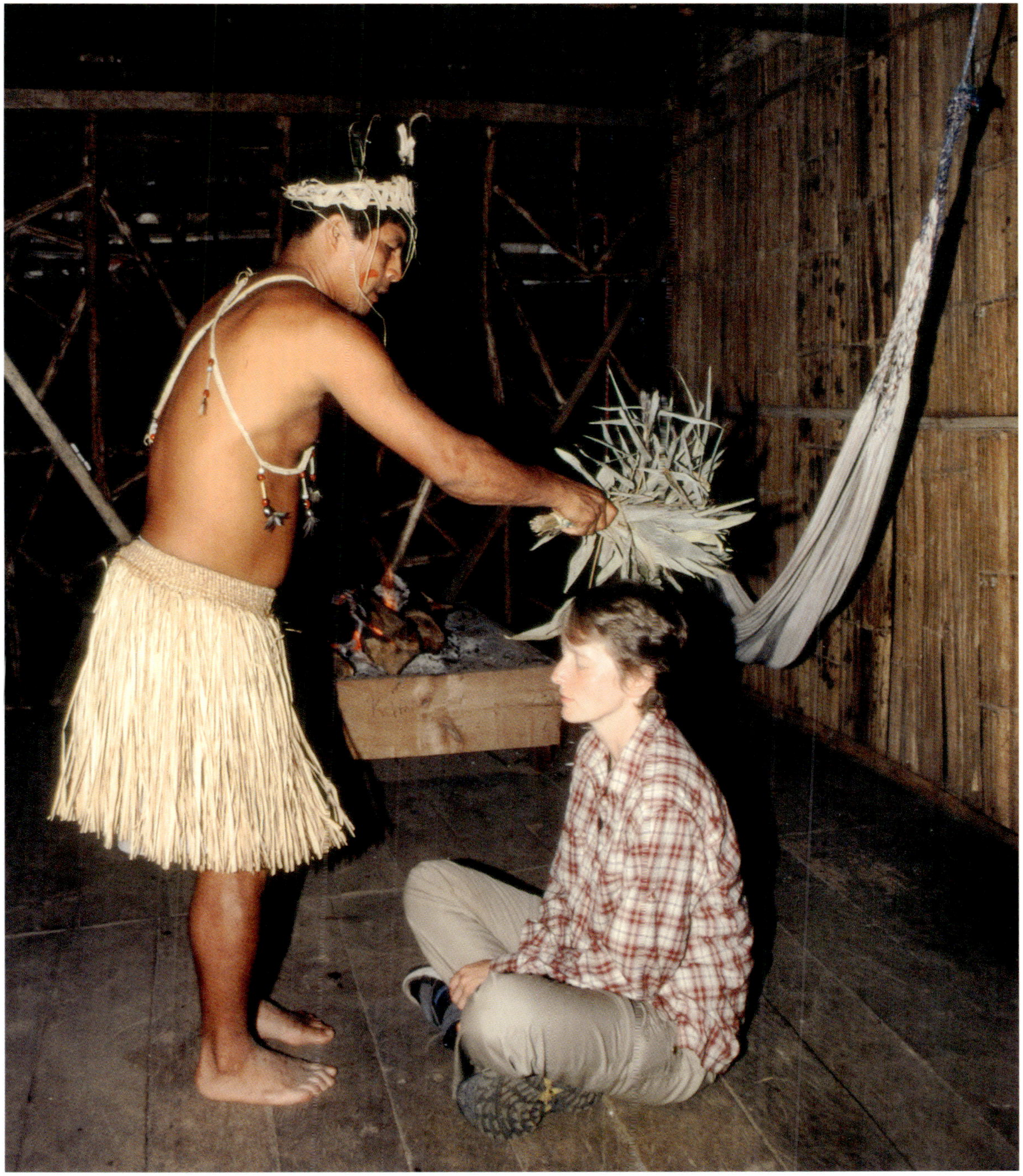

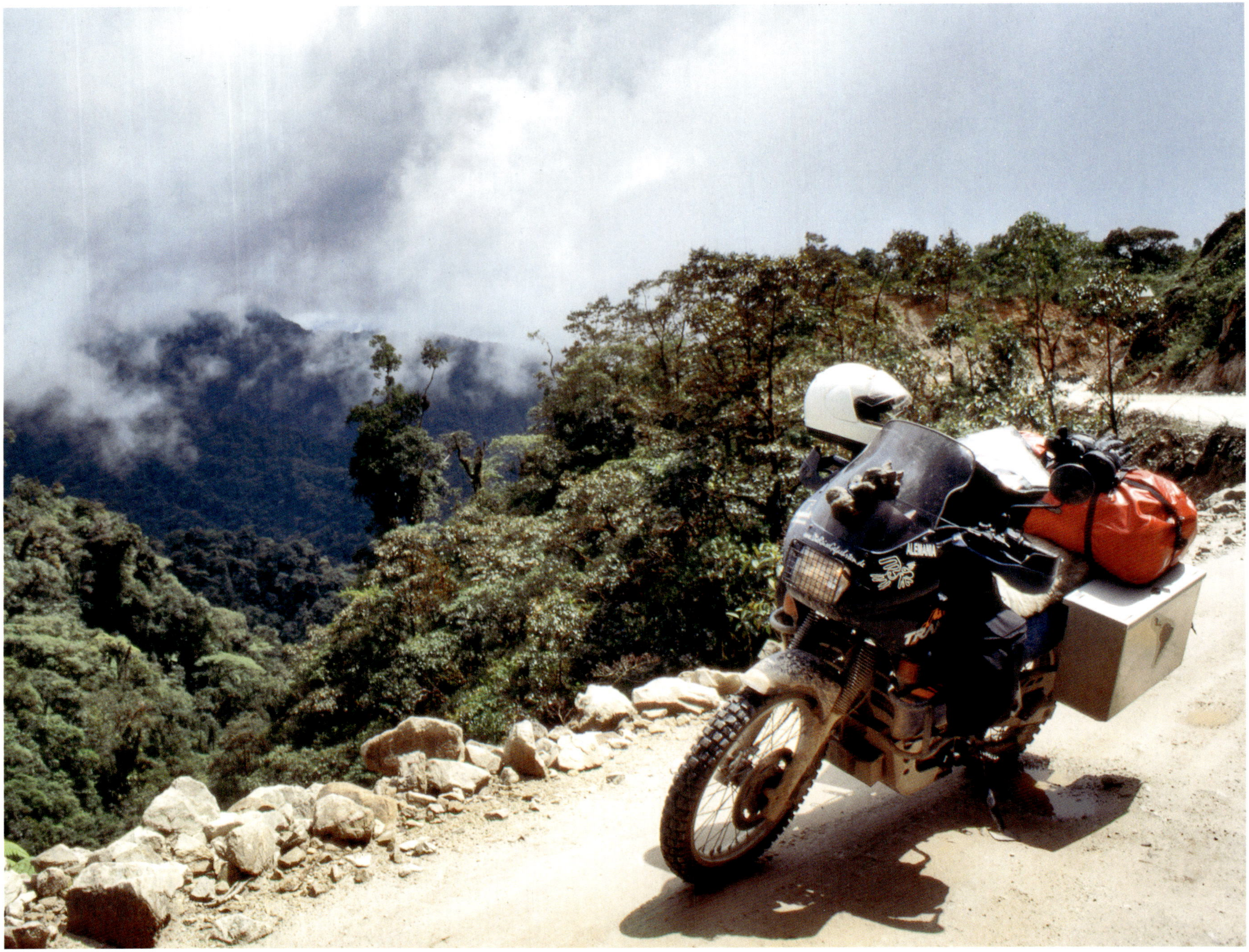
ALEMANIA

THE NORTH-SOUTH DIVIDE

Students and indigenous demonstrators have erected street barricades towards the capital in order to protest against the cutbacks in public benefits. We stay a day longer in Tena. Negotiations with the government are unsuccessful. The roadblocks are expanded to the entire country. The next morning, the all clear is given on the radio – the road to Quito is free. Only a collapsed bridge is an obstacle for us. The detour ends in a traffic jam. A bus on the other side is stuck in the mud. A few people push wooden beams under the tyres to give the driver a better starting position. It takes time. As I park the Transalp on the side of the road, my boots sink into the mud. At last, the bus is free and I hurry to find a way through the mud without jostling. On a rutted mud road littered with big rocks, we skid back to the safe road.

In Quito, Ricardo welcomes us at his house, a boarding house for bike travellers. Argentineans on 2 Honda NX 400 are preparing their trip to Brazil. We need to change a tyre and organize the transport of the bikes from Ecuador to Panama. Ricardo helps us with his great commitment and many contacts. He is Ecuador's good soul for bikers. After all, thanks to his perseverance, bikers in Ecuador don't need a Carnet des Passages anymore. At the garage, we can potter about as we please anc take special care of our bikes. At a filling station, we want to give the bikes a thorough wash so that they won't catch the eye of the customs

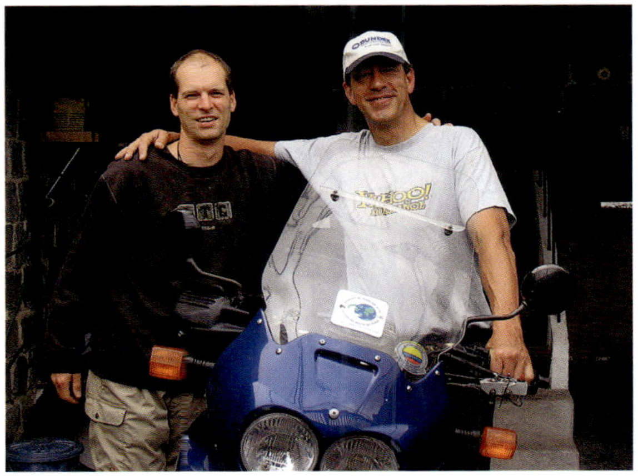

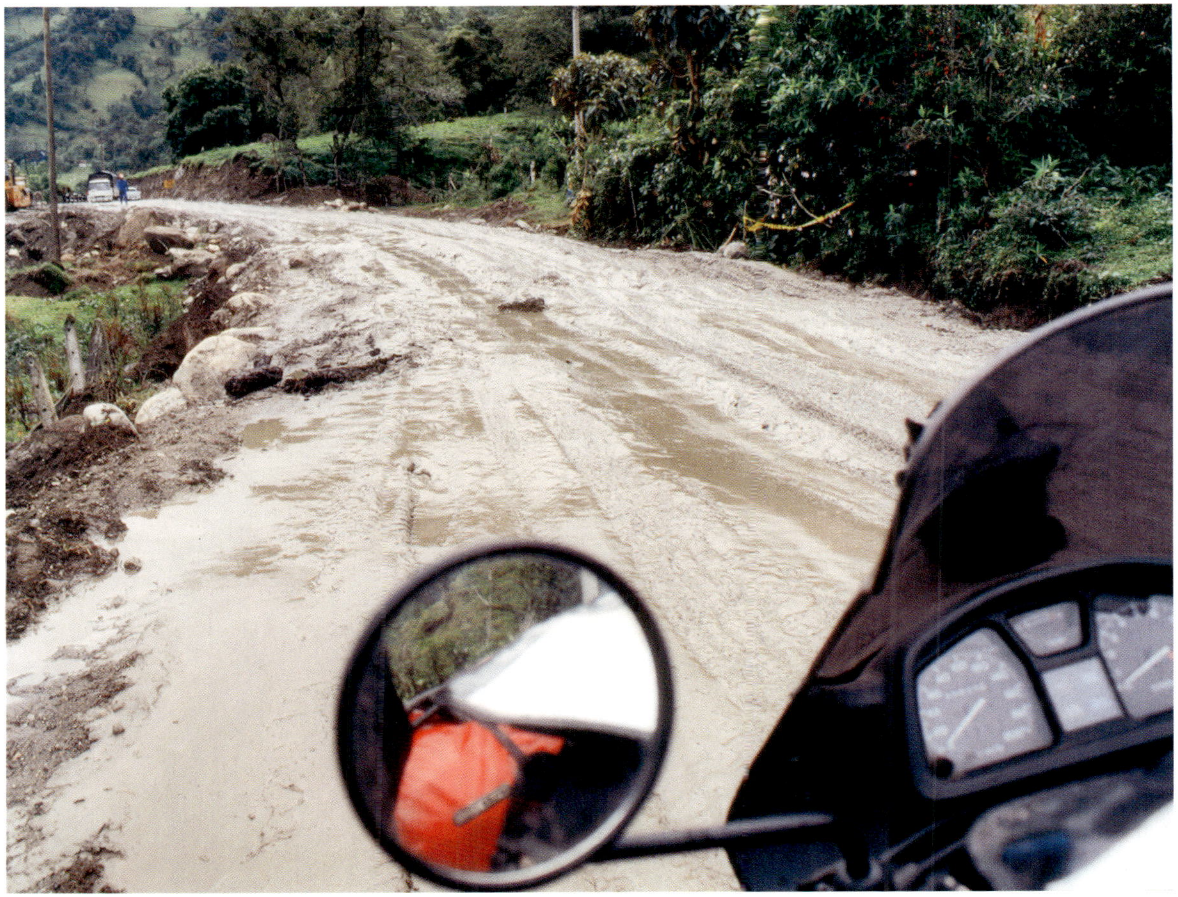

Top right: Ricardo Rocco Paz, Ecuador's good soul for bikers

Right: Detours demand driving skills

Page 168: In the mountains near Baeza

officers in Panama. From behind us, a voice is saying: "Two people from Duisburg, that's impossible." We jerk around and Bertram climbs happily out of his car. To his girlfriend Sabine, he says: "As dirty as their bikes are, they must have been travelling a long time!" The two moved here one year ago, and he drives a BMW 1200 GS. So many questions are traded back and forth so that we make an appointment for a bike tour together. Then they speed off. In the meantime, our bikes have become the No. 1 topic at the petrol station. Andrés, the owner, drives a KLR 650 and is glad that we have come to him. He tells us to come back for an extra wash appointment the next morning. The bikes are polished by hand for an hour and we are not allowed to pay a cent. Part 1 of our mission in Quito is completed.

Part 2 concerns the new tyre. We walk around for hours, ask here and search there, and finally find a shop with exactly the tyres we want. Luckily, they are in stock for both bikes. We take them home in a taxi, take off our rear tyres, take a taxi to a „vulcanizador", who takes off the old tube and puts the new one on. Accidentally, he tears off the valve of one of the hoses. He wants to repair it and I decide not to watch him do it. We use the waiting time to go back to Ricardo's house. We remove the front tyres from both bikes. I clamp a replacement tube from my box under my arm and then we dash back to the shop. He has mended the tube. It doesn't look bad, but I'm not sure that it will really hold. I unpack the replacement tube – but I grabbed the wrong one: it is the long thin front tyre tube. Once again, I go to the house and back. Despite the work time and all the going back and forth, we only pay about US$ 200 for everything. Now that part is done, too.

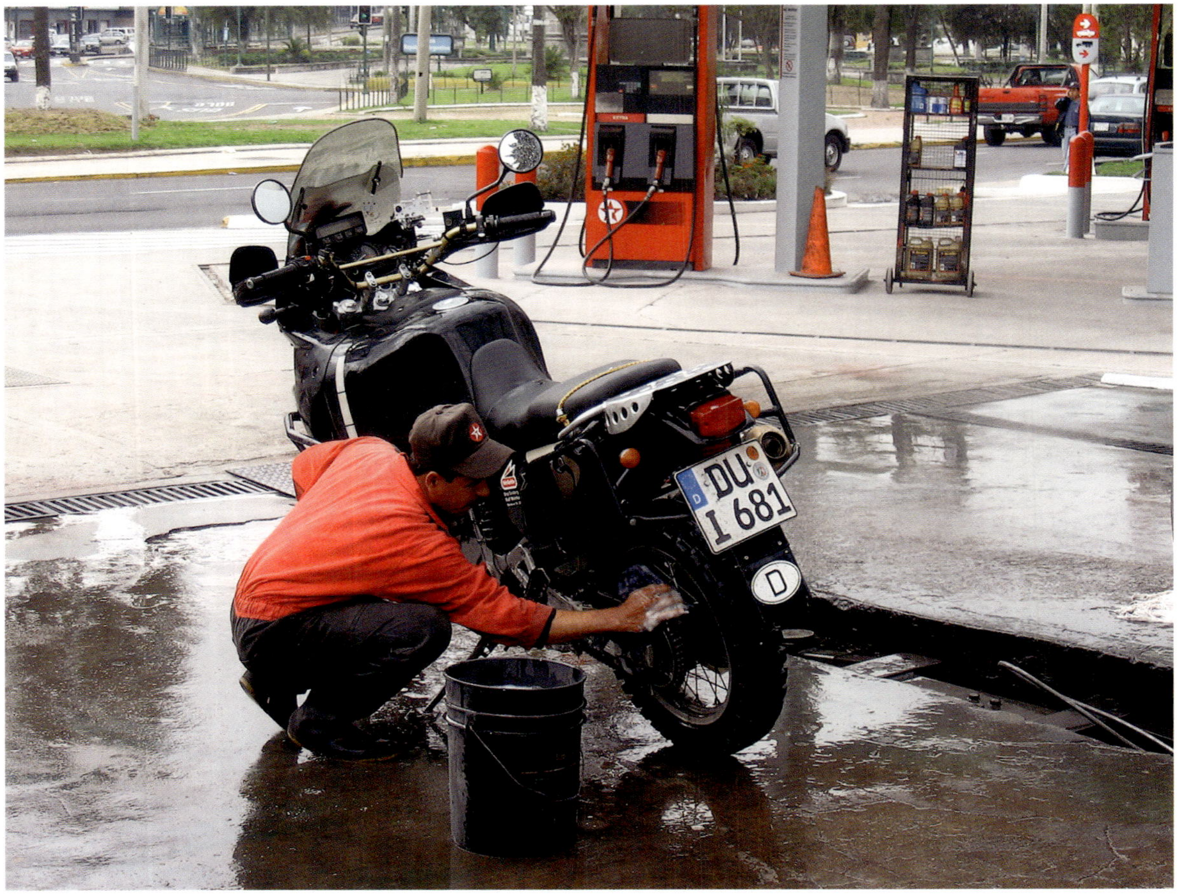

Part 3 involves the transport of the bikes, which isn't easy because Valentine's Day is approaching and all freight planes are fully booked with rose transports around the world. The prices of the carriers increase accordingly, which we have to accept grudgingly. We have to be glad that we can even find a transport in the next few days. We hand our documents to the agent we have hired to take care of all the paperwork with the authorities. A very trusting decision on our part because we would be lost without the originals. But they are in good hands, and he is even able to copy our signatures in a very short time. Then everything is organized and we can relax and meet up with Bertram to go on a tour to the north. He teaches us a quick lesson in slalom through the Quito traffic – at 80 mph and always in front of everyone else. I feel as if I were part of a computer game with a joystick, only I'm sitting on my motor-

Page 170: The dirt of the last few months needs to go before the air transport

Bottom: 0°00.000', Mitad del Mundo

bike and experience everything live. This is great fun and the best way to get through the masses. 20 km north of Quito, an artificial village was created, "Mitad del Mundo". At the centre, there is a monument with a globe at the equator line. With some diplomatic skill, we manage to drive the Transalp and the Twin to the parts of the monument that are closed to traffic in order to take a picture. After half an hour of persuasion and patience, the manager of the day agrees. This is the wonderful and astonishing thing in these countries. Even if something seems completely hopeless at first, there is always someone who can make almost everything possible. 2 security guards walk ahead and clear a path through the tourists. We follow very slowly on the wheelchair ramp to the stairs at the base of the monument pedestal. I park the Transalp on the northern hemisphere, and Axel takes his Twin to the southern hemisphere. What a strange feeling being in different hemispheres, but still very close together. Even though the actual

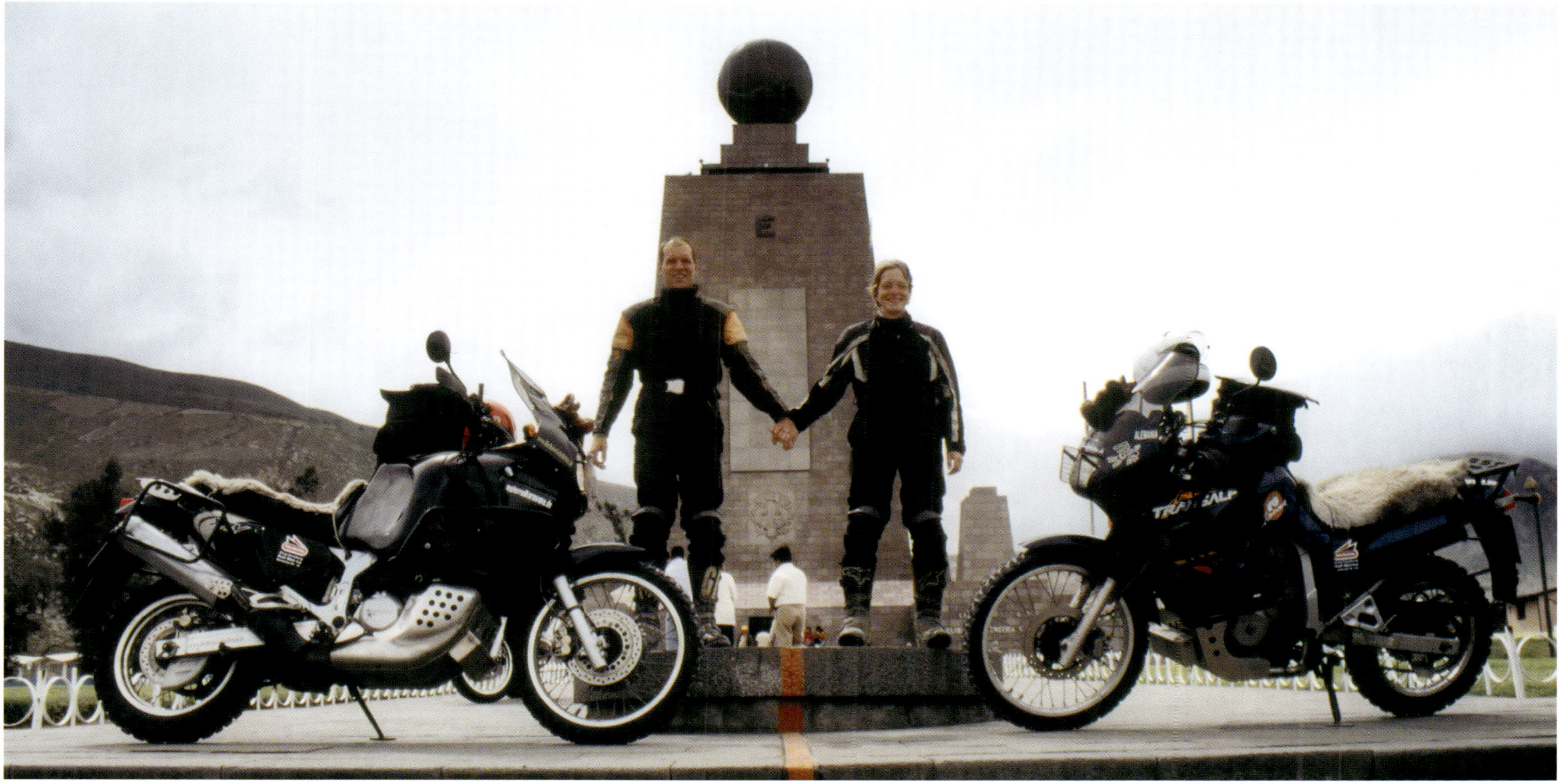

zero is 200 m away from the monument... if we started from here and drove along the equator, we would circle the earth after about 12.756 km.

Sabine and Bertram invite us on another tour to Lago Caricocha. Immediately, I sense that this is Bertram's home route, one that he drives almost every weekend with friends. I can barely keep up as he leans into the curves at 130 km/h. And he is even showing consideration for us because our bikes have new shoes. After all, during the past months we have rarely achieved speeds over 80 km/h, driving very defensively in order to survive. I can't hold the tempo and can only catch up with him when he stops close to a BMW driver whose bike broke down. The two of them are loosely acquainted from Quito. A friend has already been notified and is coming to help. Bertram leaves him a few tools. We stop at a restaurant and have breakfast. Barely 15 minutes later, the man enters with his friend to bring Bertram's tools back. They must have flown here!

The last night in Ecuador falls. What an exhausting day we have had: seen from a typical German perspective, meaning planned and perfected to the last detail, our trip to Panama went completely pear-shaped until the last minute. The tickets I pick up at the travel agency the next morning show the wrong month. They try to change the reservation but can't promise anything because the plane the next morning only has a few empty seats. Then I have problems withdrawing the money to pay for the motorbike passages. The cashpoint display says that the demanded amount is too high. I ask a clerk if I can debit the amount with her. This is not a problem, for a fee. She prepares the documents and scans my credit card. Nothing happens. My account appears to be overdrawn, which means that they can't give me any money right now. I'm getting a little restless, imagining that somebody might have emptied the account, that our travel budget is gone, we can't pay for the passage, need to look for another source of money. Our last hope are the cards for the other accounts. Axel and I go to another cashpoint in another neighbourhood. Then the relief: we are able to get all the money we ask the machine for without any problem. What a load off my mind! Now we just have to wait for the call from the agent about when to meet up to leave the bikes with the carrier. In the meantime, he has left us a message that everything was postponed to tomorrow afternoon. Something has to happen because we are supposed to fly in the morning – if we get the tickets. On this journey, I have learned that problems are approached in a different way here, but a solution will be found nevertheless. While people in Germany are quick to vent their anger, this is the wrong approach in South America. Sometimes, it has the opposite effect because people feel insulted. I get on the phone but can only reach the agent's voicemail. I dial all the numbers he gave me. Nothing. A few hours later, he returns my call. In the end, we are able to take the bikes to the warehouse not tomorrow afternoon, not tomorrow morning an hour before our flight, but today. Phew!

For the first time, the two are weighed. Remarkable 250 kg and 288 kg! Admittedly, we packed all the heavy things in the cases so that we don't have to check them as carry-on luggage. They need a diet. Maybe we should send a few things home again. We disconnect the batteries and let the air out of the tyres. Then the agent tells us that the bikes will reach Panama City a day later than planned, on a Saturday. This could mean that there will be problems with opening hours at customs, but I will think about that when we are there. We return to the travel agency and get our tickets for tomorrow's flight. Seen from here, everything is going great. It all depends on your own inner calm and optimism, and on the faith in finding solutions with sensitivity and improvisation if things don't go as planned. Now we can leave South America for Panama tomorrow morning.

Page 173: In Quito we say goodbye

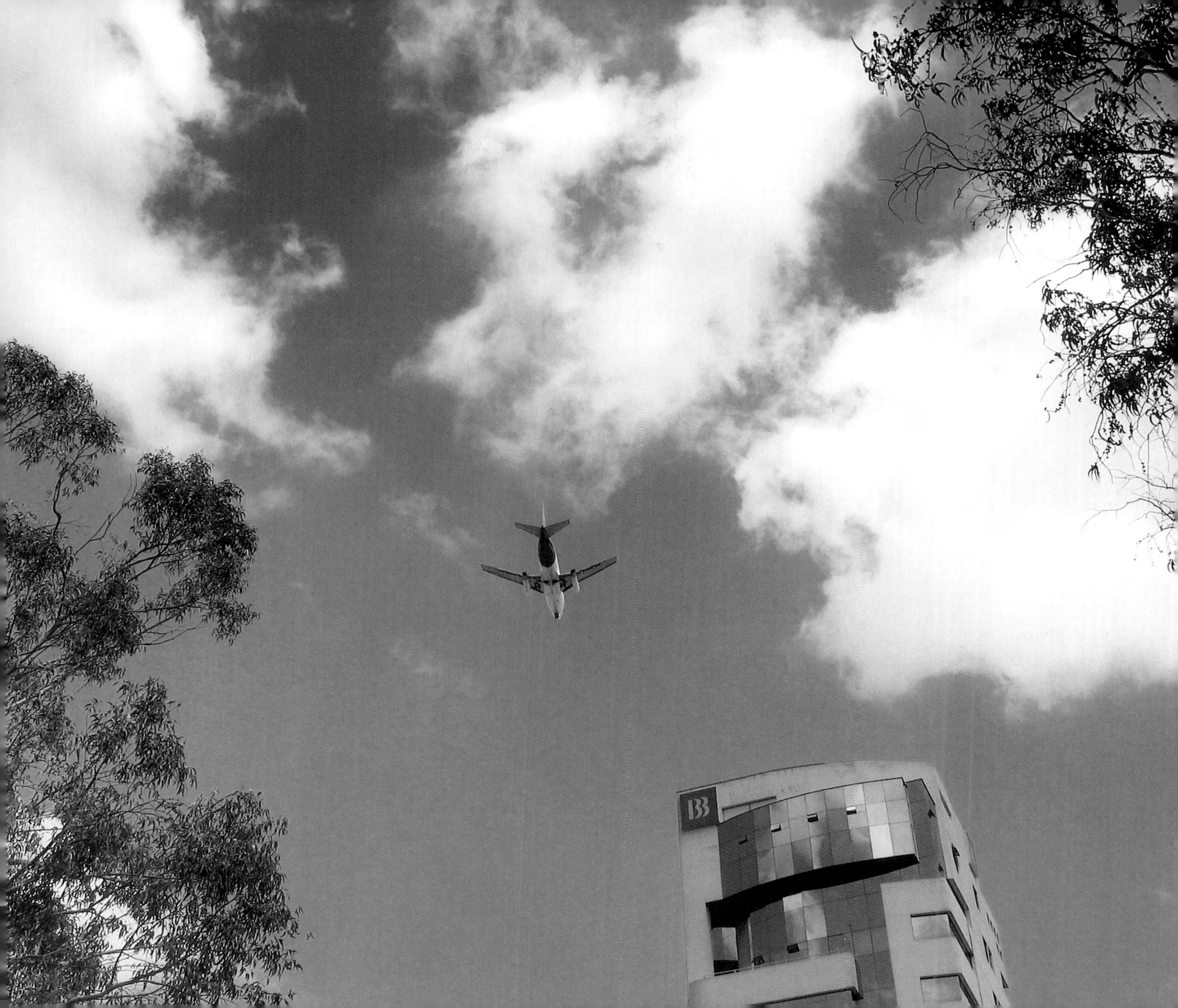

Look forward to volume 2 with which Angela Schmitz takes you
to her journey through Central America.

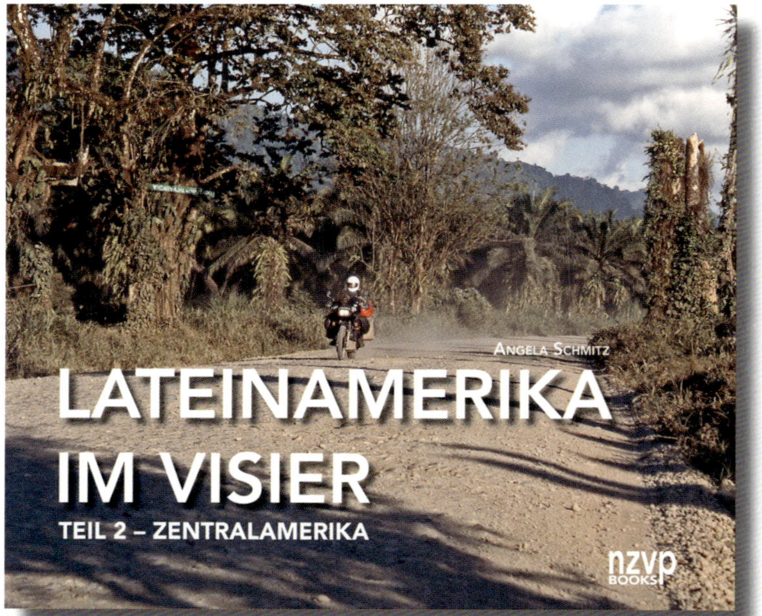

ISBN 978-3-938446-71-3

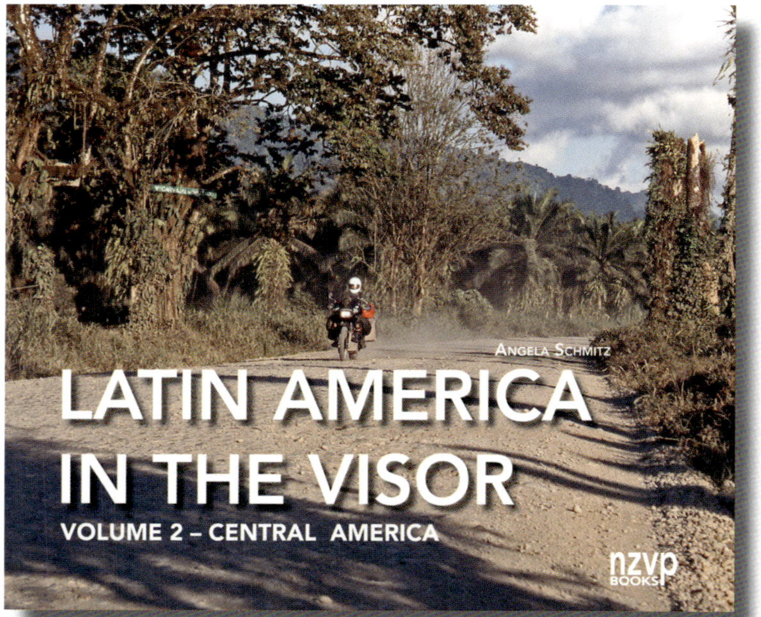

ISBN 978-1-877339-56-1

Page 175: Preview on volume 2: The Volcano Arenal in Costa Rica in the rear-view mirror of the Africa Twin

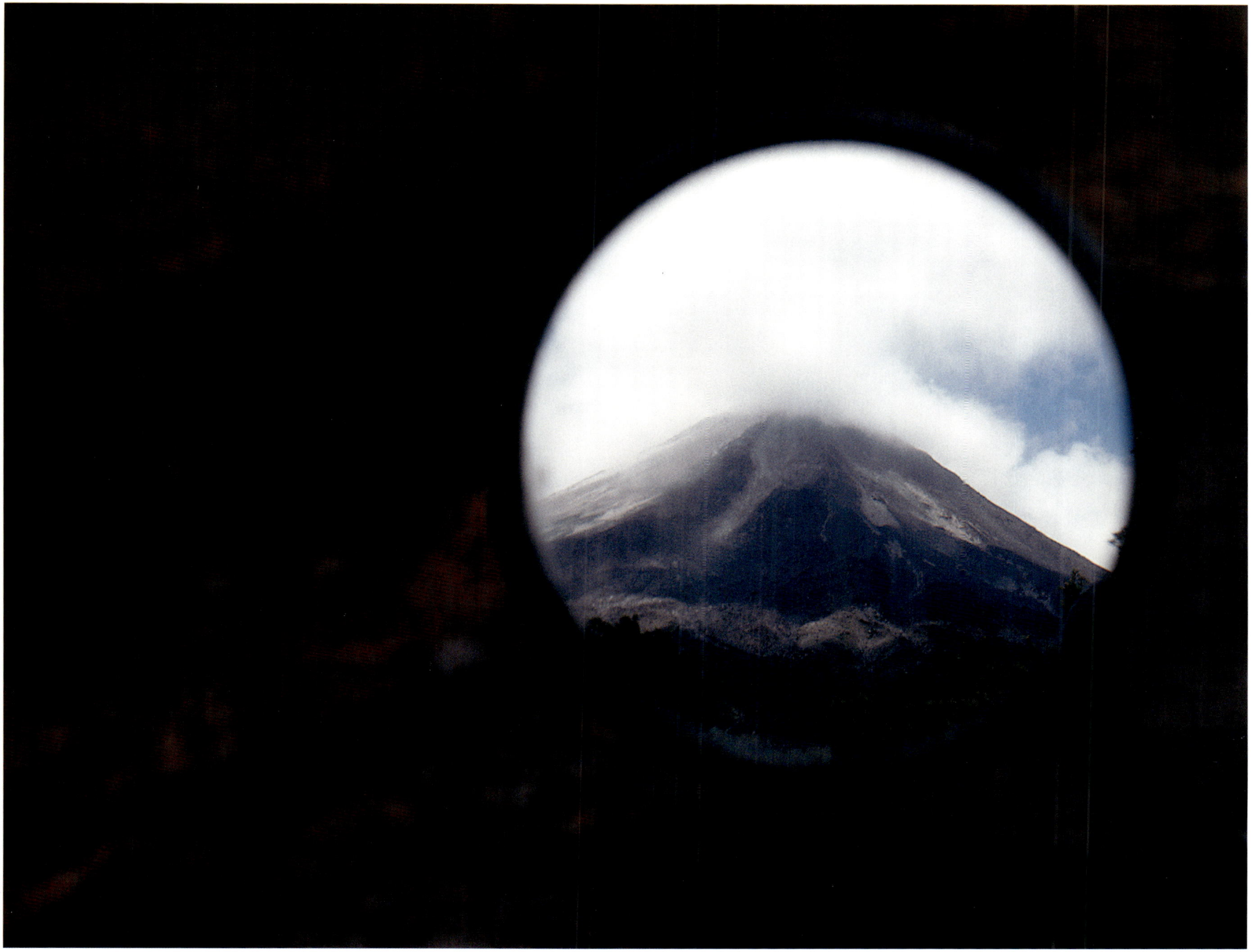

Latin America in the Visor, Volume 1 – South America, 1st Edition

ISBN 978-1-877339-55-4

Layout and typesetting	Helga Neubauer, Wolfgang Vorbeck
Author	Angela Schmitz
Photographs	Angela Schmitz und Axel Heß
Editorial Office	Studiotextart, Schwalbach a. Ts., Germany
Translation	language networks bv, Amsterdam, Holland
Printed by	Everbest Printing, China

We cannot guarantee that this book has not been struck by erronitis. Should this be the case, we would be greatful if you could point out any errors to us. You can contact us at:

NZVP Ltd.
Level 27, PWC Tower, 188 Quay Street
Auckland, New Zealand
or email us at:
editor@nzpublications.com